A LEGACY OF AMERICA'S GLOBAL VOLUNTEERISM
International Voluntary Services (1953-2002)

A Legacy Of America's Global Volunteerism
International Voluntary Services (1953-2002)

Edited by

Gary Alex

Mike Chilton

Frederic C. Benson

Peace Corps Writers Book
2022
Oakland, California

A Legacy of America's Global Volunteerism
International Voluntary Services (1953-2002)

A Peace Corps Writers Book—an imprint of Peace Corps Worldwide

© 2022 IVS for Development

This publication is licensed for use under a Creative Commons Attribution 4.0 International License (CC BY 4.0). Subject to attribution, you are free to share (copy and redistribute the material in any medium or format), adapt (remix, transform, and build upon the material), for any purpose, even commercially.

The author and publisher gratefully acknowledge permission from Wiley for use of extracts from E. Timothy Smith, "Roots of the Peace Corps: Youth Volunteer Service in the 1950s" from Wiley's Peace & Change, Volume 41, Issue 2, April 2016 © 2016 Peace History Society and Wiley Periodicals, Inc. All rights reserved.

Cover photo:
Laos: IVS volunteer (second on the right) meets with Naikong (tribal district chief) and local villagers in Houei Kong Cluster, Attapeu Province (1964-1965).
[Photo from https://search.library.wisc.edu/digital/ASageImages
(University of Wisconsin's Southeast Asia digital collection)
"William W. Sage collection on Laos."]

Printed in the United States of America
by Peace Corps Writers of Oakland, California.

For more information, contact:
peacecorpsworldwide@gmail.com.
Peace Corps Writers and the Peace Corps Writers colophon
are trademarks of PeaceCorpsWorldwide.org.

Designed and produced by Fourth Lloyd Productions, LLC

ISBN 978-1-950444-52-6
Library of Congress Control Number: 2022915620

First Peace Corps Writers Edition, September 2022

Contents

List of Acronyms ix
Foreword xv
Preface xvii

SECTION I History of International Voluntary Services, Inc.

Chapter 1
IVS Origins And Early Years 1953–1957 23
Paul A. Rodell, Georgia Southern University

    IVS Origins: An Historical Convergence (WW II–1953) 24
    Creating IVS: Organization And First Programs 28
    Adding An Executive Director: Preparing IVS for Growth (1953–55) 30
    1956: Starting The Shift To Southeast Asia 37
    1957: Endings And Beginnings: IVS Emerges Anew 42
    1953–1957: Overview Of The Years Of Origin And Founding 45

Chapter 2
Initial Programs Set-up, Structure, And Experience 47
Don Mitchell and Cherie J. Woodcock Mitchell

    IVS/Egypt (1953–54) First Volunteers in the Field 48
    IVS/Jordan (1954–55) Short-lived Support to a Private Development Project 49
    IVS/Iraq (1953–57) A Comprehensive Rural Development Team 51
        Project Team 52
        Living Conditions 55
        Project Activities 56
        Program Changes 62
    IVS/Nepal (1956–58) Training Community Development Workers 65
    IVS/UNRWA Agreement Jordan, Syria, Lebanon, and Gaza (1963–65): Working with the UN 67
    Reflections On Initial IVS Country Programs 69

Chapter 3
Volunteers And The Cold War Conflict In Southeast Asia 71
Frederic C. Benson, Mike Chilton, and Hugh Manke

    IVS/Laos (1956–75) Nation Building: Community Development and Education 72
        The Advent of IVS in Laos 73
        Expanding Rural Development Activities 74
        Establishment of an IVS Education Team 75
        Kong Le Coup d'Etat Diverts Volunteers to Relief Efforts 76
        Education Team Program Expands 77
        New Direction in Rural Development 78
        Forward Area Program and Deteriorating Security 81
        IVS Withdrawal from Rural Laos 82
        IVS Distances Itself from USAID 83
        IVS Realigns Its Programs 85

Chapter 3 (cont'd)
    The Demise of USAID and IVS in Laos *87*
    The Perseverance of IVS Volunteers *88*
    What Inspired IVS Volunteers in Laos? *88*
IVS/Vietnam (1956–72) Volunteers in a War Zone *89*
    Early IVS Team Activities *90*
    Diversifying Programs *92*
    A Changing Vietnam:1965–1971 *95*
    Vietnam Program Ends *101*
IVS/Cambodia (1960–63) International Tensions End a Promising Program *103*
IVS and USAID in Indochina: Who Left Whom? *106*

Chapter 4
Going Global With A Maturing Volunteer Program *111*
Gary Alex and Willi Meyers
    IVS/Liberia (1960–63) Village Education Program Taken Over by the Peace Corps *113*
    IVS/Algeria (1963–66; 1968–74) Soil Conservation to English Teaching *117*
    IVS/Morocco (1968–74) Range Management Challenges *120*
    IVS/Zaire/Congo (1970–74; 1986–1989) Agricultural Credit Troubles and Public Health *121*
    IVS/Yemen (1971–79) Varied Assignments and Later Focus on Agriculture Research *126*
    IVS/Indonesia (1972–76) A Long Gestation Period for a Small Program *129*
    IVS/Sudan (1973–83) Diverse Projects under Difficult Conditions *132*
    IVS/Mauritania (1975–79) Great Need but Questionable Demand for Volunteers *136*
    IVS/Papua New Guinea (1975–84) Business Development and Sustainable Agriculture *138*
    Other Country Initiatives: Failure to Launch *140*
    Mixed Results: Good Work in Difficult Places *142*

Chapter 5
Reinventing IVS: New Approaches And The End Game *147*
Gary Alex
    IVS/Bangladesh (1972–2002) A Long-running, Evolving Program *151*
    IVS/Ecuador (1974–2002) Diverse Low-key Support to Indigenous Communities *158*
    IVS/Bolivia (1975–2001) Cooperatives and Coca Substitution *161*
    IVS/Botswana (1975–88) Horticulture, Cooperatives, and Forestry *163*
    IVS/Honduras (1975–87) Soybeans, Health, and Construction *166*
    IVS/Caribbean (1983–89) Regional Enterprise Development Services *168*
    IVS/Zimbabwe (1983–92) Small-scale Cooperatives and Community Development *170*
    IVS/Southeast Asia (1991–2002) HIV/AIDS Prevention *171*
    The End Game Reinvention Failure *174*

Chapter 6
Administration: Running A Nonprofit NGO *181*
Frederic C. Benson and Gary Alex
    IVS Pressures And Turning Points *181*
    IVS Objectives And Strategy *183*

Structure And Leadership   *186*
Program Initiatives And Performance   *188*
Funding   *192*
End Game   *196*
Final Note   *200*

SECTION II   Volunteer Experiences And Impacts

CHAPTER 7
Volunteers Out Of Their Comfort Zone   *213*
Gary Alex with Volunteer Stories

Risks In Life Overseas   *214*
Rapport With Different Cultures   *216*
Responsibility Could Come Quickly   *223*
Resourcefulness Was Essential   *230*
Romances Blossomed   *233*
Reflections   *236*

CHAPTER 8
Impacts Of International Voluntary Service   *237*
Willi Meyers and Gary Alex with Volunteer Stories

Direct Results From Volunteer Assignments   *239*
Development Of Local Human And Institutional Capacity   *242*
Influence On National Or Development Programs And Policies   *245*
Personal Influence On Volunteers   *246*
International Goodwill   *251*
From Anecdotal Testimonies To Their Implications   *253*
IVS Organizational Impacts   *254*

SECTION III   International Voluntary Services Partners

CHAPTER 9
Mission And Service: The American Churches And IVS   *259*
William W. Sage

Engagement Abroad By American Churches Before World War I   *259*
Religious Society Of Friends American Friends Service Committee (AFSC)   *261*
The Mennonite Church Mennonite Central Committee (MCC)   *266*
Church Of The Brethren Brethren Service Committee (BSC)   *269*
Forging Ecumenical Cooperation International Relief And Development   *273*
Some Thoughts On Why TCA Encouraged The Three Peace Churches To Form IVS   *275*
The Faith Community And Volunteerism Today   *277*

Chapter 10
IVS And The Origins Of The Peace Corps 279
E. Timothy Smith
    BVS, Humphrey, And The Seed 281
    International Voluntary Service, Inc. 281
    Reuss, Humphrey And The Creation Of The Peace Corps 283
    The Creation Of The Peace Corps 287

Chapter 11
USAID: Recent Volunteer Service Involvement 293
Jack Hawkins
    Farmer-to-Farmer Program: An Impactful Peer-to-Peer Volunteer Service Program 293
    Volunteers For Prosperity (VFP): A Promising White House National Service Initiative 295
    USAID Sponsored Activities 300
    USAID Volunteer Funding And Program Design: Assessing the Future 301

SECTION IV Implications And Questions For Future International Voluntary Services

Chapter 12
Lessons Learned:
Implications For The Future Of Volunteering For Development 307
Cliff Allum and Benjamin J. Lough

    Emergent Themes And Lessons Learned 307
      The Challenge of Young and Low-skilled Generalist Volunteers 308
      Diversification of IVS Activities:
        Response to Changes in Cultural and Historical Contexts 310
      Localization of IVS Programs 311
    Challenges Confronting IVS And The U.S. Government 313
      Resourcing the Drive to Diversify: IVS Resourcing from Public Funding 313
      Maintaining IVS Distinctiveness: Differences in IVS, Peace Corps and USAID Personnel 315
      IVS's Diplomacy and Development Objectives 316
      Safety And Security Concerns Of IVS Volunteers 318
    The Long-term Legacy Of IVS 319
    The Future Of International Volunteering 320
    Conclusion 323

Appendix A: IVS Country and Regional Programs 325

Appendix B: IVS Corporate Objectives and Strategy 327

Appendix C: IVS Leadership 333

Notes 335

Readings: On Volunteerism, IVS, and IVS Volunteers 357
Index 359
About the Authors 365

List of Acronyms

4-H	Farm youth development program
501(c)3	U.S. nonprofit that enjoys special, tax-exempt status
A&M	Agriculture and Mechanical (in university names)
ACASR	American Committee for Armenian and Syrian Relief, Church of the Brethren
ACPO	Accion Cultural Popular (Columbia)
ACRNE	American Committee for Relief in the Near East, Church of the Brethren
ADAB	Association of Development Agencies in Bangladesh
AFSC	American Friends Service Committee, Religious Society of Friends
AIEN	Association Indigena Evangelista del Napa (Ecuador)
AKLHUe.V.	German NGO - Office and Network for International Personnel Cooperation
ALOZ	Adult Literacy Organization of Zimbabwe
APBHU	Asociacion de Promocion Humana (Honduras)
APSO	Personal Service Overseas (Ireland)
ARAMCO	Arabian American Oil Company
ARVN	Army of the Republic of Vietnam
AUCW	Sudan's Ahfad University College for Women
AVID	Australian Volunteers for International Development
BAPPENAS	Indonesia's National Planning Board
BRAC	Bangladesh Rural Advancement Committee
BSC	Brethren Service Committee, Church of the Brethren
BUTSI	Badan Urusan Tenaga Kerja Sukarela Indonesia
BVS	Brethren Volunteer Service
CAPS	Caribbean Advisory and Professional Services (West Indies)
CARE	A global NGO (previously: Cooperative for American Relief Everywhere)
CCORR	Church Committee on Overseas Relief and Reconstruction
CDAA	USAID Community Development Area Advisors
CDC	Community Development Centre (Iraq)
CDS	Community Development Service (Bangladesh)
CEDEN	National Evangelical Committee for Development and Emergency (Honduras)
CEVER	Evangelical and Reformed Center for Vocational Education (Honduras)
CIA	Central Intelligence Agency
CIDG	Civilian Irregular Defense Group (Vietnam)
CO	Conscientious Objectors
CODEL	Congressional delegation

COR	Committee of Responsibility (Vietnam)
CORDS	Civil Operations and Rural Development Support
CPS	Civilian Public Service, service camps for conscientious objectors
CRA	Commission for Rural Affairs (Laos)
CWS	Church World Service
DED	German Development Organization (Deutscher Entwicklungsdiens)
DMZ	Demilitarized Zone
DPG	USAID Development Support Grant
E.O.	Executive Order
ENI	Etude Normale d"Instituteurs (Laos – Teacher Training School)
ERC	Emergency Relief Commission, General Conference of the Mennonite Church
F2F	USAID's Farmer-to-Farmer Volunteer Program
FAT	Forward Area Teams (Laos)
FIVDB	The Friends in Village Development, Bangladesh
FNSC	Friends National Service Committee
FOA	Foreign Operations Administration, U.S. Government
FY	Fiscal Year
GK	Gono Shasthya Kendr (Bangladesh)
GOB	Government of Botswana
GOJ	Government of Jordan
GSG	USAID General Support Grant
GVN	Government of Vietnam
HELP	Homeless European Land Program
HHS	U.S. Department of Health and Human Services
HIV/AIDS	Human immunodeficiency virus infection and acquired immunodeficiency syndrome
HPI	Heifer Project, Inc.
ICA	International Cooperation Administration
ICCO	Interchurch Organization for Development Cooperation, a Netherlands-based NGO
IDS	Institute for Development Studies
IRIS	University of Maryland Department of Economics research center
IVCO	International Volunteer Cooperation Organizations
IVS	US-based International Voluntary Services, Inc.
IVS/EDUC	IVS/Education
IVS/RD	IVS/Rural Development
IVSA	International Youth Service Agency
JOBS	Job Opportunities and Business Support (Bangladesh)

JOCV	Japan Overseas Cooperation Volunteers
KRDA	Kweneng Rural Development Association (Botswana)
LPF	Lao Patriotic Front
LWA	USAID's Leader with Associates Award
LWF	Lutheran World Federation
LWR	Lutheran World Relief
MAAG	Military Assistance Advisory Group
MACV	Military Assistance Command (Vietnam)
MCC	Mennonite Central Committee, Mennonite Church
MDGs	UN Millennium Development Goals
MEDICO	An international NGO
MEPI	USAID's Middle East Partnership Initiative
MISEREOR	German Catholic aid organization
MP	Military police
MRCWS	Mennonite Relief Commission for War Sufferers
MSA	Mutual Security Act
NATO	North Atlantic Treaty Organization
NCCUSA	National Council of Churches, USA
NDF	National Development Foundation (Dominica)
NEC	National Education Center (Laos)
NECC-CRW	Near East Church Council Committee for Refugee Work
NGO	Non-Governmental Organization
NLF	National Liberation Front
NRDF	National Research & Development Foundation (Guyana)
NSBRO	National Service Board for Religious Objectors, U.S.G. agency responsible for administration and oversight of the Civil Public Service camps.
NV	National volunteer
NVA	North Vietnam Army
NVP	National Volunteer Program (Bangladesh)
NVS	National Voluntary Services (Vietnam)
OAC	Operations Advisory Committee
OIAA	Office of Inter-American Affairs
OPG	Operating Program Grant
ORAP	Organization of Rural Associations for Progress (Zimbabwe)
ORD	St. Vincent Organization for Rural Development
OSROS	Methodist Infrastructure de la Santa Rural Dans L'Ouste de Shaba Congo)
PACT	A global NGO
PC	Peace Corps

PCV	Peace Corps Volunteer
PEPFAR	USAID's President's Emergency Plan for AIDS Relief
PGNU	People's Government of National Union
PL	Pathet Lao
PL-480	U.S. international food assistance program
PN	Provincial Nutritionist (Papua New Guinea)
PNG	Papua New Guinea
PROSHIKA	A national NGO (Bangladesh)
PVO	Private Voluntary Organization
RLG	Royal Lao Government
RN	Regional Nutritionist (Papua New Guinea)
SAP	South Asia Partnership (Bangladesh)
SCS	U.S. Soil Conservation Service
SDGs	UN Sustainable Development Goals
SERRV	Sales Exchange for Refugee Rehabilitation and Vocation, Church of the Brethren
STD Clinic	Sexually Transmitted Disease Clinic
SUCAP	Sub-Central de Cooperativas Agropecuniarias Villa Paraiso, Ltda. (Bolivia)
TCA	Technical Cooperation Administration
Tet	Vietnam's Lunar New Year Festival
TUP	Trickle Up Foundation
U.S.	United States
UK	United Kingdom
UMCOR	United Methodist Committee On Relief
UN	United Nations
UNDP	United Nations Development Program
UNICEF	United Nations Children's Fund
UNRRA	United Nations Relief and Rehabilitation Administration
UNRWA	United Nations Relief and Works Agency
UNV	United Nations Volunteers
UOWR	United Orphanage War Relief, Mennonite Brethren
USAID	United States Agency for International Development
USG	United States Government
USIS	U.S. Information Service
USOM	United States Operations Mission
VARDA	Voluntary Agency for Rural Development Administration (Laos)
VDTP	Village Development Training Program (Bangladesh)

VEGA	Volunteers for Economic Growth Alliance
VFP	U. S. Volunteers for Prosperity
VISP	USAID's Volunteers for International Security and Prosperity Program
VITA	Volunteers in Technical Assistance
VSO	UK-based Voluntary Service Overseas
VV	Village volunteer
VVP	Village Volunteer Program (Bangladesh)
WAND	Women and Development Unit (Antigua)

Foreword

Watching the Mekong River roll by from the banks of Vientiane, the capital, was a cherished pastime for IVS volunteers in Laos. It certainly was for me as a volunteer teaching English at the Dong Dok Teachers College from 1971-73. It was a time during the most active years of America's war in Indochina. When I returned to Vientiane in 1976 as a first tour Foreign Service Officer at the U.S. Embassy, much had changed under the new Pathet Lao regime. The American presence had been reduced abruptly from thousands before 1975 to the lonely nine of us who kept open the only American Embassy in Indochina.

My fondness for gazing at the swift moving waters of the Mekong had not changed. And so it was that I found myself on the banks of the Mekong on an especially memorable hot, humid, Sunday afternoon in 1977 chatting aimlessly with a teenage Pathet Lao soldier as he guarded the riverbank. BAM! BAM! BAM! his AK-47 rifle shots broke the still peace. I looked at his young face only a moment ago relaxed in idle banter, now tight and intent on killing. I was immediately fearful that the swimmer fleeing across the Mekong was one of the orphan boys from the Vientiane orphanage I had coached on a swim team only a few years earlier as an IVSer. I would never know for sure. Nor could I be certain he made it to one of the refugee camps in Thailand although I have convinced myself that he did. I do know that several of the orphan swimmers whom I coached on a swim team as well as some of my Dong Dok students, made it to Thailand during that unsettling period. The swimmers used their aquatic skills that they practiced enthusiastically every Sunday morning with the support of generous USAID officials at the KM6 compound pool.

The history of IVS from its early beginning in the fifties to its final days at the turn of the century takes the reader through the evolution of American aims, attitudes, and approaches to international development. The chapter on Laos and Vietnam poignantly captures the idealistic dedication of young agricultural technocrats in the 1950s and 60s who worked hand in hand with USAID on rural development projects. You will learn in this book that by the early 1970s America's involvement in the Indochina War complicated the mission of IVS and endangered its volunteers. Tragically, volunteers in Laos lost their lives to Pathet Lao ambushes and fatal accidents while in Vietnam some were killed and others captured by the Viet Cong and held as Prisoners of War. As the divisions deepened domestically in America over our role in the war, IVS struggled with its identity. The role of development as an instrument of policy or as an end was still very much an issue when I served as

Assistant Administrator for Asia and the Middle East during the early days of the Afghan and Iraq wars in 2002-2004. It remains so today.

It is often said that successful volunteers are measured by what they leave behind. By this standard the dedicated IVS volunteers whom I met and worked with in Laos and elsewhere were successful by any measure for the lives and numerous communities they impacted with the skills they taught and the training they provided. The less spoken truism is that each one of us learned just as much from the people and communities we served. In my case, more. I returned to Laos in 1995 as the American Ambassador. Dong Dok had expanded to become the campus of the National University of Laos. One of my former students had studied at Harvard and was a high ranking official. Many others returned to visit Laos from their new homes in Australia, France, Canada, and the United States. All had built their lives on the foundations many IVS volunteers had left behind.

The book you are about to read offers ample evidence of the value of IVS as a volunteer organization. Its volunteers have worked and impacted the lives of people in Asia, the Middle East, Africa, the Caribbean and Latin America. Of particular pride, IVS occupies a special place as a pioneer for fielding volunteers which later became a model for the Peace Corps.

The world has changed dramatically since IVS was founded in 1953 and with it the institutions and priorities for international development. One fundamental truth so graphically illustrated in this book is the value of people-to-people engagement and the impact of the experience on both the volunteer and the community they served. I know my experience served me well numerous times during my many years of international service.

WENDY J. CHAMBERLIN
IVS Laos, 1971-1973
U.S. Ambassador to Laos, 1996-1999
U.S. Ambassador to the Islamic Republic of Pakistan, 2001-2002
Assistant Administrator for USAID, 2002-2004
UN Deputy High Commissioner for Refugees, 2004-2007
President, Middle East Institute, 2007-2018, President Emeritus

Preface

International Voluntary Services, Inc. (IVS) was a 501(c)3 private voluntary organization founded in 1953 to provide services of American volunteers to international relief and development programs. The name "IVS" has often been confused with other organizations of the same name and with its use as a generic acronym for 'international voluntary services'. Over its 50-year existence, IVS provided volunteers for 1419 assignments in 39 countries, as listed in Appendix A.

IVS came into being during post World War II period while the world was beginning to recover from the unspeakable tragedies and disruption of war. In the past, the term "volunteer" often applied to those volunteering for military service. The public-private partnership that launched IVS expanded the options for individuals to selflessly serve the public good. Over the seventy years since IVS was founded, many international voluntary service programs have come into being, innovating in the use of volunteers and raising the question of "what is a volunteer".

A first book, *The Fortunate Few: IVS Volunteers from Asia to the Andes*, which was published in 2015, grew from the desire of former volunteers to tell their personal stories. The IVS Alumni Association put this together as a collection of highly personal stories involving excitement, danger, hardships, and personal satisfaction. These individual stories contribute to understanding development and the volunteers' experiences.

A Legacy of America's Global Volunteerism: International Voluntary Services (1953-2002) builds on the previous book by telling the story of IVS's philosophical and organizational origins, describing its field operations, and analyzing the experience for lessons learned for the future. The idea for this book came from a 2018 IVS Alumni Reunion in Newport, RI, where Dr. David Schleich, friend of IVS and President of NUNM Press, which published the earlier book, encouraged IVS Alumni to document the IVS story in greater detail.

Contributors to this book include IVS alumni and academics with experience in international volunteerism. Excerpts from individual volunteer stories are used throughout the book to give field level insights on the volunteer programs. Other resources were drawn from IVS archives housed in the Mennonite Church USA Archives in Elkhart, Indiana. With about 58 percent of volunteer assignments in the two countries of Laos and Vietnam, volunteer insights are sometimes limited for other programs. Contributions from specialists outside of IVS complement the

IVS history and frame it in a broader perspective of international development and volunteerism. The authors and editors gratefully acknowledge the written, financial, and other contributions by the many supporters of this book project, with special thanks to Ann Wright-Parsons for research support in the IVS archives.

This book has four sections. The first six chapters cover the history of IVS from its start in 1953 to it close in 2002. Chapter One describes the formation of IVS; Chapter Two covers initial country programs, most in the Middle East; Chapter Three covers the extensive IVS involvement in Indochina during the Vietnam war; Chapter Four describes other countries roughly from 1963 to 1973 when IVS sought to expand its volunteer-based programs; Chapter Five covers country programs from 1973 to 2002 as IVS relied on local volunteers and struggled to survive; and Chapter Six describes IVS corporate management and strategies over its lifetime.

The second section includes Chapters Seven, highlighting diverse experiences of individual volunteers, and Chapter Eight, with insights on the difficult question of assessing impacts of volunteers and volunteer programs. The third section explores partner programs that influenced and were influenced by IVS. Chapter Nine looks back to the origins of the historic "Peace Church" volunteer programs; Chapter Ten recounts the origin of the Peace Corps; and Chapter Eleven looks at more recent volunteer initiatives of USAID, the major funding agency for IVS over its lifetime. Finally, the fourth section analyzes lessons learned from the IVS experience and implications for future international volunteer activities.

IVS volunteer stories could not be used in their entirety and can be found in the Mennonite Archives together with documentation collected throughout the life of the organization. IVS Alumni offer their warm appreciation and thanks to the Mennonite Church USA Archives and its Director, Mr. Jason Kauffman, for support in putting together this book. Thanks also goes to the IVS Alumni and friends who have contributed financially to production of this book and to the authors, who have contributed their time and insights.

In putting the book together, we found the IVS story to be much deeper and more complex than we knew from the perspective of an individual volunteer. Antecedents in the form of privately funded voluntary services were extensive and a solid base for the IVS experiment. The international environment of the 1950s provided fertile ground for expanded international volunteer work. However, much changed over the years in developing country needs for volunteer services, foreign assistance strategies, and the pool of potential volunteers. IVS evolved with these changes to its operating environment. This is the core story of this book.

International volunteerism remains relevant, as described by Sherraden, et al (2006). Dr. Benjamin Lough (2015) reported that between 800,000 and 1,100,000 Americans volunteered internationally each year from 2004 to 2014. More than 241,000 Peace Corps volunteers have served in 143 countries since 1961, and about 7,000 Peace Corps volunteers were overseas when the pandemic started in 2020. Despite questions of relevance and appropriateness of Peace Corps programs that have circulated for some time, the program retains strong support.

International volunteer programs are diverse. Four types of international volunteers are recognized: short-term volunteer tourism; short-term unskilled volunteerism for cross-cultural understanding; short-term skilled volunteers for development; and long-term (nearly a year or longer) volunteers for development (Lough 2019). These four types overlap and have different motivations and issues appealing to different pools of potential volunteers..

What long-term impacts the COVID-19 pandemic will have are unknown, but need remains for cultural/professional exchanges, developmental and humanitarian assistance, and citizen diplomacy to improve international understanding. We hope that this book may provide some guidance for improvements in future programs. Future international volunteer programs will have to adapt to the changing environment with innovative approaches to meet needs of volunteers, funding sources, and host countries.

MIKE CHILTON
IVS/Vietnam, 1960-65

SECTION I
History of International Voluntary Services, Inc.

Geographic Distribution of All Countries of IVS Services
Source: *IVS Developments Newsletter—Fourth Quarter 1989*

1

IVS ORIGINS AND EARLY YEARS
1953–1957

PAUL A. RODELL, Georgia Southern University

International Voluntary Services, Inc. (IVS) was founded in 1953 and remained active in its mission of extending help to the world's less fortunate until 2002. Shortly before IVS finally closed, its last Executive Director, Anne Shirk, told me that after the attacks of September 11, 2001, the organization's already limited funding sources dried up making its continued operation impossible. During nearly a half century, IVS placed 1,368 volunteers in over thirty-one countries and the Caribbean region.[1] Over the years, funding had come from the U.S. government plus a variety of partnerships including: World Neighbors, the Ford and Rockefeller Foundations, ARAMCO (the Arab American Oil Company), international service branches of many Protestant churches, the Roman Catholic Church, among others. For most of its existence, however, the primary financial supporter was the United States government: initially under the Technical Cooperation Administration (TCA) created in 1950; then the International Cooperation Association (ICA) founded in 1955; and finally, today's United States Agency for International Development (USAID) established in 1961 under President John F. Kennedy.

A headquarters for IVS was established in Washington, DC in 1953 with a small clerical staff, an executive director, an influential board of directors and an active executive committee. This central IVS leadership built on early connections with the U.S. government agencies and cultivated connections with new partners to advance its agenda. Service operations were built on creative volunteer recruitment strategies and training methods. All of its programs were founded on the idea of a "people to people" experience that would develop local people and their skills rather than delivering completed projects to them with only minimal in-put, at best. The first IVS programs were based in the Middle East and then Asia, especially Southeast Asia, and these became the models for the organization's lifelong work. During these first few years, IVS set patterns and dealt with challenges that continued throughout the organization's life.

IVS Origins
An Historical Convergence (WW II–1953)

Historical events do not emerge in a vacuum but rather from the context of their time. While there may be notable individuals who help create those events, even the most notable among us cannot create an event if the historical context is not favorable. So too was IVS created within an historical context, the aftermath of World War II and the development of the Cold War that brought about the policies of President Harry Truman which combined with the work of the "peace churches". The result was a joint venture from which IVS emerged.

By war's end, the world's combatants in both Europe and Asia were in desperate straits. As well, the world's colonized peoples felt the impacts of the global conflagration and post-conflict rivalries, even if indirectly. The situation, especially for these people, was dire as they emerged from colonial subjugation, oftentimes with little if any preparation or practical assistance for independence provided by their former colonizers. Only the United States remained relatively unscarred by the war, and it soon offered post-war recovery assistance to its European allies and its former Asian enemy, Japan.

In 1947, former General George C. Marshall, then Harry Truman's Secretary of State, proposed a bold plan to rebuild Europe with American assistance. Enacted on April 3, 1948, the Marshall Plan represented a radical departure in American foreign policy with its sponsorship of direct assistance to Europe with little expectation of a financial return. The Truman government realized that a fully recovered and democratic ally was America's best hope for continued post-war peace. The program of assistance soon began to work wonders, but did not extend to the Soviet Union or the countries it occupied after the war. This division of control in Europe was a major factor in the complex emergence of the Cold War.

Having come into office with the death of Franklin D. Roosevelt in 1945, Truman was elected to his own term of office in 1948. In his January 1949 inauguration speech, Truman proposed a radical departure for U.S. foreign relations. His speech became known as the "Four Point Speech" and laid out a new vision that revised and extended the Marshall Plan concept. Truman challenged his country and its political parties to support the United Nations and aid the world's economic recovery, not only that of its European allies. He spoke of strengthening and supporting "freedom loving nations" against Soviet communism.

... the United States and other like-minded nations find themselves directly opposed by a regime with contrary aims and a totally different concept of life ... Misled by that philosophy, many peoples have sacrificed their liberties only to learn to their sorrow that deceit and mockery, poverty and tyranny, are their reward. That false philosophy is communism.[2]

In addition to supporting the United Nations (Point One) and continuing our assistance to Europe (Point Two) we must " ... strengthen freedom-loving nations against the dangers of aggression" (Point Three). His most radical point was the fourth which he elaborated at length " ... we must embark on a bold new program for making the benefits of our scientific advances and industrial progress available for the improvement and growth of underdeveloped areas." He stated that only democracies can supply the needed force to ". .. stir the peoples of the world into triumphant action, not only against their human oppressors, but also against their ancient enemies: hunger, misery, and despair." The result, he proposed, would be the rise of free nations living in abundance, peace and justice.[3]

An earlier concept that seems likely to have influenced the Point Four agenda originated in a wartime program run in Latin American under the direction of Nelson Rockefeller, who headed the Office of Inter-American Affairs (OIAA) created in 1939. After the war, this wartime agency was transformed into a government owned corporation that coordinated all assistance programs in Latin America, with Rockefeller still supervising. Significantly, the new agency incorporated a "Deweyian" pedagogical approach that stressed "learning by doing" where American advisers would instruct the locals who would then carry on after the foreigners left.[4]

In his memoir, Dean Acheson claimed that the initiative for Point Four came from the president's legal counsel, Clark Clifford, who first suggested a global assistance program to Truman. According to Robert Schlesinger, it was Benjamin Hardy, a young state department official who then strongly promoted the Point Four concept.[5] Finally, White House aide George Elsey followed up with Truman to ensure that it was the centerpiece of the inaugural address. Despite the presidential authority behind the initiative, Stanley Andrews, the second director of the Technical Cooperation Administration (TCA), described the new agency as staffed by "castoffs" from various federal bureaus and departments and never having the budget it needed.[6]

The other part of the IVS equation was a grouping of the "peace churches": the Religious Society of Friends (Quakers), the Mennonites, and the Church of the Brethren. All three were opposed to waging war and in their pasts had frequently defied the demands of rulers to join in their countries' military services. Their histories have many tales of persecutions by secular authorities who did not respect their deep adversity to violence.

In the twentieth century their pacificism was put to creative use during World War I when they formed their own agencies to serve without being combatants. The American Friends Service Committee (AFSC), for example, was founded in 1917 to assist civilian victims of the "Great War." After the armistice of 1918, AFSC continued relief efforts in Europe and the new Soviet Union. Later, its work continued in the United States when service in the AFSC became a constructive alternative for their young men to gain a "conscientious objector" deferment to military conscription. During World War II AFSC ran rescue missions for Europe's Jewish communities and the victims on both sides of the Spanish Civil War. Meanwhile in the United States AFSC gave aid to Japanese-Americans interned in American concentration camps. For these and many other peace and humanitarian works, the AFSC was honored in 1947 as a recipient of the Nobel Peace Award.[7]

Similarly, the Mennonite Central Committee was founded in September 1920 to provide disaster relief. Later, in World War II, young Mennonite men served in Civilian Public Service camps which provided an alternative to military service for qualifying conscientious objectors. The camp facilities were maintained by their families and congregations while the young men worked in a variety of useful projects.[8]

The third church that was instrumental in IVS's creation was the Church of the Brethren, which in addition to holding similar beliefs with regard to violence, also had an especially notable commitment to service. In a statement of beliefs, basic Brethren principles include, "peace and reconciliation, simple living, integrity of speech, family values and service to neighbors near and far." The last point is especially applicable to IVS, which became another vehicle for Brethren members to serve even beyond the church's own Brethren Volunteer Service. The well-known Heifer Project founded in 1944, and SERRV International (Sales Exchange for Refugee Rehabilitation and Vocation), started in 1949 were both launched by the Church of the Brethren before they became ecumenical.[9]

Although the political leadership in Washington and the peace churches might often have little in common, they nonetheless found a mutual interest in creating IVS. From the government side, a special initiative was undertaken by two men from the newly created TCA, Stanley Andrews and Dale D. Clarke. Both were keen to utilize the talents of the religious community to further the goals of the government's new initiative. In an extensive oral history interview conducted in October

1970 and housed in the Truman Library, Andrews described at length the recruitment of the peace churches into forming an independent organization that might provide the TCA with able volunteers. As Andrews described it:

> As we said in the beginning, this Point IV idea was a kind of white hope to church people, to just good solid American citizens who were willing to do good. . . . There were about 75 religious organizations that had various kinds of programs all over the world. . . . They probably knew more about the real situation than the other groups. I courted opinions from the missionaries and in one case I gave the Presbyterian Board of Missions money to run a hospital in Thailand.[10]

Andrews' problem was that he had limited funds and giving money to missionaries could raise objections regarding the separation of church and state. Nor could he hire missionaries into the TCA for a variety of personnel rules and considerations peculiar to civil service regulations. Instead, he reached out to some seventy-five religious groups, which he did not identify in the interview. He said that was on the order of, "You people all get together and form a non-profit organization and set up a board of directors and select a thousand of these young people who want to go out. The idea is to work in the villages, not in the town, right in the villages. I'll find them something to do."

Beyond speaking to religious groups, Andrews recognized he needed someone to assist and organize church people to bring such an organization into reality. For this task he transferred Dale Clark from his assignment as an assistant in the TCA's Middle East division and put him in charge of what he called the International Agency Development Board. Clark gladly accepted the task and went out with this clear assignment of what he was to do.

In one of two oral interviews, Dale Clark described how IVS came to be and his role in its founding. He mentioned Andrews and his "go ahead" to work on the voluntary service approach. Clark became its proponent in the TCA. One day one of Clark's co-workers told him that the folks he was looking for had just dropped by asking about the Point Four program and collaborative possibilities. Clark immediately searched for the group and found them just as they were leaving the building. That group included Mennonite Central Committee representative William Snyder, W. Harold Row of the Brethren Service Committee, and Benjamin Bushong, a founder and executive director of the Brethren's Heifer Project. Clark explained generally what they might accomplish together and set up another organizational meeting.[11]

CREATING IVS
ORGANIZATION AND FIRST PROGRAMS

At that initial planning meeting, Clark stressed the need for an interdenominational approach that could adopt to the needs of Point Four. He wanted to be sure that they could all work together. The religious representatives noted that they had already done so in a number of common activities. With that assurance, the discussion shifted to personnel, project staffing, fund-raising, and other organizational basics. Even the name was determined at this planning session when W. Harold Row proposed International Voluntary Services. When talk turned to the new organization's mission statement, Clark took a copy of the Near East Foundation's charter, used it as a model, and wrote a statement as the group discussed what they wanted.[12]

Turning to immediate service projects, the religious representatives suggested placing an initial group of six men in a poultry program in Jericho, Jordan run by Musa Alami who also had a large orphanage. While planning this project, an opportunity arose to place agriculture instructors at a university in Assiut, Egypt. This second project proposed a partnering with World Neighbors as the first IVS "hyphenated project".[13]

The first recorded meeting of this IVS preparatory committee was chaired by Harold Row on July 8, 1953. The participants reviewed the concepts upon which IVS would be founded and the committee's tasks which included selecting an initial board of directors and taking action to bring the organization into formal, legal existence.

The meeting's morning session began with a discussion that reaffirmed the desire that IVS be a "people-to-people" program where local people were participants in IVS projects and not just recipients of foreign assistance. This first point easily achieved group consensus and the discussion then turned to a more critical topic, the relationship between IVS and government agencies funding its programs. Dr. John H. Reisner, a previous dean of a missionary agricultural college in China, cautioned that IVS must ensure that all contacts between IVS and the U.S. government offices "should reflect the independent nature of IVS." He was joined by Captain William H. Tuck, former director general of international refugees during World War II, who expressed the hope that government funds would not "adversely affect" IVS programs, which should be private in nature. Even in this first formal meeting, the issue of IVS independence was discussed in the context of a potential conflict with government priorities. In retrospect, this discussion was quite prescient. Over the course of its history the nature of the relationship between IVS and government funding, selection, and support of programs sometimes became active concerns and bones of contention.

Before taking a lunch break, the group decided who would be permanent board members. Reisner and Tuck volunteered and were accepted as were Dr. Carl C. Taylor of the Ford Foundation and Roy A. Burkhart, President of World Neighbors. The sole woman present, Margaret Hickey, expressed an interest as well, but she said that she would first have to secure the approval of her organization before she could make a commitment. The group then selected Burkhardt as Chairman Pro-tem and William T. Snyder as Secretary Pro-tem until the next meeting when the permanent Board with its chair and secretary would be chosen.

After lunch, the Board ratified the Articles of Incorporation and created an Operations Advisory Committee (OAC) composed of Row, Peters of World Neighbors and Snyder to take steps to create a functioning organization including, securing an office, hiring a secretary, and beginning the process of selecting an executive director who could be presented to the board at its next meeting. Benjamin Bushong was named IVS Director of Program Activities and a Roy L. Hiteshew was appointed Treasurer.

A commitment was quickly agreed upon to co-sponsor two college teaching positions for volunteers in Assuit, Egypt. However, the next item, a contract already signed by Bushong with the TCA for an Iraq program engendered contention and serious discussion. The newly created IVS Operations Advisory Committee was instructed to clarify and amend eight points with the TCA before the contract could finally be accepted. Most of these points were critical clarifications assuring IVS control of the volunteers and their work assignments. The list was very much in line with that morning's discussion regarding a clear delineation of IVS autonomy. The morning's discussion was not an abstract exercise. The participants already knew IVS might have to face serious issues in its partnering relationships even with friendly government agencies.

After the important business of the Iraq program was discussed, approval was given for the Jericho, Jordan, agriculture settlement program and authorization was given to the OAC to begin its planning. Before adjournment, the decision was made to register IVS with the Department of State and the Treasury Department, which would facilitate the business end of a future working relationship with the TCA and other government entities.[14]

From late July through November 1953, the OAC ran the new IVS organization with only one board of directors meeting, which was held in September. In addition to its original members, the committee was frequently assisted by Dale Clark. Ruth Early, on loan from the Brethren Service Commission, provided secretarial assistance. Elmer Neufeld, described in the records as a local Mennonite representative, assisted Clark in setting up the first IVS office. In its July 28 meeting, the OAC's principal agenda item was the proposed Iraq program. The contract with the TCA, renamed on August 1, 1953, as the Foreign Operations Administration (FOA), was reviewed and plans were made to recruit a three-person team to be sent there by mid-October and interview other potential volunteers. Volunteer training would take place in New Windsor, Maryland, with language training at the State Department's Foreign Service Institute in Washington, DC.

On August 3, the OAC met again to approve the volunteer personnel and budget for the Assuit College project in Egypt. The volunteers for Iraq were given a final approval and initial steps were taken to begin the project in Jericho with Musa Bey Alami, whose volunteers could arrive by the first day of 1954. Those latter details were to be worked out when Mr. Alami visited the United States in October.[15] The OAC held a second meeting on August 28, which would be its last before the opening of a regular IVS office at 1025 Connecticut Avenue on the first of September. After reviewing details of the Iraq program, the committee's other task was nominating individuals who would be invited to become members of the permanent board of directors which would meet on September 11.[16]

Thanks to these early OAC meetings, a full agenda was ready for the board meeting. In attendance were members Roy A. Burkhart, President Pro tempore, OAC members Row, Snyder, and Clark, and secretarial assistant, Ruth Early. John H. Reisner, Executive Secretary of the Agricultural Missions, Inc. in New York and a former dean of an agricultural college in China attended as a new member. With regrets, two other members—Dr. Franklin S. Harris of Salt Lake City and Dr. E.B. Evans, President, Prairie View A & M College, in Texas—could not attend, and Captain Tuck had been called away to Europe. After a review and approval of the organizational work by the OAC, the Board approved the names of four people to be invited as board members. They then confirmed the Iraq program's Chief of Party, the six volunteers, and their training. A report was heard regarding the satisfactory joint program with World Neighbors for Assuit College in Egypt.[17]

Adding An Executive Director
Preparing IVS for Growth (1953–55)

By late 1953, the IVS's founding leaders realized that their new organization needed a full-time officer who could develop the fledgling organization. The first programs in the Middle East had come about due to preexisting contacts that a few individuals already had, especially Dale Clark's background in the TCA and others associated with World Neighbors and other efforts in that region. Creating programs in the Middle East may also have held a strong attraction for IVS's religious leaders who would be understandable inclined to this area of the world so central to their faith. So, in a very real sense these were relatively easy programs to launch since Clark had a number of contacts and familiarity with the area because of his work in the TCA's Middle East division and the keen interest of the churches in programs that could be based in the "Holy Lands."

However, once these first programs were launched the question of what would come next soon arose. An additional difficulty the leadership faced was that they all had substantial, time-consuming commitments to other organizations which had to be their primary concern. All recognized the need for someone to coordinate efforts, prepare initiatives, follow-up on programs approved by the Board of Directors, explore new program options, initiate and follow-up on a variety of communications, and generally oversee IVS programs and volunteer personnel.

Following the September board meeting, the Operations Advisory Committee met on October 20 and November 18, 1953. In both meetings the OAC's primary concerns were overseeing the Iraq and Egypt programs, discussing the possibility of additional programs in the Middle East, and reviewing lengthy and upbeat reports from the two volunteers in the World Neighbors-IVS program at the agricultural college in Assiut, Egypt. Additionally, the immediate need for an executive director was discussed and various names were suggested. Of special interest was the guest attendance of John S. Noffsinger at the November meeting.[18]

Noffsinger's presence at the November meeting is interesting because his name had already been mentioned for the executive director position at the October meeting. There may never be an answer to why a potential job candidate was present when other potential candidates were being discussed. This strange wrinkle is in the minutes, but Dale Clark did not mention it in a subsequent interview I had with him from the last IVS office in Washington, DC shortly before the organization finally closed its doors in 2002. In the interview, Clark only said that Noffsinger's name was advanced by Harold Row who knew him from their work on the Brethren Service Committee. As fellow Church of the Brethren members, both worked together on their Church's charitable international work, and they shared some of their own life stories. Row was especially impressed that Noffsinger, when in his twenties, had worked in a government teaching program in the Philippines. In that position, Noffsinger gained direct personal experience with development work of a type IVS volunteers would encounter. In his interview with me, Clark said, "... it was a similar kind of experience that we were contemplating." Row appointed Clark and one other person, whose name Clark could not recall, to meet Noffsinger and interview him. They arranged to meet at the Willard Hotel in Washington and the result, Clark claimed, was immediate. According to him "... we went there and had lunch and talked with Noffsinger and at the end of the luncheon, Noffsinger was the administrator." Clark emphasized that, "He was perfect and that's all there was to it."[19]

In fact, Noffsinger had served in an American colonial program during the earliest decades of the United States governance of the Philippines, a consequence of the Spanish-American war. The local name for the youthful English teachers was "Thomasites", named after the ship, the USS Thomas, that brought approximately 500 of these young Americans to Manila in 1901. The program lasted well into American rule. Noffsinger arrived for his two-year assignment in 1910 and was assigned to a town in the far northeastern province of Cagayan. There, he taught English and helped implement the colonial government's program of public education based on an American model. After his two-year experience, Noffsinger returned home and spent his adult working life in education, having received a Ph.D. in Education from Columbia University. By 1953, Noffsinger had retired, but he still possessed a desire to become a part of programs to assist people overseas.[20]

Confirmation of Noffsinger's hire as executive director was made at the January 8, 1954, meeting of the board of directors. The Operations Advisory Committee was formally dissolved, Dale Clark's status was changed to "consultant" to IVS, and Noffsinger's first assignment as executive director was to work with Clark and the board's executive officers to investigate possible locations for new projects.[21] With these changes, IVS prepared to continue its work in the Middle East while also expanding to new areas of the world.

Between January and July 1954, The IVS Executive Committee met four times with the primary objective of administering existing programs. Musa Bey Alami's visit to Washington, DC and his attendance at the March 5 meeting proved critical in solidifying IVS's commitment to his project in Jericho, Jordan. Additionally, detailed contracts for volunteer hirings were established. Among the many issues decided were pay and support commitments ($60 per month for single volunteers) and ($100 per month for married couples), clothing allowances, vacation leaves, health and life insurances. Noffsinger also recruited Richard A. Norris, President of Lincoln National Bank in Washington, to act as the new IVS treasurer.

During this critical period when the new organization began to explore future options, Noffsinger undertook an around-the-world trip in late April first visiting existing programs in the Middle East. The remainder of his journey indicated the future direction of IVS as he went to Pakistan, Burma, Thailand, Vietnam, and the Philippines. On June 21, he submitted a detailed report to the executive committee. For all the new countries he visited, Noffsinger reported his contacts with U.S. and host country government officials and the gist of their discussions for IVS programs. Of these countries, Noffsinger was well received in Pakistan, where he addressed a joint conference of U.S. and Pakistani officials. The director of the United States Operations Mission (USOM) in Pakistan and Pakistani officials promised to work on a program invitation. American officials in Thailand and the Philippines were quite interested in volunteer programs, but an IVS program in Burma did not appear feasible at that time because of American mission cutbacks. American officials in Vietnam were also very interested in future IVS programs, but they advised that at present this was not possible due to security concerns.[22] At that very moment, French forces were fighting for their lives in a remote mountain stronghold they originally developed to lure communist forces into what they hoped would be a trap. That place was Dien Bien Phu and it became General Henri Navarre's great miscalculation that led to the end of France's colonial empire in Southeast Asia. Noffsinger was seeking proposals for new programs at a very interesting and dangerous time in Southeast Asia.

In addition to the country-by-country report Noffsinger also submitted a paper he had written titled, "Youth's Opportunity in Point Four." In this revealing document he noted his profound religiosity and linked that with Secretary of State John Foster Dulles' revision of the Truman administration's Point Four program. In his opening paragraph, Noffsinger stated, " . . . it comes nearer to the Christian concept of how we as a nation should deal with underprivileged countries than anything we have known heretofore in U.S. Foreign Policy." He then applauded Dulles for suggesting " . . . a rather revolutionary proposal—that the American Government through Point Four should assist and encourage the various voluntary agencies . . . to spread American technical 'know-how' and efficiency methods . . . ." He then praised W. Harold Row, William T. Snyder and Dr. Dale D. Clark for founding IVS to carry forth "people-to-people" programs. He noted IVS's emphasis on recruitment of young men and women "motivated primarily by the idea of service". He further described the good work being carried forward in Iraq, Egypt, and Jordan and how this same model would soon spread to the countries he visited, and he noted an invitation to send an IVS team to Korea.

Noffsinger's essay continued with a description of the profile for an ideal IVS volunteer which included six points such as a small town or farm origins of single individuals from 20-30 years of age and who had completed all or at least a significant part of a college degree. He then gave a long list of needed skills essential for volunteer success most of which reflected a small-town rural background. He concluded with his last two points which were a dedication to service and "last but not least" volunteers should have a "Christian character". As a sort of afterthought, he allowed the acceptance of older individuals without any particular skill who could serve as team leaders, thanks to qualities in leadership or administration.

Near the end of his four-page statement, Noffsinger turned to one issue that IVS would have to deal with over time—the issue of "alternative service". Would IVS service be acceptable to the Selective Service in place of military service? From time-to-time IVS was viewed by critics, especially in the military, as nothing more than a draft dodger's means to escape their obligation to their country. When Noffsinger wrote his document, there was little issue with young men seeking a "CO" or "conscientious objector" status rather than serving in the military. Later, however, the issue would arise as the U.S. commitment to South Vietnam escalated along with youth opposition to the war effort. In future years, IVS would have to explain that the conscientious objector status was not necessarily automatic, and young men had to petition their local draft boards who were anxious to fill their quotas with able bodied young men. When he wrote his thoughts in June 1954, Noffsinger's only suggestion was to tell people where they should go for information and application forms for CO status.

The Board of Directors July ninth meeting began with the usual financial reports, a welcome of new board members, and announcements concerning members not present. Board President, Captain William Tuck resigned, due to a new government oversight commission appointment. He was replaced by Dr. John Reisner, who had earlier held the office with an "acting" status. Meanwhile, Dale Clark was added as a regular board member instead of his special position as "consultant". Clark announced that he would be leaving the Foreign Operations Administration and returning to Utah to work in the bank that his grandfather established years before. Clark's departure was not immediate, and he continued to serve IVS and attended occasional meetings through November of 1957.

The work of the July meeting included detailed reports of Middle East projects and possible expansion and a request from the United Nations Reconstruction Agency overseeing the rebuilding of South Korea in the wake of the conflict there.

The Agency was requesting a five-member IVS team to arrive as early as January 1955. After asking Noffsinger to assess the request's feasibility, the Board listened to Noffsinger's report of his extensive travels in April and May. The Board was especially interested in the feasibility of potential sites and asked him to "keep in close touch" with the contacts he made while maintaining "the development of high-grade programs in each of the projects now in operation".[23]

In the following months, IVS was busy with its projects in the Middle East. In November, Noffsinger visited Iraq when John Reisner would also be there. Additionally, the Arabian American Oil Company (ARAMCO) dedicated a year's worth of support for the Jericho project, a memorandum of understanding was signed with World Neighbors to sustain the two member IVS team in Assiut, Egypt, and negotiations were conducted with the Ford Foundation to administer certain unspecified grants and projects. The result of these follow-up measures was clear by the first days of January 1955 when the executive committee met to review the progress. The Committee determined that two recruits should be sought for a new literacy program in Minia, Egypt, and that there was a "real possibility" for IVS personnel in a Ford Foundation program at the American University in Beirut. Meanwhile, all seemed well in Iraq and some volunteers wished to extend their tours for a third year, especially if they could earn a bit more money. Noffsinger reported that a project in Pakistan looked promising and a proposal was now with the Foreign Operations Administration awaiting approval. The previously bleak situation in Burma appeared to be improving, thanks to the Ford Foundation being more willing to work with IVS than had the United States Operations Mission in Rangoon. Thai officials were already talking to the Foreign Operations Administration in Washington about two IVS agricultural teams for their country.

Despite these encouraging reports, Noffsinger's assessment of the situation in Vietnam was bleak. He reported that American officials in Saigon were pleased that the "hot" war was over and that travel was currently safe. However, they also cautioned that communist forces had infiltrated much of the south and "will probably" take over the country within one year. They requested IVS teams that would work with others to reach out to the villagers in a "hope against hope" initiative that they might prove effective at halting the communist advance. The American officials asked Noffsinger if eight IVS teams could be dispatched immediately. In his statement to the executive committee, Noffsinger said that IVS would be better off sending volunteers to Cambodia and Laos. A motion was made and approved endorsing Noffsinger's assessment, and U.S. officials were notified accordingly.[24]

In preparation for its late April board of director's meeting, the Executive Committee met at the end of March. Much of the meeting was spent reviewing developments in existing programs and personnel in IVS Middle East, but news of real progress for any new programs was kept to the end of the meeting. At that later point, the committee was told that the FOA director in Laos requested that the IVS dispatch a IVS Chief of Party as soon as possible to begin working out the details of a program there. William W. Ralston was tentatively selected, and it was decided that he would join the executive director on his May inspection trip to the Middle East. The two would then push on to Laos. Of the possible new sites in South and Southeast Asia, this was the first to gain true fruition.[25]

When the Board of Directors met on April 27, the Laos initiative was greeted warmly and seconded. The Board also recommended that Noffsinger remain with Ralston in Laos for ten days to two weeks to help develop the program. The Board also met with their guest Milton J. Esman, Director of the Foreign Operations Administration's Indochina Division. Esman underscored the government's support for this new program and gave assurances that the contract for the volunteers would be expedited. In other board actions, the Middle East programs were given a thorough review, and Dale Clark was asked to explore the possibility of additional financing from the Ford Foundation. The Board then added new members, including: Dr. Louis M. Hoskins, Executive Secretary of the American Friends Service Committee, giving the Board a representative of the third "peace church"; the Right Reverend Luigi G. Ligutti, Executive Director of the National Catholic Rural Life Conference; Mr. L. Melvin Nelson, Vice President of the Evanston Council of Churches in Illinois; and Dr. John L. Peters, President of World Neighbors. Additionally, Dale Clark was authorized to confer with Stanley Andrews, his former boss at the TCA, about joining the board, since he was no longer in government service.[26] It was hoped this broadening of the board to include such influential members would help assure IVS success going forward.

With Noffsinger travelling to the Middle East and Asia and summer being filled with vacations and family travel, the next meeting was in early August. At that meeting Noffsinger gave a positive report about the three sites in the Middle East. He did, however, note that the volunteers in Iraq needed to get the Iraqis to do more of the work themselves rather than volunteers doing it for them. The situation in South Asia was mixed with nothing developing in Pakistan, so that country was skipped. Three days were wasted in India in fruitless meetings with Indian and U.S. officials. However, there was an excellent meeting of the minds in Nepal, where arrangements were made for the introduction of a seven-person team, already recruited thanks to Dale Clark. The USOM Nepal director, Paul W. Rose, assured Noffsinger that he would soon return to D.C. and speed a contract for the volunteers through the system. A Chief of Party could arrive by the first of October with the entire team joining him by the year's end.

Since the Ford Foundation's director was out-of-country, nothing could be done about a program for Burma. However, officials in Thailand drafted a tentative proposal for a team of seven that could arrive sometime in 1956. A stop in Cambodia was frustrating because nothing could be considered until after national elections in mid-September, but the hope was that a seven-person team could arrive sometime in early 1956. The bigger news came from the Noffsinger's visits in Laos and Vietnam. Laos turned out to be frustrating due to glitches on the U.S. side. The U.S. Operations Mission (USOM) director, Carter de Paul, was absent, thus delaying work on the budget for approval in Washington. A further delay was predicted until after the 1956 U.S. Presidential election. The watchword now was "economy" until a new administration came into office. Meanwhile, the volunteers already recruited would have to wait until a contract was signed. Although riots in Saigon preceded Noffsinger's visit, he was positive that a program to help resettled Catholic refugees from the north could be viable. The highlands where they were resettled was generally peaceful, and the refugees were fiercely anti-communist and receptive to Americans. As well, there already were Catholic and Mennonite relief groups in the area. Noffsinger recommended that a further visit be undertaken in the fall by W. Harold Row and Monsignor Ligutti, who would be on a visit to Asia for the Catholic Church. These board members could also meet with USOM officials to further develop and confirm an agreeable program.[27]

1956: STARTING THE SHIFT TO SOUTHEAST ASIA

Harold Row reported on his overseas trip at the mid-December 1955 meeting of the executive committee. While the Jericho project of Musa Alami suffered damage due to a local riot, the project had been running especially well, so Row viewed the riot damage as a minor setback. To restart the program, gifts from the Heifer Project would arrive after the facilities were repaired. Additionally, the prospect for a new community development program in Lebanon was looking favorable and might even require up to 80 volunteers. On the downside, there were tensions between Egypt's Assiut College and the Ford Foundation, but fortunately, the issues did not directly involve the two IVS volunteers.

The biggest potential challenge was a new Iraqi government directive nationalizing all community development programs. What this new local initiative might require of IVS and what its impact might be was unclear. Row had learned through Iraqi officials that some unidentified USOM officials saw IVS Chief of Party Dr. E. R. Burke as too successful, which accounted for "handicaps" placed on his work. "Because of this and other personal reasons," whatever those might be, Burke had decided to resign at the end of his present term. Despite these forebodings, IVS informed James Goulden of the ICA's Community Development Division that it was still very interested in having its community development volunteers placed in Iraq.

While these developments in the Middle East were unfolding, the program in Nepal had yet to get started, but Row reported that the outlook was positive from the standpoints of both USOM and Nepalese officials. Meanwhile, in Laos the site in Xieng Khouang was ready for the incoming volunteers, and two additional sites had been tentatively selected for expansion. In Cambodia, both local and USOM officials looked forward to preparing a contract for a future program, and there was still hope for a refugee resettlement program in Vietnam, especially one that could expand to community development after the transition of the refugees from the north was completed.[28]

There were no further meetings until April 9, 1956, when IVS hosted an all-day affair at the Hotel Washington. There was a morning executive committee meeting, then a luncheon with a guest speaker, and an afternoon session of the board that lasted until 6:15 that evening. During the executive committee's morning meeting photographs of the destruction of Musa Alami's facilities in Jericho in the December riot showed that damage was worse than first indicated. The photos elicited a decision to extend whatever assistance possible to get the project up and running again. The other programs in the Middle East were continuing with no immediate difficulties. In Nepal, the first of the small contingent was getting settled. Others would follow shortly. The same was true for the new Laos program that was now welcoming its first members. On the other hand, the Vietnam initiative had hit a snag that required some important revisions in the USOM/Vietnam contract. It was suggested that Monsignor Ligutti (then in Saigon) confer with the executive director to iron out remaining issues before advancing the program.

The Executive Committee was joined at the luncheon by all additional members of the board and guests from the International Cooperation Administration (ICA), the Department of Agriculture, and private organizations such as the American Farm Bureau Federation and the International Farm Youth Exchange. The importance of the luncheon was soon apparent because the speaker was Eldon Burke, who had just completed his term as the Iraq Chief of Party. He discussed the IVS program there in detail. His speech, more effective than a typed, end-of-term report, educated the invited guests on challenges involved in working "on the ground" in a host country.

In the afternoon board meeting, country reports and actions of the executive committee were reviewed and approved. The Board welcomed Stanley Andrews as its newest member.

The Board then focused on New Business, which proved an important exercise in light of possible dramatic future growth:

> *Inasmuch as three ICA contracts have now been signed and a fourth is in its initial stage, thus making it probable that within a period of one-year IVS shall have increased its number of teams under ICA contracts from one to six and the number of its field personnel thereunder from nine to approximately 45-48, the matter of IVS policy regarding expansion was discussed at some length.*[29]

While advising caution in the expansion process, the Board reaffirmed IVS's commitment to remaining in the "Near, Middle and Far East" and to recruiting only qualified individuals. In addition to contracts with the U.S. government, IVS would also try to secure contracts and working relations with non-governmental agencies, all the while continuing to work on a "people-to-people" basis, primarily in community development. At no point, the Board affirmed, should IVS become a mere fund-raising agency. The Board also reaffirmed its religious origins and commitment to work for the betterment of the poor without making efforts to "propagandize or to proselytize". In fact, the non-denominational nature of IVS, as it had evolved, was shown very clearly in an attached listing of the executive committee and board of directors officers—to which a denominational listing was included. That list showed that the leadership was comprised of members of ten denominations: Baptist, Brethren, Catholic, Episcopalian, Lutheran, Mennonite, Methodist, Mormon, Presbyterian and the Society of Friends. IVS, an organization formed at the behest of two 'Peace Churches" had evolved in ways that could not have been anticipated when Dale Clark, the Mormon government worker, first met the three-man delegation of Brethren and Mennonite leaders only a couple of years earlier.[30]

Approximately seven weeks later, the Executive Committee met on May 24, 1956, and reviewed the progress of each of the organization's projects. The three Middle East programs seemed to be in unsettled states. Personnel at Assiut college were in a state of uncertainty with one member on leave and another due for replacement at the end of his contract. Meanwhile, no real progress had been made repairing Musa Alami's poultry project in Jericho. A number of measures were discussed hoping that the situation would be rectified, but further clarification had to wait until the executive director's upcoming inspection trip. The Iraq program warranted special consideration because of changes being considered and implemented by the government there. While the current contract had been extended for a year, future contracts would probably be negotiated with the Iraq Community Development Agency rather than with ICA. The situation would remain fluid until important program particulars were actually worked out with local authorities.

The outlook in Southeast Asia was more upbeat with the American ambassador to Laos, Mr. Charles Yost, praising the initial IVS work and looking forward to the arrival of a second team in early 1957 to be placed in the southern Bolovens plateau near Pakse. Meanwhile, thanks to the work of Monsignor Ligutti in Saigon, the Vietnam program was on track with U.S. officials agreeing to all IVS contract requests. Already the program had recruited its first volunteer, Mr. Gordon Brockmueller and two others had been sent overtures. Monsignor Ligutti agreed to locate nurses for this project as well. The first team was to be ready by late summer or early autumn. All programs in the Middle East and Asia were to be visited by the executive director on a supervisory visit from June to mid-August.

In a new development, a staff member of ICA Washington suggested that a field or program director specializing in community development be hired by IVS to supervise all IVS sites to ensure that the best techniques were being constantly employed. The Executive Committee's unanimous belief was that such an individual would be a strong addition to the program. Their only concern was how to fund such a position. At this meeting nothing could be done, so the issue was tabled for the present.[31]

The Executive Committee did not meet again until September 7, 1956, since Noffsinger was traveling and little could be done until his late August return. Most of the meeting was devoted to his report and ensuing discussion. As usual, his report began with the Middle East projects.

In Egypt, IVS workers at Assiut College had been so successful that two of the school's graduates were now doing much of the work that the IVSers had originally come to do. Therefore, the committee recommended that future volunteers have not only farm experience but also a college education. It seems that IVS was successfully working its way out of a job. Meanwhile, volunteers were not needed with Musa Alami's poultry project because post-riot repairs were incomplete. William Snyder, the Executive Committee Chair, and Stanley Andrews offered to follow up with the Ford Foundation, which largely funded the project. These two projects were clearly changing with little prospect for further growth.

The discussion turned to Iraq. The project there was described as being in a "critical period" due to the Iraqi decision to take over and supervise all community development programs. Doubts about the capability of Iraqi personnel to successfully manage these programs had caused a significant decline in the IVS team's morale. Coincidentally, there had been a change in the IVS program's leadership. Both Dr. Eldon Burke and the public health nurse, Dorothy Paxton, had resigned. On a positive note, USOM/Iraq had asked that the current contract with IVS be continued for at least another year.[32] The program's future was very uncertain and might lead to a closing of that door for IVS.

Meanwhile in Nepal, work on the building to house the training center was proceeding and the school for village workers was scheduled to open on October 1. Yet, during his negotiations with USOM/Katmandu officials, Noffsinger was disappointed to learn that a second team of IVS workers was now "improbable". In contrast, the Laos program had begun and was praised by the U.S. Ambassador who was glad that technical assistance was now offered to Laotians outside the capital. And finally, Noffsinger reported that an ICA contract for two IVS teams for Vietnam should be ready by early October. Volunteers could be sent by the first of January 1957. One team would be located in the Mekong Delta about 125 miles southwest of Saigon, while the second would be placed in the upland station of Ban Me Thuot, where a Mennonite medical team was already in place.[33]

Reports given during the final meeting of 1956 were not very positive for reasons unrelated to the quality of the volunteers or the efforts of IVS Washington. On October 29, conflict broke out in the Suez Canal and Gaza Strip between Egypt and a coalition of Israel, England, and France and inflamed the Middle East. The Suez Crisis led to the evacuation of nearly all Westerners from Egypt and many surrounding countries. This included IVS volunteers in Egypt and Jordan. Because of the situation in Egypt, a return of the volunteers was very uncertain. Meanwhile, there was no word from Musa Alami in Jericho, and few other organizations had even begun to return to Jordan.

Iraq's situation was also unsettled because the Iraqi government's initiative to take control of all community development programs was proceeding slowly and with notable lapses in professional and bureaucratic competence. This led to frustration among the volunteers. Nor had the ICA produced a revised contract that was supposed to provide an increase in the IVS presence. A somewhat similar situation in Nepal had also arisen. There, IVS was taken by a surprising turn when, after spending seven months building and getting a community development training center built, Nepali officials announced, suddenly and without warning, that the IVS team would be transferred to another location some 150 miles to the east. A team of community development workers from India would take over the facility the IVS volunteers had taken months to prepare. No explanation was given for this abrupt decision, but there had been no reason to think that the Nepalese were dissatisfied with the IVS team's work. So, while the programs in Egypt and Jordan were dealt severe blows by a major international conflict, those in Iraq and Nepal were hobbled by abrupt changes in their host governments' policies.

At the same time, the situation looked very different in Southeast Asia, where positive reports continued to praise the Laos program in Xieng Khouang Province and a second site was being readied on the Bolovens Plateau. Personnel for the first Vietnam program were ready to depart in mid-January 1957. Meanwhile, Pakistani expressed renewed interest in IVS in light of the prospect of a large irrigation project that could use American volunteer assistance. There were renewed program interests in Burma, thanks to the Ford Foundation, and in Thailand and Indonesia.[34]

1957: Endings And Beginnings
IVS Emerges Anew

The fate of the first IVS programs and the possibility of new ones became realities in 1957—one of the most pivotal years for IVS. Its programs in the Middle East would recede and cease, while new ones would emerge in Southeast Asia. The new programs in Southeast Asia would quickly become the main IVS focus until the mid-1970s, although there would be small programs in Africa, including Algeria, Morocco, Zaire and Liberia. Without the groundwork laid in 1956 for work in Southeast Asia, it is very likely IVS would have closed its doors by 1957. However, the large programs in Laos and Vietnam would live on in the IVS mystique and have outsized importance in defining the organization down to its final demise in 2002.

On March 27, IVS had its annual board of directors meeting preceded by a meeting of the smaller executive committee and a luncheon. In these meetings the IVS program in Egypt was discussed only in terms of the financial details that remained to be clarified with the co-sponsor, World Neighbors. The situation in Jordan was still uncertain since Musa Alami still hoped to restore his old program and sought financial assistance. IVS could only urge others to support this effort in the hopes that Alami's efforts would result, as he hoped, in a large community development initiative that might encompass approximately 120 frontier villages that the Ford Foundation had offered to support.

The real blow was the dissolution of the Iraq program, which had become a sad tale of governmental mismanagement wherein both the Iraqi people and IVS were the losers. Competent Iraqi personnel, who were on-site when the government took over, were dismissed and replaced by political appointees. Promised funds were not delivered, so work on the project came to a "standstill". Nonetheless, IVS persisted and worked out a new contract with USOM Iraq only to have it stalled in Washington and finally killed after ten months of waiting and making numerous inquiries and entreaties. Perhaps USOM Iraq didn't "sell" community development strongly enough to Washington or maybe Washington wanted tighter control of overseas projects which would not include third parties such as IVS.[35] While this approach represented a reversal of former policies, it seems the U.S. government had originally suggested to the Iraqis that there should be a transfer of the community development programs to their control. Whatever the reasons behind the switch, new recruits would be turned away or assigned to other programs. For the Iraq volunteers still in the field other options had to be made.

In Southeast Asia, the soil at the second Laotian program's site in the Bolovens Plateau was not as fertile as hoped, causing a delay in that team's introduction. In Vietnam, a Chief of Party for the second Vietnam team, John Barwick, whose son Peter had been an IVS volunteer with the Iraq team, was on-site, and the team was being selected. Good news involved a potential program in Indonesia that would involve almost 200 new college graduates who would work in that government's civil service at the same pay grade as the locals. IVS would be tasked with recruiting about 25 of the students.[36]

The Executive Committee did not meet again until May 24, at which time discussion centered on closing the Iraq program and the continual problem of finding funding sources for Musa Alami to restart his program in Jerico. Meanwhile, the Nepal program seemed to be in serious trouble due to complaints by the Indian government about the number of Americans in Nepal, which is strange that they should have a say in the internal affairs of a neighboring country. In any event, USOM Nepal decided not to renew the IVS contract set to expire in February 1958. The Laos and Vietnam programs continued to be praised by all parties. Winning special praise were the two teams in Vietnam, thanks to the excellent leadership of their Chiefs of Party, Par Danforth and John Barwick. Three or four other countries expressed interest in programs, but the possibility of a program in Indonesia seemed the most promising, although Noffsinger and the Indonesian government had many details to work out when meeting in July.

While all of these program reports and concerns were important, the committee also took time to consider possible "Problems Ahead." These "Problems" included the nature of service that IVS should render, especially with respect to the

Indonesia proposal which might not be a true development program. There was some talk, too, about the type of personnel to be recruited by IVS and whether chiefs of party could be selected for terms of more than two years. Noffsinger seemed to have solved one potential problem with an office of the national Selective Service System agreement. He reported that IVS could petition for a deferment on behalf of a volunteer but should not advertise this possibility. The committee saw the wisdom of not advertising, since this might attract applicants that IVS would not necessarily want.[37]

The Executive Committee did not meet again until October 3, since Noffsinger had been on another site visitation from June 11 to September 11. Noffsinger's series of visits confirmed that the final details of the Iraq program were in order, but it was discouraging to learn that ARAMCO had decided not to continue to fund Musa Alami's program in Jericho. Nonetheless, small funding continued to Alami from some sources. In addition, he was taking produce and poultry to Beirut once a week providing sufficient revenue to restore the farm and support the boys orphanage he runs. Noffsinger had approached the Mennonite Central Committee for support, which they may render, and appeals would be sent to state poultry associations for donations. In other equally depressing news, it is official that ICA Washington would not renew an IVS contract for Nepal, even for a limited period. Even arguments that a team of two or even three IVS volunteers could do more work than one U.S. government employee, which made IVS a splendid economic deal, did not win the argument. The program would end with the current volunteers.

For South and Southeast Asia there was mixed news of disappointment for Pakistan, short-term hiccups in Laos and Vietnam, and only dim possibilities in some other countries. It was actually the ICA in Washington that decided against funding an IVS program in Pakistan for volunteers to work with fishermen. In Laos, a change of the USOM director delayed paperwork for the second team's funding, but the first site was up and running. Meanwhile in Vietnam, there was a more serious problem. The site in the Mekong Delta had to be evacuated for security reasons with most of the volunteers shifted to Ban Me Thout in the Central Highlands. Two nurses in that group were reassigned to hospitals in Saigon. Noffsinger met officials in Indonesia, but was doubtful about the viability of that program as proposed. Finally, there seemed to be only a small chance for a program in Burma and very little in the way of immediate possibilities for either Thailand or Cambodia.[38]

The final 1957 IVS meeting of the executive committee was held on November 7. There were two parts to the meeting: first, a country project review, and then, an important consideration of where IVS should go and how it should proceed in the future. By this time, IVS was virtually out of the Middle East. The work of Musa Alami was barely subsisting on aid from the Heifer Project. Volunteers were still in place in Nepal, but a termination date was set for May 17, 1958. The situation in Laos was interesting in that the USOM in Vientiane and the Laotian government were very keen on the IVS volunteers, but ICA/Washington was being very negative, especially its Agriculture Programs Division. This disconnect between Washington and American in-country officials revealed a serious potential problem for IVS and its future. The problem of relocating volunteers from south of Saigon to the Central Highlands would soon be resolved, while the two nurses shifted to Saigon left the program for personal reasons. And finally, an ICA decision not to fund the proposed Indonesia program led to a discussion of whether the Ford Foundation might be interested in funding this initiative.[39] Whether it was Indonesia, Laos, or Nepal, there seemed to have been a consistent pattern of questioning, and even obstruction, from ICA/Washington that was not present when IVS was first founded. Perhaps, for this reason, the bulk of the meeting was devoted to what was termed simply as "The Future of IVS".

Playing a prominent role in the discussion was a new board of directors member who was indirectly responsible for the IVS's very creation. Stanley Andrews, the former director of the TCA, who had initially assigned Dale Clark to reach out to interested religious leaders to form IVS, had joined the Board in September 1956 when his government service ended. He, Carl Taylor, and John Reisner used their government connections to reach out to former colleagues. They stressed the need for IVS to confer with Washington agency heads and certain congressmen to explore issues of government funding in regard to private contractors working on overseas development programs. After a lengthy discussion about what should be the objective of meeting with agency heads, Andrews stepped forward: he would meet with the ICA Administrator, James H. Smith, Jr.; Taylor and Reisner would meet with ICA officials in their Community Development Division; and Reisner and Monsignor Ligutti would contact selected congressmen who were interested in foreign aid programs.[40]

1953–1957: Overview Of The Years Of Origin And Founding

From late 1953 to the end of 1957, IVS emerged from its founding to become an established organization. Despite some real success, IVS's first programs became casualties of local government policies, the international Suez Crisis, a devastating riot in Jericho, and the shifting objectives of sponsoring agencies in Washington.

However, with the IVS office strategically located in Washington, DC, overseen by a dedicated and involved board and executive committee, and run by an executive director with personal international experience, new options were explored. When initial programs ended, others arose to take their place. In future years, IVS would continue to struggle with local hurdles to overcome and the dilemma of its relationship with U.S. government agencies. Although IVS always searched for non-governmental funding and partnerships, none were sufficient to fund the organization. As well, the possibility of IVS as alternate service would have to be clarified, especially in the years of American military involvement in mainland Southeast Asia. As a Private Voluntary Organization (PVO), IVS would always have to struggle, but the dynamism shown in its first years never wavered and continued until IVS's unfortunate demise in 2002.

2

INITIAL PROGRAMS
SET-UP, STRUCTURE, AND EXPERIENCE

DON MITCHELL AND CHERIE J. WOODCOCK MITCHELL

While a post-World War II world sought to rebuild, IVS programs, as introduced in Chapter One, were initially established in Egypt, Jordan, Iraq, and Nepal. In response to the horror of the holocaust, there was great empathy for the creation of a Jewish state in Palestine. With support from the U.S. and Great Britain, the State of Israel was created and recognized by the United Nations (UN) in 1948. The takeover of land for the Jewish state resulted in Arab land and business owners fleeing across the Jordan River to hastily established refugee camps. If peace was to be in the Middle East, the U.S., UN, and other governments recognized a need to improve the health, education, and economic well-being of villagers in the Arab countries. With time and in conjunction with the UN, IVS Middle East assistance was extended to include a Palestinian refugee program.

These early programs varied, but the preferred model was that of an interdisciplinary community development team—headed by a senior team leader—working at the village level. Iraq and Nepal were examples of this model, which was later used in Southeast Asia. The five country programs described below represent IVS's experience and lessons learned in launching its volunteer programs. The Iraq program is described in some detail, because it reflects the environment and types of work expected of volunteers during that era.

IVS/Egypt (1953–54)
First Volunteers in the Field

IVS/Egypt
PROGRAM:
• Demonstration Farm
VOLUNTEERS – 4
FUNDING: USOM and Ford Foundation

The first IVS team, assigned to the Village Improvement Program at the American College in Assiut, Egypt, followed a somewhat different pattern of assignments than later teams. Kenneth Imhoff (formerly with the Mennonite Central Committee Pax Program in Europe) and Otis Rowe (formerly with the Brethren Voluntary Service in Europe) had been working in Europe for World Neighbors. In an agreement between World Neighbors and IVS, "The project administered by IVS under contract with the government will be an IVS project and not World Neighbors."[1] Funding was from the Ford Foundation and USOM/Egypt.

While the two-person team's headquarters was at the American Mission College in Assiut, the Village Improvement Program was located 25 miles south along the Nile River at the village of Afadra. The 33-acre demonstration farm was surrounded by a high mud-brick wall. Within the compound a spacious mansion type house (once a dwelling for a rich landowner) provided a second floor as living quarters for two IVS volunteers and two Egyptian co-workers. There were few modern conveniences. Running water was pumped to a storage tank on the roof. There was no electricity, and light at night was by lantern. A pressure gas burner was used for cooking. First floor rooms were used for storage, offices, first aid, and a reasonably well-equipped workshop.

The Village Life Improvement Center served as an outreach program to farmers in surrounding villages. The farm was planted for crop trials and feed for cattle, goats, and poultry. A small herd of native cows was penned in mud-brick barns, with forage cut by hand and hauled to the cows by donkeys. American Jersey bulls from the Heifer Project were kept to cross breed with native cows in surrounding villages. Offspring were expected to produce twice as much milk as native cows. The farm served as a showcase for improved management and breeding stock for participating farmers. Outreach visits were routinely made to 125 participating farmers.

As often happens, introduction of an innovation sometimes conflicts with local culture, thus requiring a little creative thought for the innovation to gain acceptance. Traditionally, native cows and bulls were used, as oxen, to pull crude farm equipment. Some farmers objected to the introduction of the purebred American Jerseys because it was thought that they would not work in this way. During the harvest season, Otis asked a farmer skilled in handling oxen to train a Jersey bull to work. To the amazement of the farmer, once the Jersey bulls were trained, they worked just as well as native cattle.

White Leghorn and Rhode Island Red chickens, imported as chicks by the Heifer Project, were maintained at the farm and distributed to farmers. Eggs of highly productive Khaki Campbell ducks were imported from Holland and hatched, and the improved ducklings distributed to farmers. Outreach visits checked on disease and parasites and recorded progress.

After two years, Otis and Kenneth returned home, and IVS administrative support for the project ended. They were replaced by Brethren Volunteer Service and Mennonite Central Committee volunteers. Because of the Suez crisis in 1956, all foreign volunteers were evacuated from Egypt, and none were replaced. Egyptian co-workers continued the project for another year before the Village Life Improvement program was terminated.[2] In the 1980's, Otis returned for a short visit to Afadra and was pleased to learn that the community had become a major area for exporting dairy products to other parts of Egypt.

The Egypt Program was highly regarded and received good press, as described in Chapter One. Unfortunately, as IVS was to learn in later years, international politics can relatively quickly bring promising programs to an end.

IVS/JORDAN (1954–55)
SHORT-LIVED SUPPORT TO A PRIVATE DEVELOPMENT PROJECT

IVS/Jordan
PROGRAM:
 • Poultry Production
VOLUNTEERS – 2
FUNDING: USAID

IVS activity in Jordan started with a young farm-experienced volunteer assisting to establish a poultry facility at a boys' vocational school for Palestinian refugees near Jericho. A 2000-acre farm was established there under the charismatic leadership of Musa Bey Alami, Director of the Arab Development Society. Wells had been drilled for irrigation of vegetable and field crops, and there were promising prospects for employing refugees to provide fresh vegetables, meat, and eggs to ARAMCO for their employees in Saudi Arabia. While the project had considerable merits, it by-passed government channels with IVS assigning the initial volunteer directly to the project.

Jim Baile, a young farmer from the Midwest, had recently signed on with Brethren Volunteer Service to work with the Heifer Project at a Maryland holding facility for livestock being shipped overseas. Before he had settled into the job, the organizations recognized that he was well qualified for the Jordan assignment, and an agreement was reached to seamlessly transfer Jim to IVS. In rather fast action, travel arrangements were made, and Jim, with 5,000 baby chicks from the Heifer Project, was on a flight to Jericho in early 1954.

Jim hit the ground running, helping staff and refugees build poultry growing facilities and setting up a hatchery using incubators donated by a Brethren farmer. He was well liked by his workmates, but, once the project was operational in July 1955, he was transferred to the IVS/Iraq team to complete his contract.

Unfortunately, in December 1955, an Arab uprising led to the destruction of the facility and many of the birds were killed. The reason for the riots is unclear, but it seems not to have been directed against the poultry project or the vocational school. Dr. Noffsinger, IVS Executive Director, visited Jordan in the summer of 1957 and reported to the IVS executive board.

> *The poultry project in Jericho now seems to be rehabilitated. . . . The project as a whole still bears the evidence of the destructive raid. . . . A flock of more than 10,000 birds appeared to be present due to the beneficence of an Englishman.... Because of the destruction, Mr. Alami was compelled to use his personal funds and borrow additional funds to keep the operation going and even so was unable to pay the costs of pumping irrigation water. . . . The contract with ARAMCO was cancelled by mutual agreement largely due to quality issues. . . . He was pursuing other marketing avenues including opening a shop in Beirut.*
>
> *Mr. Alami was seeking additional assistance from IVS to expand the poultry flock to at least 20,000 birds, build a small slaughter plant and purchase a refrigerated truck to haul poultry and vegetable products to more distant markets. . . . Plans to build a small dairy were considered but placed on hold. He had taken steps toward official recognition by the Government of Jordan [GOJ] including the support of the King as the first steps of officially requesting ICA (USOM) funding for IVS assistance. However, for such assistance, the GOJ would require the project be turned over for government operation to which Mr. Alami was unwilling to agree.*

At the time, there was little IVS could do but seek support from other organizations such as the Mennonite Central Committee and state or national poultry associations. Mr. Alami received a $500,000 five-year grant for a Frontier Villages Program for 12 villages along the Israeli/Jordan border, but the Jericho project never revived. IVS's assistance was critical to project start-up and proof-of-concept, but local political unrest was disruptive, and the need for resources beyond the services of volunteers became evident.

IVS/IRAQ (1953–57)
A COMPREHENSIVE RURAL DEVELOPMENT TEAM

IVS/Iraq
PROGRAM:
• Rural Development
VOLUNTEERS – 20
FUNDING: USOM

The U.S. Embassy in Baghdad opened in 1950. A year later, a formal agreement with the Iraqi Government provided for the exchange of technical knowledge and skills. During the following year (1952), the U.S. Operations Mission (USOM) opened to administer these activities with technical specialists in agriculture, irrigation, public health, home economics, community development and other fields assigned to work with Iraqi Government agencies at both national and regional levels.

J. Sheldon Turner, USOM Community Development Advisor, worked out an agreement with the Ministry of Social Affairs to create two regional community development centers with IVS to train village level workers: one in Shaqlawa serving the Kurdish area and the other in Mahawil for the rest of the country. A contract to provide volunteers was signed on June 30, 1953, by Stanley Andrews, Administrator of the International Cooperation Administration, and Benjamin G. Bushong, Acting Director of Project Activities, acting on behalf of IVS. The agreement established a model for public funding for IVS to deliver technical assistance at the village level with commitment for financial and administrative support from the host government. Edward D. Harmon, Jr., the last IVS/Iraq team leader, framed the overall attitude and understanding of rural development in his final report.

> *Few in the Iraqi government and even fewer in the educated class understood the concept of community development. Indeed, many felt the villagers were ignorant and made little or no contribution to the economy. Many felt that the construction of large irrigation projects, major highways, hospitals and other infrastructure projects were the keys to economic development without working with illiterate villagers.*

Still, with the urging of USOM Community Development advisors, the concept of community development was taking root in the Ministry of Social Affairs. Few Iraqis trained in agriculture, public health or other community needs were willing to live in remote areas. Community development centers, with resources to solve village problems and sufficient status to gain the support of political leaders, could be an avenue for social and economic development in the countryside. Bringing enthusiastic young Americans along with supplies and equipment into a community development center was seen as a way to quickly start the program.

Project Team

The first IVS volunteers to Iraq, Carl Jantzen, Everett Jenne, and Martha Rupel, were accepted on August 3, 1953, and started language training in Maryland with assistance from the Foreign Service Institute.[3] They arrived in Baghdad on December 26, 1953, to continue language training and to visit USOM projects around Baghdad. Dr. Eldon Burke, the IVS team leader, arrived in March 1954, coming from a position in Europe as coordinator for all U.S. relief assistance flowing into war-torn Germany and Belgium. The team moved to the Kurdish village of Shaqlawa, about 30 miles northeast of Erbil, in July 1954 to establish a pilot demonstration farm and village worker training center, as part of the Village Life Improvement Program of Iraq's Ministry of Social Affairs.

Dr. Burke, a persuasive leader, convinced officials in the Iraqi Ministries of Social Affairs and Agriculture and USOM advisors on the value of his vision of a rural community development center. He was given considerable latitude in developing the program to include a wide range of activities: training; well-drilling and spring improvement for clean drinking water; food and nutrition programs for children and mothers; an operating farm to demonstrate improved farming methods and simple farm equipment; an orchard to test adaptability of various fruit trees; imported dairy cattle to crossbreed with local cattle; a poultry flock to improve bird size and egg production; and a business incubator for light industries (e.g., furniture making, weaving, and building blocks and latrine slabs).

USOM and the Minister of Social Affairs had confidence in the Shaqlawa model plans, and there was considerable discussion of funding an additional five-to-six teams for other parts of the country. This over-optimism led to the purchase of equipment and supplies without adequate planning and over-buying of food supplies for volunteers who never materialized. This led to later financial constraints.

The project site was in Erbil province in the heart of the Kurdish area. Shaqlawa was sufficiently close to Erbil for government supervision and sufficiently near the village to provide high visibility. Shaqlawa had approximately 3,000 residents, about a third Kurdish Christians and the rest Kurdish Muslim. The village was nestled in a mountain valley fed by about five large springs that provided year-round water. Houses lining the hillside were built with stone and mud-brick walls. Their reasonably waterproof flat roofs were made with poplar poles for structural support and covered with twigs and layers of straw and clay. People lived in these warmer houses during the winter months. In the summer they moved to gardens in the valley floor where cool shade of fruit and poplar trees provided a respite from the summer heat.

It may be difficult for readers today to comprehend the primitive conditions that existed in the Iraq of the 1950's. Despite the oil wealth of Iraq, life in villages had changed little since biblical days. Farmers tilled their soil with stick plows pulled by oxen or donkeys; village houses with livestock pens were often built uphill from a spring that provided drinking water for the village; sanitary toilets were scarce; infant mortality was high and malnutrition common. It was into these primitive conditions that the first volunteers arrived to establish their own living accommodations and to begin the task of community development with the expectation that they show results as quickly as possible.

The three volunteers set about establishing a home base while Dr. Burke spent most of his time in Baghdad talking with USOM and Iraqi officials. Initially, volunteers lived in the only, very basic, hotel in town and in a tent at the project site. Carl Jantzen set about establishing living quarters and making basic furniture, such as tables and chairs, since none were available locally. Everett Jenne gained early entry into the villages by assisting the local livestock officer with a sheep and goat dipping program to control scabies, a mite that causes a rash on people and livestock. Since villagers often shared living space with livestock, control of this irritant was a high priority. Martha Rupel, a former missionary and the first woman on the team, was an experienced nurse who became an instant hit. Working with the local doctor, they established well-baby clinics for distributing UNICEF milk to babies and nursing mothers in Shaqlawa and surrounding villages.

Meanwhile, Peter Barwick, Rudman Ham and Albert Holloway set sail from New York in October 1954 on a freighter with the cattle, poultry, and rabbits, arriving in Beirut on November 2, 1954. On arrival at Shaqlawa, Holloway and Ham worked with Iraqi staff building barns and corrals for livestock, locating feed sources, and training Kurdish staff on basic animal and poultry husbandry. They built chicken houses to grow chicks to be distributed to villagers. Holloway developed an artificial insemination program using the semen of the imported Jersey bulls to cross with village cows.

The Community Development Center (CDC) was to recruit and train Village Level Workers. The Ministry of Social Affairs hired Hanna, a well-respected Chaldean Christian and former school master from Shaqlawa as Center Director. He spoke English, Kurdish, and Arabic fluently. All day laborers and other employees were paid under the IVS contract with Dr. Burke bringing in cash to meet the monthly payroll. Since Village Level Workers were Iraqi government employees, there was considerable competition for positions and opportunities for hiring favor-itism. Village level workers were assigned to a village or a cluster of villages to work with village leadership (most often the sheik controlling the area) to identify needs and access CDC resources to meet those needs. Dr. Burke worked with the Governor, sheiks, and center director in selecting recruits. The job of IVS volunteers, with translation assistance and in cooperation with Iraqi trainers and occasional UN advisors, was to train the village level workers. Peter coordinated the training and taught English and the math they would use on the job. Of the initial class of 25, about 15 completed training and were assigned to villages. Additional IVS team members arrived, including the following:

> BETTY HUTCHESON, a home economic graduate from Ohio State University, worked with Martha in the well-baby clinics. Later, she worked with village leaders of Harir, an Assyrian village in the next valley, to establish the first girls' school in the area.
>
> DON GOODFELLOW, a young farmer from Kansas, worked on development of farm equipment and on crop production. His work was indispensable in harvesting forage and threshing grain with a German threshing machine.
>
> JIM BAILE was transferred from Jordan for two weeks before moving on to Sulaymaniyah, where he was responsible for cleaning and treating wheat seed until his departure in September.
>
> DON MITCHELL, who grew up on an Idaho farm and had a degree in agriculture from the University of Idaho, worked on the poultry project at the CDC and surrounding villages and later on extension services for field and vegetable crops.
>
> CHERIE WOODCOCK, a farm girl from upstate New York with a degree in home economics from Cornell University, worked with the well-baby clinics, food and nutrition and other activities including canning tomatoes.
>
> ED WISER, who had grown up in villages in northern India and had agricultural engineering degrees from Iowa State and North Carolina State Universities, was assigned to develop farm implements for subsistence farmers.[4] Ed was responsible for maintenance of project vehicles and farm equipment and was often found up to his elbows in a greasy engine—blowing a hole in the belief that an effendi (educated man) did not get his hands dirty.

LIVING CONDITIONS

Two trailer houses from the U.S. were set up at the CDC as housing for team members with one used as a temporary artificial insemination laboratory. The trailer houses with sleek appliances and furnishings amazed the villagers and created considerable discussion in the community. The trailers were fitted with bunk beds: one trailer for men and the other for women. Electricity from a generator provided lighting and air conditioning (A/C), although the A/C was seldom used. Water was piped in from the irrigation well. Since electricity was not dependable, kerosene was used for refrigeration, cooking, and heating water. The first person in the shower had hot water, the next person maybe.

Two adjoining stone houses with a large, fenced courtyard were rented for storage, food supplies, a kitchen/dining area and a gathering place for team members and visitors. These buildings were conveniently located just across the street from the Post Office—home to the only phone in town and a lifeline to the world outside.

Because of the amazing amount of time it took for just the daily tasks of living, Betty persuaded the parents of two Assyrian young women that it would be safe for them to share a room at the IVS house where they did the cooking and laundry for the team. There was no grocery from which to buy pre-packaged foods, vegetables, fruit, meat, and dried staples at any time of day. Shopping in the village market for meat and fresh produce was an experience. Cherie usually went with a maid and a male driver (there always needed to be a male present) to the early morning market for freshly slaughtered lamb and goat. Sometimes beef of either water buffalo or bovine origin was available. Hunks of meat were carved from the bone and weighed by kilo—with no such thing as a standard cut like sirloin steak. Since IVS was paying the grocery bill, she had to have a receipt. Cherie would write out a receipt (in English) and the butcher, who was illiterate, would dip his thumb in blood to sign it!

In Baghdad, there was considerable discussion of expanding IVS teams into other areas, possibly expanding up to 35 volunteers. Since IVS provided team members with food and lodging, this required advance planning. Dr. Burke drew on his connections in Germany to obtain food supplied by a Hamburg wholesaler. Since excess canned food left from the war was available at bargain prices, the wholesaler sent two truckloads to Shaqlawa in December 1955. With no refrigerated storage and only a bedroom in the IVS house for dry storage, the team was ill equipped to manage this volume of food.

Team member health was always a concern. Digestive upsets were common due to unclean water, open sewers, and lots of flies. Having a nurse on the team was a definite asset for minor health issues. Any hospitalization required an overnight train ride or a full day drive over dusty roads to the Seventh Day Adventist Hospital in Baghdad. All team members were required to have and keep immunizations up to-date.

Having a cook trained in basic sanitation and food handling skills was essential; but even so, three team members had hepatitis, one typhoid and most tragically in the spring of 1955, Albert Holloway came down with polio and had to be medically evacuated. PETER BARWICK wrote:

> Just as the artificial insemination program got into full swing, Albert came down with Polio. Diagnosed as flu (as it often was), it took five days to get him to the 7th Day Adventist hospital in Baghdad, where he required the only iron lung in Iraq. Then he had two episodes of loss of consciousness when the power failed, first in hospital, then en route to Germany by air. . . . He subsequently went on for three decades to do scientific abstracts for a living, typing with his tongue. . . .

Anti-polio serum was ordered but was diverted for use by the U.S. Embassy staff in Baghdad before it could reach the IVS team. When a second shipment of vaccine arrived, there was not enough for all team members, so Nurse Rupel reduced the dosage so that everyone had some immunization. Hijacking the serum certainly could have been grounds for a schism between IVS and the U.S. government!

PROJECT ACTIVITIES

The program goal was to develop the center to train village level workers and support village project activities. All team members—sometimes with Iraqi co-workers—were involved in the activities described below.

Potable Water

Understanding the accomplishments of IVS volunteers requires some understanding of village conditions, many of which had changed little in centuries. Villagers wanted "clear" water; not necessarily potable, but clear was a priority. Peter Barwick described an all too typical village water system.

> It is unbelievable a village can survive the filth that each member comes into daily contact with at the springs. The spring is usually two cement pools, each about two yards square. The water comes in from underneath or from one side of the cement enclosure. It goes into the men's pool first, and the overflow goes into the women's pool. Most of the time the supply is very meager, and late in the fall it gets smaller and smaller till some of them dry up completely. If the spring completely dries up, and there is no other source of water near, the whole village is forced to migrate to another spring till the rains return. Since the supply is rarely the equivalent of

a small faucet at home and must feed as many as two hundred mouths besides providing bathing facilities and water for the animals, it is not hard to imagine how filthy the water must be even before leaving the first pool. The water is already what we would call sewer water, but goes next door to the women's pool, where it goes through the same treatment.

Barwick went on to describe CDC efforts to improve springs:

Our mason, Sayyid Taiib, was in charge of fixing springs. First, he had a trench dug between the pool and the source of water. Then the villagers brought the materials, while he built a wall behind which the water was to be stored. He ran pipes through the storage wall to each of the pools above the level of the water. This way they each had clean water to drink, which was, of course, our primary concern. . . . This work was always slow, and the results were never as good as we would have liked them to be. Dr. Burke realized that springs were basically difficult to work with, so he brought hand pumps from Germany for use with wells.

The first pump was installed in November 1955. From the start, we worked through a village worker whom we had posted in the area. His requests, advice, and work were our biggest help. The first well that we did was in Darbent, a village near to Shaqlawa which is owned by the most influential sheikh in the area. It was a shallow well (about 15 ft.), and there was no difficulty. It is still working very well. Unhappily the field above it has since been fertilized with manure which can be tasted in the water from the well. The second well was put in at a depth of 54 feet.

Since[installing] those first two pumps, two others have been installed and both work well, even though the one is at 60 ft. There are countless other villages waiting till Sayyid is free to come and install a pump for them. The program cannot be on sound footing till we have a fairly large supply of strong, but reasonably cheap pumps.

Village Visits

Early in his tour, Don Mitchell spent time in villages together with an interpreter to learn about local farming methods. The first village level worker visited was also the Imam for the village who provided hospitality and a place to stay. Spending the night allowed for more leisurely conversations with villagers.

Most villages were owned or controlled by a sheik, who would own the best crop land and control all irrigation water. Depending on the beneficence of the sheik, the villagers would receive 25-30 percent of the crops grown, with the lion's share going to the sheik. If the villagers owned farmland, it was in upland areas suitable only for growing dryland wheat or barley, or in some areas, un-trellised grapes. It was truly a subsistence existence.

Crops grown by villagers largely depended on the availability of water. Wheat and barley were usually planted in the fall in upland areas to take advantage of winter rain and summer harvesting. All harvesting and threshing were done by hand or by using animal power. Grapes were grown with or without trellises but pruned annually. Grapes were sold to larger markets or dried for later use as raisins. Since there were no forests, growing poplar trees was profitable for construction poles. Tobacco was a popular cash crop, as were tomatoes that were used in many dishes. Other vegetables grown were eggplant, okra, cabbage, lettuce, radishes, and squash.

Villagers in upland areas often had small flocks of fat-tailed sheep and goats that were milked for family consumption or to make a hard cheese (curds) to eat during the winter. Wool was used by the family or sold or bartered to larger villages. Animals grazed on hillsides for what they could find, often competing with Bedouin herds that migrated through the area to the mountains for summer pasture and back to the desert for the lambing season. Villagers cut small branches of live oak to stack for winter months when they were fed to livestock. It was a very rough diet for the animals but kept them alive until the next season. Only native breeds of cattle were raised. Best described as scrawny, they subsisted on a very marginal diet, produced little milk, and calved only once in two-to-four years.

Dairy Cattle Introduction

One of the first and most visible CDC projects was the introduction of Jersey and Brown Swiss breeding stock supplied by the Heifer Project. Jenne and Jantzen, together with Iraqi staff, built the initial barns and corrals, which were later completed after Holloway and Ham arrived with the cattle. The dairy cattle attracted a great deal of attention, with visits from the Prime Minister, other Ministers in the Iraqi government, UN officials, U.S. and other ambassadors, the USOM Director, IVS board members, and many others. It was a flashy show. Visitors could see imported Jersey bulls and perhaps even pet them.

The first problem encountered with the introduction of the new cattle was finding feed, especially forage. Grass, hay, and straw were available in some villages, and, with the cooperation of the sheik and the sweat of IVS volunteers, the CDC was able to harvest enough hay. Barley and wheat were readily available. A mill in Erbil had mill by-products. With mineral and vitamin supplements, this provided an adequate, but not ideal, ration.

Most bulls assigned for artificial insemination were transferred to a research station at Abu Ghraib near Baghdad, where there were trained personnel and facilities to manage a cross breeding program. At the time, artificial insemination was gaining popularity among small U.S. dairy farms as a means of breeding cows to outstanding bulls without the expense of keeping a bull on the farm. This was made possible by stud farms where bulls with superior pedigrees were kept, semen collected, processed, and stored in straws at sub-zero temperatures using liquid nitrogen. When a farmer had a cow ready to breed, he would call the AI technician who would go to the farm, thaw the semen, and breed the cow. None of this infrastructure was available in Iraq in the 1950s.

Albert Halloway had grown up on a dairy farm and was familiar with artificial insemination (AI). It was absolutely amazing the way Albert trained Ellya, an illiterate Kurdish "cowboy", to be an AI technician. Ellya could neither read nor write Kurdish, Arabic or English; yet Albert mentored him in elementary animal husbandry and the steps in artificial insemination from collecting the semen, checking viability of the sperm under a microscope, diluting the semen with egg yolk and preparing the vials for insemination. In a matter of months, Eilya committed to memory everything told him by his highly regarded mentor, "Mister Albert". What might Mister Albert have accomplished had his tour not been cut short by polio?

In hindsight, introduction of dairy cattle at the CDC was not a wise decision. While it achieved the goal of attracting attention, a community development center was not an appropriate place to start an economic program that was light years ahead of where subsistence Kurdish villagers were striving to exist. Villagers cutting live oak twigs as forage to keep their livestock alive until the next rainy season were hardly prepared for purebred dairy cattle. This was not a program to be undertaken by a community development center, but rather work more appropriate for a research station with trained personnel and adequate levels of management. If the goal was to improve the diet of villagers with a quality protein, a dairy goat program would have achieved this goal at much less cost, albeit with less show.

Village Poultry

A chicken house and fenced yard were constructed for about 100 mature chickens plus additional space for brooding chicks. Perhaps the farm's most valuable resource was Mahmoud—the Chicken Man, as he was known locally. Mahmoud took care of the poultry flock at Sermedon and mentored village level workers on poultry husbandry. Mahmoud had little more than an elementary education but could read and write Arabic and Kurdish; he learned to speak, read and write passable English and had a genuine interest in chickens. He read all information he could find on poultry.

New Hampshire chicks from the U.S. Heifer Project arrived between December

1954 and March 1956, requiring Rud Ham, and later Don Mitchell, to make monthly trips to Baghdad to receive them. The chicks were grown to maturity at the CDC then distributed to villages. No doubt, many died of disease or were eaten, but the volunteers soon saw evidence of cross breeding with local chickens.

Introducing dual-purpose chickens into Kurdish villages to improve meat and egg production was well intended, but, as a long-term poultry production strategy, it was not well thought out. The distribution program was reasonably successful in introducing improved poultry genetics, but the cost was substantial and would not have been sustainable without the generous support of the Heifer Project. Perhaps a less flashy way to improve village poultry would have been to improve the diet and management of local chickens. At Sermedon, Mahmoud had a pen of native chickens received in exchange for American chickens. When compared to New Hampshire Reds with the same feed and management, the native pullets started laying at a younger age and were more productive than the American chickens. While the birds were smaller and laid smaller eggs, they likely had more disease resistance and suffered less climatic stress than their American counterparts.

The most significant aspect of the poultry project may have been the selection of Mahmoud as an International Farm Youth Exchange delegate from Iraq to the U.S. in 1957. He was scheduled to live with farm families with poultry flocks in the U.S. Midwest. While it is unknown what happened after his return to Shaqlawa, he had the interest and willingness to develop a flock large enough to supply the surrounding area with poultry and eggs.

Well-Baby Clinics

Martha, working with the local doctor, was instrumental in starting well-baby clinics, where the babies were weighed, eyes washed, and both lactating mothers and babies given vitamins A and D and UNICEF milk. Anyone with fevers, diarrhea, rashes, or major cuts or bruises was sent to the Iraqi doctor. Seeing vitamin and nutritional deficiencies for the first time, Cherie commented:

> I had never seen deficiency diseases except in text books and here we were seeing scurvy and mild forms of other deficiencies. . . . Children didn't have kwashiorkor but we often saw the color traits in their hair. . .all the infants had cradle cap because of the way they were swaddled in their cribs.
>
> When I first arrived, I knew no Kurdish. The Kurds were a little more liberal about having men interpreters, but it was obvious that we had to learn Kurdish very quickly. I will never forget the phrases in Kurdish for "my baby has a fever or headache", or "my baby has diarrhea. . . .

Girls' Schools

Betty Hutcheson was instrumental in establishing a school for girls in Harir by starting informal home economic classes. Home economics classes started in 1955 were much like beginning 4-H sewing projects. Girls made simple items of clothing for use in the home. In autumn of 1955, a qualified Iraqi woman teacher was assigned to the village and the first school for girls in the area was begun. Subjects included reading, writing, arithmetic, religion and home economics. The room was small and plain, but since this was a new building, it had glass windows and a black board. Desks were rough wood, with two or three girls sharing the same desk. They didn't have textbooks, but each girl had two or three copy books. Most instruction was in the form of recitation, and it often sounded like a football game as they recited their lessons.

In the second year, Betty and Cherie helped start a school garden. For the girls it was a lot of work, but it was a good gardening demonstration and would be useful for a school lunch program the following year and for lessons on food preparation.

Canning

Both Cherie and Betty worked on food preservation with interested village women. While there was an abundance of tomatoes during the growing season, the only means of preserving them was to make a thick paste and spread it on grass mats placed on roofs to solar dry. The resulting dried "leather" had little nutritional value but offered flavor to stews and could be stored for off-season cooking. Cherie recalled, with some amusement, teaching village sheiks how to can tomatoes.

> . . . probably the most lasting accomplishment I made was teaching the sheiks of a village how to can tomatoes. IVS had imported some European canning jars, [so] we decided to put them to use. Since this was a rather scientific process, so thought the sheik, the women were obviously not capable of learning this process! While the women watched from the shadows, I instructed the men to peel the tomatoes (that's like asking an American man of the 50's to do the dishes!), boil the water and sterilize the jars. I was dubious that this would work as the jars were the wide mouthed European type and I was more familiar with Ball or Kerr canning jars and lids. Checking back later they all sealed!! Must have had a lot of acid in the tomatoes. Later I ordered bottle cappers from Sears & Roebuck to use with readily available soft drink bottles and taught the villagers how to bottle tomato and grape juice.

Grain Harvest

For subsistence farmers, mechanized tillage and harvesting equipment was almost unimaginable. Traditional harvesting involved cutting grain using a small hand scythe, hauling the grain to a packed clay threshing area, and laboriously trampling livestock over the straw to separate the grain from the straw. On a windy day, the grain was tossed into the air for the winnowing.

A tractor and small German threshing machine were added early in the program. "Farm boy" volunteers with experience in operating machinery were able to set up and operate the thresher. The hand-harvested grain was brought into a central area and fed into the threshing machine producing straw to feed livestock and clean grain to be milled into flour.

Sulaymaniyah Sub-center and Seed Cleaning Service

A Community Development Center sub-unit was established in Sulaymaniyah at the Beckerjo Agricultural Research Center. Volunteers lived in very rustic tent and clam shell camp trailer conditions, cooking food on camp stoves. The volunteers established a seed cleaning service of great benefit to farmers in fighting black smut, a serious disease, causing poor grain quality and reducing wheat and barley yields up to 50 percent. Carl cleaned and treated more than 250 metric tons of seed for the first planting season. During the following harvest, the farmers could easily see the benefit of planting treated seed. Volunteers also worked with an Iraqi crew in drilling shallow wells for village drinking water. Building a house where volunteers could live required supplies and materials from a rather uncooperative local contractor. In the absence of support from the experiment station administration, the house was never completed.

Program Changes

In early 1956, as Dr. Burke's contract was ending, his mother became critically ill, and he hastily returned to the U.S. The new Chief of Party, Edward D Harmon, Jr., had been approved by the USOM and the Ministry of Social Affairs, so there was little lapse in leadership. Ed had been an Air Force Captain in logistics and with his wife, Marjorie, and three sons had a farm in California. USOM provided Ed, Marjorie, and son Peter with housing in Baghdad. Ed used the IVS sedan rather than trains for long trips to project sites. On arrival, Ed met with USOM and the Ministry of Social Affairs members to rewrite the IVS contract, reporting:

> As of June 30, 1956, a new contract was drawn up by USOM and IVS personnel in Iraq and sent to ICA/Washington for approval. This document was tailored to facilitate the transition of IVS to a new plan of community development work in Iraq. For almost eight months both IVS and USOM have had to meet an extremely difficult series of problems while working under an extension of an obsolete contract. Lack of clear lines of authority to handle such matters as disposition and acquisition of IVS

property, changes in status and compensation of personnel, etc. have not only hindered IVS-USOM relations, but they have even more seriously affected dealings with the Government of Iraq.

During the months prior to July 1, 1956, every effort was made by both IVS and USOM to have the Ministry of Social Affairs make preparations for the assumption of responsibility for the operation of the Shaqlawa Project; however, Iraqi officials seem either unwilling or unable to understand what we carefully explained to them. As the date of cessation of IVS control approached, it was obvious that nothing short of actual withdrawal of IVS financing and supervision would impress those responsible for taking over the administration of the project. In view of this, every effort was made to prepare for the transition period by stocking up on feed for the poultry and cattle and by putting all equipment in as good a shape as possible.

Within a week or two after July 1, Project operations were at a virtual standstill due to lack of gasoline for transportation and farm maintenance. In addition, many of the employees who had been on the IVS payroll had left because no provision had been made to accept them on the Ministry payroll. Some did remain on in loyalty to the Project. This state of affairs continued until about August first, when the Minister of Social Affairs paid a visit to Shaqlawa. Acting on inaccurate information, which was very damaging to both IVS and to Americans in general, he proceeded to summarily dismiss the Project Director and a large percentage of the staff from all categories. These people were not replaced. The Minister's action left the operation in a complete state of collapse. IVS personnel were completely demoralized at viewing what they considered to be the ruin of their work.

The visit of the Minister proved to be the low point. . . shortly thereafter, the Director General of Ministry who had been out of country returned. He was a strong supporter of community development and a co-director of the Iraqi American Cooperative Community Welfare Services (Joint Fund). With his influence he was able to reinstate much of the staff that had been terminated.

It was decided that the IVS team in Shaqlawa would continue. Yet, all the early volunteers had left by late 1956. Betty Hutcheson's tour was due to end in January 1957, and Ed Wiser had plans to return to graduate school. Betty and Ed left in January to return home. Cherie and Don were married in Baghdad on January 5, 1957, and transferred to Mahawil until their tours ended in June 1957. Ed Harmon, in cooperation with USOM, transferred all remaining vehicles and equipment to the Ministry of Social Affairs at the end of December 1956, closing out IVS's participation in the Shaqlawa Community Development Center. Hanna continued as CDC director with an Iraqi staff. Ed closed out the IVS/USOM contract on June 30, 1957, and was then hired by USOM as a Community Development Advisor until the

U.S. assistance program was terminated after a bloody coup ending the Hashemite monarchy on July 18, 1958.

Perhaps the IVS team lives on in the folklore of Kurdistan, just as the Iraqis live in the memories of volunteers who lived there in the 1950's. Revisiting Shaqlawa in 2013, PETER BARWICK wrote:

> My wife & I did revisit Shaqlawa six years ago (2013) with a small group tour. Unfortunately, we couldn't talk them into staying around long enough to look for old landmarks. What was the village is now a small town with a casino and a honeymoon hotel. It was a rainy evening and traffic was heavy with no evidence of the old village whatsoever. We learned that Saddam Hussein had literally wiped the village off the map, not once, but twice. . . .Our experience can never be relived, I know, but I was disappointed to see such complete replacement of the culture we were privileged to witness.

One lesson is clear. While volunteers have little control over political turmoil in a country, in the final analysis, it is the people with whom they meet and work who make the difference in the future of a country. It is not the volunteer who will shape the future of the country, but it is his or her friendship, technical skills and philosophy that will influence those who remain. It is unknown what happened to Mahmoud or any of the other Iraqis that worked side by side with their IVS team colleagues, but very likely they will remember a friend who happened to be an American that came to work in their village. Volunteers gained political insights, as did DON MITCHELL, who came away from Iraq with new perspectives on the Palestinian issue:

> A well drilling team of two or three people was assigned to drill the wells and install hand pumps. Working with two Iraqi counterparts, the chief of our team was a Palestinian named Nabil, who was a civil engineering graduate from the American University of Beirut. Nabil did not fit the stereotype of an Arab—black hair, mustache, and brown eyes. Instead, he was in his late 20's, blonde, blue-eyed with an early tendency to go bald, and no mustache. He spoke English fluently, was handsome with a warm friendly personality making communication easy. He was one of those memorable people we meet along the pathway through life.
>
> One morning Nabil and I were having coffee and talking about project activities as well as other things friends discuss. I knew that he was a Palestinian refugee, but little else. I began to ask about his family and the story he told provided a far different story than that related in the U.S. press. Nabil told of his family that had lived for several generations in Palestine (now Israel) and that the family had accumulated a rather large farm where they cultivated fruit crops, mostly citrus that were sold throughout the Middle East. The extended family lived in a large compound

with comfortable surroundings. They had a happy and successful life until one early morning in 1948, Israeli tanks and artillery came blasting through their compound and orchards, killing several members of the family. The rest had to flee to Jordan with only the few possessions they could carry.

They were assigned to a refugee camp where they could look across the border and see the farm they had once tilled. They had hopes of one day returning to their home, but months turned into years, and they continued to live in temporary shelters. Nabil was not willing sit idly and wait in a refugee camp but was able to get a scholarship to go to AUB to study civil engineering. He seemed to accept his fate, but not without a lot of deep-seated anger at the Israelis and by extension to the American government that supported Israel's efforts to establish a Jewish state in the Middle East. Nabil was telling this story to an American friend. Having grown up on a farm and knowing how attached my family became to a piece of ground; I could only empathize with him and feel for the injustice that had been dealt to his family. I have often wondered what happened to Nabil.

Under those circumstances, it does not seem there was time for a negotiated price on the land!! It is complicated. Many years later there was an offer to pay the Palestinians for their land but the main reason the refugee camps remained in Jordan was the Palestinians held hope they would be able to return to their land. It seems that it is antisemitic to recognize there was a very painful birth at the end of WWII and the creation of the Israeli state. In some small measure IVS resulted from the conflagration of world events focusing on the village level.

IVS/Nepal (1956–58)
Training Community Development Workers

IVS/Nepal
PROGRAM:
• Rural Development
VOLUNTEERS – 4
FUNDING: USAID

In the 1950s, Nepal threw off rule by the hereditary Rana prime ministers and began opening the country to the rest of the world. Located between India and China, Nepal was strategically important in terms of Cold War competition. The U.S. established an aid program in Nepal in 1951. Need was great due to the limited infrastructure and widespread poverty.

An IVS/Nepal program, funded by USOM, launched in March, 1956, with the arrival of Willard Patton, Chief of Party for a team assigned to a Rural Development Training School in Nepalgunj. The site in western Nepal on the border with India was remote from Kathmandu and received few government services. The team included volunteers: Ms. Patton, Gareth Lease, and Jacques Kaufman.

On arrival, there was some immediate confusion over the team's terms of reference, because the USOM Director was out of the country and the USOM Village Development Advisor responsible for the IVS project had changed.

Work began, but the IVS team seems to have had an evolving set of advisory and support responsibilities to: the Rural Development Training School, a regional Rural Development Center extension program, a mobile elementary school teacher training program, and an Insect-Borne Disease Department spraying program (essentially DDT spraying to combat malaria). It was soon determined that IVSers would not teach at the training school; rather, they would be charged with supporting Indian trainers hired to teach in Hindi. Initial work focused on completing construction, equipping, and establishing procedures for the school and launching Rural Development Center extension work.

Reports suggest that the programs started successfully. The Training School began with 41 trainees and a curriculum that emphasized agriculture. IVS volunteers facilitated practical training on student vegetable gardens. The Rural Development Center had 14 village development workers to manage rice and other crop trials and demonstrations and a well drilling program. Village-level workers met monthly at the Center for training and to review progress. Still, start-up was a struggle with construction and procurements continuing even as Training Center classes were starting. A major problem was "fluctuation" of staff due to turn-over and absences of Nepali staff. Also, government funding was limited and often late, leading to IVS (controversially) lending funds to the programs to enable them to continue operations.

The IVS team stayed quite busy with work, frequent visitors and invitations to village events, weddings, and other functions. Willard Patton noted that he attended a pleasant (though not understood) Christmas service in Hindi in a village church in India.

Relations with USOM were less smooth, and by 1957, USOM indicated that it would not extend the IVS contract. The reason given was cost and too many Americans in the country. Still, USOM reportedly offered employment to several of the IVS team at salary levels considerably above the costs through IVS. With the contract due to end, the IVS team was unexpectedly transferred to Birgunj in August 1957 to help establish a Rapti Valley Village Development Center. Team efforts in the final months of the program focused on oversight of construction and preparation for start-up of the Birgunj Center to operate similarly to Nepalgunj.

The real reason for not extending the IVS/Nepal program is obscure, but the IVS rural development program was likely caught in political influence competition between India, Nepal, and the US. India had complained about the number of Americans working in Nepal. Indian interests in taking leadership on rural development in Nepal seems to have been the reason for Indian trainers replacing IVS volunteers at the Nepalgunj training center.[5] The abrupt move to Birgunj would have shifted IVS to an area more accessible to Kathmandu and perhaps less sensitive to Indian interests.

Reports suggest significant accomplishments by IVS/Nepal. The vague documentation leaves one to wonder whether undocumented personality conflicts with local counterparts or USOM staff might have contributed to the termination. The program ended in May 1958.[6]

IVS/UNRWA Agreement
Jordan, Syria, Lebanon, and Gaza (1963–65)
Working with the UN

IVS/UNRWA Program
PROGRAM:
- English Language Teaching
- Athletics

VOLUNTEERS – 8

FUNDING: Private sources; UNRWA

In 1963, IVS entered into a joint project agreement with the UN Relief and Works Agency (UNRWA) and the Near East Church Council Committee for Refugee Work (NECC-CRW) to provide volunteers for work with Palestinian refugees in Syria, Lebanon, Jordan, and Gaza.[7] One or two volunteer agricultural volunteers would work with NECC-CRW in frontier villages of West Jordan. The others would teach English and physical education at refugee vocational and technical (VTC) schools.

Volunteers on this short-term program were recruited under contract to UNRWA with IVS providing their day-to-day management and supervision. UNRWA covered costs of housing and in-country subsistence with IVS funding other costs. The volunteers were assigned as individuals embedded in VTC schools and the MECC-CRW program. They did not function as an IVS "team", which was common in other countries to that point.

MICHAEL CALL, a Canadian, was assigned to the school near Damascus, Syria, and provides some interesting insights into the program.

> We spent about a week as a group in the hills above Beirut in an orientation program where we learned about UNRWA and its mission, something of the recent history and current events in the region, a cursory introduction to Arabic culture, religion and family, as well as a few words of Arabic. . . .

The Damascus VTC was a large complex with classrooms, workshops, dining hall, dormitory buildings, offices and covered walkways. . . . I was the only non-Palestinian living at the school, my room was on the second floor down the hall of a large dormitory with meals provided in the school's dining hall for students and staff . . . . Students—all male and some older than I was—spent most of their day in workshops for various electrical, automotive and mechanical trades in addition to a few hours a week of general studies that included English.

On a personal level I got on well with my students and was the frequent recipient of the noted Arab hospitality and generosity. Students with little or no visible income (two or three pooling their coins) would insist on paying for my bus fare into the city, the movie ticket and following treat of coffee or orange juice, my attempts to reciprocate consistently dismissed out of hand. . . . Our chats almost always focused on current political issues, what are Jews like, did I have any Jewish friends, the perceived injustice of the U.N. and Western support for the state of Israel, the dim chance of finding employment and securing any kind of stable economic and family life given the lack of legal status and the many restrictions placed on Palestinians in Syria.

My limited time in Damascus and the nature of my work as a classroom teacher resulted in there being no real impact on the school and certainly none on UNRWA and its education programming. I might have offered a slightly more 'human', friendly and accessible face for some of the Palestinian students and staff, who I think generally viewed U.N. personnel and westerners as—if not the 'enemy'—at least antithetical to their dreams of a return to Palestine. . . . This factor likely formed an important part of the rationale for the whole UNRWA volunteer programme.

My assignment with IVS/UNRWA in Syria constituted the first steps on the road to thinking more critically about the political, economic and social issues at play in the world of that (and indeed the present) time and how they impacted on individuals and local institutions and communities (such as Palestinian refugee students), a way of looking at the world that my prior college education, surprising to me now, did little to foster.

Volunteer DeWade Creveling in Jordan concluded that a volunteer is someone who is willing to work where he is needed most:

The climate in Jordan was very similar to where I was raised, except, we had more snow, and it was colder. I felt I adjusted well to the climate, the people and the living conditions. I first lived in a Boys Orphanage in Hebron, a town on the edge of the desert. I enjoyed working with the poor people in the village, for I knew what it was like to be poor. If you want to help someone improve their station in life, education, to me, is the most important. First, they have to learn to read. I would say 99 percent I worked with could not read. Book learning is good but after that you need to have hands-on learning. To get water you can change the system from a rope and bucket to a hand pump, but if you don't teach the person to read with hands-on experience to repair the pump, it is just wasted US dollars. When you first meet a person, give him the benefit of the doubt. Let him do most of the talking, you may learn something.

Despite start-up problems of poorly-defined roles for volunteers, lack of understanding of what a volunteer is, and poor support arrangements, volunteers completed their assignments.[8] Feedback on volunteer performance was positive, and UNWRA asked for an expanded team. However, IVS was not able to raise sufficient private funding to support volunteers, and UNRWA was unwilling to cover full costs of volunteers, in part because European volunteers were available at no cost to UNRWA. The program ended in June 1965.

REFLECTIONS ON INITIAL IVS COUNTRY PROGRAMS

These five early IVS programs all had quite positive experiences. Four were in the Middle East and three used a "team" approach. The UNRWA program was an outlier, coming a bit later and assigning individual volunteers to teaching positions. All projects received positive reviews and highlighted U.S. commitment to rural development.

Despite the positive aspects of the programs and the demonstrated effectiveness of engaging a private agency and committed volunteers to development efforts, all ended quickly. Political factors—the Suez crisis, local riots, Indian-Nepal relations, and Iraqi bureaucratic conflicts—disrupted programs. USOM (later USAID) could be a strong supporter, but its support could be uncertain and changeable.

The Iraq rural development program at Shaqlawa Community Development Center was the longest and most substantial of these programs. In a report closing out this program, Ed Harmon made several observations and suggestions worthy of consideration for future consideration of IVS or IVS-like teams.

> *The Project at Shaqlawa was under pressure from USOM and the Iraqi Government to make a showing. During the first year of work, the IVS Chief of Party had been given direct instructions by the Director of USOM to use his resources to accomplish this end. Any method, other than that which was used, might have impressed officials so little that Community Development work at Shaqlawa would never have been continued at all. No one can legitimately criticize IVS for aggressively moving forward in hiring personnel, ordering supplies and equipment and construction facilities at the center, while under IVS financing and control.*

In many cases Team members did all the work of carrying out a project without training anyone in the job being done. This got many things done quickly, but it resulted in an immediate cessation of work upon the departure of the team member. IVS cannot be faulted for this because the Iraqi Government was unable to field suitable counterparts for American personnel. One measure that would have reduced the over-participation of IVS personnel in project work would have been a reduction in the size of the team.

The introduction of American breeds of poultry and cattle into Shaqlawa has not proved to be as successful an experiment as it was expected to be. The reason behind this is that livestock and poultry in the village are kept on a bare subsistence level.

From the experience of IVS/Iraq there seems to be little reason to doubt that there is a place for young people in community development work. It is not necessary that they have extensive job training; however a farm background is advisable and at least a BA degree in a field related to community development is essential. It has been demonstrated that they can do a job on the village level that it is difficult to obtain more experienced people to undertake. Their lack of family responsibility, their willingness and ability to withstand adverse environmental conditions and their vitality of approach make them ideal for the job.

A problem that must be faced by IVS is to continue to make progress in building and retaining a nucleus of trained personnel. There is no better place to look for prospective leadership material than among the ranks of those who have completed a contract term. While many young people are willing to give two years of their life to an experience such as IVS offers, few can afford or will accept another term without adequate remuneration and prospects for advancement. Unless steps are taken to offer retiring volunteers of superior ability sufficient inducement to remain with the organization, it seems likely that IVS will be unable to maintain a cadre of motivated volunteers with a one hundred percent turnover.

These issues with the Iraq program were not unique to IVS. Program sustainability, local ownership, institutional capacity, technology suitability, and challenging working environments were issues that bedevil development programs of many kinds. Yet, the projects did provide proof-of-concept for international volunteers. Young Americans could adapt to work in rural areas overseas and could offer relevant technical skills and contribute to development issues of the time.

3

VOLUNTEERS AND THE COLD WAR CONFLICT IN SOUTHEAST ASIA

FREDERIC C. BENSON, MIKE CHILTON, AND HUGH MANKE

While tensions in the Middle East over the formation of Israel had led to initial IVS programs there, the situation in French Indochina was equally worrisome and would prove to be transformative to IVS as a private volunteer organization. After Japan's withdrawal, France had fought to reassert authority there, only to be forced to withdraw. This left a communist North Vietnam committed to re-unifying Vietnam and holding influence throughout Laos and Cambodia. In the mid-1950's, the U.S. was desperate for means to shore up South Vietnam, Laos, and Cambodia against the communist threat and what it saw as the beginning of a "domino effect" throughout Southeast Asia.

Rural areas were seen as vulnerable to communist infiltration, and rural development, particularly agricultural development, was viewed as an important means to counter such insurgency. Experience from Malaysia and the Philippines supported such an approach. The United States Operations Mission (USOM), consequently, turned to IVS to provide teams in rural areas, as a visible and effective means of promoting rural development. IVS leadership in Washington was aware of the potential security issues but was in agreement with the general objective and the potential for IVS to serve a long-term development role. Thus began major IVS programs in Laos and Vietnam and a brief program in Cambodia. These programs proved effective, but ultimately became enmeshed in, and somewhat defined by, the pain and controversies of the Vietnam War.

IVS/Laos (1956–75)
Nation Building: Community Development and Education

> IVS/Laos
> Programs:
> • Rural Development
> • Education
> Volunteers – 384
> Funding: USAID

Following the collapse of French Indochina and the acceleration of the Cold War, the Eisenhower administration increased U.S. commitment to the region. It was said that "in Washington's eyes, the Laotian civil conflict, which began in 1955, was not an isolated instance of internal violence; rather, it was but one manifestation of an attempt by Asian communists to exert hegemony over all of Southeast Asia".[1] In addressing this perceived challenge, foreign aid was seen as "simply one of various means a government has at its disposal to influence events in another country, with the ultimate purpose of advancing its own interests".[2]

The first U.S. ambassador to Laos arrived in Vientiane on September 22, 1954. Shortly thereafter, on January 1, 1955, the United States began supplying direct assistance to the inexperienced Laotian regime. The Foreign Operations Administration's (FOA)[3] mission in Laos began with a skeleton staff that relied on technicians borrowed from other missions.

During the years that followed, the United States and its allies fully supported the entire Laotian economy, including the Lao military, with the objective of Laos becoming a neutralized, stable, and independent state—thus preventing it from coming under communist control.[4]

In 1959, Under Secretary of State for Economic Affairs, C. Douglas Dillon, testified that:

> The principal objective of our foreign policy in Laos since the cease-fire in the Indochina War in 1954 has been to assist the Royal Government to overcome communist efforts to overthrow it from within. Our basic policy has been to encourage the establishment of the strongest practicable non-communist government, and the development of the broad popular support which such a government would require in order to defend and strengthen its independence. Specifically, it has been and is our policy to assist the Royal Lao Government in reducing the internal communist threat by the extension of economic and military assistance—working with the Royal Lao Government we have carried out joint projects in the fields of administration, public works, village improvement, health, agricultural improvement, and information.[5]

THE ADVENT OF IVS IN LAOS

In January 1955, FOA officials in Saigon told IVS Executive Director J.S. Noffsinger that they would like IVS "to send village teams to various parts of Vietnam, 'hoping against hope' that they might prove to be effective." FOA's director of program asked if IVS could send eight teams 'at once'. The IVS Director seriously questioned the wisdom of such a move and indicated that IVS's preference would be to send teams to other countries first—"even in Indo-China we would probably prefer to send teams to Cambodia and Laos rather than to Vietnam." The IVS Executive Committee agreed with Noffsinger's position, and FOA was advised accordingly.[6]

Shortly thereafter, FOA/Laos conducted a survey, and, based on its findings, a cable from the FOA director of Laos to the IVS executive director in Washington requested that an IVS chief of party be sent to that country as soon as he could be cleared. The IVS chief of party would then work out a program with Laos and FOA officials, after which, the IVS team members would be sent to the country.[7] IVS tentatively selected W. Wendell Rolston, a retired Iowa farmer, as chief of party. Rolston traveled to Laos on June 30, 1955, to undertake a more detailed feasibility study together with FOA technicians on loan from Thailand.

Shortly after Rolston arrived in Laos, IVS Executive Director Noffsinger visited the country and became more familiar with the environment that volunteers were about to enter. He observed that "most of the northern and eastern borders of Laos touch Red China or the Vietminh and considerable fighting between democratic and communistic forces is continuously taking place—at least two provinces of Laos are now being held by the Communists. It appears that the United States is pouring great quantities of war material and money into this country to check the communist flow into this primitive but rich area."[8] Rolston reported:

> When I came to Laos, I hoped, along with [ICA/Laos], to better the educational, health and agricultural programs, as well as to improve the living standards of Laos. We hoped to do this through a teaching and demonstration program, emphasizing the self-help process.
>
> The proposed project was drawn up and submitted to ICA/W on September 1, 1955. It was cleared and approved on October 26, 1955. The next step was the draft and approval of the project agreement between ICA/W and the American Aid Committee, an agency of the government of Laos. This agreement was consummated and approved. . . . October 26, 1955 by both the United States and Laos governments.
>
> In the meantime, International Voluntary Services, Inc. was negotiating with ICA for a contract. This was completed and signed by both parties February 3, 1956.

Upon the signing of the contract, three team members were [initially] sent to Laos, arriving at the project site March 1st, 1956.[9]

The IVS project started in 1956 in the mountainous eastern part of the country at Phonesavanh on the Plain of Jars. Although this was a rural development project, the Lao Ministry of Education was IVS's official government counterpart. The project, named the Xieng Khouang Development Project, was to be "a teaching and demonstration program, emphasizing the self-help process".[10] The project began as a model farm and a community worker's training project, but both activities were discontinued in 1957 because the area was found to be unsuited for a farm site and because the Royal Lao Government (RLG) preferred to concentrate on other activities in the area.[11]

A new IVS Project Agreement with ICA, dated June 25, 1957, called for a transition from a strictly agricultural project to a village development project and outlined steps to be taken to implement the project.[12] In mid-1959, IVS shifted the team headquarters in Xieng Khouang Province to a nearby location where IVS had carried out successful community development projects. Over IVS's first years in Laos under the ICA contract, the agency's administration in Laos changed hands several times and the direction and aim of IVS was altered with each change.[13] Despite the challenges, the program was well-received and praised.

Expanding Rural Development Activities

In September 1959, the U.S. Ambassador to Laos, Horace Smith, requested that IVS recruit and send eleven additional community development teams to that country at the earliest date possible.[14] The discussion "brought out the fact that Ambassador Smith of Laos considered that the most outstanding piece of work accomplished through ICA in that country to date was being done by the IVS community development team and that political conditions in the province of Xieng Khouang were probably better than in any other province due to the presence of the IVS team. Therefore, ICA requested that one IVS team be recruited for each of the twelve provinces of that country." The points discussed in the meeting were outlined by the Chief of ICA's Cambodia, Laos, and Vietnam Division on September 14.

Before a new IVS rural development contract was to be signed, IVS's executive committee member, John H. Reisner, visited Laos as part of IVS's annual inspection. Mr. Reisner noted that "the deep interest in this project shown by the United States Ambassador and by the Director of USOM[15] [Laos] was a source of great satisfaction. The spirit of cooperation within USOM was most assuring. In some ways this would be the most difficult project that IVS has undertaken. We would be less than fair if we did not recognize the very complex and difficult problems it poses for [ICA's] Division of Rural Development."[16] Reisner went on to say that it was "unanimously agreed that serious attention would need to be given to the matter of language study for all the IVS team members. It was also agreed that, while the Division of Rural Development would be administratively responsible, the professional resources of other divisions would be available to the IVS teams as needed. The pioneer character of this project is evident. There will be a great many things to learn as well as to teach."[17]

The Interim Report for the 1959 Annual IVS board meeting on Laos stated that "anyone wanting to work for IVS should be led to believe that they could be a government employee in the strictest sense of the word. The present success of the team in Laos is due to the fact that at last it has been shown that IVS is USAID, and that because of the relative independence of IVS it can do a better job in the field."[18] Indeed, as one USAID man put it at a later date: "IVS'ers are the scouts in advance of AID's 'front lines' in the provinces."[19] This close working relationship or partnership with USAID characterized the first decade of IVS in Laos.

Although ICA promised to sign the new rural development contract by January 1, 1960, signing was rescheduled for April 1, then, July 1, and finally for September 15.[20] The contract provided for seven teams of seven members each, with team leaders directing activities under a chief of party in coordination with ICA's Rural Development Division.[21] The contract called for "53 men, general utility men rather than specialists".[22] This new Voluntary Agencies in Rural Development Activities (VARDA) contract set the stage for IVS's expanded engagement in rural development and agriculture.

Despite these frustrating delays, it was reported by the IVS Field Program Officer during his four-week trip to Laos in mid-1960 that "frank, free, and open-minded spirit of cooperation [prevailed] among all the [rural development and education] field party chiefs, contract parties, ministries, public officials, provincial and local officers and technicians. Nothing quite like this has been observed anywhere by the IVS program officer in Asia or Latin America."[23],[24]

ESTABLISHMENT OF AN IVS EDUCATION TEAM

In August 1959, in response to a long-standing request by the head of ICA's education division in Vientiane, the first IVS education team of nine arrived in Laos. The team was to work at the National Education Center (NEC), known as *Ecole Superieure de'Pedagogie* at Dongdok near Vientiane.[25] Composed of vocational and English teachers, the team was qualified in the basic skills of nursing, home economics, electrical work, plumbing, agriculture and gardening, and carpentry.[26] It became the second element of the long-running IVS/Laos program complementing the rural development program initiated in 1956.

During the French colonial years, France had invested little in the Lao education system. At independence, there were only six secondary schools throughout the country, and instruction was in French. Fewer than 30 percent of the children had attended school. Of those students, few had completed primary school. Consequently, following independence, education became a priority to meet peoples' demand for education, to train personnel for governmental positions and economic development, and to develop a shared sense of nationhood. Accordingly, ICA and later USAID supported an ambitious program of school instruction and teacher training.

The role of an IVS education team volunteer differed from the rural development volunteer in that the volunteer came to Laos with a fixed teaching job. One of IVS's primary goals was to help Laos develop a strong national identity by improving the educational system and training enough teachers so that the instruction could be given in Lao instead of French.[27]

Kong Le Coup d'Etat Diverts Volunteers to Relief Efforts

Before new IVS teams could be recruited and placed throughout Laos, Lao Army Captain Kong Le staged a coup on August 9, 1960, against the rightist government and occupied Vientiane. Kong Le invited Prince Souvanna Phouma, a former prime minister, to form a Neutralist government, which he put together in November. In December, the Battle of Vientiane took place, and Kong Le's Neutralist forces were forced to withdraw to the Plain of Jars by the political right led by General Phoumi Nosavan. Kong Le then joined forces with the communist Pathet Lao faction, which was aligned with North Vietnam and received support from the Soviet Union.[28] As a result, the only progress IVS made during 1960, after signing of the VARDA contract, was basic planning and development of operational policies.

Following the Kong Le coup, the Royal Lao Government (RLG) Commission of Rural Affair's operations were thrown into turmoil.[29] Most Americans (including IVS personnel) were evacuated to Bangkok during the latter part of 1960. On January 10, 1961, USOM reorganized a task force in Laos and a support group in Bangkok to cope with the existing hostilities and limited security in Laos.[30] The Task Force Program had three areas of responsibility: relief and rehabilitation, rural self-help, and sub-projects of provincial significance.[31]

In 1961 when the Task Force Program began, only a few of the displaced IVS Xieng Khouang team members were still in the country. Also, only a small number of new IVS volunteers were scheduled to come to Laos in 1961. Nevertheless, IVS'ers from both the VARDA and Education groups, who were in place during 1961, played an important role as members of the Task Force Program, especially in the refugee relief sub-project. One-third of the task force personnel were IVS'ers; indeed, IVS'ers were on the verge of exceeding the number of USAID personnel.[32] It was not until late 1961 that USAID personnel, with IVS'ers in the foreground, were able to return and take over program management.[33]

As of September 1961, there were seven rural development and five education volunteers in Laos.[34] IVS volunteers then began to arrive in force. During 1962, IVS teams were positioned in major Lao provincial capitals including Luang Prabang, Sayaboury, Ban Houei Sai, and Pakse.[35] With this new recruitment push, the IVS Board found that there was a reduction in applicants due to strong competition from the Peace Corps.[36]

USAID's Task Force Program continued until mid-1962.[37] During the latter half of 1962, the original Rural Self-Help project resumed as a sub-activity under the "Development of the Rural Economy" program established by RLG's Commission for Rural Affairs (CRA) in November 1958.[38] The other sub-activities introduced were Rural Public Works, Well-Drilling, and Support for the CRA.[39] Under the Rural Self-Help sub-activity, USAID community development advisors and IVS volunteers were in a position to stimulate village initiative and self-expression, and to help establish a rapport between villagers and local officials on the one hand and provincial and central government officials on the other.[40]

Education Team Program Expands

In July 1961, negotiations began for a second contract for IVS education team personnel in Vientiane. Because of the political unrest and evacuation of all personnel to Bangkok, it wasn't until October 1962 that nine of the twelve positions were filled in Vientiane.[41]

The primary goal was training. All IVS'ers would teach themselves out of a job and turn responsibilities over to the Lao. Such change usually took more than two years, and the volunteers didn't get to see the fruits of their work. In addition, there was the added frustration that after training, people often left and went to work elsewhere.[42] Nevertheless, the Education Team continued to grow in numbers with additional positions for secondary school English teachers and for agriculture and English teachers at the regional teacher training schools (*Ecole Normale d'*

Instituteurs (ENIs). A unique element of the early Education Teams is described by Volunteer BERNARD WILDER:

> When I arrived…in July of 1963, I was the average age of the IVS/ED team members, 32. Most of us had left jobs and were not fresh out of school. I had resigned a tenured associate professorship at what is now the University of Wisconsin, Platteville Campus. All but two of us had master's degrees. We were not the average group of volunteers.

An important by-product of teaching was the cultural exchange of ideas and customs; something that was indulged in by both the Lao and Americans through classroom work and extracurricular activities.[43]

The IVS Educational Team was covered by a separate USAID contract from that of the IVS Rural Development Team.[44] However, in early summer 1969, the IVS Rural and Education Teams were joined into one organization, and the IVS Education Director was appointed Director of the new IVS/Laos team.[45] As of 1968 there were four staff and 36 volunteers on the education team. Twenty-two of these positions were at Dongdok. Furthermore, by 1968 Lao teachers were completing training and beginning to take over teaching responsibilities, reflecting the program's success. Thereafter, the Education Team dropped to 30 positions for 1968-1971.

In the 1969-70 IVS/Laos Annual Report, an education team member noted that "IVS/EDU can be considered as one of the most productive groups in Laos today. Due to the mundane type of work we are doing, i.e., the routine teaching situation as opposed to some of the adventuristic, exciting programs that reporters and congressmen like to check into, much of our work has not been publicized…."

NEW DIRECTION IN RURAL DEVELOPMENT

Following the Kong Le coup, the Development of the Rural Economy activities provided the framework for input of USAID resources into a *Mu Ban Samaki* program.[46] This program engaged IVS volunteers and was designed to revitalize those rural areas of Laos containing the majority of its people. In addition, it had the goal of improving RLG relations with rural populations by introducing improvements in agriculture, public health practices, transportation, public works, and education facilities.[47]

Beginning in 1963, rural activities shifted emphasis from scattered and difficult-to-supervise areas to concentrated more manageable areas. To this end, the Cluster Program was introduced on September 29, 1963.[48] A "cluster" was a grouping of villages selected for improvement based on its "visibility" to other rural villages, as well as for economic, social, and political-strategic reasons.[49] Cluster activities

—most of which were self-help projects—were channeled through the RLG in each area in cooperation with USAID Area Coordinators or Community Development Area Advisors. This staff, in turn, was assisted by IVS volunteers.[50]

Initially, the RLG with U.S. assistance carried out these activities in a pilot rural development program staffed largely by IVS volunteers in six rural areas of Laos. Security was an issue, but the Lao military provided security within the cluster areas.

As development activities in original cluster villages and forward-area locations progressed, the boundaries of both were extended to include additional villages. Most clusters, and some forward areas, were expanded to include entire districts (*muangs*), thereby engaging the district chiefs (*chao muangs*), to become the local leaders of the community development programs.[51] In some areas simple rural marketing and credit cooperatives were established.[52] A wide range of development-related training programs were conducted for villagers and RLG personnel. [53]

Some non-cluster activities, such as aided self-help activities begun in earlier years and new activities of extreme need and urgency, justified diversion of resources from cluster and forward-area activities. These occasionally involved enlargement of existing clusters to encompass outlying villages.[54]

Between July 1963 and June 1964, IVS placed volunteers in thirteen locations outside Vientiane, including six clusters and seven non-clusters. However, as of July 1964, IVS rural development was still far below contract strength of 72, partially due to IVS Washington's preoccupation with staffing IVS teams working with USAID Vietnam.[55]

The VARDA contract was to expire on May 15, 1964, but was extended for six months while a new contract was being readied.[56] To manage these expanding commitments throughout Laos, in May 1964, IVS divided Laos into northern and southern regions for administrative purposes. The two IVS regional leaders worked out programs with USAID and the RLG.[57] To free up IVS for this more important work, USAID assumed full logistic support, a function previously borne by IVS Vientiane.[58] USAID provided much appreciated strong support to IVS volunteers, but this also raised problems regarding appropriate channels for reporting and supervision.[59]

During this period, IVS worked closely within the framework of the USAID Mission under the general direction of USAID field personnel. Many remote IVS field positions became more accessible and communications with Vientiane improved. Although security was still an issue, the RLG regained control over wider areas. And finally, increased engagement by the RLG in rural areas led to enhanced working relationships with RLG counterparts.[60]

USAID/Laos Director Charles Mann assessed the role of IVS in his introduction of IVS's July 1963–June 1964 annual report:

> The main purpose behind the presence of IVS here is to bridge the "last six inches" in the extension of American diplomacy in this part of the world, and I believe that its "person-to-person" approach has contributed greatly toward that end. Those among us who fear that the American pioneering spirit is dying or dead can take heart on perusal of this IVS/RD annual report—a straightforward, factual chronicle of young American men and women venturing into a strange land, and meeting and overcoming strange situations.[61]

Although rural development programs were designed to combat insurgency and "win hearts and minds", volunteers approached their work on the basis of a participatory community development mindset. Creative IVS'ers worked directly with the USAID's rural development division engaging in wide-ranging rural development projects that were designed to benefit the remote agriculture-based villages typical of Laos. Agricultural projects included: demonstration farms, livestock, vegetable garden, rice improvement, agricultural cooperatives, fish ponds, etc. Other community development projects were construction-related (schools, roads and bridges, dispensaries, dams and canals for irrigation, etc.), home economics, school health and sanitation, wells, water-seal toilets, village industries, information services, youth work, and social welfare-related refugee resettlement projects.

KEN ULLUM, IVS/Laos (1965–1969), pointed out the uniqueness of the USAID and IVS relationship:

> USAID is the bread-and-butter source to which IVS is presently related, and USAID goals and objectives are limitations which will confine the present range of IVS operations... One will have to go a long way before he can find a situation where so few can affect so much, particularly in Laos. It is indeed a rare opportunity for young idealists to command such large quantities of material and technical resources. The scope of this opportunity, for both the individual and IVS as an organization, is unique, and we should capitalize on it and promote it rather than lamenting our USAID ties and hedging around a definition of those ties in the recruitment process.[62]

IVS volunteer JIRO OI (1968–1970) observed:

> [The] IVS experience to each volunteer must be like the parable of three blind persons describing an elephant—depending upon where one person touched, [the] description of an elephant may be completely different from the others.[63]

Following the RLG's significant territorial losses to the communists beginning in 1968, the growth of the rural development programs in Laos waned as advances were made by the Pathet Lao and North Vietnamese, and USAID's attention was increasingly drawn toward providing refugee relief and resettlement assistance to the large numbers of people displaced by the war. Furthermore, in some instances, the point was reached when the original clusters were no longer distinguishable as separate entities within the overall development program.[64]

IVS/Laos volunteer, RANDALL IRESON (1967–1969) also expressed his views on the role assumed by IVS in increasingly war-torn Laos:

> While IVS is not primarily concerned with implementing political development in the countries we assist, we cannot blind ourselves to its necessity. Modernization cannot proceed rapidly within the context of a feudal political system, nor can it proceed at all in the midst of a civil war. Thus, any developing agency must make a number of political decisions, because modernizing and increasing the efficiency and responsiveness of the host government can be a valid byproduct of any development project done in cooperation with the government of that country. And such modernization is usually an avowed goal (publicly at least) of the host government.
>
> To ignore the fact that everything done in the name of development and modernization has a political effect will almost invariably be counter-productive to one's best efforts at modernization, as has been the case in Laos. . . . Obviously, it is necessary to involve the host government in the development process, and the government must also have significant control over that process. . . .[65]

In his December 1967 Christmas letter to IVSers, Executive Director, ARTHUR Z. GARDINER, wrote:

> IVS is serving in controversial programs, and in troubled regions [in both Vietnam and Laos]. Many IVS volunteers, and the IVS Board and Staff, have had to face squarely problems of conscience—should they help to forward policies which they oppose and possibly be identified with tactics which they abhor? . . . The Board's decision is that IVS is duty bound to continue to work in Vietnam and in Laos, always upholding the right of dissent, but equally wishing to keep alive the flame of service. As a member of the Board put it, 'IVS is a small candle, but we must keep it lit'.[66]

FORWARD AREA PROGRAM AND DETERIORATING SECURITY

While cluster programs were put into operation at sites throughout Laos, it became clear in early 1965 that there was need for short-term, beneficial programs in isolated areas recently cleared of communist Pathet Lao troops. Such programs were to convince villagers of the good intentions and ability of the RLG and American government to stand behind them and provide necessary government services.[67] Two-man Forward Area Teams (FAT) were staffed by a combination of IVS and

USAID direct-hire or contract personnel who were supervised by USAID's Deputy Assistant Director of Rural Affairs, Loren Haffner (known as "Haff"), a retired Marine colonel. The IVS Chief of Party retained administrative control over FAT's IVS personnel. By the end of 1967, the Forward Area Program had reached its maturity with only eight of the twelve original positions still active. There is no indication that any new Forward Area field positions were established.

Security was of concern in selecting Forward Area locations and posting IVS and USAID personnel at these sites. As Haffner pointed out, "it should be noted here…that regardless of precaution taken at any time or place, no persons or area in a war situation such as in Laos can be assured positive safety against attack."[68]

IVS Withdrawal from Rural Laos

As fighting intensified, both IVS and USAID employees became more security conscious in 1968. Pathet Lao forces roamed the countryside, and it was almost impossible to determine when and where they would appear. During the first eight months of 1969, three American volunteers (Chandler Edwards, Dennis Mummert, and Art Stillman) and three Lao IVS Field Assistants were killed in ambushes. The house of another volunteer was attacked at night, although he was unharmed. Prompted by these assassinations, the administration of IVS/Laos and its members were forced to re-examine what IVS was doing in Laos and whether or not their service should continue.[69]

There were two fundamental issues: security, on the one hand, and involvement with the American presence and programs in Laos, on the other. IVS administration decided that no volunteer should continue to live or work in a situation where he or she had to be unduly concerned about their personal security or where they were exposed to an abnormal amount of danger.[70]

Volunteers in Laos engaged the issues of safety and purpose during their annual team meeting in early 1968, summarizing the issues in a newsletter:

Are the losses of IVSers lives worth the possible changes IVS is [promoting] in Laos or is IVS supporting an elitist or corrupt situation which it, along with the U.S. Government, is unable or unwilling to change for fear of alienating the elite group?

As IVS volunteers our motto has been "people to people"—in the belief that the key to social and political change is through the formation of personal relationships. We would rather not be in Laos if our presence creates a sense of resentment on the part of the Laotian.

Finally, among other things, we must decide, as individuals, whether or not we want to make the name of International Voluntary Services come true.[71]

The volunteers' "consensus" was to propose two alternative courses of action to the IVS board of directors: (1) That within a specific period of time IVS phase out of Laos, and (2) that, while IVS remained in Laos, certain changes be made to better ensure the safety of the volunteers and to establish a more independent role for the organization.[72] The Board's immediate response was to schedule a visit to Laos by a committee of their members to review the situation first hand.[73] When the Board met in November 1969, it was decided to lessen program involvement with USAID, engage in closer cooperation with the RLG, and establish a more austere standard of living for the volunteers.[74]

Before a final decision could be reached by the board, the administrators of IVS/Laos decided to withdraw IVS volunteers from all rural areas located outside provincial capitals, either because security was a prohibiting factor or because the close identification with the USAID program was perceived to be incompatible with the values and ideals of IVS. By January of 1970, there were no volunteers stationed anywhere in Laos other than in provincial capitals.[75]

IVS Distances Itself from USAID

As early as the mid-1960s—when the war accelerated and intensive U.S. bombing began, IVS administrators and some volunteers began to view the country as being slowly destroyed by a civil war brought on by international Cold War rivalry. They saw an American military presence contributing to this destruction. They also saw a USAID program that in many ways, but on a different level, contributed to the military program and found most of its rationale for existence in the support it was giving to the military effort.[76]

In this context, there were those who began to feel that it was necessary to be independent from American foreign policy and programs in order to have the freedom to really perform the people-to-people service that IVS was organized to provide. It was believed that IVS found it extremely difficult to operate effectively in a situation where the program and the policy become paramount and the people of secondary importance.[77]

But the question remained, why was IVS in Laos in the first place? What concerned IVS/Vietnam volunteers Jay Scarborough and Jeffrey Long also applied to IVS/Laos volunteers:

> What, philosophically, politically, historically [does our work mean]? This is the kind of question that each of us will have to answer to his own satisfaction, and everyone in IVS seemed to have a different idea of how to go about it.[78]

They went on to observe:

> Who, after all, is an IVSer? He is supposed to help better Asian living conditions as well as to translate cultural resources into authentically Asia social realities. The question is, whose cultural resources? We bring to our work thought processes, institutional models, and conceptions of man-in-society that have no roots in the Asian's historical experience. Improving the physical conditions of his life necessarily involves subverting many of his fundamental values and replacing them with our own. This is imperialism, but hopefully it will be an imperialism of wise and honest men. But can we speak any more of a progress that is authentically Asian?

Finally, Scarborough and Long asked the question:

> Is it possible to divorce socioeconomic improvements from their political implications...where just entering the country defines one's de facto allegiances?

Along these lines volunteer RANDALL IRESON pointed out the following:

> The increased polarization of the war, the polarization of the factions in the government, and the increased U.S. military activity in Laos all combine to preclude any possibility for impartial economic and social development in the country. Not only has IVS become an integral part of the U.S. effort to stop communism, but security has deteriorated to such an extent that IVS can no longer plan a program for more than three to six months in the future. It is impossible to have any positive effect on the people of Laos when we cannot stay in a village long enough to know and gain the trust of the villagers....[79]

Indeed, IVS's Forward Area Program veteran (1968-1970), KEN STEINER, noted:

> We were young, idealistic, and perhaps a little overconfident that we could make a difference. But the distinguishing trait was that we were a group of young people willing to risk the convictions of our faith and idealism. It was an extremely intense experience—one in which I was keenly aware of the closeness of death, while also being intensely alive....[80]

IVS/Laos concluded that given the nature of the two organizations, it was logical that in many areas IVS and USAID would come to a parting of ways. Not that they couldn't work in cooperation with one another, as it was sometimes to their mutual benefit, but that USAID's direct involvement with and control over IVS was no longer acceptable. Accordingly, it was concluded that IVS should work in closer cooperation with the Lao Government and that their activity should be coordinated through RLG's Ministry of the Plan.

Consequently, as IVS withdrew from rural areas, IVS became a "perplexing organization". Not only did IVS severely cut the number of personnel and the geographic areas in which they worked, IVS slowly began to move away from direct involvement with USAID and their programs. To many this was upsetting and difficult to understand.[81]

Volunteer HOWARD LEWIN (1963–1965) pointed out:

There were those who complained a lot and felt that IVS was too dependent on USAID for its support. Many felt that given the military situation, IVS should not even be there. I felt that if they truly came to Laos to help the Lao, what was wrong with using USAID-furnished cement? If everything we needed to implement a project was readily available and furnished from USAID, what was wrong with that?[82]

IVS REALIGNS ITS PROGRAMS

A three-way Letter of Agreement between USAID, the Royal Lao Government Ministry of Plan, and IVS/Laos signed in December 1971 called for a long-term plan to mesh with the RLG Five-Year Plan, dated November 1971. IVS/Laos prepared a Two-Year Plan (July 1, 1972-June 31, 1974) as a first step towards fulfilling the Agreement with a primary purpose of putting the IVS program more in line with Royal Lao Government programs and plans. IVS would then prepare a five-year plan to start concurrently with the next RLG Five-Year Plan in 1975.[83]

Procedures in the Agreement provided for the various ministries to request IVS assistance in their programs. The Ministry of Plan would, in conjunction with IVS and USAID, oversee the entire program.[84] The Letter of Agreement indicated that volunteers would be functionally responsible to the ministry under which they were assigned. Day-to-day support and supervision of volunteers would be done by IVS staff, with periodic consultations with the Ministry of the Plan and with USAID.[85] The Agreement was intended to enable IVS to consciously set objectives and improve its programming towards the general objectives of IVS,[86] defined in the plan as:

- To contribute to human betterment and social justice by cooperating with the people of host countries in their efforts to satisfy their needs and overcome their most pressing problems.
- To further international understanding and cooperation.
- To assist the people of Laos to develop the human resources necessary in their national development.[87]

Weaknesses and inefficiencies in the program's procedures, as well as disagreements in their interpretations, arose during the initial year of the Two-Year Plan. Issues included: procedures for evaluation of volunteer performance, opportunities for engagement at the village level, and assignments of counterparts for volunteers.

Nevertheless, IVS viewed the operations as having proceeded relatively smoothly. The idea of working in a systematic way in close coordination with the RLG continued to be one that IVS sought to achieve.[88]

The bulk of IVS's work, as defined in its Two-Year Plan, would focus on education, but there would also be a scattering of positions in several other fields. The variety of these non-education activities made this part of the program seem more significant than the number of volunteers involved would indicate. IVS/Laos administrators learned something about what volunteers were best able to do and what they probably should not attempt to do.[89]

During a mid-1972 visit to Laos, IVS Board Member Winburn T. Thomas indicated that "the emphasis upon education by IVS/Laos is due to at least two factors: (1) Education is the first priority of the Royal Lao Government. The French Government [development agency], the [Colombo] Plan countries, and Japan assist in providing funds and personnel towards the educational goal. (2) Rural insecurities have restricted IVS activities largely to urban areas."[90]

Former IVS rural development volunteer, JIM GINGERICH (Laos 1967–1969; Washington 1972–1973) expressed his opinions on the subject:

> I think my major criticisms of IVS as a volunteer were probably similar to many of the other volunteers at the time in Laos. They were closely connected with the role that IVS was playing as being complementary to what the American government was trying to do in Laos, which was mainly based on political goals. To spell those out a little more specifically, IVS volunteers, especially in the rural development team in which I was involved, were mainly placed in positions that were of high priority to AID and the U.S. Government to maintain an American presence and to do the hearts-and-minds type thing. That has all changed considerably now, I think, because IVS is not in a rural development program in Laos… I think that everybody, from the Board to the staff and volunteers, is much more aware of trying to stay out of those kinds of situations. I think getting out of Vietnam was an indication of this.[91]

While IVS' rural development activities wound down, the agenda increasingly centered around education, with approximately two-thirds of the IVS volunteers assigned to work with schools.[92] Still, after formal termination of the Rural Development Program in 1971, IVS attempted to fill non-education position requests in a wide range of fields.[93] These included support to the Vientiane Orthopedic Center, Department of Fisheries, Child Nutrition Center, Salakham Agriculture Research Center, Ban Amone Skills Training Center, Ministry of Plan's Human Resources

Center, Ministry of Youth and Sports, and Refugee Affairs. All were based in Vientiane, except for Refugee Affairs which was in the royal capital, Luang Prabang.[94]

THE DEMISE OF USAID AND IVS IN LAOS

From 1965 to 1973, the war in Laos seesawed back and forth, and it was perceived that "by the late 1960s, the [IVS] programs in South Vietnam and Laos had become caught up in the turmoil and controversy of the war".[95] In the meantime, however, negotiations between the conflicting parties in Indochina were underway. In October 1972, the major components of a cease-fire and political settlement in Vietnam were reached, and the Paris Agreement on Vietnam was signed on January 27, 1973; two months later, the last U.S. combat troops left South Vietnam. In February, just a month after the Paris Agreement, the Laotian factions signed the Vientiane Agreement, which provided for a cease-fire and for a coalition government composed of factions from the RLG and Pathet Lao. A year later, on April 5, 1974, the new Provisional Government of National Union (PGNU) was established in Laos. Ministerial portfolios for the ten most influential ministries were distributed equally between the political Right, or "Vientiane-side", and the Left, or Lao Patriotic Front (LPF) faction.

As political control in Vietnam tipped toward the communists, the Pathet Lao gained political ascendancy in Laos. When the Vietnamese communists marched into Saigon at the end of April 1975, the right-wing forces in Laos lost heart, and most of their leaders fled, permitting a bloodless takeover by the Laotian communists in mid-1975. A campaign of intimidation against RLG members and Royal Lao Army officers gathered momentum during the spring of 1975, and anti-American demonstrations spurred by the communist faction took place throughout the country. USAID compounds were occupied, forcing the termination of the aid program.

On May 27, 1975, agreement was reached between the PGNU and the American Charge d'Affaires that the USAID mission would be terminated no later than June 30, 1975. Termination was completed on June 26, 1975, when the Acting USAID Director, Gordon Ramsey, departed Vientiane and an American Embassy Diplomatic Note to that effect was delivered to PGNU's Ministry of Foreign Affairs. As described by journalist Arthur Dommen, the departure of the U.S. personnel "was stage-managed in as humiliating a way as possible."[96]

Shortly after USAID and most IVS volunteers departed, Ramsey was asked: "After all these years, all the expenses, and now to have it all end so ingloriously, was it worthwhile?" Mr. Ramsey's response was, "I think we've done a hell of a lot of good things for this country. Maybe we did them wrong, but the results are here".[97]

The Perseverance of IVS Volunteers

Lawrence Olsen, IVS/Laos Program Officer from October 1973 to May 1975, identified, implemented, and supported IVS volunteer projects. Lawrence helped close out IVS programs when the Royal Lao Government collapsed, and the IVS-USAID contract was voided. However, after most IVS'ers left Laos at the end of June, three volunteers chose to remain and continue their work with their cost-of-living allowance provided from private sources.

Remarkably, Lawrence elected to remain to support the three education program volunteers working at Dongdok Teacher's College. Work also continued with a science experiment textbook written in Lao and intended for publication by the United Nations Development Programme (UNDP). Lawrence prepared and submitted to the Ministry of Foreign Affairs a written proposal (hand-written in Lao script) for the continuation of IVS work in Laos. IVS was hopeful, but very uncertain, that a future program could be mounted.[98] Time passed, and Lawrence did not receive a response from the new government. Since his visa expired in late October, he had no choice but to cross the Mekong River to Thailand.

What Inspired IVS Volunteers in Laos?

During IVS's nineteen years in Laos, approximately 372 IVS volunteers served on the rural development and education teams in fifty locations throughout the country. What attracted so many volunteers, and how did they benefit from their diverse experiences?

LAWRENCE OLSEN (1965–1970; 1973–1975) wrote:

Much of the richness of IVS came from the level of responsibility we were given along with the freedom to try, to fail, and to try again. I like solving problems and inventing things." He went on to say that "I learned to listen. I learned better ways of interacting with others, and I gained a measure of humility... The biggest impact of IVS has been the people, friends, and contacts made. . . . IVS was—and still is—huge in my life.[99]

WIN MCKEITHEN (1962–1964) realized that:

We, in IVS, had received the priceless gift of hospitality among people who taught us much more than we could ever conceivably have taught them. I am still in awe.[100]

KEN STEINER remarked that:

[T]he Indo-China War and our responses to that moral and ethical dilemma severely tested the consciousness of a whole generation of students.[101]

JIM MALIA, former IVS/Laos volunteer and Chief of Party (1967–1971), summarized, in retrospect, IVS's program in Laos in his paper entitled, *We Want to Build; They Want to Destroy: The Dilemma of Volunteering in Laos*:

> The seeds of the ultimate demise of IVS in Laos were sown at its inception. Like any classic tragedy, only time was needed to work through to its inevitable conclusion. Early leaders in Laos and Washington, D.C., put on blinders and ignored the military and political ramifications of volunteer work in Laos. To someone on the "other side" within the context of a people warring against one another to gain control of land and villages, when subtleties distinguishing American from American were not obvious, IVS'ers were seen as part of the total picture and treated accordingly. Our good intentions and perceived good works were not sufficient to hold us aloof from the turmoil that was Laos in the late 1960s and early 1970s. The time to have left would have been early on, but we were hopeful and it was an adventure. And so we stayed on. At the end it was too late. We stayed to contribute and to learn until it was no longer possible. It seems only right to have done so.[102]

Between 1956 and 1975, a foreign policy scholar wrote: "IVS placed [372] dedicated young workers at dozens of locations in such fields as agricultural development, home economics, education, public health and community development. In addition, no one has been able to calculate the amount of good will towards the United States that IVSers have generated."[103] At the same time, no one has been able to calculate the amount of good will toward the people of Laos that volunteers generated…

Indeed, it can be said without doubt that the IVS 1953 Mission Statement was fulfilled in its entirety during the years IVS dedicated to Laos: "International Voluntary Services. . .is [an] organization designed to promote 'people-to-people' cooperation in improving health, productivity and living standards and fostering better understanding among peoples." [104]

IVS/Vietnam (1956–72)
Volunteers in a War Zone

IVS/Vietnam
Programs:
- Refugee Resettlement
- Agriculture
- Education

Volunteers – 416
Funding: USAID

In the aftermath of the French Indochina War, the Geneva Accords of 1954 provided for partitioning Vietnam at the 17th parallel. People in the north, who chose not to remain under the emerging communist rule, were given the opportunity to move to the south, where the relatively weak but non-communist government of Ngo Dinh Diem was being set up. This resulted in large movements of refugees (predominantly Catholic) from the North to South during 1954-1957. USOM contracted with IVS for volunteers to assist with the resettlement process. The IVS assistance was centered in two locations: (1) the villages of Halan A and B in the southern central highlands of northern Darlac Province, and (2) the Cai San project located near Long Xuyên in An Giang Province in the depths of the Mekong Delta.

The first volunteers arrived in 1956. This began a 15-year program that included at least 416 volunteers.[105] It was clear that IVS was engaging in a country with a serious conflict underway, and volunteers seemed committed to helping counter the communist insurgency. Still, it is unlikely that any foresaw the scale of the conflict that was to develop and the destruction and loss of life that would ravage the country and engulf IVS in its own crises and controversies. Despite these developments, many volunteers served there and left with a feeling of accomplishment and with life-long friendships and attachments to the country.

Early IVS Team Activities

The role of IVS changed based on needs and circumstances after completing urgent refugee resettlement. IVS then moved to longer term development objectives involving research and extension for important cash and food crops. Later, volunteer assignments diversified and became more urban-focused as conditions changed and rural areas became less secure.

Basic Resettlement Needs

In the Highlands, in the 1950s, Vietnamese populations fleeing communist rule in the north were being settled on southern virgin jungle lands which needed to be cleared. Constructing rudimentary living structures was a first priority. Local food production was an immediate and urgent need and became an early priority for the IVS team.

At the same time, a major movement by the newly established Diem government created the high-priority Commissariat of Land Development to open new lands in the Central Highlands to people of coastal South Vietnam. These fertile highland areas had been populated solely by Montagnards or tribal people with distinctly different ethnic origins and cultures. Their customs and means of livelihood were unfamiliar to newly arrived, traditional Vietnamese. This set the stage for conflict. The large movements of ethnic north and south Vietnamese into southern tribal lands was exacerbated by an expanding North Vietnam Army (NVA) political cadre presence there and the beginning of long-term strife and instability.

Before these ethnic Vietnamese moved into the area, French colonialists had developed scattered rubber plantations as the main agricultural and economic activity of the region. Since plantations required six to seven years before economic returns were realized, it was a system neither accommodating of, nor familiar to, newly relocated populations from coastal fishing and rice growing areas. The NVA political cadre incursions, the expediency of North Vietnamese resettlement in the area, and the politics of moving in coastal Vietnamese all carried potential for serious friction with the indigenous people.

Other Government of Vietnam (GVN) resettlement efforts were undertaken in the far southern region of the country at Cai Son, a small, under-populated area along Vietnam's west coast facing Cambodia between Rach Gia and Long Xuyen. These were unoccupied lands either belonging to absentee landowners or to the GVN with only a minimal presence of small nearby Army of Republic of Vietnam (ARVN) detachments. A six-person IVS team, including two women (one nurse and one social worker), was dispatched to help the settlers become established. Volunteers focused on water supply and irrigation development but were withdrawn after only a few months because of safety and insurgency issues. This left a single IVS location in the central highlands of Vietnam, Darlac Province.

Agricultural Research and Development

After the urgent needs of resettlement were addressed, IVS volunteers transitioned into an early agricultural development phase. In 1958, near Ban Me Thout where the first IVS teams had been assigned, volunteers began working with local GVN extension agents and villagers clearing jungle and establishing initial production trials for food and cash crops. This began what became a major focus: experimental work on fiber crops (particularly kenaf and ramie); multiplication of grain and vegetable crops (i.e., sweet potato cuttings) for distribution to the surrounding villages; irrigation development; and crop pest and disease control. The station became known as Ea Kmat and was well supported by the Ministry of Agriculture and Forestry in Saigon. It was the headquarters for work of two to four IVS agriculturalists and became a model for development of other experimental stations around the country.

By 1960, a 20-person IVS team was working at ten stations around the country, including the IVS headquarters at Ton San Nhut Livestock Station on the outskirts of Saigon. In addition to Ea Kmat near Ban Me Thuot, locations included: M'Drak in the highlands, for livestock; Nha Ho on the central coast, for forage and feed crops; Dalat in the highlands, for vegetables; Di Linh in the highlands, for lacquer; Bao Loc in the highlands, for tea, coffee, and rubber; Hung Loc near Saigon, for grain and forage crops and a nearby livestock station; and My Tho in the delta, for rice. From late 1961 onward, additional IVS agricultural extension teams were assigned to: Qui Nhon, Nha Trang, and Phan Thiet on the coast, for extension, and Can Tho in the delta, for rice.

From about 1959, IVS enjoyed a close working relationship with the Ministry of Agriculture and USOM/Agriculture in the conduct of station activities throughout the country. Howard Harper was an early contract representative with USOM and served a major role, along with Directorates within the Ministry and the Ministers themselves, in giving IVS an important focus in the experimental development of Vietnamese agriculture and husbandry.

Montagnard Training and Development Centers

In the late 1950s, the tribal people in the highlands became a target for the Vietnamese communist (Viet Cong) village insurgency, and the Army of the Republic of Vietnam (ARVN) relocated villages closer to Vietnamese population centers. This added to resentments and local conflicts with the tribesmen. In 1961, IVS undertook the first steps to create "Montagnard Training and Development Centers" in about eight principal provinces of the Highlands. This involved one or two IVS volunteers at each center to specifically encourage village gardens, health projects, elementary schools, etc. in tribal areas. This was a new direction both for IVS/Vietnam and for GVN cadres as well. The communities were grateful for the external private assistance, and the program grew over time, representing a meaningful attempt to bring tribesmen closer to Vietnamese society. In addition to USOM support, some private support came from the Asia Foundation and other U.S. donors. This program was taken over ultimately by the Ministry of Education, an indication of favorable acceptance by the Vietnamese government. Unfortunately, socio-economic unrest continues to this day with Vietnamese encroachments into the traditional tribal areas. Volunteer David Nuttle's experience with the Montagnards is described in Chapter Seven.

DIVERSIFYING PROGRAMS

From 1962 the IVS program continued agricultural activities while expanding into new program areas.

English Instruction

Male and female volunteers assigned as English teachers became a large part of IVS's total in-country presence. The first group of eleven English teacher volunteers arrived in Vietnam during the latter half of 1962 and were posted in Saigon and provincial sites throughout the country. Many found they could use their assigned role as English instructors to expand into other useful community activities appreciated by villagers. English instruction had wide general acceptance within Vietnamese communities.

Mobile Science Teams

In 1962, IVS worked with the Ministry of Education and USAID to create a program that came to be known as the Mobile Science Programs. It was designed to teach elementary school teachers the basics in science through hands on demonstrations and experiments. The goal was to replace the French approach of teaching science entirely through texts. Volunteers were assigned to provincial offices of elementary education, where they worked with counterparts on presentations that rural school teachers could replicate with their students. These teams travelled throughout the countryside making their presentations. The program faced opposition from teachers used to the "old school" teaching techniques, but gained some success. The travelling teams unfortunately became increasingly vulnerable to the rural insurgency.

Malaria Suppression Team

USOM had made a major commitment to malaria eradication in Vietnam and offered strong support to eradication teams throughout the country. In 1963–64, five volunteers were assigned to work with these USAID-supported teams to resolve operational and technical problems they frequently faced in the difficult working environments around the country. Two volunteers worked with field stations in Di Linh and Khe Sanh on unique problems of malaria transmission and control. Two other educational-support volunteers worked country-wide in the design and dissemination of educational material for malaria control. And, one mechanic volunteer supported automotive transport operations, resolving problems throughout the country.

Rural Youth Program

Initially, IVS, in conjunction with the University of Saigon School of Agriculture, designed a program that involved students in weekend and summer vacation work assignments. Agriculture students would volunteer for up-country assignments which would ultimately result in village participation projects. The program was primarily designed to familiarize university students with rural Vietnam and develop leadership skills. Modest support was available through USOM and from various private sources. Students participated by taking part in field trips, weekend residence within target villages, and extended village stays in assignments during an entire summer. Many of these students became agricultural and community activists, and several went on to get advanced degrees primarily in the U.S., before moving into political and government leadership positions.

In the mid-1960s, the agricultural program led to work with the National Voluntary Services (NVS), a local Vietnamese organization that was not directly linked with school programs but with youth and community organizations in various urban communities. NVS involved its volunteers in village improvement and community enhancement projects. It attracted a broad spectrum of youth, particularly idealistic, young Vietnamese struggling with the disturbing effects of the ubiquitous country-wide military presence and activities—both American and Vietnamese. Volunteer RICHARD BERLINER, who worked with NVS in 1966, describes the ambiguities of volunteer service in Vietnam and of working with the local volunteer program:

> In the spring of 1966, with graduation from Earlham College imminent, I faced the balancing act shared by thousands of other young men that spring: How to frame the next few years of my life in a world where the Vietnam war and the draft loomed as overwhelming and very personal realities?
>
> After two years of study and conversation about the war as a student at a Quaker college, I was persuaded that the U.S. needed to withdraw from military engagement in the country. But I was not a pacifist, opposing all wars on religious or moral grounds. I thus had no basis for seeking conscientious objector status. I considered the Peace Corps, and various graduate schools, but ultimately was recruited by a supportive faculty member to apply for a volunteer position with the International Voluntary Services in Vietnam.
>
> Going to Vietnam to avoid going to Vietnam to fight had a certain irony to it. So why Vietnam? First, I wanted to be like a Peace Corp type volunteer–living humbly, learning the local language, and 'making a difference' in the lives of the inhabitants. Second, I wanted to confirm my own thoughts about the nature of the war in Vietnam. I believed the U.S. was fighting in Vietnam for its own geo-political interests and not to protect or serve the Vietnamese people. I wanted to see things for myself, and IVS gave me that opportunity.
>
> Once in Vietnam it did not take long for me to realize that, while I could certainly learn more about the Vietnam conflict, including the tremendous suffering caused by the war, I would have little opportunity to achieve any of the development successes of my predecessors in IVS. The war kept getting in the way.

My first assignment was with the newly formed Vietnamese Youth Council and its related organization, the National Volunteer Services ("NVS"), which emulated the U.S. Vista program by sending Vietnamese volunteers into rural communities to pursue community development. One group went to Phan Rang, near the coast, where it established a demonstration vegetable garden and a health clinic. Another went to An Khe, in the Highlands, with similar goals. Back in Saigon I edited the Council's newsletter and helped the Council respond to inquiries from similar student groups around the country and across the world, eager to know how their counterparts in Vietnam viewed the war and their role as youth in shaping their country's future.

While enthusiasm for the work of NVS was high, the war stymied the growth of the program. Recruitment was difficult, especially for young men who kept getting drafted into the Vietnamese army. The Phan Rang house was hit by a mortar, injuring several volunteers and destroying the project. The An Khe program was forced to shift its focus to working with the growing number of 'shoeshine' kids, children orphaned or abandoned and left to live on their own as mendicants near the U.S. army bases. Needless to say, the opportunity to promote economic development was minimal.[106]

This program brought IVS Community Development volunteers into close contact with talented young Vietnamese, who were often dreaming of a different, better government, but were caught in the middle of a devastating civil war. The sentiments of these Vietnamese and the stories they shared with IVSers highlighted the damage that the war and U.S. involvement was causing their country. This person-to-person contact had an understandable impact on the IVSers, and, ultimately, on IVS.

A Changing Vietnam: 1965–1971

The working model for IVS had been reasonably well-established by the middle of the 1960s. In mid-1964, IVS/VN had 69 volunteers in 28 different locations. In addition to research and varietal introduction from the ten station locations, agricultural activities expanded with more extension activities in villages throughout the country. This involved pest control, improved varieties and new crops, production system improvements, and marketing developments, all under the auspices of the Ministry of Agriculture. Many younger Vietnamese were affirmatively responding to the new economic opportunities that required English language competency, technical skills, and entrepreneurship. The educational teams continued to grow to the delight of USAID and the GVN. There was heavy demand for English language and science teachers. General liberal arts graduates from the U.S. were recruited to for community development projects in ever-expanding refugee camps.

USAID support was excellent.[107] Those were the halcyon days of IVS in Vietnam. A Vietnamese Advisory Board that included a least one Ministry of Agriculture official loved what IVS was doing, and the priorities of the GVN and USAID fit well with the goals of IVS.

Unfortunately, volunteers increasingly experienced interruptions in their daily work environment. For example, there were delays and changes in both ground and air transportation, communications, local personnel availability, equipment, and supplies. These issues often required program plans to be modified or cancelled. The changes were incremental, growing subtly as insurgency levels increased. Changes were not always anticipated or fully understood by volunteers, by IVS management staff in the field or by the home office in Washington. Volunteers were deeply affected by these operating issues, the growing conflict, and the incompatibility of development and war. These issues were festering below the surface and in 1967 were ready to explode.

After reviewing the IVS Vietnam program in 1964, Washington Program Officer GORDON BROCKMEULLER had noted the dilemma of working in a conflict area:

> My final recommendation to the team encouraged them to resist evaluating their accomplishments and failures on the basis of winning or losing the war. It is tempting for a volunteer to become totally discouraged when a community in which he has lived for months or even years suddenly raises the Viet Cong flag. We share this despair, but we believe strongly enough in the ideals of IVS to have confidence that something of value will remain beyond the change in political allegiance.

Even as the war heated up, volunteers continued to work on rewarding and useful development and relief projects, while establishing good relationships with the Vietnamese people. Community development volunteer STEVE SWIFT retains strong memories of places and people from his four years in Vietnam over the late 1960s and describes some of the dangers, weirdness, and joys of his assignment:

> Quang Tri Province lies just south of the Demilitarized Zone, at about 17 degrees north latitude. Cold and rainy in winter monsoon. Won't see the sun for two or three months. Rice paddies totally under water, sections of north-south highway also under water. Need to wear layers of sweaters and a rain cover. Vietnamese wore conical hats and sheet of clear plastic or a traditional palm-leaf "poncho." Still get wet and cold. Adds to the depression of poverty and war.
>
> And personal behavior. Urchins from the sampans just down from our apartment door, see you coming, and ask for things: "Ok Salem"; "beaucoup chop-shop (c-rations)"; "You like boom-boom (bung-bung, i.e. stomach to stomach.); "You dinky dau." And you could not leave anything valuable behind a locked door: my two still cameras and a movie camera went missing!

One bright morning, I was driving north from Quang Tri to Dong Ha, and got stuck behind an old, slow French bus very packed with people and goods. I was 10-15 feet behind. Couldn't pass. Then "pow"! The bus hit a mine. Soy sauce, chickens, mats, and passengers—blown away. One man face down in a rice paddy; an old woman lying down with right leg almost totally severed. I filled my International Scout with the ambulatory injured and headed to the Quang Tri provincial hospital. I would go to Dong Ha another day. I wasn't very far from that mine! Really, I wasn't very far from that mine. . . .

My job was to find a project to help the generally poor people of Quang Tri. My Vietnamese was hardly up to speed. I had worked with two interpreters, just my age, but they, not surprisingly, didn't have any clear ideas how to start a project. CORDS, the American aid program for Quang Tri, couldn't suggest any projects. I was beginning to feel a little inadequate.

But another accidental solution presented itself. I decided to motor up to Dong Ha City where Viet Nam Christian Service volunteers resided and where they were trying some projects. It got late. After 5:00 p.m., I worried that the VC might be waiting to ambush some foreign dude returning to Quang Tri. So I was invited to stay over. Upon returning to Quang Tri, I noticed black-clad Viet Cong bodies lying dead here and there. I checked with the CORDS office—finding a telegram from Don Luce: Pack up all your belongings and fly back to Saigon. Sage advice.

To Thai van Thach: Native to Cam Lo town, west of Dong Ha, on the road to the mountains and Laos. Just my age. His father fought and died for the French Army. Thach, his mom, sister, and brother fled west to the mountains to live among the Bru Montagnards, whom Thach fondly remembers. I met him in Quang Tri where he attended Nguyen Hoang High School. He studied English assiduously and taught me all the Vietnamese I could absorb. And he was a poet in his own right; used to recite his poems in Vietnamese and then explained to me—in English—the thoughts in his poem. I attended his wedding in Cam Lo to Miss Ai. After several years of translating for CORDS/Quang Tri, Thach moved his family to a safer environment in Saigon, where Sabina and I caught up with him in 1999. Nice.

During the late 1960's, U.S. and Vietnamese military actions grew in intensity, especially at the village level in key areas of the country. The GVN was creating an embryonic democracy and political campaigns led to arrests of many people, including some working with IVS or the National Volunteer Service. Feelings between Vietnamese and Americans were becoming frayed. The IVS volunteers were becoming more polarized regarding the direction of the growing war and its increasing effect upon volunteer activities. The IVS program administration became more complicated, and new security issues emerged as areas experienced heavier military action. Volunteers were relocated, programs were delayed or abandoned, and in some cases injury or death became a reality. Emotional trauma was on the rise. IVS volunteers had strong feelings for what they were assigned to do, but circumstances on the ground often prevented them from carrying out their assignments or doing what they saw was necessary. Destabilization of project activity was a problem, and it increased for all kinds of volunteer assignments. There often seemed to be no good alternatives. Volunteer RENE MOQUIN reflected on the social disruptions from the war:

> My team leader introduced me to the Director of the Technical High School where I would teach English as a secondary language to vocational students. I had no formal teaching instruction or experience, and although he appeared skeptical about my motivations for being in Vietnam, the director invited me to begin teaching his vocational students conversational English. My daily teaching schedule at school went from 8 a.m. to noon, followed by a lunch break and rest. Then we resumed teaching from two-to-five p.m. My evenings were devoted to teaching in informal settings with adults.
>
> I was also introduced to a school in Dien Khanh, about ten kilometers from the coastal city of Nha Trang where I would teach. Beyond those assignments, I was on my own. IVS, I found, was not keen on holding your hand and telling you what to do.
>
> The schools were overcrowded, noisy, and lacking books. Many of my students' lives were unsettled, with young men being drafted and with too frequent funerals of relatives killed.
>
> Although I went to Vietnam without any preconceived notions about the merits of the war, my close association with teachers, Vietnamese families and youth began to paint a picture for me regarding the war and our involvement. . . .
>
> In my opinion we should have never Americanized the war. It was essentially a civil war. We should not have become more involved other than just serving as advisers and observers. The South Vietnamese stand: "Here is the United States; let's let the Americans do the fighting for us." In my opinion we were being used by the leadership of South Vietnam. Increasingly their leadership did not even have the support or respect of its own people. . . .
>
> Corruption seemed to exist in the entire infrastructure of the Vietnamese society, and it seemed to increase in direct proportion to American intervention and escalation. The South Vietnamese Government seemed incapable and unconcerned about doing anything about it. . . . Moral degradation became increasingly evident among a number of high school students. "Live for today and to hell with tomorrow" was becoming a common student philosophy. . . . During my two-year tour in Vietnam, I watched sisters, girlfriends and wives go off to work in bars frequented

by Americans, which added to the growing malaise, frustration and undercurrents of dissatisfaction and violence. A significant portion of the young male population was dying. Juvenile delinquency was far more significant in Vietnam than it was in the United States. . . .

In 2007 Joanne and I joined a bike tour of North and South Vietnam. . . .The Technical High School where I taught in Nha Trang has been transformed into a four-year college with tourism as the fastest growing field of study. The accommodations related to tourism are first class with an impeccable focus on service delivery. The food is to die for. While visiting in Nha Trang, I was invited to meet the former director of the Technical High School. Upon seeing me his first comment was "I think you were with the CIA during your tour in Vietnam, and I think you are still with the CIA." Laugher followed.

The growing issues of an unstable working environment, often most reflected by military presence and action, began to create serious questions for what was to have been the real purposes of a volunteer presence. The country also was becoming more dangerous. From 1965 to 1968, four volunteers died in Vietnam—one in a vehicle accident and three from military action. Several suffered bullet wounds. Two were taken and held as prisoners of war in North Vietnam. Many others had narrow escapes, as Volunteer STUART RAWLINGS reports from his time there in 1967–68:

> On the night of January 25, 1968, IVSer Lem Shafer and I sat for four hours in the living room of an American agriculturalist called Bob Hall. We had a lengthy discussion about new varieties of seeds and machinery which could be made available to local farmers. Lem and I then got up to leave, we walked 100 feet to my jeep, and we climbed inside.
>
> At that instant a rocket exploded inside the house. "CAAR-ACCK!!" Then another one. CAARAACK!! Lem and I raced our jeep away from the direction of the blast and back to our Phan Rang homes.
>
> The next day we found that, indeed, two rockets had exploded in the room in which we had been sitting for four hours, and that that whole section of the house had been leveled to the ground. Bob, the agriculturalist, had been sitting in the bathroom upstairs when the rocket struck, He was injured in one leg, and his face had been cut by glass. Both his ear drums had been ruptured. Another USAID man living upstairs had been wounded and burned by shrapnel. The Vietnamese maid who had served us tea had suffered severe shrapnel wounds and burns, and she had lost an eye. And Lem and I were extremely lucky to be both alive and well.

These fragile times within the IVS community ultimately climaxed with issuance of a letter addressed to the President of the United States and published in the New York Times in September 1967. The letter brought into the open what had festered in the minds of many team members for some time. It described the devastating impact of the U.S. military presence on the Vietnamese people and announced the resignation of four IVS team leaders and noted the open dissatisfaction by 49 IVS team members with the U.S. war effort. There was dissention within the organization, with those who desired to continue assisting the Vietnamese as best they could during their time of strife stayed on with the blessing of the letter signers. No doubt, the issues raised affected all team members and created a less solid foundation for all volunteers, but the IVS country team continued to receive support from the U.S. Embassy for an additional four years.

The Tet Offensive at the end of January 1968 was a watershed moment for the United States' involvement in the war and certainly for the IVS role in Vietnam. For the 180 volunteers in the country at the time, almost all were seriously at risk as the Viet Cong and North Vietnamese attacked almost every province in the country. Three volunteers were taken prisoner and two were released five years later. One was released in less than a month. Two Korean volunteers were hidden in a latrine outside Quang Ngai City in Central Vietnam for several days, while the Viet Cong moved freely through their village. Volunteers in Can Tho and Hue were especially threatened as Viet Cong and the NVA occupied a large part of these provincial capitals for extended periods. A far-reaching program that endangered volunteers could no longer be justified. Further, young male Vietnamese co-workers were drafted in large numbers as the government responded to the offensive. The IVS leadership decided to retrench, sending more than 100 volunteers home in the course of several months and re-examined the criteria for placement of volunteers. Security was the paramount criterion.

Without stability, serious volunteer work could not take place. Placements were often limited by the absence of available male co-workers. Mobile science programs had to be restricted because visits to village schools could be dangerous. Agricultural extension work often faced the same limitations. This meant that volunteer placements had to be made in locations that were relatively secure, such as the Hoa Hao and Cao Dai areas in the Delta and some Montagnard areas in the Highlands. Unfortunately for IVS, those areas were not priorities of the GVN. That mismatch became a problem over time, as the GVN was fighting for its life and their priorities were short-term and political. Refugee work was a priority of the host government and USAID, but most volunteers felt that such work was not what attracted them to IVS. Matching IVS and government priorities became increasingly difficult.

Between 1969 and 1971, the level of anti-American sentiment rose dramatically as the U.S. withdrawal policy became more and more obvious to the Vietnamese. Refugee populations ballooned as villages were destroyed and casualties increased. In response to increasing anti-American sentiment, IVS increased recruitment of non-American volunteers. Well-qualified agricultural specialists from Taiwan, Japan, India, and the Philippines were less vulnerable to local hostility than American volunteers. Still, this did not fit within the model that USAID or the U.S. Embassy envisioned for IVS.

In early 1971, IVS was planning to recruit additional non-U.S. volunteers to expand existing agricultural research, extension, irrigation, and cooperative training activities. Twelve volunteers were already working in these program areas with significant successes in introducing new "miracle" rice varieties, irrigation pump innovations, and village marketing initiatives. Private funding efforts were being undertaken to make ten volunteers fully independent of the USAID contract. The strategy appeared sound but was not to be given a chance.

Vietnam Program Ends

In 1971 the IVS dilemma came to a head. The Government of South Vietnam was fighting for survival, controlling less and less of the countryside, and relocating tens of thousands of Montagnards from the Highlands. In urban communities, disabled Vietnamese veterans rose up in protest against government treatment and lack of benefits. They took over public parks and set up armed camps beyond the reach of police authority. One of those camps was very close to the IVS office headquarters at the edge of Saigon. IVS leaders in Saigon had to negotiate with the group in order to retain their office. The fabric of society was unravelling from within, and the increasing area controlled by the Viet Cong and NVA was shrinking development options everywhere.

As had happened four years earlier, some in IVS leadership again spoke out about the disintegrating situation. The public commentary of some of the volunteers was the last straw for the GVN. Country elections were about to be held in 1971, and President Thieu felt that the continued presence in-country of a disenchanted IVS would be detrimental for an up-coming election. Not only was IVS not supporting the government's top priority programs, it was not universally supportive of the government's war efforts. USAID did not renew the IVS contract. The termination begs the question as to how a volunteer program can solve the dilemma of working where its program priorities do not match those of the host or funding agency, where volunteer placement locations are dangerous, or where the host government's behavior shocks the conscience of volunteers.

The termination of the IVS/VN program marked the end of fifteen years of continuous IVS presence and the largest IVS country program ever. In its early phase of involvement with refugee resettlement, agricultural research, and educational programs, volunteers had found their work highly productive and satisfying. However, as the war heated up, IVS activities became more politicized and difficult. Volunteer productivity and satisfaction declined until the situation became untenable. Still, 28 volunteers remained in Vietnam until June 30, 1971, when IVS was finally forced to withdraw.

An IVS/Washington retrospective assessment of the IVS/Vietnam program termination concluded simply that IVS no longer satisfied the desires of the Vietnamese Government. IVS had changed.[108] In early days IVS was acceptable as volunteers worked with common people—students, farmers, extension agents, teachers, refugees—at the grass root level to improve their lives. Over time and never formally or completely, a "New IVS" emerged with "an almost opposite character". The "New IVS" took on roles of witnessing war atrocities and inhumanity and of supporting Vietnamese political activities. IVS developed links with the press corps, a role not appreciated by the government. When the issue of program extension came up at the senior government level, some people in the Government of Vietnam and in the U.S. Mission remained positive towards IVS but did not oppose the program termination.[109]

With IVS in Vietnam closed, IVS was ready to embark on new directions and new country activities under new organizational strategies and programs. There were two key takeaway lessons of note for IVS as it looked to the future: (1) recruiting technical volunteers from countries other than the U.S. under certain circumstances is beneficial, and (2) creation of a host country volunteer program, such as the Vietnamese National Volunteer Service, can leverage greater change, and where there is political stability, can provide for continuity. Ideally, for good programs, voluntary service organizations needed to be in a stable country with a government that respects basic human rights, although such are not easy to find, nor in greatest need.

A different retrospective holds that USAID's transformation of its mission from pure economic development to counter insurgency meant that USAID left IVS, rather than IVS having left USAID.[110]

IVS/Cambodia (1960–63)
International Tensions End a Promising Program

IVS/Cambodia
Programs:
- Agriculture
- Education
- Rural Development

Volunteers – 25
Funding: USAID

More than three years of IVS activities in Cambodia began in August 1960 with the arrival of George Eason, Chief of Party. A former farmer from northwestern Iowa, he was accompanied by his wife, Jean, and their seven-year-old daughter, Wendy. They had just spent two weeks becoming familiar with IVS personnel in nearby Vietnam, learning details of IVS team operations, direction, and support. As in Laos and Vietnam, nearly all Cambodian support for IVS team logistics and project activities came from the USOM mission in-country.

Cambodia was more peaceful than its neighbors, but, as IVS was to find, it too was politically fragile. The IVS/Cambodia program began with familiar work areas—agriculture, education, and rural development.

Agricultural Station Development

In collaboration with the Cambodian Ministry of Agriculture and Forestry and supported by USOM Agriculture/Cambodia, a team of five agriculturalists arrived in 1960. Their task was to establish a research station on land carved from the dense jungles located at Stung Keo on the route south of Phnom Penh heading towards the southern coast.

Since land had been cleared and initial buildings constructed, team members were able to live and work at the station full-time. The facility became a livestock station, ultimately housing several head of Murrah buffalo imported from India by the Cambodian Government. This buffalo was considered to be good for both dairy and meat production. Other breeds at the station were large, imported animals (Hariyana) with potential for crossing with local stock and use for agricultural draft purposes. An irrigation system was developed to support year-round feed production.

During the second year, the agricultural team expanded to four locations with two volunteers at each. The larger plan for the third year was for a full complement of twenty-five volunteers. In Siem Reap areas with upgraded irrigation, agronomic work began to develop better cultural practices for rice and dry season crops.

Volunteers worked on the technical challenges of establishing a seed corn improvement program at a center near Phnom Penh. This work was later supported by the Rockefeller corn breeding program in Southeast Asia. Extensive forage trials were initiated as a part of the seed program at the Stung Keo Agricultural Center.

By the third year, IVS activities were moving from an emphasis on initial construction (i.e., the Stung Keo agricultural center) to development, organization, and training of an agricultural and educational cadre for different locations of the country.

Classroom Instruction

Two ten-person teams of educational volunteers were planned for IVS's third year (1963) in Cambodia. The first team of ten arrived and finished three-months of English as a second language training, just prior to receiving word that all Americans would have to depart Cambodia at end of 1963. Volunteer-teachers had been assigned to various area schools in and outside of Phnom Penh, including Siem Reap, but assignment duties were not to be realized. A USOM advisor, Dick Constantino, had worked closely with volunteer preparation, and when the program was cancelled, he moved on to USOM/Laos. Many of the IVS educational volunteers transferred from Cambodia to Laos and worked with him on educational programs in that country.

Rural Development

Near the end of IVS's time in Cambodia, a new project was started in eastern Cambodia, and a few volunteers were assigned to Ratinakiri. The program was for rural development with a focus on water resource development. However, the project had just begun when political disruption forced the sudden departure of all Americans.

Sudden Withdrawal

At the end of 1963, a series of events created unusual instability in SE Asia, and rapidly changed the political climate in Cambodia. These included the coup in Saigon and the death of President Diem (Nov 01), the death of the strongman premier of Thailand, Sirit Thanarat (Dec. 08), and the assassination of President Kennedy (Nov 22). Prince Sihanouk in Cambodia decided to take a neutralist position and asked the Americans to leave in haste. IVSers that didn't return home were reassigned to either Laos or Vietnam. The experience of volunteer TRACY ATWOOD reflects the short duration of the program:

> My time in Cambodia was probably the shortest of any of the volunteers as I arrived

a week after the others in my group. I did not have a cholera vaccination and was not allowed on the plane in Chicago. I went back to Connecticut and found that the only place to get cholera shots was in Hartford. I took the bus in three times, got the shots and was as sick (miserable and uncomfortable) as I have ever been.

I was sent to the Stung Keo livestock station that had a sizable contingent of IVS volunteers. They had most of the activities covered for development of this livestock station that was being carved out of the jungle. Harlan, the team leader, suggested that I study Khmer in the mornings with our interpreter, Sam An Keo, and work on the farm in the afternoons.

There were eleven Murrah water buffalo on the station that Sihanouk bought from India. He wanted to start a dairy industry in Cambodia. The buffalo were initially kept at the livestock facility in Pochentong just outside of Phnom Penh. No one seemed to know what to do with them so they sent them to Stung Keo. Since they were milking water buffalo, I decided to milk them. That was a niche that no one else was filling. The Cambodians would not drink this very rich milk unless it was laced with gobs of sugar making it similar to the sweetened condensed milk that they drank in their tea. We made some great ice cream with this milk using the hand crank freezer that I got from Tom Wickham, who bought it from some departing French nurses.

I was at Stung Keo for a little more than two months when everything fell apart. Ngo Dinh Diem was assassinated on November 1, then Sarit Thanerat, the Prime Minister of Thailand died, and then Kennedy was assassinated. At the same time Sihanouk decided he did not want any more American aid, which he declared very loud and clear in one of his marathon speeches that was broadcast nationally. As a result, USAID closed the next day. A USAID official drove to Stung Keo and told Charlie Simmons and me (we were the two remaining volunteers) that he was to bring us back to Phnom Penh and that we had an hour to pack our things.

There was no room for us at the IVS House on Trask Paim (sweet cucumber) because it was full with volunteers who had been pulled in from throughout the country. Charlie and I were sent to the Mondial Hotel. The next morning the desk clerk told me that my president had died. I was sure that with my limited knowledge of Khmer I had misunderstood him. Later that afternoon someone arrived from the IVS house with mail that had accumulated. There was a letter from my father, who never wrote, telling me that my favorite cow, Dolly, had died. It was an eventful 24 hours that I will not forget: I was pulled out of my first overseas assignment; my President was assassinated, and my favorite cow died.

We sat in Phnom Penh for more than a month. Don Luce came from Vietnam and Walt Coward from Laos to tell us of the opportunities for us in their country's IVS programs. Eleven of the 'us' volunteers signed a letter to Prince Sihanouk telling him that we would like to continue to work in Cambodia. Eventually there was a reply that we could stay as long as we had no funding from the U.S. Government. IVS secured sufficient private funding for one volunteer, Martin (Marty) Klish who stayed on for a year and a half at his station in Cheri Dong.

The IVS withdrawal was immediate but not final. Volunteer Martin Clish returned with the Asia Foundation and private funding to resume work with the Cambodian Commissariat of Agricultural Cooperatives, which was interested in starting with three or four volunteers and later expanding.[111] The U.S. Embassy was supportive, and the Cambodia Government was open to a program—if U.S. government funding was not involved. Further funding did not materialize, and Clish left when funding ran out.

IVS AND USAID IN INDOCHINA: WHO LEFT WHOM?

In February 1971, prior to the withdrawal of IVS from Vietnam later that year and the repositioning of its relationship with USAID in Laos, IVS board members and staff met at Harper's Ferry, West Virginia, to chart a new course for IVS.[112] The Board was comprised of members with varied and dedicated backgrounds. Stanley Andrews, an important board member for eighteen-years, was deeply troubled by the problems and risks inherent in working in a country torn by civil and/or international war, particularly when the American government was involved. It was difficult, if not impossible to do development work and remain free of political or even military involvement.[113] The basis for the meeting's discussion was the following set of questions:

> *Can a volunteer organization receive United States Government funds and still operate successfully in developing countries? Are other funds available? What should IVS as an organization strive to do, educate American youth so they can become agents of international communication? Or dedicate itself to becoming an agency to promote economic development of the poor countries? Are these two aims mutually exclusive? What do we mean by "development"? by "volunteerism"? Can IVS become more multi-national? Should IVS get out of Southeast Asia? Is IVS worth saving?*

Volunteer JIM BOWMAN, IVS/Laos, notes the dilemma faced by a conscientious objector serving in a conflict area.

> I joined IVS and went to Laos partly because it provided a means for performing alternative service. As a conscientious objector it was my conviction that I could never kill another person for any reason, whether in war or otherwise. Although we lived and worked near a war zone (this was during the Vietnam War, which was constantly spilling over into Laos), the fighting never came really close to us

and this conviction was never challenged. However, the close friendships that were forming with Lao colleagues certainly made me begin to question my beliefs, and I began to wonder what would happen if the fighting did come to us, and sensed that some of my Lao friends might go to extremes to protect me, perhaps even killing to save my life. What would I do under such circumstances? Would it be morally correct to let that happen? Would it be wrong to be unwilling or unable to protect their lives in the same way? What about my responsibilities towards their family members? And what about my responsibilities towards my own family in the future? I was never able to resolve this philosophical dilemma while in Laos, and luckily it was never put to the test during those years.

Given the magnitude and complexity of the questions, and the varied backgrounds of the attendees, the development and unanimous approval of the "Harpers Ferry Charter: IVS in the 1970's" was a considerable achievement.[114] There was also excitement as the Harper's Ferry conference drew to a close—"what contributed to the excitement of the conference was the growing realization that not only was IVS worth saving, but that recent world events had increased the need and the possibility of success, of a financially independent, multi-national, volunteer organization pledged to work for development and social justice. The most important question of all, 'Was IVS worth saving?' was answered resoundingly in the affirmative."[115]

On June 30, 1972, less than one year after IVS closed in Vietnam, DR. WINBURN T. THOMAS wrote *The Vietnam Story of International Voluntary Services, Inc.* It was a Terminal Report to USAID by a man who, being an NGO staff member and a professional in the international development community, knew about being a volunteer. He starts his IVS Terminal Report with a well-deserved statement of appreciation to USAID.

> International Voluntary Services, Inc., with offices at 1555 Connecticut Avenue, N.W., Washington, D.C. 20036, wishes to express appreciation to the United States Agency for International Development, Washington and Vietnam, for the support and assistance rendered to it in the development and implementation of the IVS program in Vietnam from December, 1956 to August, 1971. These were trying times for both agencies. It is significant, especially in view of the turn of events after 1967 that it was possible to continue the relationship for four additional years. Given the terms of its own mandate and assignment, the staff of USAID has demonstrated considerable flexibility and great cooperation in its dealings with IVS.

As an integral part of the pacification program that was the strategic complement to the military effort against the Viet Cong and North Vietnamese, USAID had a difficult mandate. USAID and other parts of the U.S. Mission were racing against time to help build a viable government that could stand on its own after the withdrawal of American troops and the serious reduction in U.S. financial assistance. Their job was to make the best with whatever talent existed in the Government of Vietnam (GVN) headed by President Nguyen Van Thieu.

Dr. Thomas spreads "guilt" for the demise of IVS in Vietnam among the IVS Board, USAID, the GVN and the IVS/VN leadership in the country in 1971. Early in the Terminal Report, Dr. Thomas writes: "The IVS/VN team suffered from the brashness of youthful idealism, from the assumption that the rights the volunteers enjoyed as individual Americans also pertained in Vietnam, and from insensitivity with respect to the institutional character and relationships of IVS/VN." He suggested that the "brashness" and "youthful idealism" of most volunteers who were then in their mid-20's may have been linked to their limited experience in institutional employment.

The implication in the Terminal Report is that IVS/VN failed to be part of the team with its institutional partners: the GVN and USAID, in effect saying that IVS walked away from USAID. The reverse could also be the case. Parting of the ways may have begun in the early 60's with the strategic hamlet program, accelerated in the mid-60's with the huge military buildup and intensification of the pacification program, and ended in the final years when IVS worked in relatively secure areas of low priorities for GVN/USAID pacification efforts. This program shift in the final two years was an attempt to return to the halcyon days of 1957-61, when IVS could work freely with its Vietnamese counterparts to address their needs.

In 1972, one year after IVS closed, Ambassador Ellsworth Bunker, a man scrambling to keep the GVN intact, wrote the following to Dick Peters, IVS Executive Director:

> Viet-Nam still benefits from the talents of several former IVS volunteers who have chosen to stay on here as Fulbright-grant teachers. As you may know, since the North Vietnamese Army invaded across the DMZ three weeks ago, students at Hue University and other schools in MR 1 have halted classes in order to help the refugees flowing south. I have just received a report that two former IVSers assigned to Hue University, John Schafer and Thomas Malia. They have been working with their students to move rice and other supplies from Danang to refugee camps in Hue.

The letter is a wonderful tribute to two outstanding IVSers, who did what a good guest in the midst of a crisis would do, and perhaps harkens back to the time when the objective of IVS and the needs of the GVN were closely aligned. The letter also reveals the fundamental problem of IVS in Vietnam in the 1960's and 1970-71, and perhaps, the fundamental problem of volunteer programs all over the world to varying degrees. The fundamental goal of developing countries over the past 50 years has been to strengthen national governments and bring disparate ethnic and regional groups into the national political fabric. By itself, this goal creates a degree of tension between a guest Non-Governmental Organization (NGO) trying to work people-to-people at a village level and the central government.

Even assuming the guest is comfortable working with the host government, what happens when corruption and despotism increase, and local counterparts of the NGO are ignored or abused? Volunteer Tom Luche was instrumental in providing technical agricultural support to strategic hamlets in 1960-61, in what might be considered the early "good days" of the Diem regime. These hamlets became the models for a creative, reasonable counter-insurgency program. In the subsequent "bad days" of the regime, however, these models became core elements of a quasi-police state. How long can the "idealistic" guest NGOs be expected to align with the host government during such a transformation?

Conflict areas typically are characterized by extensive human suffering and break-down of institutions. Services of external volunteers to work in relief and development may be critically important. The continuum of relief-to-development is well recognized and important to resilience in "building back better" to avoid recurring conflict. That said, a voluntary organization and volunteers must go into such a situation with their eyes open. It is extremely difficult to remain neutral while working in the midst of a civil war, especially when funded by a benefactor that supports one side in the fight. IVS and the USAID started out with the same objectives in Southeast Asia, but as conditions changed, the common commitment eroded.

4

Going Global With A Maturing Volunteer Program

Gary Alex and Willi Meyers

Much has been communicated about IVS programs in Southeast Asia because activities there were so long-lasting and operated amidst political strife: Laos, 1955-1975, Vietnam 1956-1971, Cambodia 1960-1963. This chapter looks at the larger global IVS institution in the 1960s and the pivotal 1970s. By the 1960s, IVS had a history of mature volunteer programs and institutional successes, and its administrators understood the need to expand programs beyond the conflict areas of Southeast Asia, to diversify funding, to fulfill institutional objectives, and to confirm IVS's relevance and identity as a premier, global development volunteer service.

With the formation of the Peace Corps in the early 1960s, there were expectations that IVS program funding would come via the Peace Corp. However, the first partnership program in Liberia resulted in disappointment, and IVS faced the problem of finding countries for its programs that would not compete with the Peace Corp. Such countries tended to be "difficult" places that a cautious Peace Corps might avoid, or places that might not welcome a program with U.S. government volunteers. IVS was able to establish productive volunteer-based programs in ten countries, nine of which are summarized in this chapter. Initiatives in eight other countries failed to develop beyond a few initial assignments.

Throughout the 1960s, IVS retained its original objectives, as listed in its certification of incorporation (see Appendix B) and maintained them throughout its existence. A March 1970 IVS newsletter includes a document, *Purposes and Policies*, dated 1953, as a timely reminder of the origins and reason for establishment of IVS. It noted that there had been a "natural evolution toward other methods of attaining its basic goals," most notably an expansion into non-agricultural programs and the use of non-American volunteers.[1]

In February 1971, an IVS board and staff meeting at Harper's Ferry, West Virginia, led to a major pivot in IVS's operational strategy but presumably without changing objectives. The meeting addressed three fundamental questions: (1) Was there a continuing role for international volunteers? (2) Could IVS make a significant contribution? (3) What structure and program changes would be necessary for an effective IVS contribution?[2]

The meeting concluded that an era of U.S. international affairs and the U.S.'s dominant role in the world were ending. At the same time, globalization trends were evident, and the poverty gap between rich and poor was widening. The U.S. Government (USG) appeared poised to increase development assistance while separating it from other foreign policy programs. Still, there remained a critical need to improve international understanding and provide middle-level technical skills to developing countries. Thus, meeting participants concluded that IVS had a continuing role to play, but to do so, it must broaden its financial support base, initiate additional and diverse programs in Asia, Africa, Latin America, and the U.S., and have multinational representation among its volunteers, staff, and board. It set a target for placing 500-1000 volunteers in five years. The new strategy was disseminated in a paper "International Voluntary Services, Inc: New Directions—1992."

In retrospect, the meeting's conclusions were premature regarding the changing global status of the U.S. and naïve in envisioning a change delinking foreign assistance from broader foreign policy objectives. There may also have been excess optimism in the targets and the benefits of internationalizing the organization's personnel. However, the meeting provided a clear call for change and a new direction for IVS. The Harper's Ferry meeting and subsequent IVS management initiatives receive greater analysis in Chapter Six.

Ten new country programs were launched between 1971 and 1975, with five of them in 1975 alone. Thus, the number of IVS country programs increased from five or six in the 1950s and 1960s to an all-time high of 14 in 1975. New programs remained focused on providing voluntary technical assistance, although post-Harper's Ferry programs had an increased emphasis on non-U.S. volunteers. This chapter summarizes the experience of nine country programs started between 1960 and 1975 that emphasized international volunteers. The Bangladesh program, which also began during this period, is described in the next chapter, because it changed in nature along the lines of IVS programs in other countries and continued until IVS ceased operation in 2002.

IVS/LIBERIA (1960–63)
VILLAGE EDUCATION PROGRAM TAKEN OVER BY THE PEACE CORPS

IVS/Liberia
PROGRAMS:
• Primary Education
VOLUNTEERS – 24
FUNDING: USAID - $445,000

Liberia, never formally a colony, was founded in 1822 by freed slaves from the U.S. Rubber plantations and iron ore mines attracted foreign investors and provided much of the limited state revenue. The governing elite reaped most of the benefits from rubber and iron ore contracts, leading to a wide gap between rich and poor. Still, the period from 1944 to 1971 was one of relative economic growth and prosperity, although with strong repression of any opposition to the government. Poverty remained endemic and rural infrastructure and social services extremely limited.

In early 1960, ICA (renamed USAID in 1961) proposed a project for IVS to field a team of 50 teachers with one chief of party. The IVS teachers were to organize, establish, and teach in community primary schools and, as a side activity, provide leadership for community development. There were delays in getting the contract signed, but by March 1961, seven IVS teachers were in the country, and a contract was in place for 45 volunteers over two years. Volunteer RONALD JOHNSON described volunteers' assignments in a March 1963 letter:

> I briefly mentioned, in an earlier letter, what IVS is and why we are here. We are most directly responsible to the United States Agency for International Development Education Division which works with the Department of Education in this country. The IVS teacher serves as a co-principal in each location. He also teaches one or more classes and teaches the principal's classes when he attends a semesters in-service teachers' training program which has been started in the past year. We are to provide in-service training to the other teachers on a day-to-day basis. This is often a difficult thing to do when we need to spend the necessary time our own classes require. Although most of our efforts are school centered, we also participate in community development, agriculture, literacy, etc. projects where they are needed or our time, effort, and abilities are available.

Volunteer assignments were challenging and quite varied. Often, on arrival in a community, volunteers had to construct or coordinate construction of school buildings and/or their own housing. Teaching assignments were uncertain, because Liberian teachers came and went for various reasons. Side projects in agriculture, adult education, or community development varied. For a time, improved chicken raising was popular, but the project ran into problems when the required poultry feed imports were delayed. USAID also asked volunteers to take on special assignments, such as assisting in establishing new schools or developing a school feeding program in conjunction with Cooperative for American Remittances Everywhere (CARE).

The relationship with International Cooperation Administration (ICA) appears to have been close and collegial. Volunteers received mail through ICA, reported on their activities to ICA, as would be expected with an ICA-funded program, and relied on ICA for technical support. One volunteer even described IVS in a letter to friends as a "recruiting agency for ICA, the U.S. Government foreign aid program". Undoubtedly, volunteer motivations varied, but DAVID BLANCHARD in a February 1963 letter home discussed why IVS was in Liberia, disagreeing with what was often considered the organization's rationale.

> Some of you have mentioned motivation towards and value of the work IVS men are doing here and I would like to sum up what I think our general attitude is. Probably nowhere among the Africans does a true Communist exist. Liberia is one of the most anti-Communist countries in Africa. To the uneducated, abstract philosophies are meaningless; to the educated here, nothing can divert them from their headlong drive to copy everything American. No! We are not here to fight Communism.

Relations within communities were very good in many cases, although it required time for volunteers to be accepted. Food was scarce and living conditions basic, but local missionaries working in education and development were quite supportive. Motorcycle accidents, political violence, and poisonous snakes were threats, and health was a major concern. A smallpox epidemic luckily struck no volunteers, but other illnesses were common, as when amoebic dysentery combined with malaria hospitalized volunteer George Francis.

The IVS/Liberia program became a joint program with the Peace Corps' establishment. In early 1962, Cliff Doke of IVS arrived with four others as part of the management team for 90 Peace Corps/IVS teachers who were to arrive a month later. The partnership did not last long. In an August 1962 letter to friends, David Blanchard gave his view of what happened:

> Like the winds of a tornado, the Peace Corps has torn the Blanchard family from their foundations and flung them to the far corners of the world. Both my mother and myself are today where we would not be except for this storm, and by September we will have moved again....
>
> My mother's story first for many of you know of it already. Last year (I cannot remember when for time has lost all relevance in this seasonless existence), she took the Peace Corps (PC) exam in English for the experience, for in her public life

she is often quizzed about the PC; and, secretively probably, to see if she qualified. In May this year, her acceptance arrived for training as a remedial English teacher in some university in the Philippines. . . .

My own experience with the PC, while less revolutionary, is also less voluntary. In February, PC executives breezed into Liberia like the messengers of God implementing divine will. Theirs was a program of bringing in about seventy Americans to teach in Liberian high schools a few of which are up-country. By March, we learned that the PC felt that there should only be one government service contract in a country, and that they had therefore forced IVS to stop recruiting for Liberia and pressured USAID not to renew our contract when it expires about April 1963. Recently our contract has been renewed to July 1963 to allow us to complete the school year. Later we were told that an IVS/PC team of nearly thirty would arrive along with the high school teachers to teach in the village elementary schools. Apparently, for we have never been officially informed, this is truly a PC team with an IVS-recruited Chief-of-Party. These teachers will get sixty dollars a month more than we receive (we are not complaining for our allowance is more than enough to cover our expenses) because the Liberian Government is contributing part of the amount. There will always be two Americans to a location and only the more sophisticated towns and previous IVS locations will be used. . . .

USAID on learning that PC was considering placing two teachers in Ganta decided to pull us out and put us in new locations. PC will, of course, move directly into our house, for it has been substantially improved since IVS acquired it a year and a half ago.[3]

Newsletters from IVS/Liberia volunteers suggest a high degree of satisfaction with their assignments and experience. Volunteer David Blanchard returned to Liberia in 1967, while in a U.S. university program and completed a study on rural development needs and options for Liberia. After two years teaching and living in two different communities, volunteer DAVID FRANCIS wrote of his commitment to the country in his final newsletter:

> My term ended there with a "send-off" by the school committee and a double row of waving school kids for a mile or so. Leaving Dubli Island was not easy, but the sadness soon left me upon arrival at Ganta [his first school posting]. My contract with International Voluntary Services has now officially ended. Upon return to the States I will be attending the new Methodist Theological School in Ohio, near Delaware. Since classes don't start until September the time from now until July will be spent teaching at our mission here in Ganta. So far the schedule includes the seventh and eighth grades of the Mission School in the mornings, grades three,

four, and five out at the Leprosy Colony school in the afternoons, and probably more studying Mano at night. . . .

My goal: to return to school for one or two years and return (with wife!!) to Liberia and build an Agricultural School. A school with technical two-year program leading toward establishment in farming.

Volunteer GEORGE BEESTMAN also had very positive memories of the assignment to Liberia:

The mission of IVS in Liberia was to replace the teachers in village schools so that they could be sent to teacher training. Most were headmasters because they had completed all 6 grades themselves and were the most knowledgeable. Off I went to the village of Palala as their new teacher. My mode of transportation was a trusty chain-driven Zundap motor bike. Throughout my stay in Liberia I travelled 5000 kilometers on the bike over the rough laterite roads.

During my second year I was sent to Cuttington College in the center of Liberia. A large Agricultural Experiment Station about a mile from Cuttington campus had been closed. All of the scientists who had taught at Cuttington were gone. Because of my Agricultural background, I was sent to provide a course in tropical soils to their graduating seniors in agronomy. I had the library at the abandoned experimental station as my resource to prepare a course. I was deeply committed to give them a credible college level course in tropical soils. Now, all of my colleagues were Masters and PhD people. So when it was time to return home, I applied to the University of Wisconsin Soils Department for graduate work.

The two years with IVS in Liberia were more formative of me than four years of college had been. I gained a sense of maturity and a direction forward.

The IVS/Liberia program had a substantial number of volunteers working in primary education with reasonable support from USAID and other organizations, and it seemed poised to have an important developmental impact. Country conditions were difficult, but volunteer morale was high. A critical mass of volunteers with a clear and defined objective probably helped. The early phase-out due to the Peace Corp arrival was unfortunate.

IVS/ALGERIA (1963–66; 1968–74)
SOIL CONSERVATION TO ENGLISH TEACHING

IVS/Algeria
PROGRAMS:
- Soil Conservation
- English Teaching

VOLUNTEERS: 122
FUNDING: USAID; State Department; Government of Algeria; private

After independence in 1962, Algeria was recovering from a devastating eight-year civil war and the mass exodus of one million Europeans. Unemployment was widespread. The IVS/Algeria program began in this context and became IVS's third largest program with 122 volunteer assignments over 14 years. Projects were split with two periods.

In 1963, USAID funded a Rural Rehabilitation Project—the "Four Areas Project"—to provide employment and address a nationwide soil erosion problem. The project included technical assistance from the U.S. Soil Conservation Service (SCS) and 24 IVS volunteers with training in agronomy, soil science, civil and agricultural engineering, and forestry. Volunteers were assigned to four field offices to manage 200,000 person-days per month of labor on the following: food-for-work or for-cash activities for construction of terraces, contour cropping, land leveling, small dams and water control structures, and reforestation. Later, this was expanded to include water and sanitation infrastructure. The project was to train Algerians to replace the SCS advisers and IVS volunteers. Implementation delays plagued the initial years of the program and frustrated volunteers. Still, much was accomplished in building relationships and activity planning.[4] More fundamental problems arose when SCS technical assistance was terminated early.

A second project, "Secours National Program" or "Algeria-Tefeschoun", was designed to take homeless children off the street and put them in a more positive situation. In 1966, IVS provided volunteer teachers and medical workers to orphanages caring for orphans from the civil war. Here, too, implementation problems and lack of clarity on volunteer roles affected the program, to the extent that all six volunteer positions planned for the program were not filled. The U.S. State Department was also to fund 12 volunteers for four English Language Centers offering intensive English training to Algerians with work-related need for the language. This was to expand with demand and was intended to train Algerians to take over the centers. There is no documentation as to whether the program ever started.

In 1966, the Algerian program ran into difficulties.[5] The Secours National Program became unviable, and USAID cut back on their staff and funding. Despite encouragement from the U.S. Ambassador to continue with a program of 30 volunteers, funding was uncertain and IVS activities in the country ended.

Then, in 1968, at the request of the Ministry of Education, IVS reengaged with private funding for English language training at lycées (high schools) and the University of Oran to train a cadre of future English teachers. Twenty-two volunteers were assigned in 1972 in response to a government request for up to 100. Volunteer TINA MARTIN (Algeria 1974-76), a former Peace Corps volunteer to Tonga, shared in letters home some of her frustrations with teaching English in a girls' school in Medea.[6]

> Indeed, life was difficult for an unmarried woman. There was little or no socializing with members of the opposite sex, and friendliness was often misinterpreted. I knew not to smile too much or talk too readily. I'd heard it all and learned it by heart, like catechism. . . . Now the truth is that I'm not miserable and have no intention of being so unless it is absolutely necessary. . . .
>
> After I finished going over all the questions [from students] and they've given me their suggestions on how to improve the English language to make it more comprehensible to foreigners, I ask for their complete attention and they give me some of it. I begin by saying that in my four years of teaching, I have never met students more gifted for dramatics. They have impressed me from the very beginning with their theatrical talents, so instead of directing their energy to moving me to tears and convincing me that life cannot go on if I don't change their grades and for the better, why don't they just concentrate on understanding the errors, correcting them, and learning from them?
>
> At five, the students gather around my desk and sing for me in Arabic. Ms. Banyekleft gives me some Algerian bread she'd made called Galette and the recipe. The students are always so generous with cakes and breads. They know bribery is their only chance. No, I'm not that cynical (or perceptive?) and I really appreciate their generosity. I think how much I'd like them if it weren't my responsibility to teach them English.

The English language program had its controversies. Some volunteers questioned the developmental value of teaching English, and others felt volunteers were simply filling positions that Algerians could have filled. For part of the period, less than 50 percent of volunteers completed two years assignments. A counterargument was that Algeria had on its own initiative requested volunteers, was willing to fund a significant share of costs, and English and volunteers could serve to expand international communications and understanding. Volunteer dissatisfaction was due in part to their relative isolation, having little contact with students outside of class and difficulty developing other social relationships. In the August 1969 "IVS Reporter" newsletter, IVS Chief of Party DOROTHY YOUNG justified English language training:

> If I have not painted a very gay picture of life and teaching in Algeria it is because Algeria has not yet had time to be a happy country. It is certainly not the romantic Arab World of the Barbary Pirates or "Kismet" or Lawrence. It is a strikingly beautiful country, but a country that will bear the physical and spiritual scars of war for years and perhaps generations to come. It is also one in the family of developing nations, a family which we need to know better. It is also part of the Arab family, a family which has had an unhappy relationship with the West and with whom we Americans risk stifling all meaningful dialogue unless we build some constructive and durable lines of communications—not only economic but cultural and spiritual as well.

The IVS program continued and evolved. By 1971, the program was funded 50 percent by the Government of Algeria, 35 percent by private funds, and 15 percent by the U.S. State Department.[7] The Government optimistically requested 117 agricultural volunteers and 50 English teachers[8] and by the next year, two agricultural volunteers were in the field supporting a broad program of modernizing Algerian agriculture, working with government counterparts on research trials, seed production, and extension. In August 1974, seven new teachers arrived—six for the University of Oram and one for a lycée.

Volunteer DOROTHY YOUNG, who spent six years in Algeria—four with IVS as a volunteer and Country Director, noted some of the unique aspects and problems in the program:

> The program in Algeria, unbeknownst to me, was to IVS a sort of landmark agreement in the midst of a great debate on what IVS' relationship should be to the U.S. Government, especially in Southeast Asia. In the field, we had the view that IVS/Algeria was an Algerian program, paid for by the Algerians, and it was practically self-sufficient. The Algerians provided our lodging (this often, including in my case, meant weeks to months WITHOUT lodging). Algeria paid our stipend. This was generally a huge hassle—first to get paid and then to try to expatriate any savings to the U.S. as IVS did not pay our stipend or our vacation allowance.
>
> The Algerian Ministry of Education wanted to replace all the French "cooperants" with native English speakers and requested a minimum of 50 IVSers. IVS averaged about up to 15 volunteer teachers/year.

The IVS/Algeria program ended in 1974. It had strong engagement from the Government of Algeria to address defined developmental objectives, and volunteer numbers were sufficient to be a viable country program. The initial conservation project could have had important employment and environmental impacts but was terminated by USAID for foreign policy reasons. Under the later, government-funded program, volunteers appear to have had problems fitting into local society. Funding from the Algerian government was limited and somewhat irregular, leading to logistical problems that may have also impacted the "volunteer experience". Additional IVS staff resources to support volunteers might have been helpful but would of course have added to costs.

IVS/Morocco (1968–74)
Range Management Challenges

IVS/Morocco
Programs:
• Range Management
Volunteers – 12
Funding: USAID ($500,000)

In 1966, the Government of Morocco requested USAID assistance to improve management of eroding common pastureland. IVS was funded to provide technical assistance, with four volunteers arriving in 1968. The project started with high expectations for developing 12 range management areas covering 325,000 hectares over three years. Shortly after its start, the project was reduced to four areas totaling 95,000 hectares and later to just two areas covering 70,000 has. The focus changed from rapid range improvement to intensive research on 6,000 hectares. Notably, the project relied heavily on qualified volunteers with range management expertise with several others placed in positions in the Forestry Department.

The project failed to engage local livestock producers, who were suspicious of the government's plans and resisted the program. Local officials had neither decision authority nor budget, and national level officials did not provide the needed logistic and budget support. Perhaps not surprisingly, at least four volunteers resigned before their contracts were completed. Still, the project had some important results. Seven Moroccans received U.S. training, and project personnel assisted in formulation of a Royal Proclamation providing for local grazing organizations to manage communal grazing lands. The project demonstrated the feasibility of reseeding and deferred grazing and led to the establishment of a National Feed and Range Service.

The Morocco program was IVS's first attempt at a comprehensive project with a defined objective for national level impact. This came nearly a decade ahead of other such projects and, in contrast to many other IVS host countries of the time, was in a generally stable country environment. In providing specialized technical skills in range management, the project was a chance to shine.

Unfortunately, the Morocco project suffered from a lack of adequate planning by IVS, USAID, and the Government of Morocco. A three-year timeframe was too short, even without the major changes in scope, which must have also been quite disruptive. As well, early departure by several volunteers could not have helped IVS's reputation. Under a follow-on range management program, USAID contracted a team of range management specialists from Utah State University with Peace Corps volunteers assigned to work at the community level. That project also had major implementation problems.[9] The IVS program closed with the end of USAID funding, although Moroccan counterparts were said to have requested volunteers to continue their work.[10]

IVS/ZAIRE/CONGO (1970–74; 1986–1989)
AGRICULTURAL CREDIT TROUBLES AND PUBLIC HEALTH

IVS/Zaire/Congo DR
PROGRAMS:
- Agricultural Credit
- Cooperative Development
- Public Health

VOLUNTEERS – 19
FUNDING: USAID; other

The Democratic Republic of Congo (DRC) (known as Zaire from 1971 to 1997) is a vast country, as large as the United States east of the Mississippi. It has great diversity in climate, topography, and peoples. After independence in 1960, it faced formidable social, political, and administrative problems, when withdrawal of Belgian civil servants left an inexperienced, but highly centralized, government with limited resources. Civil strife soon broke out and continued through 1965. Even when some political stability returned, poverty and dysfunctional government systems remained the norm, despite the country's wealth in natural resources.

In 1970, a five-year $704,000 Supervised Agricultural Credit Project was initiated by USAID and the DRC Government to establish an agricultural credit system in three pilot areas linking loans with advisory services for farmers. USAID funded IVS to provide ten field credit specialists and a team leader to work under an Agricultural Credit Advisor. The team leader was responsible for credit operation logistics and management, while volunteer credit specialists—considered employees of the Ministry of Agriculture—would work with regional agronomists and counterparts to prepare loan documentation with farm budgets and management plans, supervise loan use, and track repayments.

IVS excelled in recruiting volunteers and fielded eight volunteers before project activities really got started. This allowed time for language study and orientation but, unfortunately, left volunteers with little to do for too long because implementation did not begin until January, 1971—a full year after project signing. Volunteer DAVID DAMASKE wrote, in an October 1970 letter:

> The IVS/Congo team has been in the Congo for eight months, and our accomplishments are still few. Our team reached its full strength in late September with the arrival of two Nationalist Chinese (Won & Kwan). The Chinese are a valuable addition, if for no other reason than the fantastic boost they have made to our drab menu. After many meals of diligent apprenticeship, Won and Kwan have certified me as a qualified fried-rice chef. . . .
>
> Our team consists of 10 IVS men (seven Americans, one Englishman and two Chinese), all having graduated from an agricultural college with a major in Agricultural Economics. Four of our team started French language training in Washington, D.C. in January of this year and continued their training in the Republic Democratic Du Congo in March. Since finishing training in late May, they have been waiting for the program to receive its official structure from the Congolese Government.
>
> The purpose of IVS/Congo is to help administer a pilot Agricultural Credit program. The program has $1,000,000 of loanable funds to be spread over three pilot areas: The Bas Congo (i.e. below and west of Kinshasa), the Bumba region (i.e., on the northernmost point of the Congo River), and Kasai (i.e., the region around Laluabourg). Each IVS volunteer will be working with one or two Congolese counterparts in the handling of loan applications in his area. Each loan application is approved or disapproved by a central Board of Directors, appointed by the Ministry of Agriculture to the program, with the recommendation of the IVS volunteer and his counterpart carrying considerable weight.
>
> The Congolese Ministry of Agriculture has great expectations, dependent upon the failure or success of this pilot program. If it succeeds, the Ministry hopes to establish a National Agricultural Credit Bank designed to hasten agricultural development in the Congo.

Given the conditions in the Congo, the project would have been a challenging undertaking under the best of circumstances. But, despite the delays and other problems, some volunteers had positive experiences. Volunteer JIM JENSON, who spent a year at two different sites, described a Congo village visit in this September 1971 letter:

> The president of the cooperative gave us the house of one of his wives to live in. After each day's work we bathed in a small stream and then settled down to a meal of cooked bananas, chicken, and pineapple. We even had a taste of roasted monkey.
>
> At night we sat around a kerosene lamp to answer questions about moon exploration and the astronauts, about snow and winter, about the tremendous distance to

go to America and about American life in general. By their tradition the first night was reserved for the men, the second for the women and the third for the children. Since there are radios throughout the area villagers are informed about world affairs. Even with their knowledge, some surprising misinterpretations result. Some elderly women were curious to know if I had been to the moon. They knew that an American had landed on the moon and I was the first American they had met.

The study indicated that Bumba was not economically ready to use a credit program so, with some regrets, I moved to Thysville where the credit office had already been in operation for a short period of time. Economically Thysville provides what Bumba is lacking. There are many Congolese farming at an impressive level who need the extra capital that agricultural loans can provide.

In September 1972, Loring Henderson arrived in the Congo as the first of three volunteers to serve on a regional advisory team for a Canadian-funded cooperative development project. The project was to work with local community groups as quasi-cooperatives, helping with marketing, business development, adult education, and community development. This project also suffered implementation delays. Henderson spent six months making preparatory visits to cooperatives in the Bas-Congo region near Kinshasa. He found a dismal track record for cooperatives, dating back to pseudo-co-ops of colonial times. He concluded that conditions were not yet conducive to successful cooperative growth. The planned project appeared to fizzle out, and Henderson left early. LORING HENDERSON reflected on his volunteer experience in an April 2, 1973 letter:

> One of the most gratifying of these first six months' experiences has been discovering that qualified, knowledgeable Zairois are available to work with cooperatives. These include the government men in the regional offices, the trained personnel returning from their courses and older, experienced, successful businessmen and farmers who live in the rural environment and have some association with the cooperative in their area but are too busy to devote full time to its management. These men represent a tremendous resource for cooperatives and we hope to coordinate them into our program. In many ways, cooperatives are an ideal institution for Zaire. The land is generally held communally in the name of the village or clan. It is the custom to work together and share the benefits. The difficulty comes from the conflict between this generous way of life and the lack of appreciation of the profit motive which is necessary even in cooperatives. This is why the exceptional men who have broken with the traditional pattern can be such an effective influence in cooperative development.
>
> The most unsettling thought to occur in my time in Zaire is that, perhaps, we are being counter productive. The continued individual and government

reliance on foreigner assistance is a force acting against the growth of national self-confidence. After 80 years of colonial experience and the tribal and regional battles of the early 1960's, Zaire's awareness of its own abilities and limitations is very fragile. I often wonder if it would not be better to stand aside while the country goes through a period of adapting all the imported knowledge to its indigenous culture. To this end, I work as non-directly as possible and support the government's authenticity movement and measures to determine its identity without cutting relations with other countries.

Along with the efforts for cooperatives, I have had my share of memorable personal experiences. With my 4-wheel drive International Scout, I have travelled more than 3,000 miles over the roughest roads imaginable, through deep mud, torrential rain, choking dust, and repeated breakdowns; I have voyaged on the Zaire River; I have spent many pleasurable nights in villages enjoying the chiquange (cold, rubbery chunks of mashed, boiled manioc) and company of the sociable Zairois; I have been sick from bad water, gone through a cholera epidemic, had malaria and been robbed; I have gained a conversational fluency in African French and learned a few words of Kikongo; I have gone spelunking to see stone age drawings in nearby caves; and, I have delivered a baby girl on the dining room table of a mission. Fortunately, for everyone concerned, I had recently asked a midwife what to do in the bush if. . . .!

Relations with USAID were not always good, partly due perhaps to frequent turnovers of USAID staff. In an undated letter, volunteer CHRIS WARDLE, assigned to the agricultural credit project, expressed concerns and uncertainties and suggested that faults lay with USAID design and project management:

> My decision to resign has not been reached hastily. I have had plenty of time to think about all aspects of our program. My reasons for resigning are several. In May, 1970, I was assigned to the Kasai region. After nearly one year of waiting, I have not reached my permanent post. I feel that the chances of' getting there are minimal. With AID's attempts to cut back the program, it appears that Kasai will be permanently abandoned. This leaves nine volunteers in the remaining two regions which, in my opinion, is an overstaffing. Even if Kasai is left in the program, it will take a year just to investigate and set up our offices before we can begin. No one associated with our program has ever visited this region, and thus there is always the chance that it could turn out to be another Bumba.
>
> It appears that AID is having second thoughts about our program. An organization must evaluate its programs and judge each one of them according to its performance. I realize that the performance of our program to date has been marginal but the marginality depends upon whose eyes you are looking through. Our program has rightly come under scrutiny. However, I seriously question the tactics being

used to investigate it. The Director of USAID is, in my opinion, determined to eliminate our program. His unannounced visit to our Thysville office demonstrated the methods he is willing to use to achieve this end. His subsequent report contained several inaccuracies and was written in a tone that clearly exhibited the writer's attitude towards our program. For the past three weeks, rumors concerning the fate of our program have abounded, and I for one cannot work in this atmosphere.

IVS activities ended in 1974 at a time when U.S.-Zaire relations cooled, due to human rights issues in the country.

Twelve years later in September 1986, volunteers Mary and Scott Endsley were posted in the Congo to work with the Methodist Infrastructure de la Santa Rural Dans L'Ouste de Shaba (OSROS) as health specialists. They were to work on improving the administration of dispensaries, public health campaigns, and continuing education for local health workers to re-establish public health services destroyed by civil war. In May of the next year, with their work seemingly going quite well, USAID informed OSROS that project funding was not to be used for public health services. (This may have been the consequence of USAID's funding for a new public health project covering the region where the Endsleys were working.) Efforts to resolve this issue were initially unsuccessful, and the Endsleys decided to leave early in December 1987.[11] They apparently relented and continued to 1989. The project's focus also shifted to broader system development with one volunteer providing administrative support and three volunteers supervising reconstruction and rehabilitation of community health posts and other infrastructure.[12] Volunteer Tin Sy Nguyen was key to the construction program, which ended in 1990.

IVS/Congo projects involved placement of volunteers on some challenging, strategically important projects, where innovative, energetic technical assistance would have been quite useful. Project problems and volunteer frustration grew, however, due to design flaws and/or unrealistic expectations for projects, given the state of development of the Congo at the time. IVS might have benefitted from additional country staffing for planning assignments and support of its volunteers.

IVS/Yemen (1971–79)
Varied Assignments and Later Focus on Agriculture Research

IVS/Yemen
Programs:
- Agriculture
- Health

Volunteers – 13
Funding: USAID and various

Much of Yemen in the early 1970s was considered practically medieval. Until 1962, when the last Imam (traditional ruler) was overthrown, Yemen was one of the most isolated and feudal countries in the world. Communication with the outside world was almost impossible. Basic social infrastructure—schools, transportation, health, and civil administration services—were rudimentary. Except for Koranic schools, education was practically nonexistent. A civil war from 1962 to 1968 devastated the country but led to a gradual opening to the outside world. Ninety percent of the population was subsistence farmers, and severe drought added to hardships. USAID considered Yemen's aid absorptive capacity as one of the lowest in the world.

Living conditions were primitive in the major cities, but villages lacked even the most basic amenities. USAID came to see a need for assistance in rural areas and proposed the use of IVS and Peace Corps volunteers for rural assignments. Volunteers were considered adaptable with experience for "roughing it" where logistical problems for health care, communications, and language were formidable.

In 1971, IVS assigned Yoshikazu Ito of Japan as a volunteer water management engineer to Yemen under United Nations auspices. The UN Volunteers Program was just being formed and used IVS and other arrangements to place seven of its first-ever volunteers in Yemen. Volunteer Yoshikazu Ito describes his experience and its effect on his later career.

> In 1970, the United Nations Development Programme (UNDP) made a call for Japanese engineers to work as a volunteer for Yemen's development. I applied for this opportunity and had an interview with the International Voluntary Services (IVS), which was seconded by the UN and the UNDP Office in Japan. . . . Yemen was another reason that made me apply; Yemen has the world's oldest dam called the Ma'rib Dam, which is a sacred ground for people in irrigation, drainage, and reclamation engineering industry. . . I was officially selected as the successful candidate in 1971 and flew to the U.S. to receive an Arabic language training in Washington, D. C. and a briefing on the duty station in New York. Then I was finally assigned to Yemen. . . .

The main assignment for me and the Italian UN volunteer was to secure water resources for drinking water and irrigation. My work was to build deep wells for drinking water and farming. I assessed infiltration water using electrical prospecting, collected data, and dug wells. During the engineering process, I also trained Government staffs, including [Yemen] counterparts, enabling them to increase the number of deep wells largely. This is one of the projects I still recall as especially successful.

Despite difficult working conditions, lack of support, and infrastructure that limited accomplishments, the volunteer service was well received, and IVS received requests for English teachers, nurses training, and other health care volunteers. This launched the IVS/Yemen program, whose small teams worked on various public health and agricultural program through the 1970s.

A group of volunteers arrived in August 1973 and soon ran into logistical and assignment problems. This led IVS to recruit a Country Coordinator in December 1974. Over the following eighteen months, the program grew to include: three nurses at the city hospital, a nutritionist, four agriculturalists on a sorghum/millet project, two positions with a German aid project, and two rural development volunteers. The three nurse positions were closed out because ill-defined roles and responsibilities led several volunteers to terminate early.

Especially in urban assignments, volunteers encountered the common dilemma of sustainability. Who would replace them? Were they just filling a position that should be held by a local? What was the value of their service? CHRISTINE ANSELL, who worked on a nutrition program, expressed her concerns in a January 1978 report:

> In some ways it would seem that the time has come for us to consider phasing out. Rahman is very capable of running the department and does so. However, she is powerless to move outside it on her own to work towards involving the department in the community as a whole. It's unfortunately just the expatriates who are "allowed" to do the "bizarre" but worthwhile things like this. Another factor is that given the staff turnover there is no guarantee that Rahman will be there indefinitely, nor that her successor will know much about nutrition.
>
> I don't think it's realistic to expect much change in the attitudes of the doctors and director who see themselves as very well trained, etc. and do not intend to delegate responsibility to the nurses or redistribute power in any way at all. This is a real barrier to progress.
>
> However, I can see one very real advantage in continuing an expatriate presence in the nutrition department and that is (unfortunately) to maintain its status. Without this, I feel that those in control, who don't see nutrition work as an absolute priority

may inadvertently run the whole department down through lack of interest. For example, Rahman could be removed at any time to work in another department—the rooms could be used for giving even more injections (of which hundreds are given unnecessarily every week). Willa could be used only to hand out WFP food, etc. Someone who can answer back and prevent this sort of thing is essential and at the moment no Yemeni woman can claim to be able to do that. Expatriate involvement also means encouragement and ideas to those involved in the department. A particular point is that (unlike with nurses and midwives) there is no prospect of a trained Yemeni nutritionist as such appearing.

A 1976 USAID National Sorghum and Millet Crop Improvement Project became IVS/Yemen's highest profile project, with placement for an agricultural engineer and three research station technicians for five years each. Volunteers were support technicians for a University of Arizona technical team. The project involved a close relationship with USAID, which seemed to everyone's benefit. As one note from the field indicated, "Everyone is told that volunteers are USAID personnel." USAID was responsible for arranging housing and other logistics for volunteers.

Despite difficult conditions, volunteers saw accomplishments. A sorghum/millet project (1973-74) evaluation concluded that, "IVS's understanding of project purpose, technical qualifications, training of local technical and administration of participants were rated 'superior'.[13] In all other categories the rating was listed 'as planned'. No unsatisfactory ratings were given." In an October 1979 End-of-Tour Report, Volunteer ANDRES TACADEO noted:

> In conclusion, I can say that IVS has filled a definite contributory role, quite vital in a research programme of the type we were involved with. IVS programme is coming to an end in Yemen, but the facility established with the help of IVSers will remain, and I hope this will contribute to an introduction of better sorghum varieties in Yemen, which in turn will improve the standards of the farmers. Al Jaruba farm though, is not fully operative at this moment, but its infrastructural facilities have been established and hopefully from next cropping season sorghum research work will start there too. IVS volunteers were highly accepted by Yemeni technicians as well as AID personnel. Impact of our efforts will be reflected not in short time to come, but in a longer time frame as is the case with agricultural development elsewhere.

Relationships, or perhaps communications, were not entirely smooth. In 1979, a University of Arizona visitor to IVS/Washington concluded that IVS would not be interested in extending the Yemen Sorghum/Millet Project contract, because IVS "likes to make a commitment to be in a country in a big way or not at all. Their present force in Yemen is too small from a policy standpoint. The second reason is that IVS likes to have responsibility for a program or, at least, for a program segment. Marshall [the University of Arizona visitor] does not see such a role for IVS now or in the future."[14] How accurately this reflects IVS thinking is unclear, but it suggests some hesitancy in IVS's commitment to the project. Later, IVS participation was terminated before the end of the project. The University of Arizona Project Final Report noted that "Some changes in the Project were made unilaterally by USAID. The IVS technicians were discontinued at a time when they were greatly needed. Project progress suffered as a result."

The Yemen program ended in 1979. There was a sense that inadequate assessment of Yemeni conditions and planning for IVS volunteer assignments had been responsible for many of the problems encountered in the program. Still, the engagement on the USAID research project appeared quite productive and the initial volunteer helped pilot the UN Volunteer program.

IVS/INDONESIA (1972–76)
A LONG GESTATION PERIOD FOR A SMALL PROGRAM

IVS/Indonesia
PROGRAMS:
• Local Volunteer Program
• Development
VOLUNTEERS – 2
FUNDING: CARE

Following independence in the 1940's, Indonesia faced complicated competing interest groups vying for power. Sukarno emerged to lead the large and diverse population through varied periods of regional unrest and economic growth. The economy deteriorated in the mid-1960s, as the mix of communists, Muslims, and military broke down. An anti-Communist purge in 1965-66 resulted in one-half to one million people or more being killed. The Peace Corps, which started a program in 1963, was asked to leave in 1965. The military then gained power and brought an era of stability and economic growth.

In 1968, IVS Director Arthur Gardiner asked Willi Meyers to explore opportunities for an IVS program in Indonesia, believing a private voluntary service would be more acceptable to the host government than the governmental Peace Corps. Meyers spent three months in Jakarta in 1968 and a couple of weeks in 1969. He found that both U.S. and Indonesian officials at that time preferred to work with a non-governmental voluntary organization rather than the Peace Corps. Extensive consultations explored options for English teaching, for a Food for Work/rural development program, and for cooperation with CARE (an international non-profit) to collaborate with Badan Urusan Tenage Kerja Sukaela Indonesia (BUTSI), a domestic volunteer program. Indonesian officials stressed that international volunteers should come after the program was already launched.

The IVS/Indonesia program involved perhaps the longest launch for one of the smallest IVS programs ever. IVS assisted the fledgling domestic volunteer program, BUTSI, through a partnership with CARE-MEDICO. IVS was responsible for all volunteer costs and CARE for all other costs. The project took four years to get started and ultimately involved only two volunteers, but these volunteers may have been especially impactful. Volunteer in Asia, a program for Stanford University students that had collaborated with IVS-Vietnam, sent volunteers to work with BUTSI during this same period.

The IVS Director initially opposed reliance on CARE in favor of an independent IVS program, but eventually relented. The Johnson Wax Foundation offered funding, if IVS was invited to assist BUTSI. At the same time, the Ministry of Education called to discuss an English teaching program. By June 1969, BUTSI had requested IVS volunteers, and the Ministry of Education had requested English teachers. But, a problem of funding remained. Finally, after four years, the CARE-MEDICO-IVS-BUTSI initiative came into being when, in 1972, volunteer MARK BORDSEN visited CARE/New York to become acquainted with their program concepts and reporting procedures. Mark wrote:

> IVS viewed getting a volunteer to Indonesia as a way to possibly send more IVS volunteers there. I viewed my objective as trying to help the BUTSI volunteers to become more effective in the villages. To achieve IVS Washington's goal of an IVS expansion, I felt that if I helped the volunteers achieve solid accomplishments, that would demonstrate what additional IVS volunteers could do. . . .
>
> After I had made visits to the BUTSI volunteers in their villages, I asked them how they thought they were doing. Most were pretty frustrated with the lack of progress towards modernization. So I asked what they had been doing. It turned out that they had been trying to persuade the village chief and/or council to "modernize." They exhorted them to be more modern, think more modern and so forth. When I inquired as to how that had gone, they admitted that not much had happened. Remembering my own 4-H experience with learn-by-doing projects, demonstrations and illustrated talks, I also recalled that demonstrations had been the successful means to get American farmers to try new varieties and farming methods. So I suggested this to the BUTSI volunteers and asked them to think about what kinds of small improvement projects might be of interest to the villagers. Soon they came back to me with ideas. Some of them, like a wet season fish pond to raise fish, took labor and the transport of fingerlings from the Surakarta fisheries office to the

village. Others needed some supply of money, such as the purchase of an improved breed of rooster to mate with local hens.

When I approached CARE for such funding it was set up and I could write a short proposal for it and access what amounted to a pitifully small amount of money for each project. That small amount, however, was all that was needed to show or demonstrate something. Once a villager with a fish pond harvested fish at the end of the rainy season, other villagers decided that was a good idea. One village that had an easy and adequate supply of water even in the dry season got interested in building water seal toilets. I had found from a VITA manual (Volunteers in Technical Assistance), plans and instructions for making a wooden framework so that BUTSI volunteers could make them with cement, sand, and water. The value of each volunteer assessing the village's conditions and interest made the projects uniquely fitted to that particular village. . . .

Mark served four years, after which Volunteer Frank Welsh replaced him in the Surakarta post. Frank had a motorcycle accident and had to leave early, ending the IVS/Indonesia program. This two-volunteer IVS program was successful in collaborating with BUTSI in its initial years through a person-to-person program. The important results are the personal ones at specific times and places. These may not have moved the earth but had meaning for the individuals engaged.

Indonesia seems to have had abundant opportunities for productive IVS volunteer services, but a lack of funding and daunting bureaucratic requirements for program approvals doomed program expansion. The two-volunteer program was too small to have extensive impact or to provide a base for further program development. It demonstrated, however, that an experienced volunteer could have substantive impacts working at the field level. This may also have been the case in the several other countries in which IVS fielded "one-off" volunteer assignments, which succeeded in themselves but never provided the hoped-for entry for larger, longer-term programs.

IVS/Sudan (1973–83)
Diverse Projects under Difficult Conditions

> **IVS/Sudan**
> Programs:
> • Women's Education
> • Agricultural Rehabilitation
> • Resettlement
> • Agricultural Research
> • Small Business Development
> Volunteers – 43
> Funding: USAID

In the 1970s, Sudan was one of the 25 least developed countries in the world with a literacy rate of 19 percent and widespread poverty. The population was spread thinly across the large country with an identity founded in the local tribe rather than a sense of nationhood. This tribal loyalty was one reason for the seventeen-year civil war in the South which had led to heavy loss of life and destruction of physical infrastructure. IVS initiated a ten-year, ten-project program in 1973.[15]

Education

IVS/Sudan's longest running project was with the Ahfad University College for Women (AUCW) at Omdurman. A dozen volunteers taught there and worked on follow-up programs for graduates. AUCW had plans for a World Education project to train women to design, implement, and evaluate extension programs for impoverished adults, especially women. In 1977, IVS committed four volunteers for head of schools and faculty positions associated with the project.

Agricultural Rehabilitation

In 1975, a $150,000 USAID grant funded volunteers for a World Bank Agricultural Rehabilitation Development Project designed to restore food self-sufficiency in the South (which eventually gained independence as Southern Sudan in 2011). Volunteers were to work under the same supervision as other expatriates, assisting the Ministry of Agriculture with extension, rural road construction, seed production, testing new varieties, field surveys, and livestock marketing. Three other projects started in the South in 1976—rice production research in Aweil, a pilot sheep ranch, and well-drilling for village drinking water supply.

These projects produced mixed results. There were logistical challenges, lack of government support, and limited appreciation of development opportunities by local communities and staff. The challenges of working in the South were reflected in a 1978 IVS press release highlighting volunteer Reg Harper:

As road engineer Reg Harper can confirm, it's [Sudan's] not the easiest place in the world to work. But Reg takes the climate and conditions in his stride—even though he's just turned 68.

For the past year Reg has been supervising road-building efforts in an extensive agricultural project based near the town of Yei and financed by the Sudanese Government and the World Bank. The four-year project is designed to help farmers, and the country's agricultural sector in general, recover from the effects of the civil war, which ended in 1972. . . . In his IVS assignment, Reg is supervisor of the project's road construction unit. The unit's main task is to build feeder roads linking crop-growing areas with main roads. This enables more farmers to take advantage of the project's agricultural services.

Early progress was hampered by delays in the arrival of machinery, equipment, and materials. But, by the end of 1977, the road construction unit, under Reg's direction, had surveyed 35 kilometers of road and completed two miles of haulage road and two miles of farm road, as well as the preliminary grading and shaping of an important link route. Also, a road gang was trained to carry out road maintenance by hand. However, Reg's greatest contribution in the first 10 months of his two-year IVS contract was not—ironically—in road-building. When late arrival of supplies stymied progress on road construction, Reg and his road crews turned to other tasks. These included building a fuel storage depot, an earthen dam (capacity 200,000 gallons) to store water for irrigation, and houses for project staff. As with other IVS volunteers, one of Reg's key roles has been training nationals to take over project responsibilities after he leaves. When he arrived, the road construction unit totally lacked trained Sudanese staff. Now a senior road foreman and a road crew have learned basic skills through on-the-job training under Reg's guidance.

Resettlement

In 1978-79, IVS took on two major USAID-funded infrastructure projects: Wadi Halfa resettlement and Yambio Agricultural Research Station reconstruction. The Wadi Halfa Project was an ambitious undertaking. Completion of the Aswan dam in 1964 led to rising waters of Lake Nubia (Lake Nasser) flooding the town of Wadi Halfa and 27 neighboring villages. The population was to be resettled at Khasm al Girba 900 miles away, but the Nubians of Wadi Halfa resisted the move, preferring their relatively prosperous and independent way of life in Wadi Halfa. Ultimately, about 2000 people simply refused to leave their homeland. Over thirteen years, as lake water levels reached a new high, the "remainers" established themselves in a previously unpopulated and barren area, where the Government finally agreed to reintroduce water supply, irrigation, nutrition, and sanitation services.

The $398,000 Wadi Halfa Community Development Project, co-managed by IVS and the elected Wadi Halfa Peoples' Council, was to develop a drinking water supply system for the 30,000 population; conduct horticulture trials for fruit and dates, winter barley, wheat, sugar cane, and winter vegetables; engage 250 youth in seed production and distribution; establish cooperative marketing of crop and livestock; drill five boreholes to irrigate 500 acres; develop human waste disposal facilities with 48 public latrines; and support a health and nutrition education program for 1,000 pre-school children.

A project evaluation concluded that IVS had provided insufficient personnel to adequately monitor its Sudan program, and, as a result had delayed resolving and reporting problems to USAID/Sudan.[16] This was likely true, since IVS then had six development projects in the South and one in the North with a country staff of only three professionals, one of whom was part-time. The evaluation found problems with supply of agricultural inputs and well casings. More seriously, local people were not committed to the planned Cooperative Society, the Cooperative Youth Training Farm, or the IVS-run experimental farm. The project had significant accomplishments but fell short of expectations. Most problems stemmed from inadequate project planning and inadequate funding.

Agricultural Research

The Yambio Agricultural Research Station Project was to re-establish the station as an integral part of the research and development network for the South, with trials for cotton, coffee, tea, rice, kenaf, fruit, and vegetables. This required renovation of laboratories, administration block, stores and workshops, seed processing sheds, and staff housing with construction of three new houses for senior staff, new equipment for laboratories, and farm equipment, water, and electrical systems. Volunteers filled positions of agronomist, support service manager, soil scientist, and entomologist. The project funded M.Sc. training for a horticulturist and a pathologist, and short courses for laboratory technicians.

A 1981 project evaluation found that the expected objectives were "never achievable with the level of effort proposed for the project".[17] Initial implementation was seriously delayed by IVS problems with recruiting, fielding, and supporting project staff. However, once volunteers arrived, progress was impressive with facilities renovated, laboratories functioning, basic utilities restored, and staff training completed. After the project was completed, USAID planned to continue to support the station.

Sudan IVS assignments were not for the faint-hearted. A 1978 press release described the assignment of volunteer ALAN KERSE from New Zealand.

> Mr. Kerse managed an experimental sheep ranch near Kapoeta, a one-street town of 5,000 in the dry savannah near the Kenya border. The ranch is to demonstrate better pasture and herd management techniques. The assignment to this frontier town involved cultural isolation, requiring self-sufficiency and flexibility, raising sheep and running a mixed ranch growing maize, sorghum and vegetables. Water is a constant problem during the dry season from December to June. The only contact with the outside world was a radio link to the regional capital, Juba, 200 miles away.

SMALL BUSINESS DEVELOPMENT

Three additional small business projects in South Sudan rounded out the IVS Sudan program. Volunteers helped a local self-help organization—"ACCOMPLISH"—to establish an effective integrated rural development program in Terakera. Another volunteer helped village cooperatives establish grinding mills for sorghum and maize, but this eventually failed due to inconsistent diesel fuel supply. Other volunteers helped leather craftsmen establish a Juba Leathercraft Cooperative, but this disbanded when it was taken over by the Regional Ministry of Cooperatives.

IVS closed the Sudan program in 1983. Costs and operating difficulties in the southern region were daunting and developmental impacts limited. A worsening economic and political environment posed further risk, as the Second Sudan Civil War broke out that year.

In summary, the IVS/Sudan program saw IVS take on some major challenges in difficult circumstances—especially in the war-torn South with its lack of infrastructure and services. The World Bank reconstruction program and the Yambio research station projects required recruitment of relatively qualified volunteers with specialized professional experience. These projects encountered delays in recruitment and placement. Projects, such as Wadi Halfa and the Yambio research station, included construction, training, procurement, and other inputs that took IVS into activities beyond the provision of volunteer technical assistance. Implementation problems were not surprising in Sudan and were likely due in part to project design flaws by USAID and IVS. IVS acquitted itself reasonably well in implementation.

IVS/MAURITANIA (1975–79)
GREAT NEED BUT QUESTIONABLE DEMAND FOR VOLUNTEERS

> **IVS/Mauritania**
> PROGRAMS:
> • Rural Water Resource Development
> VOLUNTEERS – 11
> FUNDING: USAID

Mauritania, with 1.2 million people spread out at 1.2 persons per square kilometer, was a challenging country for volunteers. USAID (1975) described the country as follows:

> . . . a very new country, having been created as an administrative unit over certain remote areas which were brought under French administration only after the First World War. The French arrived late on the scene because there was no particular urgency to control an unpromising area thinly populated by camel and goat herders. Under such circumstances, no administration could pay for itself. Indeed, the French ruled the territory from St Louis, in Senegal, since no town existed in Mauritania of sufficient importance that could justify its being nominated capital. . . . The newness of Mauritania suggests that the country is critically weak in virtually every area where a modern government must be strong: staff, equipment, finance. Until independence [in.1960], there were almost no schools, almost no tax base, and little administration, little commercial agriculture, and very little promise of any early change from these conditions.[18]

By the mid-1970s, exploitation of rich iron mines and a commercial fish processing facility had stimulated some development of a modern economy but left 90 percent of the population in traditional agriculture. Seventy percent were at least partially nomadic and prolonged drought had reduced livestock numbers by half and agricultural incomes by 45 percent. Lack of qualified technical and management personnel was a chronic constraint.

The IVS program started in 1975 with the arrival of Country Director Max Goldensohn and the signing of an Agreement with the Government of Mauritania for 19 volunteers. The first volunteers, George and Linda Dungan, were assigned to a state construction corporation and a state insurance corporation in April 1976. Others arrived to set up and run a public health laboratory. By January 1977, IVS had a USAID grant to provide 13 volunteers to work with the Ministry of Water Resources and the National Rural Development Council.

Recruitment focused on individuals with professional experience and prior overseas work. Assignments were for responsible positions important to national development. But all did not go well. Most volunteers terminated early. There were issues with health and the typical inefficiencies and lack of material support common to developing countries. More problematic was a lack of counterparts or planning for eventual takeover of volunteers' responsibilities. Some volunteers felt they were not really wanted in their institutions.

Willem and Corrie Chevallier served from January 1977 to May 1978, encountering significant frustrations as well as positive feelings about their work. Their final report stated:

> My position as mecanic [mechanic] trainer at the garage of Hydraulique did not work out because of insufficient investigation by the local country director and because of malfunction of the local government.
>
> During the month of April 1977, the local director of the Lutheran World Federation offered me the position of' "chef de garage." I accepted under [the] condition I could keep six students whom I started training at the garage of Hydraulique. A contract was signed with the Lutheran World Federation [L.W.F.] and the Local Red Cross on the first of June 1977. The workshop we built was financed by the L.W.F. (we are still waiting for electricity but we installed the single phase A.C. wiring this week). The third week of July 1977 we started with the repair and maintenance of 13 Red Cross vehicles and 10 vehicles and three water pump-engines from the L.W.F.
>
> My main goal was the training of the students so they would be able to service and repair. The need for trained people is very great and the local government is unable to provide this training, no money, no teachers. During this training period the L.W.F. paid 200 UM a week per student and provided soap, coffee, and sugar. The material to repair and maintain all vehicles was also paid by the L.W.F.; without this funding my work would have been impossible.
>
> Most tools were given by the U.S. Embassy under a self-help project grant. Shortly after I started the training, one student left, and the five remaining have finished the course. I have given them a certificate stating what it was all about, duly certified with a stamp from the Red Cross and with Goh and my signature. The students are of the Poular tribe, spoke very little French, are separated from their families and habitual social environment. Because of the drought they left their villages and came approximately 300 miles to Nouakchott to look for work: they were extremely poor and ill fed. Now after 18 months, they are able to work alone, have pride in their work, are very valuable to society, earn enough to buy food and are well dressed. Three students will start working as "aide mecanicien" at the U.S. embassy garage, the two youngest will stay with the L.W.F. and the Red Cross. All will get a salary enough to live on.
>
> As part of their education, Corrie and I have taken them for a long weekend to Dakar approximately 350 miles by car, where they saw for the first time a city, experienced running water, electricity, beds, food to eat with fork and knife—*enfin*

[finally,] all things we take for granted. All had been given money to spend and they came home with each a wristwatch, rings, and all kind of goodies they never thought to have. It was as big an experience for us as something they talk about, the changing of traffic lights was something never seen before, yet they were happy to be back in Nouakchott again. . . .

My time as a volunteer has been very rewarding and I am happy that my work will be continued by a Peace Corps volunteer who is already working with me.

In December 1977, IVS/Washington ran into financial constraints that required reductions in staff and programs. Some volunteer assignments in Mauritania were cancelled, following a memo from Washington which stated, "Mauritania has had a particularly difficult program, because it is a particularly difficult country." The Mauritania program ended in 1979. Clearly, the country had a need for volunteer services but, perhaps, not an appreciation for them.

IVS/Papua New Guinea (1975–84)
Business Development and Sustainable Agriculture

IVS/Papua New Guinea
PROGRAMS:
- Business Development
- Sustainable Agriculture
- Public Health/Nutrition

VOLUNTEERS – 39
FUNDING: USAID and other

Papua New Guinea (PNG) gained independence from Australia in 1975, after being ruled by three external powers since 1884. As one of the most culturally diverse countries in the world, it had 851 known languages and an extreme diversity in cultures. Nearly 90 percent of the population lived in traditional communities. Rugged geography impeded travel, communications, and the economic development of its vast natural resources.

In 1974, IVS received requests from PNG for ten volunteers—five for the Department of Business Development, four for Public Health Services, and one agriculturalist for a church development activity. In August, the PNG Government approved volunteer placement and, by 1977, IVS had 18 volunteers in the country. Over the nine-year program, IVS worked on public health, public works, business management, agriculture, and sericulture projects with five field staff and 39 volunteers working with three Papua New Guinea government ministries, Lae University, and several private development agencies.

The initial focus was on small business development including: cooperatives, a new radio business development program, and vocational agriculture. A volunteer master blacksmith from Sri Lanka served four years to introduce metal working technologies and help students establish businesses. Two India sericulturist volunteers supported a cottage industry of silk production in the country's highlands, while another volunteer worked on carpentry and business development on the coast.

Volunteer JEAN ENG described her 1975 assignment as a nutritionist:

> My assignment was at Mt. Hagen, capitol of Western Highlands Province (5502 feet above sea level) as Provincial Nutritionist (PN) and Regional Nutritionist (RN) of the Highland Region in PNG with IVS. . . . In the beginning, listening and observing were important in understanding what was happening in the field. Going on bush patrols, visiting agricultural extension sites and village gardens, visiting schools and various levels of health facilities helped to identify the areas of focus.
>
> When bush walking to remote villages with maternal and child health services, we'd walk the trails that only the locals were familiar with. Mixed crop food gardens showed a diversity of foods that have adapted to the marginal soils. Women did most of the work. Overnighting in grass huts, we would eat a dinner of sweet potato cooked slowly in ashes, and it tasted really good. Then sleeping next to crackling fires was comforting because of the chilly evenings, but I will never forget how mice scurried over me and I hoped they would not join me in bed. Village people were very friendly and welcoming. However, they did not see the problem of malnutrition.
>
> Reflecting on my time in PNG, this was my first involvement in the nutrition planning process. I saw a big gap between the policy directions of the central government and its implementation in the provinces. Time and therefore programs moved very slowly, the further you were away from government centers and road systems. PNs were very committed along with other government workers. But life is complicated in a society that is evolving so quickly from a stone-age mentality into that of the 20th century, especially with all the negative influences of the Western World. . . .

Another nutritionist, volunteer MARIAN CAST RUGE, described her assignment and one of its quirky activities:

> I travelled to the rural clinics, often run by American or Australian missionaries, and went out on well baby clinics. It was all very amazing! Mothers sometimes came in grass skirts and bare breasts. The start of the clinic was announced by hitting a large gas cylinder left from WWII. We hung a scale on a post, put the baby in a bilum (string bag) to weigh it, and marked its growth on a chart. They also got immunizations. Sometimes the nurses and I walked for a few hours to get to the village for the clinic. . . .

Somebody in town decided to help us raise money for nutrition education by hosting the premier showing of a Pink Panther film. I have blocked out a lot of the craziness that ensued, but we ended up with a Pink Panther suit worn by some brave soul in the searing heat of PNG when we visited the schools. We also printed up lots of t-shirts with various sayings from the Pink Panther. And we showed the film; Peter Sellers did not come to PNG.

IVS's program focus became the Wau Ecology Institute, where volunteers worked to replace slash-and-burn agriculture with stable, settled cultivation systems. Volunteers conducted research on agro-forestry and sustainable technologies (mulching, inter-cropping, composting) with promising results. Other volunteers disseminated these promising production innovations through community extension activities. But it was soon apparent that research needed on this issue would require a long-term program.

After reviewing program options in late 1981, IVS decided to phase out further program development. The presence of other volunteer programs, the high operating costs, and constraints on achieving direct impact on the rural poor were key considerations. The last years were oriented to the transfer of IVS's responsibilities on subsistence agriculture to the Wau Ecology Institute, so that local staff could sustain the momentum.

IVS considered the PNG agriculture program a success—having trained research and extension staff, established a strong network of outreach contacts, and established extension staff in Lae, the country's vegetable capital. Increased availability of fresh vegetables in local markets was a notable indicator of impact. The Morobe Provincial Government's assumption of responsibility for the Wau Ecology Institute in 1984 was seen as recognition of the high regard the local government held for the IVS project.

IVS departed Papua in 1984 when the last volunteer assignments were completed. Volunteers worked successfully in a range of technical areas. Assignments appear to have been personally rewarding with positive impacts. The working environment was difficult, the activities perhaps too diverse, and the number of volunteers too few, to have had a broader developmental impact.

OTHER COUNTRY INITIATIVES FAILURE TO LAUNCH

Over the years, IVS sought to establish programs in other countries when opportunities arose. Washington staff traveled extensively to discuss potential programs in Pakistan, Korea, Burma, Thailand, and elsewhere. Several countries had initial volunteer assignments that may have been somewhat exploratory, a "foot in the door" for potential future programs. The following eight exploration programs did not lead to further work.

Ghana 1960–1961

In 1959, two volunteers spent a year in Ghana under the auspices of the Rockefeller Brothers Fund demonstrating a simple machine to make bricks from earth and cement.

Malaysia (Sabah) 1965–1967

Three volunteers, funded by the Asia Foundation, worked in Sabah for two years teaching civil servants English and developing an educational resource center.

Libya 1971–1973

Two agricultural volunteers were assigned to Libya to work on the Kufra Agricultural Company's 10,000 hectare production project.

Colombia 1975–1976

Three volunteers worked as administrators and teachers at a farmer training institute for Accion Cultural Popular (ACPO). ACPO was a private agency preparing farmers for community leadership positions. Much of the training was through educational radio programs.[19]

Madagascar 1975–1977

Volunteer Roger Page worked with Church World Service and Catholic Relief Services, providing technical advice for water project designs. He completed several village self-help water projects and began others in remote villages.[20]

Ethiopia 1984

IVS initiated a program by placing one volunteer in a medical staff position for Africare clinics in Ethiopia, hoping that this would lead to a more traditional IVS program. Funding never materialized.

Cape Verde 1987–1988

An IVS technical advisor in Cape Verde helped to plan a new cooperative project in conjunction with the Unitarian Universalist Service Committee.

Mali 1988–1988

In conjunction with the Freedom from Hunger Foundation and OEF International (formerly, Overseas Education Fund), IVS provided two volunteers to work with the Malian Groupe de Jeunes in the Sikasso region. The project was an income generation and credit program to improve the health, nutrition, and incomes of women and their families.

MIXED RESULTS GOOD WORK IN DIFFICULT PLACES

IVS's experience in expanding its global volunteer program over its second decade was decidedly mixed. The nine country programs in Asia and Africa described here provided for a diverse and ambitious breadth of activities, but many of the programs were small, overly-diverse, and fragile. The countries involved were challenging places in which to work, with six of the ten having post-conflict situations. It might have been hard to pick a more difficult set of countries. Only the Bangladesh program described in the next chapter took root, becoming IVS's largest and longest-running program with over 50 multinational volunteers over a 31-year period.

VOLUNTEER SUPPORT

Volunteers proved quite adaptable to these hardship posts, but were often frustrated by the weak, corrupt, and/or incompetent institutions they worked for. While this is a feature of developing countries, it was particularly pronounced in these cases. It became clear that in addition to volunteers' services, other resources were needed for rapid developmental impact. Helping volunteers adapt and become effective in such situations required effective support in planning projects and assignments, negotiating with hosts, counseling the volunteers, and facilitating other needed support. Most IVS programs were too small or had too much instability in country staffing to do this adequately.

INTERNATIONALIZATION

IVS did succeed in its objective to internationalize its volunteer program. By 1979, more than half of IVS's volunteers were non-US. A 1978 IVS press release stated:

> [IVS's volunteer] mix is made up of volunteers from both industrialized and non-industrialized countries. In Botswana, the only American among eight volunteers is horticulturist Dennis Magnello (PCV in Upper Volta 1972-74). The other IVSers come from the U.K. (four), the Netherlands (one) and Tanzania (one). Two of the three IVS field staff in Latin America were previously with Peace Corps. Dan Riederer, a PCV in Nicaragua from 1970-74, is now in Honduras as the IVS Field Director providing administrative support for IVSers who include three Taiwanese agriculturalists, a Colombian rural sociologist, and three irrigation specialists, two Dutch and one Filipino. Down in Ecuador, Hank Beder, a PCV there from 1970-73, whose predecessor was one-time Peace Corps colleague Jim Hindman (Ecuador 1970-72), backs up an IVS group comprising, among others, two Italian community promoters, a Sri Lankan agricultural extensionist and a West German civil engineer.
>
> IVS, committed to further internationalizing its operations, opened a European

office in Luxembourg a year ago. The office is staffed by Jonathan Otto (PCV in Niger 69-71), who is building a network of European contacts primarily to recruit more volunteers from Europe and raise more funds from European sources.

This internationalization had both positive and negative aspects. It facilitated recruitment of relevant skills and expertise—Europeans with African experience, Indian sericulturists, Taiwanese agronomists, a Sri Lanka blacksmith, Philippine agricultural scientists, etc. Teams took pride in their international composition. Programs were perhaps less obviously "American", and this may have opened some additional doors, but may not have been seen as an advantage by USAID, which remained the main funding agency. The reduced number of U.S. volunteers diminished the U.S. constituency for IVS, and recruitment and vetting of international volunteers was somewhat complicated.[21] Initial non-U.S. volunteers, who also served in Vietnam, helped establish relations with volunteer-oriented NGOs in Japan, the Philippines, and Sri Lanka. The IVS Luxembourg office had links with church groups in Germany, and the Netherlands added to recruitment capacity in Europe. IVS also switched to recruiting persons with prior volunteer service with U.S., UN, or other agencies. As IVS became more project-oriented than volunteer-oriented in the 1970s, country offices assumed more responsibility for recruitment from whatever source, indifferent to nationality. Private and project funding allowed for additional costs of international recruitment and processing.

Relations with USAID

IVS's program development benefitted from its positive reputation and the goodwill of USAID staff and others who had worked with or for the organization in other places, particularly in Southeast Asia. USAID staff reductions during this period resulted in an increased need for volunteers to work on projects at the community or field level. In Liberia and Yemen, projects appeared to work very well where there was close collaboration between IVS and USAID. This allowed for additional resources and technical support that were more likely to have broader developmental impact.

While the relationship with USAID was generally supportive, this varied with project implementation, experience, and personalities. Close collaboration on projects occasionally led to volunteers identifying weaknesses in project designs, a fact not always fully appreciated by USAID. Project design problems (as in the Sudan, the Congo, Morocco) seemed due to inadequate analysis and planning by USAID and IVS, and to inadequate time and flexibility to make changes when needed.

Most IVS programs relied on USAID (or more broadly, the United States

Government) funding, although Algeria shifted to local government funding, Indonesia had private funding, and Bangladesh diversified its funding, getting significant support funds from European and private donors. However, USAID funding remained important. Unfortunately, this USAID dependency resulted in high instability for programs in Algeria, Morocco, Liberia, the Congo, and Yemen, when changing international policies, development strategy, or personalities led to USAID terminating funding. However, alternative funding sources could have their difficulties, due to reliability (Algeria), funding limitations (Indonesia), or bureaucratic requirements (Bangladesh).

Relations with Other Volunteer Programs

Despite an IVS policy of avoiding work in the same country as the Peace Corps, several IVS countries had active Peace Corps programs. The experience in countries varied from that of competition (Liberia) to collaboration (Mauritania). In general, there seemed to be few problems.

In Yemen, IVS helped the startup of the United Nations Volunteers Program by placing an IVSer as one of the program's initial volunteers. Whether, and to what extent, the UN program was influenced by IVS procedures and approaches is unclear. The UN Volunteers Program has gone on to become a complex operation with 6,000 volunteers in 2021.

Volunteer Assignments

Initial IVS country programs were modeled on multi-disciplinary volunteer "teams" working in agricultural and rural development as change agents at the community level (Iraq, Egypt, Nepal, Laos, Vietnam). This changed to the assignment model—individual volunteers in positions, perhaps linked to larger national programs or institutions. Volunteers on such assignments worked quite independently, and the model worked well with young volunteers having practical farm experience and often with agricultural degrees. As programs matured, IVS began working and placing volunteers with more diverse partner organizations.

Volunteer Qualifications

IVS partners began to require volunteers with higher qualifications and experience (the Sudan, Mauritania, Yemen, the Congo, Algeria, Morocco). Volunteer assignments became less community focused and more work-specific terms-of-reference for a host organization, for another development agency program, or for IVS providing services to other organizations. IVS recognized the need to shift to more highly specialized volunteers as part of its aggressive program development.

IVS's evolution was apparent, as John Rigsby noted when completing a three-year period as executive director.[22] "IVS is no longer in the business of volunteers; rather IVS uses volunteers in the business of development." IVS had begun managing more complex projects, providing grants, materials, and other inputs besides volunteer services. Fielding non-U.S. and more experienced volunteers added complications, as the 60 volunteers and staff in the field in 1979 represented a total of 141 persons counting all family members. Volunteers ended up working with larger numbers of local employees. For example, there were two volunteers to 26 staff in Bangladesh and two volunteers to ten technicians employed in Bolivia. USAID direct funding dropped from 90 percent of the budget in 1975 to 65 percent in 1979, although a portion of the non-USAID funding was from other agencies that were receiving their funds from USAID. Changing work needs and funding sources were major contributors to IVS's evolution.

IVS's Program Evolves

The 1970s brought an increasing pace of change to IVS's programs and approaches. John Rigsby, an IVS staff (1975-1976) and Executive Director (1977-1982), focused on two issues: volunteer recruitment from countries other than the United States and diversifying the IVS funding base.[23] One overriding challenge was reviving IVS's original role of providing an alternative to military services for Quakers. Brethren, and Mennonites Churches. The prodigious growth of the Peace Corps offered more overseas opportunities than IVS could offer. The proliferation of U.S. NGOs with international programs also severely impacted IVS's funding base. Three IVS strategic responses were: the Luxembourg outreach office, which by 1980 led to funding from Germany and the Netherlands reaching more than one-third that of the U.S.; reorienting recruitment to attract persons with previous volunteer service; and shifting programs from filling volunteer service positions to implementing defined projects with specific two- or three-year development objectives. These changes pushed IVS towards a new business model.

5

REINVENTING IVS
NEW APPROACHES AND THE END GAME

GARY ALEX

The mission of IVS was never easy. Recruiting, placing, and supporting qualified volunteers in developing countries, designing volunteer assignments leading to sustainable change in traditional societies, navigating competing interests, and raising funds for these things were more difficult than the IVS founders ever expected. Twenty years into its operations, new challenges appeared: the needs of host countries were changing as were institutional structures.

By the 1970s, newly independent and developing countries had increased their own local capacities with many individuals who were trained through aid programs. They had established needed institutions for social and economic development including agricultural agencies, schools, businesses, local governments, among others. They had a track record of operations and a new confidence. Hence, opportunities for young volunteers to step in and influence programs were fewer, and there was less patience with foreign advisors. Costs of fielding foreign technicians—even volunteers—had increased. There were many exceptions to these trends, but in general, there were less obvious roles for volunteers in many development programs.

Development strategies and USAID's operational model also changed. Development programs worked more through established local public and private institutions. Improving management and expanding programs was more the objective than establishing new institutions. Work with local organizations required more diplomacy, status, and less practical technical knowledge than under past programs. USAID streamlined management by consolidating project implementation under larger contracts that provided equipment, construction, training, and operational costs as well as technical assistance. USAID in-country staff numbers declined with project implementation done by contractors and grantees. Volunteers continued to fit well when providing field level innovation and project monitoring, but this role was less valued by USAID or host countries.

USAID's emphasis on poverty reduction and reaching the "poorest of the poor" in the late 1970s fit well with the IVS ethos. Reduced emphasis on food security and agriculture in the late 1980s shifted funding away from what had been IVS's strength. This funding shift, in itself, may not have been as harmful to IVS as demographic changes that made it harder to recruit experienced agricultural volunteers. The USAID shift from working directly with host governments to working through private sector implementing partners, including NGOs, may have been neutral, as far as IVS operations were concerned, but this change increased the number of competitors for USAID funding.

Although IVS seldom gave formal statements regarding its organizational policies and strategies, the 1971 Harper's Ferry decisions to reduce reliance on U.S. Government funding and expand non-U.S. volunteers effectively re-invented IVS. In 1977, IVS opened an office in Brussels—IVS, Inc. in Europe—for recruiting European volunteers and positioning itself to raise funds from Europe.[1] The office closed in early 1979, having established a base of European contacts.[2] This seems to have been started with a healthy optimism, and it is hard to assess the value of the office. However, by 1988, 65 percent of staff, volunteers, and country directors were non-U.S. personnel.[3]

Improving international understanding remained an IVS objective, but with staff and volunteers coming from within the host country or region, it is not clear how this would be accomplished. Focus was less strong at the village level. The range of volunteer activities expanded. In reality, a corporate strategy mattered little, because IVS was forced to engage in projects for which there was funding.

The 1979 IVS Annual Report noted that IVS's programs emphasized peoples' retention of ethnic identity and local organizations' independence to chart their own development. Whether this was the result of a conscious strategy or the realization of a de facto situation is unclear, but IVS had worked extensively with minority ethnic communities in Ecuador, Bolivia, Laos, Vietnam, and Papua. In 1984, a mandate from the IVS Board to explore new ways of providing development assistance led to commitment for closer collaboration with a variety of overseas development agencies.[4] An initial surge of activity explored volunteer placements with Africare in Ethiopia, several organizations in Sudan, a hydro-power project, small business projects in Honduras and Costa Rica, church programs in Africa, an NGO engaged in vocational training, and UN and State department programs in Africa and Pakistan.

IVS became a more generic development NGO. A 1981 USAID evaluation of IVS found that "Unlike earlier years, when the exclusive resource of IVS was its complement of volunteers, IVS now has a management and administrative role in all of the projects with which IVS volunteers are associated. Thus, IVS is far more heavily engaged in recent years in total development project context and is not limited to the role of recruiting, placing, and supporting expatriate volunteers."[5] Further, tweaks in program direction tended to follow prevailing strategies of USAID.

A first quarter 1988 newsletter reported that IVS was committed to providing "skilled and experienced professionals to help local development groups."[6] This issue of professionalism of volunteers crops up elsewhere in IVS documents and country programs. Clearly, there were market signals from donors and beneficiary organizations that what was needed was skilled and experienced volunteers, not just well-intentioned generalists.

The IVS strategy for the 1990s was to respond to requests for assistance in: a) sound rural agricultural, health, enterprise, and conservation development, and b) organizational management. Emphasis was clearly to be on organizational development.[7] A 1990 paper on "IVS Experience with Rural Development" summarized lessons from rural development work across countries, noting issues of religion, access to land, NGO relations with governments, local businessmen, and the role of women.[8] This might have been the base for an organizational strategy for rural development but appears not to have progressed further.

In 1993, in reflecting on lessons learned under its last major USAID grant, IVS saw support for foreign assistance declining and a need for new strategies.[9] Three actions were indicated. First, IVS needed to focus where it could be most effective: working in agricultural development in ecologically fragile areas, assisting ethnic minorities, promoting income generation for women, and preventing the spread of HIV/AIDS. As well, it needed to increase developmental education in the U.S. to show the need and potential for development assistance. Finally, it needed to strengthen its financial base. Although these were not entirely new items, they were challenging, especially when there was "the need to cut staff" and budgets due to financial constraints.

In 1997, IVS entered a strategic alliance with PACT, a NGO with which it had previously worked.[10] IVS Executive Director, Anne Shirk, the only remaining IVS staff member, moved into the PACT office to work with an IVS/PACT Program Officer. The alliance made good sense. PACT had 27 years of experience developing civil society capacities, and IVS brought experience with volunteer programs that could be applied to civil society development. The alliance was facilitated by a $147,000 USAID grant to IVS for program development, with expectations to focus on local volunteer program development in Ecuador and Bolivia. Efforts did not result in any new projects, and the alliance appears to have quickly faded away with little evidence of impact. By June 1999, a group of IVS alumni was working on an Action Plan for IVS Renewal.[11] This eventually resulted in the placement of two volunteers on short-term assignments.

The varied priority statements and program initiatives previously referenced masked a fundamental change in IVS country programs during its last two decades. Earlier country programs had generally been launched in conjunction with the country USAID Mission. These later programs—except for Botswana and Bangladesh—were based on USAID Washington operating program grants. This gave IVS greater independence and less vulnerability to changing country personnel and priorities, although seriously reducing linkages to important in-country USAID support and funding.

Through the 1980s and 1990s, IVS struggled to reinvent itself to conform to the new environment for international development. Programs emphasized international volunteers as part of comprehensive development projects and then shifted towards use of local and regional volunteers and finally to establishment of local volunteer organizations. The number of country programs declined from the high of 14 in 1975, to seven to nine through the 1980s, and then to three for most years post-1990. Country operating environments were more stable than in earlier years, and IVS programs were smaller with less visibility. IVS's last eight country programs are described below.

IVS/Bangladesh (1972-2002)
A Long-running, Evolving Program

> **IVS/Bangladesh**
> PROGRAMS:
> • Health
> • Literacy
> • Organization Development
> • Agriculture
> • Disaster Preparedness
> • Micro-credit
> • Small Business Development-
> VOLUNTEERS – 58 International, 25+ Bangladeshi
> FUNDING: USAID, U.S. State Department, UNICEF, Australian High Commission, Canadian High Commission, Churches (Methodist, Baptist, Misereor, United Church Board of World Ministries, Church World Service, ICCO (Interchurch Organization for Development Cooperation), Ford Foundation, Levi Strauss, Readers Digest Foundation, PACT, Trickle Up (TUP), University of Maryland IRIS Project (USAID-funded).

Bangladesh, known as East Pakistan, together with West Pakistan formed the state of Pakistan when these two predominantly Muslim regions separated from India at independence from Great Britain in 1947. The two areas were separated geographically (East Pakistan on the southeast border of India with a warm, tropical climate; West Pakistan on the northwest border of India with a temperate climate); used different languages (Urdu vs. Bengali); and possessed different cultures and cuisines (rice vs. wheat-based diet). By1971, the relationship between the two regions had frayed to the point that East Pakistan declared independence from West Pakistan. After a nine-month-long war, East Pakistan finally gained recognition as the independent country of Bangladesh. The war had resulted in wide-spread death and destruction, large refugee displacement, and disruption of agriculture. Added to this, a devastating cyclone and resulting famine marked a disastrous beginning for the new country.

The new government sought help in rebuilding its infrastructure and resettling the millions of people displaced by the war. International aid swiftly flowed in on a scale that equaled the Marshall Plan in Europe after WWII. However, lack of functional local institutions and broken infrastructure greatly restricted capacity to absorb relief and development assistance. Foreign governments and non-government organizations worked with the few functional local organizations.

Local NGOs were quickly organized to assist with rural development. Two

NGOs were formed to work nation-wide in rural areas—Bangladesh Rural Advancement Committee (BRAC) and Gono Shasthya Kendra (GK). GK focused on healthcare while BRAC focused on literacy training and rural development. Many other local NGOs formed to work in specific areas or villages. Work groups of farmers, fishermen, artisans or other special groups formed cooperatives that then federated at the Thana (county) level. Once federated, cooperatives were then recognized by the government. These NGOs and cooperatives emerged as the extensive civil society sector for which Bangladesh is well known and which figured prominently in its development. This civil society sector formed the environment and provided counterparts for the IVS program.

In 1972, the government requested IVS assistance to work with small farmers and minimum wage earners in rural areas. Warren "Bud" Day, who had worked as a missionary with refugees on the border with India after independence, assisted IVS in this start-up. Char Cuento-Jeggle, who had worked in the Philippines training IVS volunteers heading to Southeast Asia, represented IVS in establishing the Bangladesh program. Her experience with IVS volunteers and appreciation for the IVS philosophy and goals helped in setting up the Bangladesh office and negotiating projects with the Ministry of Local Government, Rural Development and Cooperatives for potential volunteers.

Later in 1972, Winburn Thomas arrived to serve as Country Director and Char became the Associate Director of Administration. Thomas became widely respected and played an important role in the donor community. He was instrumental in establishing the Association of Development Agencies in Bangladesh (ADAB),[12] helping NGOs coordinate developmental efforts, and serving as informal ADAB leader with Char acting as resource person. IVS involvement in ADAB continued through the 30 years of its work in the country.

The first phase of the IVS Bangladesh program began in January 1973 with arrival of the first five volunteers funded by a $1.2 million USAID grant. Volunteers worked mainly in four geographic areas. Volunteers in Comilla worked on agriculture and health under the Comilla Model of co-operative approach to rural development. Those in Dinajpur worked with Bihari refugees displaced by the war and with government horticulture, health care, and agriculture projects. Others worked on varied activities in Mahakal. And in Syhlet, they worked on an Integrated Rural Development Program to replicate the Comilla Model, using a training center for village cooperatives to improve management and technical skills. This phase of the IVS program was staffed entirely by international volunteers.

As in other IVS countries, the volunteer's role was primarily to transfer skills. Initially, in most cases, volunteers did the work themselves with the help of local people, providing an example of how to do a particular task. An example of this "performer" model would be volunteers teaching English to school children. In Bangladesh, the focus rapidly shifted to the volunteer being an advisor or partner with locals in the transfer of skills, so that Bangladeshis learning skills could then train other Bangladeshis. This would correspond to volunteers working with local teachers to improve their English and teaching skills rather than teaching students directly. Over time, more educated and skilled Bangladeshis became available to replace the international volunteers.

The IVS program gradually shifted its focus to the Syhlet region, where a lack of counterpart organizations led to IVS employing field agents to work with volunteers. The Sylhet volunteers and local staff developed a new approach—that of providing a package of development activities to meet community needs. This led to a US-AID-funded Village Development Training Program (VDTP) to provide resources and extension services to local farmers through village cooperatives.[13] By the late 1970s, as USAID funding was coming to an end, volunteers and Bangladeshi staff in Sylhet saw promising results from their work but had no local organization to carry it forward. They realized also that the cost of American volunteers was 10 to 20 times that of Bangladeshi field agents. In seeking better cost-effectiveness and sustainability, IVS local staff created an NGO—Friends In Village Development, Bangladesh (FIVDB)—to manage VDTP activities and seek funding from various sources.

IVS remained committed to continuing its successful program activities into the 1980s, but USAID was not interested in continuing to fund American volunteers. This led to an acrimonious split with USAID. Facing the end of USAID funding, IVS/Washington turned Sylhet field activities over to FIVDB and encouraged weaning FIVDB from IVS support. This marked the beginning of a second and transitional phase of the IVS/Bangladesh program. Beginning in 1980, IVS pursued a policy of assigning volunteers to local organizations that could fund the volunteer costs. Few were willing or able to do so. During this period, three volunteers worked mainly with and were funded by FIVDB—Feliciano Francisco (1978-86), Peter Heffron (1979-84), and James Jennings (1980-82). They worked in agriculture, literacy, and income generation. IVS/Bangladesh staff continued to assist the independent FIVDB with program planning and fundraising, mainly from European donors.

The success of FIVDB was due to far-sighted leadership which invested in three things: IVS volunteers and other specialists to provide innovative program activities, a qualified accountant to ensure respect and trust of donors, and a communications specialist to manage project reporting and promotional materials. FIVDB's program resonated with donors due to its focus on the rural poor—emphasizing needs of the landless and women.

One highly successful activity was a duck project started by Volunteer Jim Archer in the 1970s.[14] The new "Chinese production model" introduced by Jim used improved duck breeds, vaccines against common diseases, and a system of herding ducks to forage during the day. This suited landless people and women. Volunteer Feliciano Francisco helped expand the program, linking FIVDB to Philippine sources of technology, such that FIVDB became the acknowledged center of excellence for the technology. The technology spread widely. Volunteer Freddie de Pedro (Philippines) cited one example of a landless widow with six children who herded ducks and was able to support her family through the sale of eggs.

Other FIVDB programs were health and midwife training, home visits for pregnant and nursing mothers, income generating projects for women (e.g., weaving, sewing, and food processing), as well as functional literacy courses for both men and women. Volunteers created training materials in subjects such as literacy, food production, health, management, disaster preparedness, agriculture, and local governance. David French (former IVS/Bangladesh country director, 1978-80) noted that volunteer James Jennings, when working in Sylhet, had written three primers and three teacher's guides for a functional literacy program. With modifications they continued to be used widely by government and non-governmental agencies.[15]

An independent assessment in 1984 found that the FIVDB program had benefitted 55 villages and that the institution was well regarded by other NGOs and the government for its development accomplishments.[16] The assessment team also pointed out weaknesses in limited accountability to its constituency groups and inadequate incentives to motivate staff. In 1983, IVS essentially ended support to FIVDB, which was successfully run by Bangladeshi staff able to raise its own financial support. IVS volunteers had worked themselves out of their jobs.[17] Through the early 1980s, IVS continued to work with ADAB, supporting them in advocating for NGOs in the face of increasing government oversight and regulation. FIVDB continues to function as a well-respected organization.

Beginning around 1983, the third phase of the IVS/Bangladesh (IVS/B) program saw only five recorded international volunteers over nearly 20 years. In those years, donor funding was readily available to NGOs with sound proposals, and IVS/Bangladesh was relatively successful in raising funds from European donors—

especially Bread for the World and the Dutch Interchurch Organization for Development Cooperation.

In 1987, IVS established the country-wide Village Volunteer Program (VVP) to draw on skills and expertise in one village to transfer to others. M. Farook, Regional Officer for the Bangladesh Rural Advancement Committee (BRAC), commented ". . . trainees, mostly poor and rural, feel less shy and more 'at home' with VVP training, as it occurs in the trainees' own milieu. There is no artificial teacher-trainee relationship, as the teacher is the guest of the trainees."[18] Examples of village skill transfers were beekeeping, credit management, handloom training, palm fiber basket weaving, fisheries, livestock management, and health and sanitation. Over 900 projects used 500 skilled village volunteers on short-term assignments. An USAID evaluation found the local volunteer program to be innovative, flexible, and cost-effective.[19]

A National Volunteer Program (NVP) was an outgrowth of the VVP in the mid-1990s. It provided training from local professionals in various fields to meet the needs of local development organizations. In 1999, 20 National Volunteers (local professionals) were working for IVS/B. Hiring locals as volunteers was cost effective and seen as sustainable over the long term. The NVP worked on building organizational capacity (management, accounts, documentation, monitoring, and evaluation), gender and development, livestock and fisheries, disaster preparedness, and democracy and governance. NVP volunteers also managed VVP projects.

One important area of work for NVP was disaster preparedness. In 1991, more than 100,000 people perished in a cyclone. Disaster preparedness activities, such as provision of small battery-operated radios to get weather reports, led to major reduction in loss of lives and famine from severe storms. NVP volunteer Rokeya Begum helped villagers prepare a community storm shelter and stock it with non-perishable food items and potable drinking water. A second important area for NVP was fisheries. Reduced fish protein availability had negatively impacted nutrition among the rural poor. In 1990, volunteer Francicso Noble (Philippines) introduced a program for fish production in flooded rice fields. Another NVP activity targeted control of fish diseases in the growing aquaculture industry.

An assessment of the National Volunteer Program (NVP) in 2000 found that the program, using skilled but underemployed Bangladeshis, had assisted 72 NGOs benefitting more than one million people.[20] The assessment pointed out that the NVP could be stretched too thin with more demands for assistance than personnel and funds available could meet. Villagers' (both men's and women's) thinking had changed concerning the value of women, and women themselves had a greater sense of self-worth after they became literate and learned a trade.

An evaluation of the Job Opportunities and Business Support (JOBS) Project to create sustainable wage-based employment for small, medium and micro enterprises noted that "IVS Bangladesh provided short-term training and technical assistance to many organizations through its Village Volunteer Programs. In 1990, the IVS model was a breakthrough: it revitalized NGO-MEs [micro-enterprises] and other organizational development activities by transferring successful cases from one place to another while using the locally available cost-effective specialist services of proven, field level trainers and practitioners. IVS developed this approach in close association with their partner agencies and networks—ADAB, SAP Bangladesh, and CDS [Community Development Service, a local NGO]."[21] IVS had a small but substantial part of the project, that of providing national volunteers (NVs) and village volunteers (VVs) for field implementation activities.

Although the NVP approach may have worked well in Bangladesh, it was not without problems. A 1993 IVS project evaluation by Shirley Buzzard for USAID found that nearly all innovations were introduced by international and regional volunteers.[22] National volunteers often lacked technical training and experience and, in some cases, served simply as additional staff for their host organization. Local NGOs preferred international or regional volunteers, although national volunteers were cheaper.

One of the greatest difficulties for IVS/Bangladesh was money. Funding was a constraint on IVS headquarters' ability to fund country program proposals and country directors' ability to commit to program goals. USAID provided almost 100 percent of the funding for IVS in Bangladesh over its first decade. As USAID priorities changed, funding became matching grants with USAID providing 50 percent of the total, later reduced to 20 percent. IVS had to raise the balance from other sources, but this took time from development work, and it was always difficult to meet the required match for USAID. Within USAID, a "historically negative feeling about IVS" became a problem in fund-raising.[23]

Private funding for IVS/Bangladesh came from the many different sources listed above. European funding for the NVP and VVP was important in later years. In the final decade (1990-2003), USAID provided no direct funding to IVS/Washington. However, a 1999 sub-contract with the University of Maryland IRIS Center for work on a USAID-funded Job Opportunities and Business Support (JOBS) Project provided over $300,000 to IVS/Bangladesh.[24] This was followed by a second small sub-contract and completion of the last significant IVS country program. As IVS gradually wound down worldwide, the Bangladesh program remained its largest.

Bangladesh was IVS's longest running country program—31 years. It was highly successful in many ways and long respected within the Bangladeshi government and among international and national NGOs. Over the decades, the composition of volunteers evolved from predominantly North American with some from Asian countries—Sri Lanka, India, Philippines, and Japan—to the final decade when almost all were Bangladeshis, including the entire staff of the IVS/B office.

Politics became an issue the last years of IVS in Bangladesh, due to growing government distrust of NGOs in general and suspicion of IVS in particular because of its close relationships with a large, politically active NGO (PROSHIKA) and ADAP. In January 2002, the IVS Country Director, Abdul Matin, had to rush back from a field trip because of an investigation of him and IVS by the Anti-Corruption Bureau.[25] The investigation was apparently politically motivated because of Matin's support for PROSHIKA and supposed support for an opposition political party.[26] In June 2004, Matin was forced to go into hiding with police "desperately seeking" to arrest him.[27] Later, the Government blocked the release of funds to IVS/Bangladesh, requiring Anne Shirk, the last IVS Executive Director, to write a letter in 2004 countering a charge against Matin and certifying that he had not misused development funding.[28]

In 2002, as IVS was closing, the staff of IVS/Bangladesh took action with the encouragement of IVS/Washington to establish International Voluntary Services in Bangladesh (IVS/B) as a Bangladeshi NGO.[29] This would allow it to continue to implement projects for IVS as well as to seek funding from European donors and other independent sources. Operations were still substantial with 31 total staff. A constitution and by-laws had been drafted and a Board of Directors named, but registration was uncertain as the Bangladesh NGO Affairs Bureau was not registering new NGOs—reportedly for political reasons. IVS had been subject to various harassment measures and was not allowed to access foreign funding. After IVS/Washington closed, the local affiliate also became inactive.

Information from IVS annual reports, program assessments, financial statements, newsletters, and personal letters demonstrate that IVS volunteers provided valuable assistance in Bangladesh, enabling villagers to improve their lives. Locals learned organization and management skills. Women below the poverty line established small businesses. Programs in environment and energy conservation, health and family planning, and literacy aided the national development effort. The legacy of IVS work continues in Bangladesh in many areas.

Volunteer PATTY HILL (Bangladesh 1990-92) summed up the philosophy of the IVS approach to development since its beginnings in 1953:

> I don't think IVS is a 'dinosaur.' What I was in Bangladesh to do was to work with a national NGO to help them perform better and increase their capacity. They [the local Bangladeshis] know what they are doing in the field. But what they needed from IVS was to strengthen their ability to work better. They looked for that and IVS addressed that need. That is the way IVS should work—helping local organizations address their own needs better.[30]

IVS/ECUADOR (1974–2002)
DIVERSE LOW-KEY SUPPORT TO INDIGENOUS COMMUNITIES

IVS/Ecuador
PROGRAMS:
- Agricultural Production and Marketing
- Cooperative Development
- Health

VOLUNTEERS – 48

FUNDING: USAID; Inter-American Foundation; Charitas-Australia; Chase Manhattan Foundation; others

Ecuador enjoyed rapid economic growth in the late 1970s with development of its large petroleum reserves. A new democratic government launched ambitious development programs that were then derailed by recession in the early 1980s. Cycles of economic and political optimism and disappointment continued, but through it all many rural populations struggled.

In 1974, IVS initiated what was to become a long-running program in Ecuador. Reports are not clear on funding sources, but the program's core funding appears to have been from USAID. The initial program involved agricultural training, two engineers managing road and other local infrastructure construction, and one volunteer training health workers. An early volunteer, nutritionist Susan Meunier, unfortunately died in late 1974 from incompatibility of medications.[31]

Two early IVS/Ecuador counterpart organizations were the Department of Campesino Development for work with remote communities and a church group working in the eastern Amazon region. In the late 1970s, the Ministry of Agriculture and Rural Development was a key partner, and, in 1982, an umbrella agreement for IVS activities was signed with the Government of Ecuador. IVS activities were quite varied and geographically dispersed with an emphasis on indigenous populations in three areas—highlands, Amazon, and Chota Valley.

During the 1980s, IVS worked with agricultural cooperatives in the highland provinces of Chimboranzo and Canar among Quechua communities. Volunteers assisted in agricultural training, market facilitation, and organizational development. The Union of Campesino Organizations—El Bureau—was a key partner. Volunteers Peter and Anne Clark (Australia) spent four years working in Canar Province with Promocion Humana, the private social action arm of the Catholic Church. The Clarks used agricultural courses to bring people from widely scattered villages together on a regular basis to address common problems. As a result of agricultural production improvements, farm incomes increased and migration to other areas for work decreased.

The Canar project had its problems. It was started with a bishop requesting volunteers to develop a demonstration farm. Community participation was good at first, but then fell off. At the end of the second year a group of 200 people threatened the volunteers with violence if they did not leave. It turned out that the local priest, feuding with the bishop, was preaching against the volunteers. The priest was transferred, and the IVS work resumed and was later extended.

In the Upano River valley of the eastern Amazon, IVS worked with Shuar Indian communities for nearly 20 years. Initial work centered on agricultural training. In the 1970s, volunteers established a community store and trained local managers to take over its operation. Health and nutrition services were part of the program for most of the time. Other activities were marketing, reforestation, and organizational development. The Associacion Indigena Evangelista del Napa (AIEN) became a close partner, hosting IVS volunteers for diverse activities.[32] Volunteer Su Abewickrame (Sri Lanka) worked on a food processing and nutrition education program for 100 women, ten of whom became trainers in their own community. Volunteer Bandu Abewickrame (Sri Lanka), Su's husband, trained 30 young men in carpentry and mechanical skills to produce small agricultural and fishing implements and repair river motorboats. Volunteer Eugenia de Pedro Legan (Philippines) worked as a health educator serving river villages that lacked health care. Volunteer Ariel Hidalgo (Chile) supported agricultural and community health organizations by training field promoters and setting up a revolving loan fund for income-producing activities. BANDU ABEWICKRAME remembered his assignment there:

> The Campana Cocha project with IVS was to train indigenous boys and girls to improve their life styles. Many students attended our project school from 13 indigenous communities. They all had to take a canoe to come to the project site. The project had plenty of activities. There were about 60 female students and 42 male students. The female students learned knitting, horticulture, cooking, health and hygiene, and many other things to improve their lives. The boys learned carpentry,

mechanics, agriculture, horticulture, tractor operation, house construction, two-stroke and four-stroke engine repair. They planted rice for the first time in their life.

Work with Afro-Ecuadorian communities in the Chota and Mira valleys emphasized health and nutrition but expanded to broader agricultural and livelihood activities. In collaboration with the Afro-Ecuadorian Federation, a Community Health and Nutrition Project was started in 1993 to serve 60 Afro-Ecuadorian communities. Emphasis was on women's health, safe water consumption, personal and environmental hygiene, and combatting parasites. Nutrition campaigns led to development of 40 family and two community vegetable gardens. Community chicken and guinea pig farms, along with ten community poultry and fish farms, promoted a diverse diet. This was the final area of focus as IVS/Ecuador was winding down.

In nearly all activities, IVS sought to strengthen local organizations. Chase Manhattan Foundation funded IVS through the Peace Corps to implement a Pilot National Volunteer Program in Ecuador. This was completed in 1999 with placement of eleven Ecuadorian volunteers to work on horticulture, community development, and reforestation.

Most IVS volunteers in the Ecuador program were from the region—Bolivia, Colombia, Chile—or local. Among them was Volunteer HANS CAYCEDO, a forester from Colombia.

> *[Hans] worked with the Federation of Shuar Indians to develop a program of reforestation. Hans, who supported himself during his student days in Bogota by driving a taxi, worked several years on similar projects in his home country. He worked with the Shuar on reintroduction of native hardwoods and introduction of compatible crops such as cocoa, coffee, citrus, and naranjilla. . .*
>
> *Reforestation was a challenge, as the Shuar were used to a semi-nomadic existence in an unfailingly bountiful tropical homeland. [They]had never had to plant trees, only chop them down. Slowly, the Shuar and the Colombian forester found ways to develop sustainable agriculture and protect their environment.*[33]

As its program wound down in 1996, IVS facilitated establishment of a local NGO—Fundacion para el Desarollo Communitario, or Minga, to continue the IVS-type work. "Minga", in Quechua, means "collective work" and captures the organization's commitment to self-help and local ownership. A small grant from the Inter-America Foundation facilitated its establishment. Minga's program was to focus on work with Afro-Ecuadorian communities. Unfortunately, the local organization seems to have gone dormant after IVS closed.

The IVS/Ecuador program ran for 28 years as a low-key, perhaps low-budget, operation that seems to have been held together by dedicated individuals committed to the local programs and people. While some IVS assignments were poorly designed,[34] their structure may have improved as IVS introduced more rigor in planning for institutional development.

The emerging narrative for the program was one of empowerment of minority and indigenous ethnic groups. As mentioned above, activities were geographically dispersed, involved culturally and economically different communities, and were small scale and diverse. Achieving coherence and broader impact were thus difficult, although of course, one might argue such attributes are inconsistent with the ethos of local development.

IVS/BOLIVIA (1975–2001)
COOPERATIVES AND COCA SUBSTITUTION

IVS/Bolivia
PROGRAMS:
- Camelid Production
- Handicrafts
- Agricultural Cooperatives
- Coca Substitution

VOLUNTEERS – 30
FUNDING: USAID and others

In the 1970s, Bolivia was the poorest country in South America with extensive poverty among indigenous groups on the Altiplano, a high elevation Andean plateau. Migration to settle (colonize) the eastern lowlands was a national strategy. Coca for local use was a traditional crop but became the target of crop substitution efforts as international cocaine trafficking became a major problem.

In 1975, IVS launched a program targeting assistance to the rural poor in Bolivia. Expectations were that half of the volunteers would come from within the region. The initial project supported llama and alpaca raisers on the Altiplano with veterinary services, forage production, and organizational development. Two Peruvian volunteers helped to form a producers' association from 14 Aymara kinship groups of several hundred members each. The IVS Country Director served as co-manager of the association until 1981.

IVS facilitated wool marketing through an association of 12 handicraft producers making alpaca sweaters and local musical instruments. Involvement with these handicraft producers led to longer-term IVS volunteer support, lasting until 1997. The association, Q'antati, received comprehensive support from 1989 under the Senor de Mayo Project and expanded to include 20 handicraft groups. Most of these centered in the El Alto suburb of La Paz. Volunteer ANTONIA RODRIGUEZ DE MOSCOSO (Bolivia) worked on this program.

> *Antonia Rodriguez de Moscoso, a master weaver who perfected her weaving and knitting skills to support herself and her three children, served as an IVS handicraft specialist with the Senor de Mayo Artisans Association in El Alto. Antonia trained 285 women, many of whom were single parents like herself. The project to increase women's income benefitted 1,500 people. Antonia taught craft skills, methods of textile production, quality control and marketing. She was the designer—cutting, measuring and fitting —garments and shared her knowledge of improved spinning, dyeing, weaving, and knitting techniques. Speaking Quechua and Aymara, as well as Spanish, Antonia facilitated community building, fostering cooperation among artisans from different ethnic groups.*

The association upgraded technical skills and improved business management of 14 textile producing associations in the impoverished area. Each member association would send elected representatives to serve on a "Directorio," to manage the association. The association filled major orders for textile shipments to Japan, Germany, Switzerland, Great Britain and the U.S.[35]

In 1981, IVS initiated work with agricultural cooperatives in the eastern lowlands, then being settled by colonization from the uplands. Initial work helped organize 50 farmers in 14 village associations under the Agricultural Cooperative of Mineros. Work later expanded to other cooperatives in the lowlands and in the altiplano province of Potosi. In 1984, volunteers started work in San Julian, a US-AID-supported settlement area of the 1970s. Most assistance was for agricultural production, marketing, and cooperative management, although IVS began providing health services in 1986. This program strengthening local organizations ended in 1997.

Volunteer Dudley Conneely (USA) worked with the SubCentral de Cooperativas Agropecuarias Villa Paraiso, Ltda. (SUCAP), a central cooperative launched by eight communities in the San Julian area of the Santa Cruz Department. SUCAP initially requested IVS assistance for training in cooperative development, management, and accounting. Subsequently, the cooperatives asked Conneely to work with them to improve agricultural production. Conneely also assisted the co-ops in starting a credit program funded by the Inter-American Development Bank and meeting legal and logistical requirements for a water pump irrigation system. He helped them obtain financing for a rice mill from the Inter-American Foundation, provided management and logistical support for installation of the rice processing complex, and helped with the development of a rice marketing program.

Beginning in 1991, IVS/Bolivia's largest activity was coca crop substitution work in the Chapare region. Sub-contracts with USAID consulting firms implementing large coca substitution programs funded IVS volunteers as agricultural extension agents, who assisted communities with diversification and marketing of cash crops, including black pepper, palm hearts, bananas, and others. In 1996, 33 volunteers and eight IVS staff were working on the program. The initial sub-contract was over one million dollars; the second contract ended by 2001.

IVS facilitated the establishment of IVS-Bolivia as a local NGO in 1996. This local organization managed the coco substitution work to its conclusion, after which, the organization became inactive.

The IVS Bolivia program benefited from the continuity of a 22-plus years of in-country operation, although benefits may have been lessened by considerable staff turnover and the program's relatively small size for most of its life. IVS work with camelids, handicrafts, and agricultural cooperatives was highly appropriate. These were also served by many other donor programs. IVS was well-regarded for its coca substitution work which was a challenging undertaking. In this, IVS essentially served as a manpower provider for the larger consulting firms.

IVS/BOTSWANA (1975–88)
HORTICULTURE, COOPERATIVES, AND FORESTRY

IVS/Botswana
PROGRAMS:
- Horticulture
- Environmental Conservation
- Enterprise Development

VOLUNTEERS – 33
FUNDING: USAID and others

Following its independence in 1966, Botswana maintained a fairly open democratic political tradition. There were village-level discussions guiding decisions of communities, decentralized elected district councils, and multi-party democracy at the national level. This suited conditions for a low population density spread over a large area with traditional culture in small towns and villages. There was, however, a dearth of civil society organizations due to a shortage of individuals with adequate training for leadership and management. IVS's ability to provide qualified volunteers and trainers appeared well-suited to help address this shortage.

The IVS/Botswana program started in 1975 with a Rural Manpower Development Project to train Botswanans for economic and social development. Initial emphasis was on agriculture programs (land use, horticulture, livestock) and non-agricultural rural income opportunities in health care and women's employment. This work evolved into the Botswana Horticulture Project (1978-83) to "support the efforts of the Government of Botswana (GOB) and Community Development Associations to expand both commercial and subsistence horticultural crop production" with a goal of self-sufficiency in vegetable and fruit production.[36] Volunteer LALA A. KUMAR (India) described the project.

> I worked as the Horticulture Unit Manager of the Kweneng Rural Development Association (KRDA), Molepolole, Botswana, southern Africa. My responsibilities were to supervise and train the local technical staff in various aspects of vegetable and fruit production for the smooth running of a commercial irrigated vegetable production unit of about three acres.
>
> There were four IVS volunteers in the agriculture program: Ephram (Tanzania) in beekeeping, Dio (Philippines) in horticulture, John (U.S.A) for the Farm Supply Service Center, and me (India). The goal for each unit was to run independently and economically, so that it could become a sustainable unit after the expatriate volunteer left. We were successful in producing high-quality vegetables and fruits on our commercial irrigated farm, but after one year an evaluation team concurred with my conclusion that a small commercial irrigated farm could not cover the cost of a farm manager and an accountant. As a result, the commercial farm was converted into a community garden with each participant given a plot to grow vegetables for home-consumption and sale.

Volunteer JOHN MARKS (U.S.A) remembered his work on marketing, training, and extension at the project's One-Stop Service Center for Agriculture:

> What I remember most is the great numbers of farmers at harvest time bringing in their crops (mainly sorghum) to sell. Arriving at 8:00 AM, I would see lined up in the yard dozens of carts and wagons of various configurations—ancient wagons with four huge wooden wheels pulled by 16 oxen, small wooden two-wheeled carts pulled by a few oxen, rear-ends of pickup trucks pulled by donkeys. The project filled a community need by introducing many farmers to new ideas and selling products at reasonable prices.
>
> A strong factor in making my work there enjoyable and hopefully beneficial was the strong institutional support from the rural development association and its links to government—especially the grain marketing board. This was in contrast to my Peace Corps experience in Somalia, which was by and large a failure due to the lack of local institutional or government linkages. My time at the project was two years. The fellow that I trained to be the manager stayed with the job for a few years after I left, and later became the minister of agriculture.

IVS later provided one volunteer to coordinate horticultural research and two volunteers for extension outreach. Outreach was through the national youth "brigades" movement. These were not military, but similar to 4-H organizations geared to fostering community-led vocational training and entrepreneurship. The Ministry of Agriculture's National Horticultural Officer was an IVS volunteer. It is unclear whether he was recruited by IVS for the position or named a volunteer while already in service. The first two years emphasized commercial production and experimentation, research, and training. A second phase emphasized extension to encourage smaller-scale horticultural production.

An evaluation of the 1978-83 project concluded that there had been considerable progress in horticultural production and extension. There was also a positive impact on strengthening the Ministry of Agriculture's Horticultural Unit and the Research Unit in the Department of Field Services.[37]

IVS continued its work with horticulture, while expanding activities to include environment and renewable resources, food production, and small enterprise development. In 1984, IVS helped with the development of a National Horticulture Strategy.

A Matsheng Village Woodlot Project (1983-1985) provided 26 months of volunteer services to establish tree nurseries and to improve woodlot management in the dry western region. The project quickly ran into implementation problems due to severe drought and loss or non-assignment of Botswana field personnel for the project. IVS still succeeded in establishing 24 hectares of woodlots and forming Village Development Committees for their management. Other IVS projects were Forestry Extension and Agricultural Service Development. In 1984, IVS/Botswana had seven volunteers: two on horticultural research; two on a renewable energy project (one with village woodlots and one with a bio-gas project); two on business advisory services; and one advising a parastatal handicraft marketing organization.

In 1988, as the Botswana program was closing, IVS provided grants to two local groups, the Forestry Association of Botswana and the Rural Industrial Investment Center, to continue work in areas IVS had supported. The IVS/Botswana program appears to have been reasonably successful in providing technically qualified volunteers to projects, but it might well have benefitted from longer-term engagement, not possible with the short duration of USAID projects. The IVS program appears to have evolved from providing volunteers to implement a specific USAID project to the placement of volunteers with local organizations.

IVS/Honduras (1975–87)
Soybeans, Health, and Construction

IVS/Honduras
PROGRAMS:
- Soybean Production and Use
- Health and Sanitation
- Micro-enterprise

VOLUNTEERS – 27
FUNDING: USAID

The IVS/Honduras program started in 1975 and by the next year had four volunteers teaching in vocational training schools, three engineers working on rural construction, two volunteers working on feasibility studies, and a nurse working on public health. Over the following two years, activities coalesced into two projects: a soybean introduction project and a water and sanitation project. Volunteers played varied roles in these projects. One volunteer teacher was called a "genius with junk." Volunteers introduced ways of doing things that may have been new at that time to the country.

> Students at a vocational training school in Catacamas learned how to make valuable farming tools from scrap metal, as taught by VOLUNTEER GORDON CRIPE. Gordon, a millwright by profession, proved himself something of a genius with junk. He and his students used scrap to make a 60-foot long land plane, a device to level fields for irrigated farming. Building the plane not only gave Gordon's young students a chance to practice their metal-working skills. It also enabled them to prepare 40 acres of school land for irrigation to grow rice, sorghum, and cowpeas in the dry season. Once all school land was prepared, the land plane and other hand-made tools were made available to local farmers. Since the region's six-month rainy season is unpredictable, irrigation from local rivers can prevent disaster in drought years and allow for year-round crops.
>
> The land plane was a product of the school's machine shop where the students, under Gordon's guidance, also learned how to repair and re-build vehicles and other equipment. Gordon's objective was to ensure that another expatriate would not be needed after his departure. He trained three students to take over the machine shop and teach new students.[38]

The Soybean Development Project sponsored by the Ministry of Agriculture was initially funded by USAID to introduce soybeans as a new crop in Honduras. IVS recruited three volunteers from Taiwan. Wang Chao Chin from the Asian Vegetable Research and Development Center managed soybean research, while Cheng Ching ("Pedro") Kui and Henry Lee worked on extension. Soybeans were to be a new source of income for small farmers and to improve nutrition. Not surprisingly, both objectives proved to be longer term efforts requiring changing cropping patterns and changing eating habits. The IVS work on the project was well-regarded, but soybeans did not take off during the project.

IVS partnered with CEDEN, National Evangelical Committee for Development and Emergency, a Honduran non-profit organization, for work on public health. In 1979, a volunteer public health nurse, Carol Castillo, completed a two-year assignment coordinating the CEDEN health program in the San Pedro Sula region. She trained health workers and completely revamped the health program for 20 villages in the area. The IVS-CEDEN partnership continued in a Water Resource Project to install 60 water projects in poor rural communities. Most villages served were far off hard roads and approachable only on foot or by a four-wheel drive vehicle in dry weather. Two volunteers, a program design advisor and an engineer/topographer, assisted participating communities in constructing and administering new water systems. Volunteer DAVID LAMB (U.S.A.) worked with another partner, the Evangelical and Reformed Center for Vocational Education (CEVER).

> Lamb worked in the Yoro region helping 15 rural fanning groups diversify crops, increase yields, and use appropriate technologies. He helped establish a model farm plot, demonstrated techniques for soil and water conservation, installed water wheels for improved irrigation, and facilitated access to metal crop storage silos for some CEVER-member farmers. He worked with 150 women in 15 communities in a swine production project, providing technical assistance to improve genetic stock, animal nutrition and health, farm management practices, and marketing systems. The project became a model for swine and small animal production projects throughout Honduras.[39]

In the 1980s, IVS/Honduras began work with small enterprise development. This rounded out a program to strengthen local organizations that provide services to rural beneficiary groups. Volunteers trained local counterparts to respond to local needs and facilitate linkages with public or private sources of assistance for improving agricultural production and marketing, public health, nutrition, or small enterprise development. Volunteers also worked with housing construction, as described by volunteer ARTHUR KELLY:[40]

> For the past two years, I have been involved as an engineering advisor, designer, and technical consultant in the construction of low-cost homes in two distinct colonies involving a total of 554 homes. As a volunteer consultant for the Asocicion de Promocion Humana (APBHU), I have assisted in site planning, topographic surveying, sewer piping layout and design, potable water design and construction, surveying instruction, construction technique, construction programing, sewer

lagoon design and construction, materials ordering, and budgeting for the aforementioned projects. These are projects funded by MISEREOR, a consortium of German Catholic dioceses financing housing construction in the wake of the devastation of Hurricane Fifi.

I believe my very presence on the projects was tantamount to an encouraging push to all Hondurans concerned. I worked as long as my health permitted and could see good-to-excellent response on the part of my closest working associates. I have the highest personal regard for Executive Director Pacheco and construction superintendent Jose Ramirez Soto; these are men of a distinct and singular courage.

We [IVSers] in Honduras were truly international: Holland, Philippines, Taiwan, Japan, Colombia, and the U.S. It has been a great pleasure to know them all... May it be remembered that for this writer, Honduras became the instrument for radical changes in his life. It was in Honduras that I became the sickest I had ever been in my life contracting Hepatitis shortly after I arrived. It is here also that I fell in love, married and had a son. Honduras and I are intertwined, and that is as it should be.

IVS/Honduras faced some staff health issues, and in 1984, security concerns restricted activity. The program appears to have been quite successful in many of its diverse activities even with a modest overall budget. Funding seems to have been mainly from USAID. Volunteers provided effective specialized technical support to programs of established NGOs, boding well for the sustainability of IVS contributions. The Honduras program closed in 1987.

IVS/CARIBBEAN (1983–89)
REGIONAL ENTERPRISE DEVELOPMENT SERVICES

IVS/Caribbean
PROGRAMS:
• Enterprise Development
VOLUNTEERS – 8
FUNDING: USAID and others

The IVS/Caribbean enterprise development program started in 1983. By 1984, it had four volunteers linked with local business development organizations. Activities sought to raise incomes, create jobs, develop local agriculture, and establish micro-enterprises and small-scale industrial development. All team members were to be West Indian nationals or diaspora. The volunteers worked in the island nations of Antigua and Barbuda, St. Kitts and Nevis, Dominica, St. Lucia, St. Vincent and the Grenadines, and Grenada. These countries shared problems of reliance on food imports, poorly developed market systems, and high unemployment.

The program strengthened community-based private organizations and government agencies supporting enterprise development. Volunteers worked in partnership with the Women and Development Unit (WAND) of the University of The West Indies/Antigua to promote women's access to jobs, Dominica's National Development Foundation (NDF) to help local entrepreneurs start small businesses, the St. Vincent Organization of Rural Development (ORD) to promote crop production and marketing, and St. Lucia's National Research and Development Foundation (NRDF) to improve loan applications analysis and financial management support to clients.

As an example of the project approach, volunteer Michael Seepersaud (Guyana) in St. Lucia established a financial system for the NRDF and trained its staff to maintain it. The system facilitated review of loan applications from small business people and provided follow-up support to borrowers. Seepersaud integrated computers into the agency's work and organized training workshops on use of computers for financial management, for client businesses, and staff of other National Development Foundations.

Volunteers trained local managers in skills for promoting small-scale development projects and for transferring skills to beneficiaries. The volunteers provided training in postharvest technology, marketing, small enterprise development, youth skills, human resources development, small-scale industry development, financial management and planning, and enterprise development. Over the life of the project, volunteers assisted 130 small enterprises and groups.

In 1988, the IVS West Indian volunteers collectively formed the Caribbean Advisory and Professional Services (CAPS). The Formation of CAPS, essentially an IVS spin-off, established a multi-island regional development agency and a basis for continuing support that IVS had been providing to clients. CAPS established relationships with ten development agencies and received approval for four projects totaling $240,500. Unfortunately, CAPS was not sustained and ceased operations by 1993.[41]

The IVS/Caribbean program was a focused project that was apparently effective in supporting enterprise development, a prime USAID objective at the time. The actual volunteer component of the program was relatively modest.

IVS/Zimbabwe (1983–92)
Small-scale Cooperatives and Community Development

IVS/Zimbabwe
Programs:
- Cooperative Development
- Micro-enterprises
- Agriculture

Volunteers – 21
Funding: USAID

Zimbabwe gained official independence from Britain in 1980, following a ten-year civil war between the break-away white-minority government and local independence groups. In 1983, IVS started a program in Zimbabwe and sent five volunteers in 1984 to work on cooperative development, horticulture, agricultural training, and micro-enterprise development. The program worked directly with cooperatives, with cooperative federations, and with NGO cooperative support programs. Most activities were with agricultural cooperatives and involved support for livestock, diversification, and farm management. Examples of such activities include:

Volunteer STEPHEN HUSSEY (England) worked with the Organization of Rural Associations for Progress (ORAP), an umbrella group for 300 community-based groups serving people of Midlands and Matabeleland provinces. His project was to expand a water resource development/village technology center. He established links with private and government technical institutions to set up a technical library and information center.

MARY ATTARD (England), a handicrafts specialist, assisting the Christian Marching Church to establish a center in Chegutu for rural women to acquire income-generation skills. Attard trained women in weaving, sewing and rug making; established linkages with similar training centers; and developed marketing and support systems to continue after her assignment.

ROBERT FOX (U.S.A.) working with the Adult Literacy Organization of Zimbabwe (ALOZ) to develop income-generating projects in silk production, pottery, and beekeeping for former literacy students. Fox completed a baseline survey of potential literacy group projects, identifying technical and managerial skills needed for those projects.

The IVS program strengthened local service organizations to assist resettlement of subsistence farmers from overpopulated and marginal tribal areas to more productive areas. Technical and managerial skills training promoted self-sufficiency, improved agricultural production, and linked people to local resources.

Volunteer NOLINA MAYO (Zimbabwe), an IVS Field Worker in the Filabusi area with the Organization of Rural Associations for Progress (ORAP), helped 700 families with their health, education, and economic problems:

> I am a coordinator and facilitator. Many of our families do not have toilets. To help them solve this problem, I go to the Ministry of Health or UNICEF and ask for six bags of cement. Then I get the District Development Fund to bring the cement for several families to a central place. Then the families or a neighbor picks it up with their oxcart.[42]

Nolina encouraged villagers to set up support groups of five to ten families to mold bricks for improved housing, to obtain drought disaster aid, to start a sewing project, or to dig wells for safe drinking water and garden irrigation. Sometimes an activity, like molding bricks for their own houses, became a way to earn extra money to send their children to school. ORAP Director Sithembiso Nyoni said: "Billions and billions of dollars have been spent on development, and the villagers are poorer. But with Nolina and your other workers, I see sustainable development. People are changing their own lives. Please send us more workers like Nolina!"[43]

Other Zimbabwe projects were Small Scale Vegetable Production, Subsistence Farmer Training, and Technical Resource Development. The latter worked with water resource development through the ORAP's 300 community group affiliates. There is little detail on these activities and they most likely were relatively small.

The IVS/Zimbabwe program was modest in scope and lasted less than ten years. IVS appears to have had trouble finding partner organizations although there was extensive collaboration with ORAP. Counterpart challenges, limited funding for management staff, and the country's difficult political environment likely constrained the volunteer program.

IVS/SOUTHEAST ASIA (1991–2002)
HIV/AIDS PREVENTION

IVS/Southeast Asia
PROGRAMS:
- HIV/AIDS Prevention (Thailand, Cambodia, Vietnam)

VOLUNTEERS – 3
FUNDING: Various private sources

IVS returned to work in Southeast Asia in the 1990s for its finale program initiative. Two things lured IVS back: IVS's strong identification with Southeast Asia where 60 percent of IVS volunteers had served and many still had contacts, and the reality of the global HIV/AIDS pandemic threatening Southeast Asia because of the area's active commercial sex industry.

A start was made in Thailand in 1991. IVS partnered with a local NGO—EMPOWER—to provide services to bar and brothel sex workers. Services included: condom distribution, assertiveness training, support group formation, outreach discouraging employment in the sex industry and client visits to prostitutes, and, most importantly, education about safer sex for HIV risk reduction. Volunteers provided training and helped with program development, and IVS provided operating cost grants. Later, in the 1990s, the program provided English language training for sex workers.

Beginning in 1992, IVS worked in Vietnam with the Women's Union to provide training on safe sex, distribute condoms, operate a sexually-transmitted disease (STD) clinic, and operate a family planning clinic with a maternal-child health program. The next year, in Cambodia, IVS engaged with a local NGO, the Indra Devi Women's Association, to train about HIV/AIDS prevention and provide health outreach messaging. Activities in the three countries were similar but followed approaches of the different partners and varied over time. IVS attempts to engage in Laos and Bangladesh through workshops and consciousness raising discussions never got traction. Programs worked through grants and limited international volunteer assistance to the local organizations.

Volunteer KOEN OLIE (Netherlands), one of the few volunteers on the program, worked with the EMPOWER program in Bangkok and exemplified some of the innovation expatriate volunteers could contribute.

> *Koen performed with the Honeybee Theater Group and wrote and directed their productions. These presentations were staged for bar workers and their patrons in the go-go bars of Patpong, the red-light district of Bangkok. The Honeybee group presented skits and plays relevant to the lives and health of bar workers, educating about AIDS and advocating practices that reduce HIV risks. Prostitutes were played by the bar women themselves. Koen and other volunteers played patrons and police officers. Koen was a director and performer in Amsterdam and London and brought special talents to this work. His talents as illustrator and cartoonist made him well-known in Thailand. Koen designed and illustrated a board game on HIV risk reduction. The game was played in Patpong and throughout Thailand. Koen's posters and comic books about safer sex were used by workers in the entertainment industry.*
>
> *Koen brought experience as a linguist to his work, offering bar workers lessons in English, Dutch, and German. Degrees in English and fine arts were among Koen's qualifications, but even more significant was his ability to go into bars and brothels with a nonjudgmental, client-respectful stance. His work was highly respected by colleagues and clients, who were inspired by Koen's enthusiasm and commitment.*[44]

Peer counseling was a key part of the program's approach, so some support was provided for AIDS caregivers. IVS program reporting at times cited a relatively large number of local volunteers—mainly sex workers—serving as peer counselors and sharing outreach messaging on safe sex. One impactful innovation introduced was the approach of oral application as a means of overcoming client reluctance to use condoms. These were reportedly quite effective. In 1998, Thai Volunteer THANANYA reported:

> My name is Thananya, my nickname is Ung. I am from Lampang Province in northern Thailand. Three or four years ago I came to Bangkok, and then I worked at the Japanese Bar. I was lucky to learn about EMPOWER from my friend. At first, I found that EMPOWER teaches English to women free of charge. After paying 30 Baht for the first application, we can study there all our lives. I worked in Thaniya area and study at EMPOWER for a long time. It made me want to help EMPOWER's project in English and Japanese language. I knew that EMPOWER needed volunteers to help this project for a long time, as sometimes they cancelled classes because they did not have enough volunteers.
>
> Because I have been a student at EMPOWER, I understand the feeling and needs of our students. I would like to share my knowledge with my friends who come to EMPOWER. The other reason that I decided to teach is [that] I like our students to have a good chance for their lives, make their lives better [and] have a chance to find better job. It's not difficult if they are patient and try hard. If they have dreams and goals, they can achieve them.
>
> Normally we have classes every day from 4-6 o'clock p.m. However, the first three months this year, I could not do the project every day because I have to study tour guide courses. But since May, I can teach every day. My education at EMPOWER gave me a good opportunity for a good job. We used to think that it is impossible to work for other people who had higher education, like those who have at least Bachelor's degree, but I know now that it's possible. This gives me an idea that I should try to help other people to get good thing like me.
>
> At EMPOWER our school is special because people who join our school are women working in bars. We have to work with them like friend, relatives, or sisters. This method makes them want to study, and they are not afraid to ask many questions.

This was a timely program addressing a serious need. The program had a limited budget and perhaps required a low profile for work in an area in which governments might not have entirely welcomed foreign NGO involvement. It continued with dwindling grant support to the local organizations until 2002. This final program was certainly unique, and one that the IVS founders in 1953 would never have dreamed of.

THE END GAME REINVENTION FAILURE

By the late 1990s following a decade of program decline, the IVS light was flickering. No significant new projects had been started since the Caribbean and Zimbabwe programs in 1983. The Southeast Asia HIV/AIDS program of the 1990s was an interesting initiative, but it was poorly funded and spread quite thin. As the century ended, IVS was left dependent on residual activity in Ecuador and two sub-contracts that the local IVS-Bolivia and IVS-Bangladesh affiliates had with USAID contractors. Reinvention had failed.

The change in IVS programs is demonstrated dramatically, and perhaps unfairly, by comparing 1990s Southeast Asia programs with those of 1950s-1970s, which are described in Chapter Three. The former, working closely with USAID and local governments, had substantial resources, large numbers of expatriate volunteers, and significant influence on people and programs. The latter was done independently, on a shoestring budget, with few expatriate volunteers, and by grants which directly funded implementation by local groups. Impacts were at an individual level.

IVS STRATEGIES

Nan Borton assumed the position of IVS Executive Director in 1982, a difficult and contentious time.[45] The immediate objective was to streamline and improve management and to delegate more responsibility to field staff. Washington staff outnumbered field staff, and IVS had no financial reserve at all. The IVS volunteer model appeared to be no longer financially viable. It cost IVS as much to maintain an expatriate field officer as it did for USAID. Donor interest in funding expatriate volunteers had severely diminished. By then, churches had generally created their own overseas volunteer programs. Also, sending American development workers had come to seem "disrespectful." As a program strategy, IVS stayed open and started making greater use of skilled local and regional volunteers.

The strategies IVS embraced over the "reinvention period" following the 1971 meeting at Harper's Ferry were largely developmentally sound, but they were perhaps overly idealistic and optimistic. The commitments from the 1970s to reduce reliance on U.S. Government funding and to emphasize international volunteers were understandable. Unfortunately, there were not many options for significant non-USG funding—a lesson learned by other organizations that have faced the same USAID-funding dependency dilemma as IVS. Furthermore, managing an organization to comply with USG requirements, while also aligning operations with objectives and procedures of other donors is not easy. International volunteers provided some obvious advantages, but also presented problems for systematic recruitment and orientation, promotion of common values, and standardized management. With few new U.S. volunteers, IVS was unable to expand its support base. It lost its unique model of engaging Americans in participatory community action in support of U.S. development assistance.

IVS followed, and may have helped lead, shifts in development strategies of the 1980s. Commitment to strengthening local institutions, pursuing participatory approaches, targeting basic human needs and poverty reduction, and empowering local people fit well with volunteer-based programs. In 1986, IVS emphasized a recommitment to strengthening local organizations.[46] And, again in 1990, IVS defined itself as a leader in international volunteerism engaging in, "... a number of self-help projects around the world, using volunteers from developing countries and appropriate technology to help develop self-reliant communities. At IVS the idea of 'self-help' was not merely a philosophy: self-help was put into practice. IVS volunteers do not 'mount' or 'manage' projects. Rather, they act as expert consultants to communities, helping them to solve their unique problems with their own unique resources."[47]

IVS Effectiveness

A 1985 USAID-funded study reviewed IVS programs in Botswana, Bangladesh, and Ecuador.[48] The study concluded that, with two exceptions, IVS had little impact on the effectiveness of the institutions to which volunteers were assigned. There were three reasons for this. Volunteer assignments were to implement discrete projects, not to strengthen institutional capacity. Volunteers were to deliver services, not serve as advisers. And, most host organizations were large, established institutions in which influencing change is difficult. Surprisingly, the study found that volunteers often had more impact in work with smaller, local organizations on side projects rather than in their main assignment. This may be a unique aspect of volunteer service that encourages individual initiative in identifying and building on local opportunities. The evaluation appears not to have assessed or valued the social capital development that can be a strength of volunteer programs.

The 1985 study concluded that volunteers should generally be assigned as advisers, ideally with intermediary organizations to develop organizational capacities to better serve clients. This became the stated direction of IVS strategy.[49] Advisory positions relied on good inter-personal relations. However, they could potentially provoke resentments or generate frustration when volunteers did not see or feel clear accomplishments from their work. Volunteers with technical skills frequently had limited skills or understanding of issues relevant to the development of institutional capacity. Training and staff support on such issues were also limited and not easy to arrange.[50] Volunteers may be disadvantaged as an adviser if they lack qualifying expertise, and if the host perceives a "volunteer" to lack status and value. On the other hand, there are advantages to assignments with clearly defined tasks to focus volunteers and allow them to lead by example.

In retrospect, IVS country programs trended towards three over-lapping but distinct types of activities: sub-grants to national NGOs (as funding partner), recruiting implementation personnel for larger projects (contracted partner), and general support to local organizations (support partner). For sub-grants, funding was limited and transaction costs high. Recruiting project technical staff could be difficult for meeting project timelines, especially when placing skilled international volunteers. In recruiting local personnel, it is not clear that IVS had any comparative advantage. In providing general support to local organizations, IVS differed little from other NGOs. With its reinvention, IVS lost its uniqueness and ability to offer a specialized volunteer service different from other contractors or NGOs.

Funding

Funding was a constant problem. In 1971-72, as the Indochina programs wound down, lack of funding forced the reduction of IVS/Washington staff from 12 to seven.[51] There was some success in diversifying funding, as non-USAID funding increased from $77,000 in 1973 to $736,000 in 1979. Church funding increased significantly, from $36,000 in 1974 to $378,000 in 1979.[52] But, despite efforts to diversify funding, USAID remained the dominant funder. A $2.5 million matching fund from USAID from 1988 to 1993 complemented $2.152 million private funding and $1.017 million of in-kind and limited other government funding.[53] The grant was to have been for $3.0 million, but $500,000 was de-obligated due to lack of an IVS match.[54] This matching grant funded nearly half the costs of headquarter operations plus programs in Bangladesh, Bolivia, Ecuador, and Zimbabwe. Botswana and the Caribbean programs were dropped due to their costs.

With the end of the Cold War, development assistance funding declined. Increased global food production reduced concerns over food security and led to a decline in funding for agricultural development, a major element of most IVS programs. With many more organizations competing for USAID funding, IVS was often unable to leverage its country activities to attract funding for larger programs. USAID provided another matching grant of $200,000 in 1995, but again IVS was unable to meet the match.

Continuous efforts secured private funding. In 1991, IVS received funding from 23 organizational donors, but only four exceeded $20,000, only one exceeded $100,000 and only two others exceeded $50,000.[55] This was a labor-intensive means of fund raising and not conducive to the development of a sound program. IVS was not able, interested, or responsive enough to compete for larger USAID projects and was not able to develop significant resources from other sources. In 1993, IVS was again forced to cut staff and other costs.

Scale of Operations

Economies of scale were an issue. IVS country field directors felt that at least 15-20 volunteers would be needed to justify a field director position, although Zimbabwe had only one volunteer under the field director supervision.[56] Planning assignments and supporting volunteers require technical and management expertise. Lack of such expertise threatens program quality, while their provision requires an adequately sized program to be cost-effective. Washington technical and management expertise is also essential for a sustainable program and requires an adequate number of substantial country programs for viability. Under its six-year program from 1988 to 1993, IVS had only 33 international/regional and 150 Bangladeshi volunteers. While "small is beautiful" for many community development activities, "large is efficient" in many ways.

Local Affiliates

IVS adopted the strategy of registering offices as local NGOs which came to be known as 'legacy' organization. The IVS "legacy" organizations or local affiliates—IVS-Bangladesh, IVS-Bolivia, IVS-Ecuador, and Caribbean Advisory and Professional Services—were seen as a means of providing continuity to IVS's services. These continued for a while but all too soon became inactive. Why? The legacy organizations may have been more dependent on IVS and its access to USAID and other funding than was appreciated. They may have been left as weak organizations, lacking pragmatic development strategies. And, the volunteer concept may not have been understood or accepted in their countries, leaving them with little differentiation from the many other NGOs.

What Is a Volunteer?

This final phase of IVS also highlighted questions of volunteerism's role in development. One question was, "What is a volunteer?" One definition would be "someone who does something of their own volition." Thus, a corporate executive or a highly paid consultant could be volunteers. Or, it could be "someone committed to a task and willing to make an extra effort." But this too can apply to consultants and others.

Traditionally, the term "volunteer" carries a connotation of "making a sacrifice in doing something to benefit others." The question arises when IVS's local and regional volunteers had salaries and terms of employment that were very similar to local consultants employed on other projects.[57]

In terms of developmental impact, it may make no difference whether workers are considered "volunteers" or consultants. Clearly, the IVS local and regional volunteers were well-qualified individuals—often better qualified than the typical U.S. "generalist" volunteer, and they were also very committed to the work and people they served. IVSers called themselves "volunteers," even though, as noted in the 1981 evaluation mentioned above, some were not very happy with the designation. IVS also appeared to treat them differently as many non-American volunteers were not included in the IVS Alumni Directory. This contrasts with the international expatriate volunteers recruited by IVS/Washington under previous programs (e.g., Laos, Vietnam, Bangladesh), who were clearly and enthusiastically accepted as IVS volunteers. The difference may be that all earlier volunteers went through the same central recruitment process and standard orientation towards a common "IVS mission" and philosophy, while later programs with regional and national volunteers lacked these processes.

Political support

After the end of the large Indochina programs in the 1970s, IVS retained some influential support in the U.S. congress. This ensured that USAID continued some support to IVS. That support kept IVS operating and allowed some independence, but also enabled IVS to operate without being strongly responsive to USAID strategies and interests. When Congressional support eventually waned, IVS's relationship with USAID was relatively weak. IVS perhaps took too seriously the 1971 Harper's Ferry decision to seek independence from USG funding, without fully realizing its implications.

Did IVS outlive the needs of its original Peace Churches and U.S. Government founders? Or did it fail to effectively market the unique value-added developmental benefits provided by U.S. volunteers? The answer is mixed. For the peace churches, after the elimination of the U.S. military draft in 1973, the need for options for alternative service disappeared. The churches remained engaged and probably expanded their international relief and development efforts, but they had never expected to fund IVS themselves, but rather to work in collaboration. For developing countries, education systems produced individuals with many of the skills offered by volunteers. USAID reduced field staff and began contracting out its project implementation, a move that made it more difficult to integrate volunteer assistance into programs managed by other organizations. This was reflected in a terminology change from "private voluntary organizations (PVOs)" to "non-government organizations (NGOs)."

Did IVS effectively package or sell the concept of volunteers' value-added development impact? Perhaps not, but perhaps the problem was that USAID managers rejected the validity of such benefits, or host countries may not have fully accepted volunteers. Some benefits seem obvious: innovative field-level implementation and monitoring; person-to-person mentoring and capacity development; improving citizen understanding and support for international development; improving responsiveness to local people's interests and benefits; and symbolizing assistance as being 'from the American people'. For a donor or host country, benefits are weighed against some drawbacks of volunteers, such as their uncertain availability, independence, lack of experience, naivete, or lack of familiarity with other cultures and political systems.

There remains commitment to engaging volunteers in U.S. foreign assistance programs. Chapter Eleven summarizes recent initiatives to do this. It is not easy. Programs must meet needs of host countries, align with USAID programing processes, and be attractive to volunteers. The demise of IVS and its experiment in providing an opportunity for private citizens to serve with a flexible private organization in overseas relief and development work is regrettable. Perhaps, both IVS and USAID walked away from what might have been the "sweet spot" for IVS—providing field level volunteers integrated into USAID projects with a longer-term perspective for support to the projects' development objective.

6

ADMINISTRATION CHALLENGES RUNNING A NONPROFIT NGO

FREDERIC C. BENSON AND GARY ALEX

As an historical account of International Volunteer Services, Inc. (1953-2002), this book opens with information on the origin of IVS, its formulating partners, general organization, mission or purpose, initial service programs, and volunteer guidelines. Subsequent chapters speak to specific programs and organizational issues providing historical accounts of personnel, decisions made, programs engaged, problems in the field, problems in funding, political influences, achievements, and much more. This material comes from meeting reports, archival material, and volunteer stories. Additional volunteer accounts can be found in *The Fortunate Few, IVS Volunteers from Asia to the Andes* which was published in 2015.

The effort here is to look frankly and objectively at the major organizational, management, and administrative issues affecting IVS in an effort to answer the question, "Why did IVS close?" This material draws heavily on an unpublished detailed paper in the IVS archives, "IVS From 1971-2002" by Frederic Benson, and other archival information. As IVS archives receive on-going contributions, additional analysis may shed more light on the issues engaged here.

The IVS story that emerges is one of shifting forces but stable commitment of staff, volunteers, and board members to the mission and volunteer ethos of the organization. Therefore, before engaging specific elements such as organization and strategy, structure and leadership, program initiatives and performance, funding, etc., it is helpful to briefly list some of the forces at play.

IVS PRESSURES AND TURNING POINTS

Throughout its lifetime, IVS was subject to changing pressures that influenced its programs. In a couple of instances, these resulted in significant redirections for the organization. Others may have been equally important, but not as obvious. Country program descriptions throughout this book reflect these influences, but they are summarized here.

Cold War/Middle East Tension/U.S. Global Engagement

In the 1950s, the U.S. sought to counter the spread of communism, stabilize the Middle East after the formation of Israel, and expand its influence internationally. Individual Americans were motivated to contribute to these objectives. This provided fertile ground for IVS to engage volunteers in international development, especially in rural development programs.

Formation of the Peace Corps in the Early 1960s

Modeled after IVS, the Peace Corps offered Americans an alternative public agency option for international voluntary service.

War in Indochina

From the mid-1950s through 1975, IVS volunteers were directly affected and endangered by the intensified fighting in Laos and Vietnam. This was a challenging environment for volunteers. The American public became more aware and less supportive of government foreign policies. In a meeting held at Harper's Ferry, WV, in 1971, IVS decided that it needed to become less dependent on U.S. government funding, a decision that signaled a major turning point in IVS operations.

USAID Downsizing

In the early 1970s, USAID reduced its staff by 30 percent[1] and shifted from direct project implementation to out-sourcing project implementation to contractors. This led to an increased number of organizations competing for funding and a less collegial relationship between USAID staff and IVS.

Participatory Development Strategies

From the mid-1970s through the 1980s, USAID and other development agencies emphasized poverty alleviation, participatory development, and private voluntary development approaches. USAID Operating Program Grants (OPGs) provided flexible funding. All of these were favorable to IVS program operations.

A New Era in Development

The 1990s ushered in a new era for international development work. The Cold War ended, and development assistance declined. Agriculture and rural development faded as priorities. Private sector development was emphasized. Projects became larger and more complex. Accountability and impact reporting became more important. This was difficult for small NGOs.

Private Agencies Cooperating Together (PACT) Alliance and Final Struggles

In the late 1990s, IVS staff and programs shrank and struggled to remain viable. A short alliance with PACT failed to reboot the IVS program. Other organizational revitalizations proved to be too little, too late.

IVS Objectives And Strategy

IVS's corporate objective remained constant throughout its lifetime. Its charter was: "to utilize the services of volunteers on an organized basis to combat hunger, poverty, disease, and illiteracy in the underdeveloped areas of the world and thereby further the peace, happiness and prosperity of the peoples thereof."[2] IVS pioneered the use of non-sectarian volunteers in international programs with the International Cooperation Administration (ICA), which was interested in IVS for its unique capability to place committed private individuals at a minimal cost to implement foreign assistance projects. The IVS operational strategy in support of the corporate objective evolved substantially over time.

IVS was established to work closely with ICA on community level development projects, essentially providing American volunteers to supplement ICA staff. However, by the end of the 1960s, IVS programs in South Vietnam and Laos were enmeshed in the turmoil and controversy of the war there. As the war intensified, some volunteers and staff became uncomfortable with IVS's role in support of U.S. Government policy. As a result, on November 17, 1970, the IVS Board of Directors scheduled a special three-day meeting in February 1971 at Harpers Ferry, West Virginia, to consider reevaluation and redefinition of IVS to meet the challenge of the 1970's.[3] The Harpers Ferry meeting posed three fundamental questions:[4]

(1) Does volunteer work abroad, which peaked in the mid-1960s and was declining, have an important role in the 1970s?

(2) If so, does IVS, with its concept of volunteerism, have a significant contribution to make in this new era?

(3) If IVS does have a significant contribution to make, what changes would be required in the IVS structure and program to make them responsive to the new circumstances and potential of the 1970s? What changes should be initiated in 1971 if the longer-term goals are to be achieved on a timely basis?

1970s

The *Harpers Ferry Charter: IVS in the 1970's* resulted from the meeting and was a considerable achievement.⁵ It called for IVS to build on past successes, applying these to new world circumstances in which IVS must operate. Key features were: (a) broadened financial support; (b) additional and diverse programs in Asia, Africa, Latin America, and the United States; and (c) multinational representation at all levels: volunteer, staff, and board. IVS in the 1970s was to be characterized by program independence, financial flexibility, and responsiveness to the felt needs of the people of developing countries.⁶ This was a significant redirection of IVS's operating strategy, which previously focused on American volunteers working abroad.

By January 1977, when John Rigby was appointed executive director, he observed that in five years IVS had made progress in all three areas identified by the Harpers Ferry Charter. IVS had much more financial backing from private and host institutions. Grant funding from USAID had also become more flexible. IVS had begun new programs in Latin America (Ecuador, Honduras, Bolivia), Africa (Mauritania, Sudan, Botswana), the Middle East (Yemen Arab Republic), and Asia (Bangladesh and Papua New Guinea). The number of volunteers and staff members from countries other than the United States had increased.⁷ IVS was comfortable with its new approach. Board Chairman DONALD M. FRASER described the role of IVS as follows:

> In its own quiet way, IVS is helping in the struggle for human rights. IVS extends a helping hand to those who are working to improve their own social and economic status. This is not an act of charity but of enlightenment. Especially now, when cynicism about government is rampant, the modestly scaled efforts of IVS to assist others assures us that at least something is working and working well. This assurance is reinforced by our knowledge that IVS continues to attract highly talented people to its corps of volunteers, to its staff, and to its board.⁸

Beginning with a USAID General Support Grant in 1974, IVS undertook projects in which it had a major, if not total, input to project design and responsibility for managing day-to-day operations. A USAID 1981 evaluation observed that: "Unlike earlier years, when the exclusive resource of IVS was its complement of volunteers, IVS now has a management and administrative role in all of the projects with which IVS volunteers are associated. Thus, IVS is far more heavily engaged in recent years in the total development project context and is not limited to the role of recruiting, placing, and supporting expatriate volunteers."⁹

1980s

The 1981 evaluation also questioned in what sense IVS was a volunteer organization—a question that became asked more frequently. Whatever its volunteer origins, IVS was no longer providing only international technical specialists.[10] At least half of IVS's volunteers at the time were from third-world countries, and some of them were earning as much as, if not more than they would have earned in a regular technical job at home.[11] The massive investment in education in developing nations during the 1970s and 80s had created a pool of highly trained professionals. It was harder to justify a program exclusively consisting of foreign volunteers while qualified nationals already in country were seeking jobs that would use their skills.[12]

In the 1980s, IVS therefore pioneered the "national volunteer" — the use of specialists from within the country to provide support and effective leadership for many community-development projects. This logical program adaptation helped breathe life into IVS programs. National or indigenous volunteers brought a high level of immediately useful, professional training and relevant cultural experience to their jobs. Thus, while adapting to the needs of the developing world, IVS kept its own, original ethos — the concept of voluntarism and the internationalist spirit. These principles were worthy of preservation.[13]

By 1983, IVS was heavily focused on institutional development. It had evolved from a volunteer organization whose role was placing volunteers in overseas development positions to a development organization using voluntary technical assistance to assist change and local institutional development. It saw lasting change as taking place only when local abilities and interests were organized to promote and implement change. While external technical and financial assistance might be required to facilitate this, initial dependency could and should decrease as local skills and capabilities increased.[14] There remained however a recognition that IVS needed new approaches to become more effective and competitive for funding. A 1984 Annual Board Meeting gave IVS the mandate to explore alternative ways of providing development assistance. Work was underway to develop contacts and pursue leads that could bring IVS into much closer collaboration with a variety of agencies working overseas.[15]

1990s

In 1991, IVS co-directors proposed a new programmatic thrust—education in American schools, colleges, churches, and community groups about the realities of economic development abroad.[16] This does not seem to have taken off, but their overall priority was to emphasize volunteerism and enhance IVS's reputation as a leader in small-scale development.[17] IVS seemed to be groping for a new operating strategy. Concern that IVS needed to set new directions and develop new strategies to respond to the poor and exploited stemmed from a feeling that the previous 40 years of development programs had not diminished the numbers of poor, exploited, and hungry people in the world. IVS felt the need to speak louder as an advocate for people in the economically developing world.[18,19]

STRUCTURE AND LEADERSHIP

IVS was established as a registered tax-exempt status (501(c)(3) organization with an IVS board of directors, board executive committee, and an IVS office headed by an executive director and other staff as needed. The Board and its Executive Committee were to oversee the IVS programs and institution. Typically, board members met twice annually and served defined terms. The number of board members at any given time varied. For the most part, the organizational structure served well and remained stable throughout the life of the organization. Within this structure, management effectiveness and staff numbers varied, as did budget levels.

The Executive Director was responsible to the board for operations, management of programs and the institution's assets. For the most part, the IVS office operated on a low-cost basis and drew heavily on volunteer efforts. The executive director and the Washington office coordinated work of committees and volunteers and expanded or contracted as program needs dictated.[20] Until 1959, the Washington office had only the Executive Director and one secretary.[21] In 1976, the IVS Washington office had 18 staff members, but by the late 1990s, there was only the Executive Director.

Each IVS overseas office was registered in the country in which it worked and was organized uniquely depending on the needs of the program, the level of development of the NGO community in the country, and the history of IVS involvement. Country offices were accountable to the Washington office, which arranged audits, monitored reporting, and to varying degrees, assisted with program development and implementation. Country offices came to follow two basic organizational models. (1) The "direct implementation" model had an independent IVS office in a country. (2) The "partner NGO" model had IVS working through partner NGOs. The latter became the preferred approach as local organizations developed in many countries. Under the partnership model, the head of a local NGO might serve as IVS Country Representative (e.g., in Indochina) or IVS might recruit an individual to serve as Country Director (e.g., in Bolivia and Ecuador).[22]

IVS also established a European office in Luxembourg in 1977 to boost recruitment and fundraising from European countries.[23] With this, IVS established a special European Advisory Council to advise on engagement with European organizations, recruitment of volunteers, and organizational policies.[24] By 1979, with a network of

European contacts established, the IVS office in Luxembourg closed. The office was planned for one year but was extended for a second year because of progress made.

During its fifty years, IVS had thirteen different executive directors as listed in Appendix B. Two directors served for eight years each providing institutional stability. However, many served less than three years affecting long-term institutional continuity. Until the Harper's Ferry redirection, the IVS Executive Director focused on managing the funding relationship with ICA/USAID, new project opportunities, and staffing and placing volunteers in on-going projects. New directions after 1971 added challenges for subsequent executive directors.

After 1989, IVS entered a period of instability in executive directorships. David Smock served little more than a year before leaving for the U.S. Institute of Peace. Suzanne Stafford, an IVS Board member, then served as Interim Executive Director until Don Luce and Linda Worthington were named co-directors. Both agreed to work full-time on substantially reduced salaries. Lack of role definition and personality differences made this relationship ineffective and had a demoralizing effect on the organization.[25] In May 1993, Linda resigned, and Don continued as executive director. He was succeeded by Parker F. Hallberg who served one year as Executive Director *pro tem*[26] before Anne Shirk assumed the position and served until the end in 2002, often with partial or no salary.

The IVS Board of Directors was quite stable with low turnover of members. As of 1956, officers and board members were from the top echelon of the following eleven denominational groups: Baptist, Brethren, Catholic, Christian, Episcopalian, Lutheran, Mennonite, Methodist, Mormon, Presbyterian, and Society of Friends.[27] Most came with sound experience. Seven members of the first Board of Directors had combined overseas experience exceeding 150 years.[28] After 1972, the number of board members ranged from 30 to 39 but dropped to 21 after 1996-1997. Board members included former IVS volunteers, academics, church leaders, and other prominent individuals, including some foreign members. In later years, the percentage of ex-volunteers increased considerably. The Board was always short on corporate or foundation representations. Board chairmen are listed in Appendix C.

For most of its life, the IVS Board maintained an Executive Committee to expedite operations. Representatives from the Peace Churches provided continuity and active oversight to IVS over its initial years. There is little information on the Executive Committee in the 1960s, but from 1971 to 2002, it had between seven and fourteen members. In the 1980s, chairpersons were from government or foreign affairs backgrounds and in the 1990s were IVS volunteer alumni. Executive Committee chairs are listed in Appendix C.

When the IVS Board appointed Parker Hallberg as executive director in September 1996, he took the helm of an organization in a precarious financial condition. At the time of his appointment, there were twenty board members. Nearly half of them were former IVS volunteers who had served in Vietnam or Laos—illustrating a trend to appoint board members and executive directors from within the IVS community, as opposed to more prominent individuals from national leadership positions. This may have been an attempt to draw on the commitment and enthusiasm of IVSers for the organization's volunteer ethic, or it may have been that a declining program and institutional visibility made such positions less attractive to others. Whatever the reason, the lack of nationally prominent individuals in IVS leadership positions compromised its ability to engage other institutions and raise needed resources to support programs in the 1990s.

Program Initiatives And Performance

IVS's initial programs of the 1950s and 1960s focused on rural or community development and worked in conjunction with the ICA/USAID missions. Program development depended on visiting ICA/USAID country missions to jointly design projects. Projects were not rigorously evaluated, but press reports and reviews tended to be positive toward IVS activities. After the establishment of Peace Corps programs in many USAID countries, IVS found that it was harder to "sell" its services because Peace Corps volunteers were available at no cost.

Beginning in the 1970s, USAID had become more of a contracting agency reliant on partners for implementing projects and had become a more-cumbersome bureaucracy.[29] An Office of Private and Voluntary Cooperation (PVC) in Washington was the point-of-contact and funding office for IVS and other NGOs. New mechanisms and administrative procedures facilitated the Private Voluntary Organization (PVO)-USAID partnership, encouraging expansion in the number of NGOs registered with USAID from 82 in 1970 to 441 in 2000.[30] Grants from the PVC office became the driver of IVS activities and entre into activities at the country level. Funding directly from country missions continued, and, in 1974, IVS had grants from USAID Missions in Bangladesh, Yemen, Botswana, and the Sudan.[31]

The 1974 USAID-funded General Support Grant provided $600,000 a year—$450,000 for up to 80 volunteers and field staff in less-developed countries and $150,000/year for two or three new integrated rural development projects. The grant required a matching contribution from private and host country sources, provided for strengthening IVS recruiting capabilities and volunteer support, project design, and program reporting and evaluation.[32] This central funding was most welcomed, but in enabling IVS to operate more independently, reduced its responsiveness and relevance to country USAID missions.

A 1979 evaluation by Cleo F. Shook concluded that the PVC grant, IVS's organization to utilize grant resources, and projects selected for volunteer placement were all well designed and met the stated goals of both USAID and IVS. The evaluation was quite positive, concluding that "both the letter and the spirit" of the intent of the grants were diligently carried out by IVS and that the impact of IVS-style volunteer projects was long lasting and extremely helpful.[33]

By the end of 1981, IVS had the management team and procedures in place, as well as the attendant overhead, for a program half again as large as it was at the time. Twenty-five volunteers were serving in programs focused on institutional development under 17 different projects in seven countries (Bangladesh, Bolivia, Botswana, Ecuador, Honduras, Papua New Guinea, and the Sudan) and were backed up by seven expatriate field staff. This was a very dispersed global program with few volunteers. There was a clear consensus on the urgent need for expansion by both field and Washington staff. The evaluation strongly recommended that close attention be paid to this expansion if USAID provided additional funds for IVS.[34]

Nan Borton, who was appointed executive director in 1981, believed that only through program growth would IVS be able to realize its potential in the most cost-effective manner.[35] By 1983, the number of IVS volunteers doubled. However, program exploration in new countries and increasing numbers of volunteers required more money.[36] The new Caribbean regional program exemplified the increased demands on IVS/Washington. The required multi-disciplinary West Indian technical assistance team challenged IVS's ability to recruit, screen, and place specialists with Caribbean organizations capable of sharing their skills equitably and efficiently.[37]

A 1985 USAID study of private voluntary organization effectiveness sought to develop indicators for institutional effectiveness and to assess the efficacy of different types of assistance for institutional strengthening. With 25 volunteers in nine countries, IVS cooperated in the study. The study found that projects had little or no impact on the effectiveness of institutions to which volunteers were assigned, but it noted that volunteers had greater impact on institutions other than those to which they were formally assigned.[38] There were three reasons for lack of IVS impact on indigenous institutions. (1) Most volunteers were engaged in project-oriented assistance rather than institutional development. (2) Volunteer work was aimed at delivering a service or product rather than at transferring the ability to deliver the service or product. (3) Most organizations to which the volunteers were assigned were large and well established, thus reducing influence of an individual volunteer.[39] These findings did not bode well for future IVS funding.

At that time, IVS volunteers were engaged primarily in assisting existing organizations rather than promoting the establishment of new organizations. Most volunteers were skilled technicians whose terms of reference were to improve the technical proficiency of their host organizations rather than their managerial or organizational needs. When the volunteers were effective (as most of them were), evidence of an increase in the technical capacity of the host organization was observable. However, the volunteers rarely had a mandate to work on larger policy or management questions in their organizations.[40]

In 1986, IVS had programs in fourteen countries. Many new ventures were in collaboration with other agencies, including Africare in Ethiopia, the Methodist Church in Zaire, and La Buena Fe and Project Global Village in Honduras.[41] Taking on new activities jointly with another agency made good economic and development sense. Decentralizing operations by experimenting with regional field management also led to a smaller Washington staff for support to overseas activities.[42] By 1987, IVS regional recruitment efforts led to 65 percent of all field staff, volunteers, and country directors being from the developing world.

An IVS 35th Anniversary booklet in 1988 suggested new directional thinking for IVS, noting that "the rural poor must increasingly turn to themselves, to grassroots groups and local organizations of which they are members, for answers. The lack of skills and resources which limit individuals also limits their organizations. IVS is convinced that by helping to make these organizations more effective, more responsive to local needs, and more self-reliant, it can have the most significant and most lasting impact on the lives of the rural poor."[43] In 1988, Executive Director BORTON reviewed her achievements during her final days as executive director in a memo to the IVS Board of Directors:

> I am proud of the accomplishments of IVS over the past several years. . . . I am proud that almost three-quarters of our volunteers now come from the developing world themselves. I think it is admirable that IVS works only through local organizations—that we are not just another service delivery, welfare-oriented agency, but one genuinely trying to establish equal relationships with our partner agencies. I think it is remarkable that we have doubled our impact, despite our funding problems, by finding more efficient ways of providing technical assistance to an ever-increasing number of partner organizations. We now have a clear mission statement—strengthening local organizations.[44]

IVS had evolved from directly providing service to communities to strengthening local organizations to provide such services. An approach that grew out of this was the establishment or spin-off of local voluntary organizations, including IVS-Bolivia, IVS-Bangladesh, Minga in Ecuador, and the Caribbean Advisory and Professional Services (CAPS) in the Caribbean. Unfortunately, none of these took root. They failed due to a lack of sustainable funding and, perhaps, a weak understanding or commitment to volunteerism.

In 1988, PVC funded a five-year IVS project to strengthen capacities of local institutions with the intent of solving development problems in increasingly self-reliant ways. The project covered Bangladesh, Bolivia, Ecuador, the Eastern Caribbean, Zimbabwe, and Botswana with some regional activities in Southern Africa.[45] Then, in 1991, a mid-term project evaluation by Gordon Applebee concluded that the situation of IVS was precarious. The organization lacked strong leadership and had lost part of its original constituency. IVS had raised only 70 percent of its required private sector matching funds required by USAID. This led to a significant downsizing of headquarters staff and a decline in the IVS program. Some country programs had been eliminated, and those remaining were largely in a holding pattern.[46] The evaluation concluded that IVS must clearly define a vision of its role in the 1990s and beyond. It suggested that IVS focus its resources on pioneering a model program of indigenous volunteer services which would imply greater delegation of authority to field offices and provide IVS experience for similar work in the future.[47]

An additional question was, "How effective is IVS/Washington in technical support to project design and implementation?" With the initial rural projects of the 1950s, it soon became evident that more strategic approaches were needed with more guidance for volunteers. To this end in 1959, IVS hired Daniel Russell, a sociologist, as Field Director to provide technical guidance to programs and share lessons across countries.[48] There is little documentation of the impact from this, but Russell appears to have strengthened design and planning for IVS activities. Later on, Executive Director David Smock wrote a paper entitled "IVS Experience with Rural Development: Some Comparative Reflections."[49] There were some other attempts to provide technical support to country programs, as with the HIV/AIDS work in Southeast Asia and organizational capacity development strategies for cooperatives and other local groups across countries. Generally, it appears that programs were too diverse and funding too restricted to enable IVS/Washington to provide significant technical support to country programs.

The 1991 Applebee evaluation clearly indicated that IVS was in a fragile position.

Funding

IVS always had some private support, but from its beginning IVS relied heavily on ICA/USAID funding. When founded in 1953, IVS appeared to be designed to supplement government foreign assistance efforts by providing technical assistance from experienced and altruistic volunteers. Until 1973, IVS relations with ICA/USAID were largely through service contracts with regional or country offices. Under IVS contracts, volunteers filled positions in AID-planned programs in a specific country.[50]

Though records are incomplete, available archival data indicate that ICA/USAID funds accounted for about 92 percent of IVS's total funding up to 1960. The share in the 1960s and early 1970s would likely be similar. From 1976 to 1993, the USAID share was about 48 percent, a share that tracks with the USAID 50 percent match requirement. Some of the non-USAID funding would have been imputed as in-kind contributions from beneficiaries and volunteers.

The table below lists all known USAID funding for IVS. It does not include significant USAID funding that came to IVS through third party sub-awards.

Table: ICA and USAID Funding for IVS Programs

Start Year	End Year	Program	Agreement	USG Funding
1953	1957	Iraq	(not known)	140,000
1956	1958	Nepal	(not known)	42,035
1956	1959	Laos: Rural Development	ICA-W-105-2	152,820
1956	1975	Vietnam	ICA-235-7	2,217,162
1959	1969	Laos—Education	AID-c-1110-7	978,793
1960	1963	Liberia	ICA	695,000
1961	1969	Laos: Rural Development	ICA-c-1756-RDD	1,699,976
1964	1966	Algeria	AID/afe 133	450,000
1964	1966	Algeria—Tefeschaun (Dept of State)	(not known)	24,920
1970	1974	Congo (Zaire)	(not known)	703,665
1970	1975	Laos-Training & RD	AID/ea-89-Laos	1,764,315
1973	1977	OPG-Yemen	AID/ASIA-C-1056	29,935

1973	1978	OPG-Bangladesh	AID/CM/PHA/G-73	659,019
1974	1978	Institutional Support Grant	AID/PHA-G-1099	240,000
1974	1981	Institutional Support Grant	AID/PHA-G-1065	1,300,000
1975	1978	OPG-Bangladesh-TAG	AID/ASIA-C-1154	42,334
1975	1978	OPG-Botswana	AIDAFR-G-1161	145,267
1975	1980	OPG-Bangladesh-FIVDB	AID/NESA-G-1176	366,265
1976	1978	Institutional Support-Conference	AID/PHA-G-1140	99,392
1976	1979	OPG-Sudan—Agriculture	AID/AFR-G-1214	155,696
1976	1979	OPG-Yemen—Agriculture	AID/NE-C-1266	151,521
1978	1983	OPG-Botswana–Horticulture	78-633-30	363,030
1979	1983	OPG-Sudan—Wadi Haifa	650-0026	511,035
1979	1983	OPG-Sudan-Yambio	650-0035	994,276
1982	1985	Matching Grant	PDC-0236-G-SS-0276	2,415,000
1985	1988	Matching Grant	PDC-0260-G-SS-5069	2,250,000
1995	1997	Matching Grant	FAO-0158-G-00-5039	200,000
1988	1993	Cooperative Agreement	OTR-0158-A-00-8156	3,000,000
Total				21,791,456

Source: Authors' compilation from archival materials

The Harper's Ferry decision to reduce dependency on government funding was a game changer that would have a lasting impact on IVS's future development and growth. The Board and staff stated "we commit ourselves…to working in the 70's toward financial independence of the organization through multi-funding sources. Specifically, we aim towards 51 percent of our total funding from sources other than the U.S. Government. We are well aware of the enormous problems implied in this commitment, but we will try."[51] At that time, U.S. Government contracts and grants accounted for approximately 95 percent of the total IVS budget.[52] For the future, funding was to be a perennial problem.

In the next five years, IVS hoped to cover its budget with 50 percent from the U.S. Government (e.g., USAID, Peace Corps, Cultural Affairs), 25 percent from host country sources, and 25 percent from combined sources including churches, corporations, foundations, youth groups, IVS alumni, and a broader constituency. The latter target of 25 percent was further broken down by source: 30 percent from corporations, 30 percent from foundations, 15 percent from youth, 15 percent from churches, and 10 percent from alumni and a broader constituency.[53]

The IVS program director was doubtful that the 50 percent private funding ratio could be reached by 1975 and suggested that IVS place two full-time fund-raisers operating within the United States and consider a fundraising position overseas.[54] This was necessary even though USAID was now willing to fund IVS projects with less strings attached—i.e., grants rather than contracts. The Board also recognized that greater fund raising from both public and private sources was necessary and would require adding special staff, strengthening board membership, cultivating alumni, and possibly engaging in cooperative efforts with similar organizations.[55]

IVS saw the need to be sufficiently large to be taken seriously as a development organization. This would require recruiting and retaining good staff enabling more people to be aware of its existence. Thus, a decision was made to increase the volunteer number to between 500 and 1000 by 1976.[56] This however led the IVS program director to point out that "the major problem...in terms of that kind of expansion, is the lack of availability of funds, and without the funds, we'll never get anywhere near projected sizes..."[57] Executive Director Dick Peters observed in 1974 that "while IVS has accomplished a significant metamorphosis over the past four years because it had to, there still remains the question of true viability." He went on to say "the questions for the future of IVS are many. Who is going to pay? But before asking that, perhaps the first question is what will the future function of IVS be? Will it function as a source of highly motivated and technologically competent volunteers or will its primary function be to expose American youth to the ways of other countries. Both have their value but can both goals be satisfied in one organization?"[58]

IVS began to secure substantial funding from organizations such as PACT (Private Agencies Collaborating Together), CODEL (Coordination in Development), and Appropriate Technology International which received their funding largely from USAID. Although USAID was the source of these funds, IVS regarded this as private funding since IVS's agreements were with the non-governmental project screening committees of these intermediate organizations. In fiscal year 1979, IVS funding from such sources was some $170,000.[59]

After the 1970s, USAID funding for IVS was of two types: "Operating Program Grants" (OPGs) for country-specific projects, and General Support Grants (GSG) for IVS's discretionary work in any USAID-supported country.[60] USAID grant funds could be combined with private funds to cover both field costs and IVS/Washington costs. A General Support Grant funding in 1974 allowed IVS to inaugurate a new approach—placing volunteers in priority assignments identified by host country institutions.[61] A 1975 Development Grant (DPG) further strengthened IVS's project design, management, and evaluation capability, thus enabling IVS to obtain OPGs from USAID Missions in Bangladesh, Yemen, Botswana, and the Sudan.[62]

Money continued to be a constant concern and created pressures and constraints affecting choices, pace, and direction of growth.[63] A 1981 evaluation found that IVS had a 1979 deficit of $465,000, which had been resolved with tighter fiscal control by improved IVS/Washington management.[64]

Assuming office in 1981, Executive Director Borton saw that IVS needed to be more cost-effective and attractive to donors and committed to increasing volunteer numbers by 400 percent within two years. This would improve the ratio between administrative overhead and program expenditures.[65] A 1982 USAID Matching Grant provided up to $750,000 per year, but required IVS to match each grant dollar with a private dollar—a new concept for both USAID and IVS.[66]

IVS funding continued to diversify, but most donations were country-specific, or even project-specific, including most non-governmental funding. Unrestricted or discretionary funds were very limited. For all its efforts, IVS was unable to tap any large source of non-governmental unrestricted funds.[67] During 1984, IVS approached 130 corporations and foundations. Many of these potential donors expressed general interest in IVS programs world-wide, but still no major funding came of the effort.[68]

Funding problems became more serious in 1987, when USAID funding was reduced and revenue from private sources decreased. Program activities were curtailed, thus increasing IVS's overhead ratio. Some traditional donors, primarily interested in "service delivery", were reluctant to support IVS projects which had become more focused on local organization strengthening. In addition, institutional funders were typically reluctant to support Washington overhead costs, even at IVS's very modest rate of 19.8 percent in 1997. Consequently, IVS had to rely almost entirely on unrestricted individual donations to cover these necessary expenses. While IVS's list of donors grew, it received less total private funding that was not project specific.[69] In 1988, Executive Director Borton pointed out that "once again, IVS is seriously strapped for money—strapped to an extent which not only prohibits growth, but means a much smaller field presence, unless we can turn things around."[70]

1988 and the following five years proved to be challenging for IVS fund raising efforts. Changing priorities of many traditional donors created an extremely competitive funding climate in the private voluntary sector. Donor trends included: a more direct funding link to indigenous organizations; focus on AIDS and the elderly; and geographical shifts to China, the Soviet Union, and Eastern Europe.[71] Church funding traditionally was 20-30 percent of IVS's annual revenue, but, in the late 1980s, church giving and subsequent grant making for international development declined. This trend in church giving mirrored patterns in international grant making by other private donor corporations and foundations and increased IVS's difficulty in meeting the fund-matching requirements of USAID grants.[72] Since USAID funds could not be used for fundraising, IVS had to draw on scarce unrestricted private funds for this.[73] The IVS 1993-94 Annual Report indicated that the 1993 funding of $1.1 million U.S. dollars had been supported by 288 individual donors and 35 institutional donors. This impressive number of supporters still yielded fairly modest total support.[74]

IVS accessed some non-restrictive private funding for other programs outside the matching grant, but both USAID and private funding were difficult to obtain for regional activities. Since the scale of mission projects was often too great for IVS to undertake alone, IVS began collaborating with other U.S. PVOs to carry out mission-funded projects, as in Bangladesh and Bolivia. Essentially, IVS sought USAID funding as a sub-grantee to other organizations.[75]

A 1993 "IVS Report to AID" recognized that attitudes in the United States toward economic assistance internationally were at an all-time low, and the effectiveness of economic assistance was being seriously questioned. The end of the Cold War decreased importance of "winning hearts and minds". Money sources switched attention to domestic problems—floods, teenage violence, homelessness. It was harder for a church or other donors to become involved in international work when there was a soup line of homeless people at the back door.[76] Funding opportunities for IVS had tightened up in many ways.

End Game

By the late 1980s and early 1990s, IVS was in trouble. There were questions as to its organizational strategy, its program effectiveness, and its financial viability. This was all highlighted in evaluations of USAID-funded programs. A 1993 Final Evaluation by Shirley Buzzard of IVS's on-going Cooperative Agreement undertook to assess progress in resolving problems identified during a mid-term evaluation.[77] It found that those problems had not been addressed, and the fund-raising strategy had been ineffective.[78]

The evaluation found IVS's situation to be precarious due to a lack of leadership and dwindling financial resources.[79] Evaluators discovered that IVS kept few records: reports were insubstantial; and there was no established management or project monitoring system. Although interviews suggested that many activities had been highly successful and a few had dramatic impact, most of this was undocumented.[80]

The evaluation found that IVS headquarter management suffered from serious leadership problems. There had been long periods without an executive director, and those filling the role did not stay long or suffered from health problems that limited their effectiveness. Many activities described in the initial project proposal were never undertaken. IVS had been unable to meet its required match of USAID funds, and there was a concomitant decrease in the level of program activity. The number of volunteers fell short of the number projected largely because of IVS's inability to raise matching funds.[81] IVS's program had shrunk to just Bolivia, Ecuador, Bangladesh, Zimbabwe, and a small privately funded HIV/AIDS education in Thailand and Vietnam.[82]

IVS Board Chairman Hugh Manke responded to the Buzzard draft evaluation, noting that "In the past year, the IVS board and staff have been engaged in a kind of 'shock therapy' to adjust to the phasing out of USAID support, consolidating programs, and trimming staff and administrative costs to a point that is frankly unsustainable if we are to continue to meet the needs of the people with whom we now work in participatory grassroots development programs…."[83]

The net result was that for the first time in 40 years IVS was going to be without USAID funding.[84] How could IVS best continue to serve developing communities in their fights against poverty? With no USAID grant, IVS would be challenged to raise an additional $500,000 to continue current programs.[85] Then, in 1995, the USAID PVC office relented and awarded IVS a $200,000 matching grant to strengthen monitoring and evaluation, financial management, and project development.[86] At that time, IVS had 100 local and regional volunteers in seven countries (Bangladesh, Bolivia, Cambodia, Ecuador, Thailand, the United States, and Vietnam).[87]

Another initiative to revitalize IVS came in 1996. A strategic alliance with PACT, a larger development organization with which IVS had worked in the past, was supported by a USAID grant to PACT. This certainly showed evidence of USAID willingness to go the extra mile in attempting to help IVS survive. While IVS and PACT would remain separate entities, each with its own governing board, the Alliance would draw on their complementary strengths to mutual benefit. IVS brought its expertise in volunteer programs, and PACT provided an extensive network of country programs working to build civil societies and democratic institutions around the world. The arrangement provided IVS with the space and administrative support needed to maintain a Washington staff at a bare minimum (a volunteer executive director, part-time intern, and program officer funded by PACT). The Alliance's specific objective was to establish national volunteer programs in selected countries, focusing initially on Bolivia and Ecuador, where IVS had on-going activities.[88] The initial response to the alliance was overwhelmingly positive, not only within the IVS family but also among potential major funders.

Regrettably, the IVS/PACT Alliance didn't work out. As with any merger or alliance, personalities became an issue, and organizational cultures were difficult to mesh.[89] More importantly, new USAID funding did not become available as anticipated, and PACT concluded that the national volunteer program idea was not gaining traction with funders. In late 1998, the decision was made to end the alliance, and the two organizations quietly went their own ways. This left the IVS financial situation very tenuous, and closure began to be discussed. With lack of funding for Washington office administration, IVS found it impossible (and unethical) to approach major donors for country project funding.[90]

In 1998, two IVS reunions sparked discussion of a new course of action for IVS. The following year, in 1999, the IVS Board decided to resume placing U.S. volunteers overseas in a flexible new program designed to fit the needs of host institutions and volunteers. Experienced Americans with relevant skills would be placed mainly in short assignments of two to six months. Volunteers would be self-financed by tax-deductible donations to IVS to cover assignment costs. The program began in June 2000 with the departure of two American volunteers to Vietnam.[91] These were the only volunteers under the program.

Belatedly, an "IVS Program Development Sub-Committee" composed of IVS alumni was established in 2000 to advance both the new self-financed volunteer program and other development activities. Aggressive program development efforts were to draw on IVS alumni for program development and support.[92] Then, in 2000, an audit raised concerns about the viability of IVS as a corporation noting, "IVS has suffered significant reductions in revenues that raise substantial doubt about its ability to continue as a going concern." Such a statement would make potential funders further reluctant to support IVS.[93]

In another late initiative in 2001, the Development Committee Chair Steve Nichols announced that a former IVS volunteer had pledged $50,000 toward an endowment fund to support the new IVS volunteer program. The donor challenged IVS alumni and friends to raise an endowment of $500,000 within the next two and a half years. Though raising that level of funds was a daunting task, there was some confidence the goal could be met.[94] Another note of optimism came in conversations with Volunteers in Asia (VIA) indicating that they would be pleased to resume work with IVS as they had in the 1960s.[95]

Still, the Board of Directors realized that "the real issue is that IVS has to have an on-going program in order to seek funds. Now there is almost nothing left of a program, which means IVS has very little legitimacy. The new IVS Volunteer Program is the main focus, but many other competing, well-established groups are also doing this kind of program. IVS is not unique." To continue operations, IVS would require sufficient funding committed or in hand to cover about $200,000 per annum for Washington operations for subsequent two years.[96]

The IVS Program Development Committee indicated that there was a great deal of interest in the work done by IVS, but with no funds for significant program development it was difficult to follow up. To become relatively stable, IVS would need programs of about $600,000 per year, generating $100,000-$120,000 in overhead for IVS/Washington operations.[97] However, fund-raising prospects were discouraging. Trickle Up Foundation, Readers' Digest Foundation, the InterAmerican Development Foundation, UMCOR, and Church World Services all stopped, reduced, or delayed funding. Individual contributions were low.[98]

The IVS Endowment Fund's initial goal of $500,000 by 2003 was a long way from being met and was perhaps unrealistic at a time when operating funds were top priority. At least $50,000 in unrestricted funding was needed as part of a $150,000-$200,000 yearly budget. USAID funding could be part of any IVS budget, but USAID was no longer giving institutional strengthening grants.[99]

During the November 17, 2001, board meeting, Executive Director ANNE SHIRK was instructed to develop and carry out a plan for winding down the organization. IVS was to be kept active until March 31, 2002, so that Ecuador and Bangladesh projects could receive payments for on-going activities and transition to national NGO status. The few remaining assets were transferred to those country programs. This final board meeting produced a resolution stating:

> IVS has enjoyed a rich and successful history of nearly half a century, contributing to human progress through volunteer action in over forty countries around the

world and serving as a catalyst to the creation of other voluntary movements and to the U.S. Peace Corps. In recent years, after exhaustive surveys of funding opportunities, IVS has concluded that the necessary resources are not forthcoming to meaningfully continue its mission. Therefore, with the deepest regret, accompanied by many rewarding and fond memories, the Board of Directors hereby decides to dissolve the IVS corporation effective January 31, 2002.[100]

On November 30, 2001, Board Chairman Jeanette Goodstein and Vice-Chairman Stephen Nichols announced in a memo that "it is with enormous sadness, tempered by equally enormous appreciation for all that International Voluntary Services has accomplished over its nearly half century of existence, that we write to inform you of the Board's decision this week to dissolve IVS by the end of March 2002."[101]

Final Note

Reviewing the course of IVS's fifty-year lifespan in a comprehensive case study encounters challenges in effectively analyzing the management approaches to secure domestic and international cooperation and to shed light on how IVS evolved as the political, economic, and business environments changed around it. IVS faced wide-ranging situations in its worldwide cooperation with diverse collaborating institutions. The 1971 turning point in the history of IVS forced it to confront a broad canvas of complexities over its final thirty years.

Like all organizations, IVS's success depended largely on its administration and management, both of which experienced challenges ranging from relationships with USAID and other donors to its collaboration arrangements with host organizations. Key elements were the leadership's ability to engage in strategic thinking and planning, nourish talent and motivate staff, and orient resources toward the achievement of mutual objectives. Readers can measure the performance of IVS through both successes and failures it experienced over the years.

The end was not entirely surprising. The minutes of a September 8, 1958, Executive Committee meeting reported on comments by E. N. Holmgreen, ICA Director, Office of Food and Agriculture, noted that, "voluntary agencies are vitally important and that they are the only agencies which can make people-to-people programs become a reality." He suggested that, "it would be very dangerous for IVS to devote its entire program to projects financed by the government." The minutes reported E.N. Holmgreen's comments to the effect that he was:

> . . .a strong believer that any program which is built on a sound, strong foundation has nothing to fear. If IVS has a program which really produces, it need not worry about contract renewals. There will always be required the formality of IVS submitting requests for contract extensions each year.

The danger of IVS not having a supporting constituency to rely upon in the event that government funds become unavailable was discussed by various Committee members. It was pointed out that IVS is an organization formed to implement an idea and bas no constituency in the normal sense from which dues could be collected. It was expressed that IVS can make a vital contribution in underdeveloped countries at the grassroots level, but there is a strong possibility that IVS will eventually die if it has to fight continuously for government money to finance it.[102]

Why did IVS close? There is a simple answer and a more complex one. Simply, IVS funding dried up and it had to close. Why the funding ended is more complex, involving issues of changing development needs, complicated governmental bureaucracy, management mis-steps, and strategy weaknesses.

Figure 1. IRAQ: Volunteer Carl Jantzen with a seed cleaner introduced to clean and treat grain seed to prevent yield loss and grain damage from black smut, circa 1955 [Photo Don Mitchell collection.]

Figure 2. ZIMBABWE: Volunteer Agriculturalist Eduard Ajusto (Philippines) in white cap with workers admiring bales of cotton from a harvest at Chakeoma Co-op Farm c. 1985. [Photo: by Martin de Groot in Mennonite Church USA Archives.]

Figure 3. CAMBODIA: Wayne Lepori, volunteer from Harwood, Texas on a new bridge built across the Stung Keo (Jeweled River) as part of a settlement project to open land for crops. c. 1962. [Photo: Mennonite Church USA Archives.]

Figure 4. LAOS: Lao Buddhist monks in Phone Hong hitch a ride on an IVS jeep driven by rural development volunteer, c. 1965. [Photo by Ken Wong: Mennonite Church USA Archives.]

Figure 5. LAOS: Volunteer Carole Falk with Lao Government counterpart teaching a home economics class in Savannakhet c. 1964. (Photo: Mennonite Church USA Archives]

Figure 6. LAOS: Susan Robbins, Practical Nursing Trainer, with student nurses in Thakek ready for rounds of nearby villages as part of the public health program in collaboration with USAID and the Colombo Plan, c. 1967. [Photo: Mennonite Church USA Archives]

Figure 7. VIETNAM: Volunteer Amal Chatterjee (India) with farmer in Tay Ninh Province examining attributes of IR-8 rice from an experimental plot c. 1968 [Photo: Mennonite Church USA Archives.]

Figure 8. SUDAN: Penny Hoag, psychology and child education teacher at Ahfad University College for Women in public health education class in Omdurman in 1974. [Photo: Mennonite Church USA archives.]

Figure 9. SUDAN: IVS Director John Rigby on a field visit to workers at a self-help community water system project in 1979. [Photo: Mennonite Church USA archives.]

Figure 10. YEMEN: Christine Anell, IVS public health nurse, assisted by counterpart Wala, teaching baby bottle hygiene to mothers in Sana'a in 1978. [Photo: Mennonite Church USA archives.]

ADMINISTRATION CHALLENGES: Running A Nonprofit NGO   207

Figure 11. BANGLADESH: Abdul Matin, IVS/Bangladesh Country Administrator, presenting pin to Kamini Bala IVS Village Volunteer in bamboo technology in Dinajpur in early 1990s. [Photo: Mennonite Church USA Archives.]

Figure 12. BOLIVIA: IVS volunteer attending Cemur Mothers club event c. 1988. [Photo: Mennonite Church USA Archives.]

Figure 13. ECUADOR: IVS Volunteer Bandu Abeywickrama (Sri Lanka) in carpentry class for Association Indigena Evangelista del Napa (AIEN) vocational skills training program, c. 1975. [Photo: Mennonite Church USA Archives.]

Figure 14. ECUADOR: Volunteer veterinarian Carlos Munoz, (Chile) with improved dairy cow for livestock improvement program, late 1980s. [Photo: Mennonite Church USA Archives]

ADMINISTRATION CHALLENGES: Running A Nonprofit NGO   209

Figure 15. ECUADOR: David Smock, IVS Executive Director, visiting producer group with improved guinea pigs under the Association of Independent Farmers' Organizations of Chimborazo Province in 1989. [Photo: Mennonite Church USA Archives]

Figure 16. HONDURAS: Volunteer Nurse Carol Castillo with a patient in front of village clinic. [Photo: Mennonite Church USA Archives.]

Figure 17. PAPUA NEW GUINEA: Volunteer Engineer Ed Arata with Pelton wheel for micro-hydro-electric generator developed by the Appropriate Technology Unit of the University of Technology in Lae. [Photo: by Mimi Arata in Mennonite Church USA Archives.]

SECTION II
Volunteer Experiences And Impacts

7

VOLUNTEERS
OUT OF THEIR COMFORT ZONE

GARY ALEX WITH VOLUNTEER STORIES[1]

IVS was an ambitious experiment: a leap of faith that placed young people in foreign countries and institutions to foster social and economic development. Most initial volunteers were American and recent college graduates. Later, volunteers were recruited from other countries and with greater professional and international experience. In its final years, IVS placed national and regional volunteers to work in their own or familiar culture. This in some ways represented a shift from a volunteer program to a professional recruitment program.

Young graduates, stepping into a new job in a new country, culture, language, and political environment, were going far out of their comfort zone. Whether they realized it or not, culture shock of some sort was inevitable. Most were probably astounded at some local conditions or practices, made culturally inappropriate mistakes, and had problems communicating. This often generated quirky, humorous, and endearing stories of adapting and dealing with a new environment. Many adapted extremely well.

IVS alumni often use the term "naïve" in describing themselves as they started their assignments. In fact, part of the value of volunteers was their naïve belief that things could change for the better. They were catalysts in traditional societies. Change was not easy, but without trying, it was impossible. Most volunteers gained a measure of realism in their expectations and found ways to fit in and thrive in their posts. Some became quite cynical. Many terminated early, but others maintained an optimism and longer-term perspective, choosing to serve multiple assignments.

Assignments put volunteers at risk and forced them to develop a rapport and understanding of a different culture. They often had to take on new responsibilities and become resourceful. Individual initiative was critical to success. And, unsurprisingly, with a young demographic, romances flourished. The following stories illustrate how volunteers coped and adapted in new environments with wide-ranging encounters including risk, rapport, responsibility, resourcefulness, romance, and reflection.[2]

Risks In Life Overseas

Volunteering carried an inherent risk—going to an unknown developing country with unknown living and working conditions. Initially, volunteers were assigned to teams in Iraq, Nepal, Laos, and Vietnam, with a generally older and more experienced chief of party as director. This softened the transition but also tended to isolate the volunteers from the local culture. Tension within teams was not unknown. Later, assignments tended to place volunteers alone in posts, sharpening the isolation and personal responsibility for activities.

Young people are exposed to risks wherever they are. In developing countries, these risks are more daunting—tropical disease, poor infrastructure, crime, and civil war. Sometimes volunteers could exacerbate risk with ill-advised actions. Volunteer DON SUMNER (IVS/Vietnam 1959–61) recounts one such action:[3]

> One night a friend and I decided to explore the jungle behind the Hung Loc Livestock Station. We had seen elephant dung near some tall Napier grass, so we decided to build a treehouse, and sleep there overnight. Our perch was around 25 feet above the ground, and it overlooked a clearing.
>
> After darkness came, we flashed our light around every so often to pick up animal eyes. Shortly after 11 PM we heard a crunching in the grass. We figured it was an elephant, and when we thought he was close enough to be seen, we turned the light on him. It was an old bull and after seeing our light, he crashed out of view into the jungle.
>
> A half hour later the old bull returned and proceeded to smash into pieces the small saw we had left at the base of our tree. Even if he couldn't reach us to tear us out, he might try to shake us down by butting the tree trunk. He crunched one of the two water bottles we had left near the saw. Then he turned his attention to our jeep a few hundred yards away, and he proceeded to smash the top in and push it into the bamboo before wandering back into the jungle. The next morning, we found our jeep battered but functional, and we drove back, still shaking with fear and thankful to be alive and well, to Hung Loc.

Risk was more common in countries at war. Volunteer DAVE COLYER (IVS/Vietnam, 1963–65), a conscientious objector who worked with a Malaria Eradication Team as his alternative service, provided one example.

In November of 1963, Dave and his interpreter, Thanh, who lived in an adjoining building of our IVS station house, drove from our house in Nha Trang to Hue. The vehicle might have been the buff-colored Land Rover belonging to the Malaria Office or the IVS powder-blue Jeep with IVS spelled out on its side in dark pink Vietnamese. On their return trip, they were stopped on a rural dirt road by the VC [Viet Cong]. The spokesman told them, "We know who you are, where you've been, what you do, and where you are going. We advise you to go back exactly the way came; you've already missed three land mines." Dave and Thanh backtracked their route exactly, following the marks of their tires in the dust. When they reached the city, they took a different route home.

Volunteer HARVEY NEESE (IVS/Vietnam 1959–61) may be an extreme in the many dangerous experiences he had in South Vietnam, while a volunteer and later on contract with USAID.

At Ban Me Thuot, I had my first close shave with possible injury or even worse. As I was walking around the hut where we stayed, I saw a bright green snake which looked to me like a common garden snake variety back home. I started playing with the snake by shoving it around with my foot on the ground. It would curl up as if to strike then start its retreat. This went on for a while when I cut short the game as the dinner bell had rung in the form of the cook yelling, 'an com, an com' which in Vietnamese translates into come eat, come eat.

Over the dinner table eating Vietnamese food, I mentioned to the other agriculturists on my team who were taking language training my experience with the pretty green snake. Our Vietnamese language teacher asked me to describe the snake which I did. He then said something that really perked up my ears—that this was the Banana Green snake which has a very dangerous venom. And he emphasized, a person could die from its bite. My first miracle in South Vietnam. . . .

On a tiger and deer hunt near M'drak in the Highlands, I assembled a little platform in a clump of trees to await a wary tiger. My hunting partners dropped me there for the night. I had shot a deer for bait to lure in a tiger. About midnight, I heard the tiger encircling me with his wup, wup, wup sounds. I waited and waited on the little platform. Then the sounds stopped. I then heard what I thought were rain drops, a slight cracking of leaves. Shortly, I found the rain drops were actually a jungle fire heading my way! I was there in the middle of nowhere with no means to make a quick escape. I ran from the jungle fire over tall grassy hills where tigers and snakes abound. Finally, I stopped to rest in tall grass on a hill, when I saw lights of a vehicle moving in my direction. My hunting partners had thought I might be burned alive and hurried out to rescue me.

I had several close calls with airplanes in Vietnam. An Air Vietnam plane I was in had to land with a front tire flat. . . . Another time, I took off from the Nha Trang air strip in a C-47 cargo plane and, as we circled over the South China Sea, one of the two engines stopped working. We pitched all the cargo out the door and the pilot was able to land back at the Nha Trang air strip on one engine. . . .

One day, while walking in Saigon, I saw red lights flashing in the distance. Then a motorcycle raced towards me at a high speed with a police vehicle behind it. A policeman up the street tried to knock the motorcycle over but was thrown aside and the motorcycle kept coming. Another policeman on the street started firing at the motorcycle and its two riders. Bullets landed around me. There was a sewage drainage ditch there that I dove down into as the motorcycle sped past with bullets hitting around me. Finally, I could climb out of the sewage ditch unharmed but a bit on the smelly side.

Volunteer JOHN ESSER, reflecting on his time in Laos, remembers much of the culture and some fear.

Fear is one of those memories I have from Laos that stick in my mind after 55 years, but not the overwhelming one. That would be the feeling of adventure, excitement and learning that some people have a different way of life and it's not wrong. Still, a memory of fear is in the back of my mind when I recall my almost two years working with IVS in Laos. Do other volunteers still carry a bit of fear in their memories from their time in Laos working for IVS?

The dangers faced by volunteers were real. Eleven died during their service, nine due to hostile action in Laos and Vietnam. Health risks were common and not fully documented. Even those who survived could be affected for life, as happened with Albert Holloway, who came down with polio in Iraq, and Frank Welsh, who was crippled in a motorcycle accident in Indonesia.

Rapport With Different Cultures

Volunteers nearly always gained an appreciation and understanding of the different cultures they worked in. These played out in many ways based on individual experiences.

Volunteer DIANE FOX (IVS/Algeria 1969-70) describes stories from Algeria that condition how she felt when hearing negative talk about Islam in the 2010s:

One year into our one-and-a-half-year assignment, our first child was born. What excitement, what joy—and what complications! Khedidja, a strong, warm-hearted Kabylian woman made it possible for me to fulfill my teaching assignment by babysitting the little one she called Benti Hanounti.

In those years, people would sometimes come to our door asking for bread. Despite the 30 percent unemployment and countless war wounded, many "Europeans" we knew warned us against giving anything, cautioning us that many people were merely feigning need, and we would develop a reputation as suckers easily duped.

I can still see the pain mixed with incredulity on Khedidja's face when I asked her what she thought of this. "La, la (no, no)!" she exclaimed, raising both hands in protest. Her Muslim religion taught that it was her responsibility to give to those who ask, she explained. If all she had was one baguette of bread, she would break it and share a portion.

And what if they are not honest, I asked. That was their responsibility, she replied. Her responsibility was to give. Fifty years later, Khedidja remains for me a model. This woman, who lived with her husband and two children in a room that measured 24 square meters, openheartedly gave what she could.

Volunteer WIN MCKEITHEN (IVS/Laos 1962–64) gained an appreciation for a much different culture in the tribal community in which he worked. This was common to many volunteers who worked with minority populations in different countries.

Although I didn't understand it at the time, I later came to appreciate that during my second year in Laos, 1964, I had been living among people in the transition from wandering hunter-gathers to settled agriculturalists. My year on the eastern Bolovens Plateau in southern Laos was spent in a time capsule among late-comers in the Neolithic revolution that began 8-10 thousand years ago.

The people we lived with grew rice in swidden fields mixed with other crops. They hunted game and gathered a bewildering variety of forest products from the watershed they called home. They spoke Mon-Khmer languages, not Lao. Their spiritual practices did not follow organized religions, but invariably involved the ritual consumption of fermented rice brew. And fermentation, I learned later, was a key stimulus of the Neolithic revolution.

One of the first things we did in the fall of 1963 was a general survey of the 44 villages in our area of assignment. One striking finding was that 15 percent of the rice crop was eaten, 20 percent was sold, and 65 percent was fermented and drunk. I say again, sixty-five percent of the rice crop was consumed as an alcoholic brew. But it was not drunk haphazardly, because fermentation represented a spiritual force of nature.

Drinking was often a ritualized contest between two role-players representing good and bad. It was a timed challenge: whoever drank the most during a fixed time —about a minute—won. The drinker who represented positive aspects of life was always victorious. This was never a surprise. After all, the winner was supported by the spiritual power of alcohol. We never saw the bad side win—except when we foreigners tried to role-play and screwed it up, to the horror of our hosts.

After weeks of fermentation, a sealed urn would be opened and topped off with fresh water; a long hollow reed inserted down through the mash; and the sweet liquid siphoned up by each participant. As the concentration of alcohol became more diluted with each refill, the jug became available to the women and adolescents to take their turns. The spent mash was fed to chickens and pigs. Nothing of the rice crop was left to waste. The village pigs were relaxed, and the pork was tender. . .

We were often invited to drink at every hour of the day as an expression of hospitality and friendship. To get anything done, we had to feign a religious belief that banned drink until sunset. . . .

I first returned to visit the Bolovens Plateau ten years ago [about 2010] and visited the abandoned remnants of once-thriving villages we had lived in. I saw derelict "resettlement" dwellings built by the Lao government but never occupied, located far to the west on unproductive land. The grandson of the leader I had known in 1964 spoke wistfully of the old days. Not seeing any fermentation urns for rice brew, I asked him about our finding that 65 percent of the rice crop went into these jugs. "Oh, now it's not even five percent," he said. "We don't do that anymore." What they did instead was work as day laborers and try to survive without a homeland.

I understood then that our year on the Bolovens Plateau had offered us a unique view of the final days of a culture in transition from the Neolithic era. Our hosts had been expert stewards of the environment, practitioners of sustainable swidden agriculture, but dependent on nurturing forests and rivers for survival. And I realized that we in IVS had received the priceless gift of hospitality among people who taught us much more than we could ever conceivably have taught them. I am still in awe.

The increased rapport worked both ways with host country people getting to know volunteers and becoming familiar with American culture and practices. Win McKeithan describes in a note "Getting to Know You, Getting to Know All About You . . ." how local people in Houei Kong were bemused by one American cultural practice.

"But why would anyone want to cut off their foreskin?" the naikong [local mayor] asked.

"Well, they say it's for hygienic reasons," I said, "for cleanliness, but I guess there's some question now with modern medical practices." Naikong Moun, the head of 42 villages on the eastern half of the Bolovens Plateau, was flabbergasted.

"It's also sort of a religious practice in our part of the world," I tried to explain.

The Naikong chuckled roundly behind his glasses, really showing serious doubt about anything I had said for the first time I could remember. He had trouble talking through the huge smile on his face. . . .

I don't know how we got on the subject. But I was sure that it forever changed his impression of us. We had already told him some distinctly strange things.

So it was on the evening of the circumcision discussion that we hailed the naikong up from the path in front of our house to see our latest piece of technological wizardry, a hot shower.

"What is it," he said, shining his flashlight around our kitchen area.

"Just look," I said, "you'll see," proud of our heating apparatus and the luxury of hot showers. I threw open the bathroom to expose the double drum reservoir and heater and the pump we had installed.

But the Naikong had his flashlight focused on a much more interesting object: [Volunteer X]'s foreskin, or rather lack of foreskin. Poor [Volunteer X] froze in place.

"Oooh!" The Naikong was ecstatic. "It's really gone." The Naikong kept his beam on our forestry expert who had been about to relieve himself, but under the circumstances seemed to have lost all voluntary motor control except for a squeak of helplessness.

"What did I do?" [Volunteer X] finally managed. " I'm just standing here trying to take a leak when the naikong shines a light on my dong."

"Amazing," said Naikong Moun, "They really cut it off. "Amazing."

The glow behind his round glasses lit up his face. Our credibility had been restored, confirming that we really were strange people indeed."

Volunteer MAX GOLDENSOHN, former IVS/Laos Country Director in Mauritania in 1975, faced impressive bureaucratic challenges inherent to working in Mauritania, but described his positive impression of the culture in a May 1976 letter:

I will have to start all over again and tell you about Mauritania the way I learned about it myself—through a series of banal incidents that served mostly to tear away the veils I had placed before myself to impede my appreciation of the country in which I live and the people who render it human, charming, fascinating.

"Come in! Come visit! Come with us!" These are the words I have heard more than any others from the mouths of the people of Mauritania. They talk so much about their legendary hospitality that I was very suspicious about its reality before I got to taste it—but it is as real as can be. One of the first days I spent here, knowing no one, feeling rather lost, reveling in self-inflicted solitude, I left the hotel and its brightly lit (and expensive) bar just to take a walk and let myself think a bit. Soon, I found myself wandering in the direction of the Ksar, the site of the original village of a dozen or so huts that was all that existed here before the decision to plant the Capital of independent Mauritania in the middle of the country and on the coast.

A teenager in a boubou was walking along a bit in front of me and was obviously going the same way I was. We began to chat in a very clumsy way — his French was not all that great—and the next thing I knew he was telling me that I had to come home with him to meet his brother. After a couple of polite demurrals, I was swept along to an old Moorish house, very dilapidated, where a group of four high school students lived in slightly squalid splendor. There I sat through my first Mauritanian tea ceremony and was instructed in its appropriate etiquette.

Under the almost too bright stars of Mauritania's dark, dark night sky, I listened to Mauritanians talk about their country, their history, their customs, their relations with the other groups that people this huge, barren, divided, proud country. Slaves, agriculture, Islam, food, sex, politics—we talked about it all in a way that showed the freedom with which Mauritanians allow themselves to think. After the man making the tea had poured the last glistening arc of the sweet, strong drink into the last shot glass, after sipping the last bit of foam in which the light of the kerosene lamp glittered, after four hours of talk, calm, friendship, we separated. I have never seen any of those people again. To my knowledge, I do not even remember if we exchanged names. To them, that did not matter. I was in their house, I was their guest, they shared with me what they had, they listened to my stories and views and told me their own. The Moors say that they have always and will ever receive foreigners truly. In 10 months in Mauritania, I have had no cause to doubt the absolute truth of what they say...

Volunteer LAWRENCE OLSEN (IVS/Laos 1966–68; 1973–75) describes the rich cross-cultural experience of his stay in a Lao Buddhist Wat [temple]:

While teaching English at the Wat, I had often mentioned that I thought I'd like to be a monk for a while, but never seemed to find the opportunity. As time went by, my students became convinced that I'd never do it. When finally, I did announce that I was ready to become a monk, there was a good deal of incredulity. Even Maha Soan, my adopted Lao father, had to ask me several times to be sure that I wasn't just talking through my hat. But once convinced the preparations began in earnest...

After a leisurely breakfast, my friends and some older friends of the family all assembled for my presentation to the Wat. The bed was put in the back of the truck, pictures were taken, I was seated in front, the loudspeakers were mounted on the hood, everybody piled into the other vehicles and the whole procession—with loudspeakers blaring—crawled down the main street of town to the Wat.

The whole ordination ceremony was quite a trial for me. The fact that Atchan [teacher] Mai insisted on speaking English didn't help matters any. Several times I had to turn to someone else and ask for the instructions in Lao because I couldn't understand what Atchan Mai had said. They were just trying to be helpful of course, but at this point I find it much easier to understand correct Lao than incorrect English spoken by a Lao.

As you may well expect the whole ordination ceremony was fairly elaborate. It took about an hour and a half. A substantial part of it was conducted with me sitting in an oriental flat-footed squat with my elbows resting on my knees and my hands together in front of my face. Or at least that was the position that I was supposed to assume. I found it quite impossible, and they let me get by with a rough approximation that was sheer shin-splitting torture. . . .

I was now monk with the pleasant-sounding title of "maun" indicating that I was new to the order. The ceremony and chants completed, we came out of the building and into the sunlight flooding the Wat grounds. Family, friends, and well-wishers all showed their respects to this pale awkward wearer of the robes, called for poses for group pictures and gradually drifted off to perform their mid-morning and noon chores. I was at one and the same time both relieved at having finished the ordination ceremony and in a state of mild shock. . . .

Being new, my participation was limited mostly to assuming the proper attitudes, listening or occasionally mumbling and pouring water. They were considerate of the fact that I wasn't used to these processes and kept the prayers relatively short in order to spare me. Even so, although I had been sitting cross legged for several years and had employed most of the other positions many times during Lao festivals in the preceding two years, by the third day I was so stiff and sore that I could hardly believe it. Much, much worse than any Marine Corps PT session I ever went through. At one point while sitting back on my heels and gritting my teeth with pain, I found myself thinking: "What in the hell am I doing here? I was supposed to have been raised a Christian or some such thing."

Morning was already red before I awoke. Atchan Mai took me through morning prayers which are conducted by the small groups in each of the rooms where they live, and then, indicating a sense of urgency since we had slept in (four a.m. is normal rising time), he instructed me to perform my toilet duties, take a bath and get dressed.

Having done so, I was told to report to the main gate of the Wat along with all the other full monks. Once assembled, the novices handed us our alms bowls which we took, slipping the straps up over our right shoulders for ease in carrying and allowing the robes to fall back again covering the bowls like so many pregnant bellies. In my case it proved not so simple as it looked. Always frantically clutching at the rolled rib with my left hand to keep my robe tight, I never seemed to have hands enough to do anything else, and even so, my robe always felt as though it were slipping away from me and needed adjustment even when it didn't.

After some help with the bowl and robe, I took my position in line and we marched barefoot and single file down by the river, around the Chao Khoueng's [Governor's] house and back up through the center of town with the last of the line splitting off to cover the lower street by the paddy fields. A second group of monks left from the Wat going west towards the army camp so that the whole town was covered. We walked slowly and perhaps even sedately, stopping in front of each individual or occasionally waiting for someone who was a little late, opening our robes to expose the bowls which were uncapped to receive a small wad of sticky rice or maybe a banana in each bowl, covering the bowls again and passing on to the next waiting alms giver.

I both feared and enjoyed the morning procession. I had a frightful case of crotch rot and walking was both awkward and painful. On the other hand. it was interesting to see who came out to give alms and the reactions of my friends as they put rice in my bowl. And the cackle of old ladies saying that I made such a good monk—so white and muscular—and should remain a monk forever was ego satisfying as well as embarrassing. . . .

That was largely the history of my stay in the Wat. It varied only in detail. The schedule was amorphous and subject to change much as one finds in a university atmosphere. Up at 4:00, prayers, toilet and bath, alms round and breakfast, study or work or going out on invitation or chatting with other monks or mixtures thereof, lunch, rest, study, work, bath, evening prayers, study, observing celebrations at the main temple, teaching English, bull sessions with fellow monks and novices, individual prayers, and sleep. . . .

As with my observations on Lao Buddhism the things I learned about myself are perhaps best illustrated by descriptions of the revealing incidents. I was interested for instance in how I would react to the commandments. If you remember the list of commandments, none of them appear too difficult. The Lao were most concerned about whether or not I could get along readily without supper, but I had already made sufficient experiments with dieting and eating patterns to know that I could cope with any slight discomfort which might result from missing supper. The mandate of not taking any life, though, I had never experimented with. Before entering the Wat, I had considered it in terms of mosquitoes and the stories of the Buddha brushing the little pests off his arms and thus having considered it, I was able to make it through two weeks without swatting a mosquito. Fortunately, there aren't too terribly many mosquitoes at that time of year or I might not have made it. As it was, I engaged in the exercise as a test of self-control and not in a spirit of love and compassion for mosquitoes—a form of life. After leaving the robes I found myself slapping and killing mosquitoes with a fanatical vengeance.

As regards the other animals and insects, I hadn't expected any trouble since they don't generally cause any direct bodily irritation, but I hadn't reckoned on long ingrained habits. Ants in the tropics are overwhelmingly numerous. The use of ants to metaphorically demonstrate the countless expanses of time as is often done in Eastern religions becomes very reasonable, once you have visited a tropical or semi-tropical area and seen the ants—everywhere. At any rate, I have gotten in the habit of just idly squashing ants that get too close while I am sitting around in Lao houses. And in the Wat, it was much to my chagrin that I suddenly realized during an evening conversation with some of my fellow monks that I had been idly and methodically, even if unthinkingly, squashing every ant that came within easy reach of my thumb.

After two weeks rich in experience, learning, and personal discovery, I shed the robes and resumed my worldly duties. . . .

Admittedly there was a sense of relief and regained freedom as I left the Wat and headed back to my house, but I could never have anticipated the degree to which those two weeks helped to establish me in the Lao society. I received praise, gifts, congratulations, questions, and invitations of a sort I had never received before. I was permitted to hear full discussions on matters of religion, spirits, and animism such as had never been carried on in my presence before. I was questioned as to how it had felt and gained a new title of respect. Often as not, I am still introduced as the American who has been a monk.

All American volunteers were exposed to different cultures. Reactions varied. Some probably rejected local practices as ignorant or backward; others embraced them and "went native"; and others hopefully drew from the experience to better understand themselves. Certainly, not all reactions were positive. It would be Pollyannaish to accept all host culture practices and values. Some aspects—hygiene, nutrition, education, economic systems—were things the volunteers were there to change. Many other things—class systems, status of women, livelihoods, local governance—clashed with volunteer values and would likely be subjects to change. On both sides, exposure to a new culture and values could have stimulated thinking and changed attitudes.

Responsibility Could Come Quickly

Volunteers probably rarely fully understood what they were getting into when they took up assignments, especially those in rural areas. They might have finished college in May and by October be responsible for managing large work crews or other projects in a wholly new land. This put them into difficult situations with responsibilities that they had to quickly grow into.

IVS volunteers' perspectives on grassroots conditions and issues could make them invaluable to USOM/USAID in design and financing development programs. This could give volunteers substantial influence on development strategies, or where views clashed, it could provide highly visible rejection of U.S. Government (USG) policy. Oddly, the Peace Corps seems to have never had such influence in support of or rejections of USG policy.

Volunteer JAMES ARCHER (IVS/Laos 1966–68) described a situation at his post when he was supervising loading of people into a helicopter that had landed on the airstrip near the IVS house.

> I had worked out a system of priority so that sick people could go first, and the helicopter crew depended on the IVSers to tell them who should get on. When the helicopter was fully loaded and the pilot had enough passengers, he signaled no more could get on.
>
> There was an MP (military policeman) trying to put his son on the flight so he could go back to school in Luang Prabang, but there was no room for the boy who, at his father's urging, was standing right beside the helicopter. I took the boy by the arm and led him to the side so the helicopter could take off safely. The MP went ballistic. He was carrying a gun and threatened to kill me! He finally left with his son, but not after more screaming and threats. I was left with a severe nervous tic on my left eyelid and a desire to do something about this idiot. IVSers willing to work in such difficult places had power. I called Vientiane to complain about him and soon he was removed from Hongsa. My eyelid tic remained with me for several years.

Volunteer JIRO OI (IVS/Laos 1968–70) faced a common problem of how to deal with health problems in places with little or no experience with modern medicine. In Laos, this often involved assuaging evil spirits ("phi ba") vs. modern medicine.

> One morning, I went to one of the digging projects sites. There was nobody working. I got rather pissed off as they HAD to complete the digging before the rain starts. One person came by and told me that there was a very sick person, and they were gathering at his home. So, I went to his house to see what was happening. He was laying down half-naked. Apparently, he had a high fever and looked extremely thin. There was a tennis ball size swelling in his lower right side of abdomen. People were sitting around him and an old man with a twig with leaves in one hand and a glass of liquid on other hand was performing some type of ceremony. I was told that there was an evil spirit (phi ba) eating his stomach and the old man was driving the evil spirit out of him.
>
> I was no medical doctor, but had seen appendicitis patients before, and he was in very critical condition. There was a hospital run by a Filipino organization, Operation Brotherhood, in Kengkok about half an hour away by Jeep. Since that

was the only full medical facility near us, we went there when a need arose. I told them that I would like to take him to OB hospital. The old man said that if he were moved before the ceremony completion, the evil spirit would get angry and kill him. Although, I was more than sure that it was appendicitis, I did not want to tell them that it was not the spirit eating his stomach and the ceremony was superstition. The reason was simple—if I had not happened to be there, the ceremony was the only comfort there was and denying the old man's effort would be counterproductive. I told the old man that I would be coming back to the village after I dropped him off, so he could come with me and continue the ceremony on the Jeep. He thought about it for a while, then said "You can take him now" but declined to come along. I put the patient with his family in the Jeep and drove to the hospital. I saw a Filipino doctor whom I knew, so I had a chance to explain the situation. About a month later, when I took another villager to the hospital, the doctor told me the appendicitis patient had an infected appendix just ready to rupture. If it did, he would have been gone. On my way back to Lahanam, I thanked MY Jeep for saving a man.

Volunteers with their knowledge of local conditions and contacts could have a surprising influence on programs. Perhaps the prime example of this was volunteer Edgar "Pop" Buell in Laos, who ended up running a multi-million-dollar program for USOM, while earning $65 per month. USOM eventually realized the inappropriateness of this and hired him to continue in the job. This is recounted in the book, *Mr. Pop, The Adventures of a Peaceful Man in a Small War*, by DON SCHANCHE.

Volunteer LOUIS WOLF (IVS/Laos 1964–67) experienced how volunteers could be thrust into situations for which they—or no one—could be prepared.

> One day, I heard from a villager, nearby where we lived, that there had been a bombing in one of the sixteen villages. I rushed by jeep about twenty miles on rutted dirt paths and crossing rice paddies, and reached the village some ninety minutes later. It was immediately obvious that there was wide devastation in the village, with dozens of bodies and body parts all over as well as villagers' simple thatch hut dwellings laid to waste, and carcasses of water buffalo, pigs and chickens. Knowing well that the American pilots would routinely circle around for a second run on their target, any surviving villagers had fled for cover into the jungle nearby.
>
> I ran east into the dense jungle until I heard the haunting sound of wails and cries of survivors. There, I sighted my friend Phanh, with whom I had worked just the week before digging the hole where we, and other villagers, were building a deep well—a 3-foot deep hole into which we used ropes to lower, with difficulty, the large, heavy circular cement rings. It was evident that he was badly wounded by shrapnel, was gasping, and was fast losing consciousness. As I took him in my arms, his last words while bleeding through his ears and eyes were, in Lao, 'Please understand that I am not dying for your country; I am dying for my country'.

Volunteer DAVID NUTTLE (IVS/Vietnam 1959) had influence in Vietnam on a major counter-insurgency program with the Montagnard, although this was never fully implemented. Nuttle worked at the Ministry of Agriculture research station near Ban Me Thuot and concentrated on projects in Rhade tribal villages. His knowledge of local communities, livelihoods, relationships, and attitudes could be invaluable to planning local programs.[4]

> The Rhade accepted me as a friend. For over a year, I had tried to make their lives better via the demonstration of improved agricultural practices at the village level. I traveled from village to village by jeep or by motorcycle. Having learned the customs and language by day-to-day exposure, I grew close to the Rhade. My Rhade friends were many, and there was a feeling of mutual trust between us. . . .
>
> When I couldn't solve a problem on my own, I had looked to Saigon for help. Among my sympathetic American friends in Saigon, I counted on Col. Gilbert B. Layton. He was the hard-nosed chief of the Military Assistance Advisory Group (MAAG) Combined Studies Division which was connected with intelligence work in Viet-Nam. I usually didn't get to Saigon more than once a month, but when I did, I always managed time for seeing Col. Layton's daughter, Bonnie. Col. Layton and his wife Dora would always insist that I have at least one home-cooked meal at their house. It was during and after these dinner sessions that we discussed the Montagnard problem and a variety of possible solutions. The more we talked, the more hopeless the situation seemed. It was obvious that the Montagnards had no reason to support the Government of Vietnam (GVN).
>
> I told Col. Layton that the U.S. should pressure the GVN to provide social and economic programs that would benefit the Montagnards and make them a part of the nation. Col. Layton's position was that the GVN would never provide such assistance unless the Montagnards would help to secure the Highlands from Viet Cong control. We mutually agreed that the Montagnards would not fight for the GVN or South Viet-Nam per se. The Montagnards had no concept of nation or national defense, and no use for the GVN. We further agreed that they would probably fight for family, home, and village if the Army of Republic of Vietnam (ARVN) would stay off their backs and if the GVN provided some social and economic benefits. . . .
>
> After returning to Ban Me Thuot and working ten days with the Rhade, IVS Headquarters in Saigon sent an urgent message saying that U.S. Ambassador Frederick J. Nolting wanted to see me the following day at his office… For this trip, I decided to travel via the "Frontier Highway" on my BMW motorcycle. . . .
>
> I arrived in Saigon about an hour after dark, having flipped over after hitting a big wild hog that ran out of the jungle into my path. . . .

My mental alarm went off at 6:30 the next morning. . . . The morning was free for me to check on some vegetable seeds that I had ordered from USOM. I needed these to increase the number of demonstration garden plots in Rhade villages. . . . I had located the missing seeds and was back at the embassy at the appointed time. . . .The secretary directed me to the conference room where the country team was scheduled to meet. I didn't really know anything about this group, except that they were rumored to be responsible for the U.S. assistance effort in South Viet-Nam. I seated myself at the conference table to wait and see what would happen. . . .

The Ambassador started the meeting by saying that members of the country team wished to ask my opinion on how best to stop a possible VC takeover of the Highlands. My opinion, he said, was being solicited because of my knowledge and experience in the area. Ambassador Nolting then brought the group up to date on the several options being considered to resolve the problem. The most favored plan called for isolating the Montagnards from the VC or National Liberation Front (NLF). This could possibly be accomplished by forcing the Montagnards onto types of secured reservations, thereby breaking contact with the enemy. The Ambassador said that MAAG recommended this approach because they felt that ARVN sweeps could thus be made more effective. Theoretically speaking, ARVN would establish free-fire zones and kill everything that moved outside of the reservations. The Ambassador then asked for my opinion. I noted that General McGarr and Colonel Ward had remained silent even though this was obviously a MAAG or ARVN devised concept. I also had no doubt that the military would resent any comments that I made. But I would "call it" as I saw it even if my opinion was not well received.

I ripped into the "reservation plan" by focusing on all the obvious negatives. My argument, I thought was sound and clear. The Montagnards would resist forced relocation and would be alienated against those attempting it. If relocated, the Montagnards could and would escape any reservations by slipping away into the jungle. The rugged terrain, dense vegetation, and many trails would make it easy for the Montagnards to elude capture. Living in the jungle, the Montagnards would probably come under VC control. General McGarr interrupted, saying that while my arguments may have some credibility, there seemed to be no other realistic alternative.

Colby asked a question, one which gave me an opportunity to insert a solution jointly conceived by Col. Layton and myself. We had already agonized over the Montagnard problem. . . .I looked at this as a challenge and an opportunity to help find a way to save my Rhade friends from a horrible fate. "Mr. Colby," I said, "if the GVN will begin to bring the Montagnards into the social and economic mainstream, there will be some motivational basis for a security program.

But you should not expect the Montagnards to fight against the VC to protect Viet-Nam, the Vietnamese, or the GVN. The Montagnards will, however, fight to defend family, home, and village. . . .I noted that a small pilot project could be used to test these concepts.

At this point, the Ambassador noted that I was free to leave the meeting. I did so, fearing that the military would prevail. . . .

October 3rd, and I was back in Saigon for another monthly coordination meeting. The routine was the same with one exception; Col. Layton asked me to meet a friend of his named Jack Benefiel. According to the Colonel, Jack and his wife were already expecting me for dinner. William Colby was also at that dinner. I began to suspect that something was up. Certainly, it was not the usual dinner invitation.

As a result of that dinner meeting, I found myself agreeing to sign a contract with the Central Intelligence Agency or CIA—a contract to "go forth and help the military create a pilot model of a Montagnard defended village." In brief, the "Country Team" wanted to see if I could put my words into action. First, I had to resign from IVS as I definitely didn't want to get IVS involved with my new endeavor. I immediately resigned from IVS so I could change over to my new project.

[T]he team decided to approach the village of Buon Enao to determine if a self-defense experiment could be undertaken. . . .The village elders said they would resist the VC if the GVN made certain concessions. First, the ARVN and Vietnamese air force would have to stop attacking Rhade villages. Second, Rhade, who had been forced to train with or support the VC, would be given amnesty upon declaring their allegiance to the GVN. Third, medical, educational, and agricultural assistance programs would have to be guaranteed to the Rhade.

Upon the GVN's acceptance of the above conditions, Buon Enao would act as the test village to measure GVN intentions. . . .

This was the beginning of what proved to be an effective counterintelligence network. . . . The Buon Enao complex was therefore given authority to expand to 200 villages with a total population of 60,000. Strike forces were to total 1,500 and village defenders 10,600 at the completion of this stage. The expansion was complete by October 1962. . . .

Basic distrust, dislike, and suspicion continued between the Vietnamese and the Montagnards. Many GVN officials were dragging their feet to slow the implementation of economic assistance to the Rhade. . . By August 1962, President Diem's brother and advisor, Ngo Dinh Nhu, ordered a 30-day halt to the arming of Montagnards. . . .At the same time Nhu was making his plans, the U.S. military decided that Civilian Irregular Defense Group (CIDG) programs were becoming too large for civilian control. ARVN was encouraged to quickly absorb the CIDG program.... ARVN and the U.S. military had great difficulty in understanding the Buon Enao concept because there was no traditional military emphasis on attacking the enemy. So U.S. commanders proceeded with plans to conventionalize the war.

As far as the Montagnards were concerned, the GVN and the Americans had violated the spirit and terms of their original agreements. . . .I left South Viet-Nam in October 1962, departing in protest to planned GVN violations of the Buon Enao agreement, which included disarming the villagers and drafting of strike-force personnel. I also protested the conventionalization of CIDG assets by the United States Military Assistance Command Vietnam (US/MACV). The Buon Enao Project, as well as the concepts proved by its success, had died by October 1962. Only a very few people would ever understand what had been created or what had been lost.

Later, with Americanization of the war, volunteers increasingly came to question U.S. policy and programs in Vietnam. Their testimonies in the U.S. had a major influence on American public opinion about the Vietnam war.

Volunteer JOHN SOMMER (IVS/Vietnam 1963-67) describes how 49 IVSers came to sign a letter to President Johnson, printed in the New York Times, protesting the U.S. policy in Vietnam:

That summer of 1967 is when momentum built among many IVSers to protest the U.S. policies. They were seeing the damage being done not only in countless lives lost but in the tens of thousands of refugees generated and the denigration of the culture itself. While some volunteers preferred to stay at their work sites and abstain from political involvement, a majority gathered at the IVS house in Saigon for a couple of days to consider what we should do. Having been asked to structure and moderate the discussions, I found the depth of commitment to the Vietnamese people and the sincerity of all who spoke profoundly moving. At one session, we had invited some especially close friends on a Vietnamese advisory group we'd established in order to hear their views and advice as to what we should do: stay and quietly do our assigned jobs in agriculture, community development, and education, or publicly protest U.S. policies. As I recall, they were as conflicted as we were, but a theme that clearly emerged was that if we really wanted to help Vietnam, we should speak out to our fellow Americans on what we were seeing and experiencing. That September, a group of IVSers composed a letter—really a "cri de coeur"— to President Lyndon Johnson, delivered it to Ambassador Ellsworth Bunker, and gave it to The New York Times (where it made the front page); at the same time, the top four leaders of IVS in Vietnam publicly resigned in order to be free to speak out.

For IVS as an organization working in several other countries as well as Vietnam, this was a traumatic event. I was returning to graduate school at the time and was in close contact with Executive Director Arthur Gardiner and others at IVS's Washington headquarters, including board members. One of the recommendations of the Saigon group had been that IVS should internationalize its funding and also its volunteers (virtually all were then Americans) in order to lessen our being seen so much as part of the U.S. Government establishment. With close to 100 percent government funding, and Vietnam being IVS's largest program (we had been aiming for 200 volunteers, although never reached nearly that), this raised the very question of organizational survival if AID should turn off the spigot. But both Gardiner and board members had been reading volunteer reports, understood where we were coming from, and supported us, even as they managed to keep the remaining IVSers operating with [AID] support. Four years later, however, the swell of volunteer activism led the South Vietnamese government, together with the U.S., to call an end to IVS in that country.

Volunteers became responsible for substantive decisions, including life-or-death decisions, at an individual and broader level. Most were not prepared for this. But, after time in the country, their understanding of local conditions and of outside resources and forces did make them uniquely qualified to provide input to planning local projects and policies.

Resourcefulness Was Essential

Resourcefulness was essential in many volunteer assignments. Job descriptions were vague, and often side projects, additional to the formal assignment, were the most important contribution the volunteer could make. When a formal job assignment didn't work out, volunteers might have to develop their own. This was not uncommon. Volunteer BILL CAMP (IVS/Vietnam 1967–69), who worked on an IVS Danang Street Boy Project, describes one example.

> I was a Connecticut farm boy who came to IVS/Vietnam on the ag team. BUT I never worked as an aggie!! At the 1967 Christmas party I was a frustrated volunteer when I met Steve Goldberg, an anti-war protester who worked with pickpockets and shoeshine boys in Danang. He seemed to accept me when I told him how I'd gotten one piaster coins from store merchants and given them to the beggars in My Tho, where I was when in the Army before IVS. It seemed to satisfy the beggars and my conscience! Noosh [Richard Nishihara], the Community Development leader, sent me to Danang to work with the boys. Steve Goldberg left after only 3-4 days of teaching me sources for blankets, food, etc. I was on my own in the unknown world of pickpockets and shoeshine boys in the Danang Street Boys house on: 7/7 Ham Ngai Street in January, 1968!!!!

Our common meeting ground was that I had nothing to lose nor did the boys since, by definition, theirs was a hopeless state. I did not have any goals at the beginning as I didn't understand the world these boys lived in. So, I had no choice but to feel my way as I went along, while learning about them and how they lived.

There was a hierarchy on the streets, and it reflected the strict social and economic levels of Vietnamese society. Shoeshine boys were near the bottom, pickpockets just a step above. That was mainly because the pickpockets made more money than the shoeshine boys and because they were a little older. The pickpockets ranged in age from 15 to17 years old, while the shoeshine boys were much younger—some as young as 5-6 years old. Consequently, the pickpockets looked down on the shoeshine boys. They lived in a constant survival mode with the pickpockets in almost as poor a state.

Shoeshine boys needed permission from boys higher up the scale, such as those who worked in bars, to work certain sections of the street. While the shoeshine boys didn't pay for that permission, still they were dependent on it for their only means of survival. They slept in open markets or on the street where there were rats, foul odors, and debris. They ate whatever they could and dressed in whatever they could find. Some shoeshine boys moved up the ladder and became pickpockets. They generally did not sleep in open markets, dressed better and some even had homes to go to at night. A few pickpockets set up shoeshine boys in "business" by giving them boxes and supplies. Then they'd proceed to collect money from them—a type of economic slavery!

Shortly after Steve left, Larry Peterson came and lived in the house for three-to-four months, until he was drafted. Together we decided to make some changes. I'd been overwhelmed with what little I understood, but went ahead with what I guessed needed to be done. The first action was to kick out the pickpockets as they were not allowing the shoeshine boys in the IVS house and were generally making life miserable for them. They were also using the house to stash stolen goods. We had to fight a couple of them to get them out. I had a close call when one of them, Chien, winged a brick that just missed me. Chien eventually came back to the house and behaved himself.

We stopped the practice of the pickpockets setting up the younger shoeshine boys in business and then taking money from them. Most boys could not read or write, so I started teaching them the Vietnamese version of ABC's. Some of the older boys assisted. At times I would go out on the streets and pull boys back inside the house because they were skipping their lessons. I sent some kids to typing school. I even sent a few boys to public school. They didn't last long there because of prejudice, no family, poor clothes, and low standing.

We established a schedule. The kids gambled a lot playing cards. Sometimes we'd take this card money and tell them it was to buy oil for the cook stove or other necessities. We established mandatory personal hygiene. I built a compartment type of locker where the boys could stash their personal property. I kept their money in individual containers in my bedroom. No one ever tried to steal that. At times I'd go into the streets and open markets telling boys of the IVS house as a place of refuge and take them on my Vespa directly from the streets to the IVS house. At first, I was too easy, and I nearly got overwhelmed. In order to maintain discipline, I learned to act in a way the boys understood, basically the "rule of the streets"—fear and respect! It was not a feel good, lovey-dovey situation at all. I was firm, physical at times, as a father should be when necessary. I used my age as a means of gaining respect—well understood in Vietnamese culture.

Our team leader, Rich Jones, was of great assistance. He sent over two high school boys, Hong and Thanh, to work with me. They not only took over the educational activities but were also very good influences on the boys. Rich even got IVS to pay them a small salary. These two high school students made the biggest difference in the time I was managing the house. . . .

Over the years I have thought often of the IVS Danang street boy project. There are reflections and questions I will never be able to answer. I am not sure that I accomplished anything. I don't know if I was a role model. I don't know if I left anything sustainable in the lives of the boys. I don't know if I made a difference. THEY made a difference in my life! Once I asked one of the pickpocket boys what he thought his future was. He said he was going to America with me! That was an unexpected response; it confused me. The boys who followed me to Saigon also confused me. Was I still supposed to continue taking care of them? I didn't. Instead, I sent them back to Danang by plane. Did I do the right thing? I do not know if the boys who learned to read and write and/or typing ever used these skills to have a better life. These are not reflections of guilt. They are rather reflections I, in good conscience, ask myself. I like to think I offered some stability in their lives during a period of insane chaos. Hugh Manke, the IVS Chief of Party, once told me, unlike most Americans there, I lived with the underbelly of Vietnam and survived.

Resourcefulness was also often essential for volunteers to access resources and introduce innovations to address local problems. Volunteer MIKE CHILTON (IVS/Vietnam 1960–1965) found this in his Vietnam agricultural assignment.

During the first year (1960) of my IVS assignment at the Vegetable Experimental Station at Dalat, I soon realized the amount of work being done on new vegetable varieties and kinds which were well-adapted to the cooler climates of the Vietnamese highlands (about 4,500 ft. elevation). This work was being realized by the cooperative efforts of the Taiwanese Agricultural Mission, USOM, and the Vietnamese Directorate of Agriculture. In particular, new varieties of hybrid white cabbage, Irish white and yellow potatoes, and hybrid bulbing onions were especially noteworthy: hybrid varieties of cabbage offered new textures, flavors, yields and seasonal adaptation over the traditional Late Flat Dutch types which were low in flavor and high in fiber; Irish potatoes, were essentially unknown except by the small element of French-oriented Vietnamese population; and bulbing onions, which had not been grown before except for other less day-length sensitive members of the family (for example, leek, bunching onions, chives, etc.) but were eagerly sought by the growing expatriate community.

An extension effort was undertaken to get adequate seed and growing instructions to farmers and small landholders in the area. A cooperative effort by Vietnamese and American elements to work with local farmers began to produce results in which markets were inadvertently assisted by the growing presence of primarily American population. . . a part of the expanding societal militarization and instability of that period. After the first year, production increased and market issues arose which hadn't been totally anticipated by any of the participants,....but today each of the crops hold a significant part of vegetable production in those regions, and are found in markets throughout the country. (An early marketing issue is exemplified by an illustrated article on Vietnam in the October 1961 issue of National Geographic magazine.)

As these stories exemplify, assignments typically required a level of resourcefulness with the volunteer figuring out what he or she might contribute and how to make it happen. Even teaching assignments, which may seem straight-forward, required resourcefulness in adapting curricula and teaching methods and accessing resources. Just for normal life—finding out how to get food, how to make do on a low salary, how to get around and cope with myriad nuisances that arose—resourcefulness was an indispensable asset.

Romances Blossomed

Putting healthy, active young people together in any situation is likely to lead to stories of romance. This was certainly true with IVS, which saw numerous marriages between volunteers, between volunteers and people of the host country, and between volunteers and others they met while overseas. Volunteer Tom Fox (IVS/Vietnam 1966-68) describes his "Tom and Hoa Story", which occurred after his IVS assignment while he continued to work in Vietnam.

> ...[A] study team visit and my brief arrest were by no means the most newsworthy or consequential story of that week. No, that prize goes to the story of a fortuitous meeting at the Buu home. Sam Brown, one of the leaders of the Washington

Moratorium movement and later treasurer of the state of Colorado, asked me early in the trip if I could introduce him to a Vietnamese family. I obliged one evening, taking him to the Buu home. I recall to this day being in their family room on the second floor, a spacious room with a television set at one end where I had nearly one year earlier watched the first moon landing. It was filled this evening with Buu family members, mostly Buu children—and a young woman renting a room at the time. I didn't know this woman, but immediately was taken by her beauty and eloquence. She was quiet and stunning in appearance. Her long black hair and slender body were delightfully enhanced by a set of pastel blue silk pajamas. She didn't say much that I can recall these 48 years later. But she was stunning. I didn't want to embarrass her by staring at her, but I couldn't take my eyes off her. So, I had to peek from time to time. As I best recollect, she sat leaning against a cushion on a bed or couch. Her smile was gentle, her dark eyes riveting. I wanted to learn more. I set out to make some inquiries.

I learned that this young woman worked for COR (Committee of Responsibility), as a social worker; I learned she cared for children at COR's Saigon halfway house. I learned she spoke both French and English. I learned she came from a Catholic family. The next evening, I returned after dinner to learn more. I continued to visit, and Hoa and I spent the evenings talking. Not alone. This was impermissible by traditional Vietnamese customs. My courtship continued. I learned about her childhood, her family, her education, about going away to a boarding school in Saigon and later to the prestigious Couvent des Oiseaux in Dalat....

Visiting Hoa those first evenings, I noticed in her room next to her bed a small leather-bound book, "L'Imitation de Jesus'-Christ", a devotional book written by Thomas à Kempis in the fifteenth century. Hmm, a pious Catholic! I kept returning. One evening Hoa complained of a headache. Wanting to impress her with the wonders of Western medicine unavailable in Vietnam I went back to my place to get some U.S. pain medication. I told her I knew a way to relieve the pain and asked her to shut her eyes so I could gently rub her eyelids. First touch! It was the first opportunity—harmless enough—to touch this flower person. She didn't refuse my gesture. Wow! It didn't take me long to realize this was a very special woman; no, I was beginning to think this was THE woman!...And once I felt I knew this, then, well, why waste time? I recall it was only a week or so before I asked her if she might be interested in something long term, like marriage. She didn't refuse. I recall her saying that if I were really serious, I would need to speak with her spiritual advisor, a Canadian Jesuit, Father Andre Gelinas.

My overtures to Hoa, at least publicly, were subtle, so subtle the Buu family thought I was coming there to woo their daughter, Jackie. One evening an older Chinese woman living with the Buu family and helping care for the Buu children encouraged me to marry Jackie. She told me that were I to marry Jackie I would be put in charge of the family finances at some point. Hoa and I continued to see each other. Within weeks we began talking about plans for a wedding. It wasn't easy to find the right date. Hoa's mother, Nguyen Thi Nham, had consulted with local soothsayers and had not found a day of particularly good fortune. Hoa told me her father eventually stepped in, declaring, "All days are God's days." Enough. The wedding would be January 16th; the engagement party would be December 15th.

In Vietnam an engagement party is an elaborate ceremony, scripted in advance, at which a groom's representative formally asks for the hand of a representative of the bride's family. I flew to Can Tho with a Dominican priest, Father Nguyen Huy Lich, a widely respected priest whom I had met through a friend. . . . Hoa's father stood pleased and ready to receive us in front of their home. We walked inside and a dozen or more men in suits were waiting for us. Not a woman to be seen. Hoa was nowhere in sight either, though I later saw her peeking into the room. After some small talk my representative Father Lich formally asked for Hoa's hand in marriage from Ong Nam, Hoa's father's uncle. The request was accepted. I was asked to get up from a couch and I bowed my head as I was formally introduced to the family. A grand two-hour luncheon followed.

Hoa and I had three marriages—civil, family, and religious. The civil was the easiest. It involved filing papers at an office in Can Tho. The second and third were more complicated. We were married the morning of January 16, 1971, at the Sacred Heart Cathedral. We had gone through the ceremony—and marriage vows—the day before with the priest. In most Vietnamese wedding ceremonies, the wife vows to obey her husband. Hoa and I agreed this was not for us. So, we left that phrase out. . . . Once back at the house we went through our third wedding ceremony, this time in front of the ancestral altar as I offered gifts to the family, two bottles of wine and two cans of tea leaves. I had a painting commissioned as a gift to Hoa's parents, a scene from the classic Vietnamese epic poem, *Thuy-Kieu*, by Nguyen Du. . . .

Our departure from Saigon in late 1972 is another interesting story. Hoa was alone one night when a visitor, an old friend whose name we cannot remember for certain, came to her and said the Viet Cong were thinking of either capturing me or killing me. She asked him to return the next night, which he did. He told me he was with a group of local insurgents who really did not know what I was about and were discussing my future. We told him we would leave in two weeks and asked for that time. He said all would be fine. We left before those two weeks were up. All these years later, I still take the threat seriously. Those were crazy times. There were not many of us who spoke Vietnamese and ran around the country freely. Some Vietnamese thought I worked for the CIA; others, thought I was too close to the communists. In truth, you never knew for sure the allegiances of anyone and you had to be as sincere and open as you could.

Reflections

If an individual "stays home", he and/or she will encounter risk, interact with others, accept increasing responsibilities, learn new things, and may find romance. For an international volunteer, all these happen too, but with the complexity of one unmoored in a new environment and culture.

The two-year volunteer assignment is important. For a shorter period of several months, a person is like a rock in a stream. The water (or life) flows around it but does not engage with it. After a volunteer has gone through culture shock and begun to understand and engage with the new culture, it is more like a clump of soil in the stream. The soil mixes with the water and becomes part of the swirl and flow with potentially greater consequences. Their unique experiences certainly influenced IVS volunteers and likely so influenced those around them. Hopefully, this contributed to social and economic development and improved international understanding.

8

IMPACTS OF INTERNATIONAL VOLUNTARY SERVICE

WILLI MEYERS AND GARY ALEX WITH VOLUNTEER STORIES[1]

Assessing the impact of development activities is notoriously complicated. Impacts accrue over time, often after a substantial lag, and may be transitory. Casual linkages are uncertain. Unexpected results, sometimes negative, occur. Monitoring indicators may not be straight-forward, and measurement can be costly and difficult. As an example, training farmers on the use of a new crop variety may lead to increased planting of that variety after a few years, but by only some farmers. Production may go up, but so may production costs and risks, if the new variety is susceptible to drought or disease. Large farmers earning more from the new variety may buy out smaller farmers. Then planting of the new variety may drop, if farmers and/or consumers find it tastes poorly or has other negative attributes. Also, programs other than the training being assessed may have influenced adoption of the new variety. Volunteer program evaluation faces all these challenges with the additional complication of volunteer assignments being highly diverse, scattered, and of short duration.

Most evaluations we find are positive, as an evaluation of Australian government international volunteers concluded: "AVID [Australian Volunteers for International Development] is making an effective contribution to Australian and partner government development objectives. It is also an effective public diplomacy mechanism. Volunteers benefit from their experience and bring expertise and professionalism that host organisations value highly; they are often compared favourably to volunteers from other countries or paid technical advisers. Volunteers contribute to the capacity of host organisations, develop people-to-people links and generate goodwill for domestic and foreign diplomacy."[2]

Early international volunteer programs gave limited attention to evaluations, but this changed in the 1990s when funding agencies applied pressures to document developmental results.[3] This demand for greater rigor in evaluation brought with it a view that, "Without documentation, it can no longer be assumed, as purported by ISVS [International Secretariat for Voluntary Services] in early years, that volunteers are best suited to judge the results of their work." Even so, methodologies are problematic, and most assessments are somewhat subjective.

A common heritage of IVS, the Peace Corps, and other programs that send volunteers abroad in various types of social service lies in what these volunteers contributed during their time of service and what they brought back for future life endeavors. Many volunteers feel that they benefited more than they contributed as volunteers, but judging the relative impacts or values associated with the two sides of the service experience is unlikely to be fruitful. Such experiences would vary greatly from person to person and from place to place.

Evaluations of IVS country programs did not have broad coverage. Early programs and smaller projects were generally not formally evaluated. Yet, program assessments of various types often served as the basis for continued funding. Previous chapters refer to available evaluations, which tended to be positive, but which also often noted limitations in administrative support to volunteers and delays in volunteer placement. When volunteers worked on larger USAID programs, evaluations often had little to report concerning volunteer inputs.

Not all impacts were positive. Some volunteers were unsuited to their assignments. As well, many assignments were poorly defined. Personality conflicts occurred. Volunteers may have provided inappropriate advice. Influences on individuals or institutions may have been negative. Volunteers were subject to accidents and physical and mental health challenges. Some died. A two-year long-distance break with friends and family could disrupt personal relations and career plans.

Documentation and data are not available to fully quantify the varied impacts of IVS volunteer service. However, we may gain understanding of impacts from the testimony of former volunteers, and we can trace the impact pathways that these stories provide. Five types of impacts are of particular interest:

1. Direct results from the volunteer's assignment (e.g., training farmers, teaching students, digging wells, etc.). These would be the main expected impacts.
2. Capacity of host individuals and institutions to continue development or relief programs: A direct objective of the volunteer assignments or an expected or unexpected by-product.

3. Influence on national policies or development program strategies. Such impacts are typically not expected and are less common but can be substantial.
4. Personal influence on the volunteer. This is the impact most often cited by volunteers and may be the most profound, influencing careers and personal perspectives.
5. International goodwill. Improved international understanding and friendship might be characterized as winning "hearts and minds." From the U.S. Government perspective, this impact seeks to improve attitudes towards the United States and democratic governance.

Numerous examples of each type of these impacts are found in other chapters of this book and among volunteer stories in the IVS archives. Excerpts from a few of these are provided below as examples. Overwhelmingly, volunteer stories are positive. This seems an accurate reflection of experience, although volunteers with positive accounts are undoubtedly more likely to share them and stay in contact than are others.[4]

Direct Results From Volunteer Assignments

Volunteer assignments typically outlined the work to be performed with anticipated specified or implied results. Frequently, volunteers were expected to adapt their work plans and undertake additional developmental activities as they became familiar with local conditions and opportunities. Often these secondary activities became recognized as the most important assignment benefits. Still, well-planned assignments would help optimize potential for positive impacts. However, volunteers would have difficulty seeing the impact of their work under the best of circumstances, because the two-year assignment was generally too short for observing real change.

James Archer, IVS/Laos (1966–1970) and IVS/Bangladesh (1973–75)
—*Not Ugly Ducklings*

I went to Bangladesh in June 1973. It was not a very pleasant living situation, but I made my biggest contribution there. When I arrived, I was informed that the owner of the poultry farm, where I had been assigned, was under suspicion of having murdered someone. I did not want to go there, so I was told to look around and find something. While traveling around I met Carl Ryther of the Feni Baptist Mission. He had three or four Khaki Campbell ducks and when we got to talking, we realized that we had the same "vision" of Bangladesh as a great place for ducks. Since I had the technical expertise and ideas for what to do, Carl decided to fund a small project where I would arrange the import of day-old ducklings from Thailand, set up a Rice Husk Incubation System Hatchery, and go from there.

It all worked well, and we cooperated very well. First, I went to Thailand to arrange the importation of the ducklings, and I stayed in Comilla to raise the ducklings at the vacant government poultry station. We fed the ducklings with spoiled CSM (a USAID Corn/Soya/milk mix that was to help feed the hungry). Unfortunately, a lot of it had spoiled, and that is how it came to us. Some bags were not too bad, and others were unusable, but while we lost some ducklings, we generally were successful raising a good number of them. . . .

Once the ducklings had been moved to Feni, I left Comilla and went to Feni. I set up the hatchery at my rented house in Feni. All the materials were local, and I did all the room modifications and building of incubation beds etc. on my own. It was all bamboo poles, bamboo matting, local cloth, rice straw, rice husk, rattan matting, burlap, bamboo trays, and baskets from the market. No wood, which was scarce and very expensive. This is when Samir Baroi, a young Christian man/student, was assigned by Carl to work with me.

By the first months of 1975, the hatchery was running well, but the Feni area was not a good place for large-scale duck raising. I spoke to Carl Ryther and IVS and decided to search Bangladesh for a place where people were already raising ducks with a controlled field foraging system. We found the village in Sylhet and arrived at a most auspicious time. They [ducks] were being decimated by disease and [poultry farmers] were at the point of quitting duck raising. I explained that we had vaccines (which I had located in Calcutta) and an improved breed of layer ducks. They were very receptive to the idea, and we decided to move the hatchery to Sylhet, but under IVS control. Carl had to stay in Feni, and he decided to try to continue with his duck distribution program as best he could.

Samir Baroi was the key to the sustainability of the project. When I left Bangladesh in 1975, Samir moved with IVS to Sylhet and managed the Rice Husk Incubation System Hatchery that IVS set up. Samir was the only person at that time who had been trained with me. Other IVSers came in, but they did not have the skills to take over the incubation program.

IVS used the core program of the duck hatchery to create a training program and other activities that developed from this. Without this training and extension work, the program could not have spread duck production so effectively. There are now thousands of duck raisers in Bangladesh and many of them, including many poultry (chicken) raisers, use the Chinese Rice Husk Incubation System to increase their profits.

Most raisers are using the improved-breed ducks that we initially brought in from Thailand, and now there are many other improved breeds from China, UK, India, and so on. There are estimated to be hundreds of thousands of improved-breed ducks in Bangladesh now. That was my big contribution as an IVS volunteer. It is very satisfying to see what has happened with duck-raising in Bangladesh since I left in 1975.

STEVE SWIFT, IVS/Vietnam (1966–1970)
—*Let There Be Light*

Phu Tan village has a sizeable population of Cambodians (Khmer) because the Cambodians were the original inhabitants. Then the Vietnamese migrated south in search of land and took some from the Khmer. Then came the Chinese to be farmers and small businessmen. Near as I could tell from living in Phu Tan, the three groups seem to get along. Hear tell, that in earlier times—20s, 30s, 40s—Vietnamese, Khmer, and Chinese kids grew up among each other and learned each other's languages.

One day, village chief Lam Suong (Chinese-Cambodian), a highly respected man, dropped by the village coffee shop and started talking about the failing French generator in their village, and asked if I had any ideas on how to repair or replace such a machine. Hmmm. I had heard there was a giant U.S. military junk yard at Long Binh, not far from Saigon, and maybe there were some cast-way generators there. I went to Saigon, walked the corridors of USAID national headquarters, and found there were such generators, 100 KW each. USAID gave me requisition forms to fill out. Lam Suong and his co-operators rented three big lorries, one for each of three generators they wanted. Once the machines were in the village, Lam Suong, his older brother (Phu Tam's very best real mechanic), and other wrench men, got two of those machines working. They were ecstatic. Lam Suong awarded me a gold-and-ivory Buddha on a chain, to hang around my neck. I was truly honored. Now Phu Tan village and all the neighboring villages have province-wide electricity, day-and-night.)

RUSSELL MARCUS, IVS/Laos (1966–1967)
—*Just do it!*

I was all fired up about learning Lao, and so I went to find a dictionary. I was told that USIS Vientiane published a Lao dictionary. When I got there, the Cultural Affairs Officer, Ivan Izenberg, informed me that the dictionaries were out-of-print and that he wanted to update it. I checked back two weeks later to find out how the update was coming. He told me the project was on hold because there was nobody to run the project, and besides, qualified Lao people weren't available since they were immediately hired by the U.S. Embassy. I volunteered to take on the project in my spare time and use the students at Dong Dok as language informants. And that's how the dictionary project started.

> The English-Lao: Lao-English Dictionary was my major achievement in Laos. It was soon picked up by the publisher, Charles Tuttle, and reformatted at his cost. Over the years, it has gone through over 35 editions, and it is still available as a useful dictionary of the Lao Language. Several years later, an incident occurred which brought home the significance of what I did. As you all know, many Lao people became refugees after the Pathet Lao took over the government in 1975. Shortly thereafter, I was flying on a plane from Bangkok to Tokyo and happened to sit next to a Lao refugee who was given asylum in the U.S. and we chatted in Lao. At one point he asked my name and I asked if he had a dictionary. He wouldn't believe that I was the editor of his book, but was amazed when I showed him my passport. I was quite happy to learn that my project in IVS would be contributing to his life in the USA as well as many others.

Change and impacts take time and occur because of, or in spite of, other changes in governance and the environment. Volunteer DICK AUGSPURGER, IVS/Laos, years later saw the changes in one area in which he had worked.

> I had been well trained in rural development in the Muong Phieng Cluster in Laos, a nationwide USAID Demonstration Cluster which had concentrated rice, vegetable, veterinarian, fishpond, dug well, and home economics/nutritional components. . . . . 50 years after working in Laos, my wife, Rosie, youngest son Brett, and his wife, Cindi visited Muong Phieng and Sayaboury. We hired an interpreter and a van driver to help us navigate from Luang Prabang to Sayaboury [which now has a paved road connecting them]. Pavement covered roads, electricity for everyone, running hot and cold water, restaurants, car/phone/tractor dealerships, and gas stations were the new norm in Muong Phieng. Muong Phieng Cluster had delivered and had become the "rice-exporting bowl" that some planners had estimated 50 years earlier. Sayaboury Province was now exporting rice to all adjacent countries. The Chinese had just completed the paved road and the first bridge ever over the Mekong River [between Sayaboury and Luang Prabang] and were helping to harvest the rubber, teak, and other valuable woods [like ebony] from the forests of Laos.

DEVELOPMENT OF LOCAL HUMAN AND INSTITUTIONAL CAPACITY

Developing local capacity to continue development or relief programs after volunteer departures was often a stated objective or unexpected by-product of volunteer assignments. Volunteers might impact individuals by teaching, on-the-job training and collaboration, setting examples, mentoring, or advising. Institutional strengthening might be accomplished through human capacity development, organization and program changes, fostering linkages with other institutions, or changes to policies and strategies. Capacity development—both for individuals and organizations—was very difficult to measure and was unlikely to be evident within a single volunteer's time in-country. Capacity development might even manifest with new starts after failures.

The two-way personal relationships and collaborations, established between volunteers of different agencies—IVS, CARE, Peace Church groups like Mennonite Central Committee and Brethren Volunteer Service —and volunteers with host country youth groups, work camps, and personal friendships, impacted all parties during the years of assignment and, for some, into later careers. IVS testimonials, for example, reveal that Vietnamese student and teacher colleagues and friends profoundly influenced the IVSers' 1967 decision to resign and testify about the war back home as a way to help Vietnam in the late 1960s. Other examples of such two-way influence include the Danang Street Boy story in Chapter Seven and three examples given here from Laos: Two on personal impacts and one reflecting the results of IVS's considerable contribution to establishing a Lao education system.

Steve Stone, IVS/Laos (1969–1971)
—*One Life*

One of the ongoing sagas from Laos was the life of a Laotian friend of mine, Phengphone Chantlangsy. Phone was an English teacher of mine. He applied to a program to study in the United States, was accepted and graduated from a high school in Wellington, Ohio. Upon his return to Laos, he began writing to me that he wanted to go to college in the United States. I went to the president of Manchester College and told him that I knew a poor boy in Laos who wanted to attend college. Dr. Helman said that Phone would be good for the college and offered to waive tuition if we could come up with board and room. Phone's father sent some money, Jane and I raised some money, but Phone largely put himself through college by working for the college and American factories.

Phone graduated with a BS in sociology from Manchester College. He then earned a Masters in rural community development from the University of Missouri. He met and fell in love with a refugee from Laos. He became a teacher of English as a second language in Rockford, Illinois. He worked with numerous nationalities in this position. He converted from Buddhism to Christianity at the urging of his wife. He pastored several Laotian churches. He is now retired from teaching and is pastoring full time. He has served as chairman of the Laotian association in Rockford. I recommended him as a candidate as an outstanding alumnus from Manchester College and Manchester granted him that award. He and Lang have raised three children. One of his daughters was recently awarded a PhD. He has made numerous trips to Laos and works with refugees from both Laos and Africa. His parents and siblings became refugees and located in the Rockford area. He continues to minister to Laotians, Africans, and some Caucasians. He has the ability to communicate with Americans about Laotian customs and culture.

Dianna (Dee) and Dick Quill, IVS/Laos (1963–1965)
—What Goes Around, Comes Around

Thanks IVS, for one of the most rewarding times in my life. After my tour, I extended for six months and came back for another two-year tour. In January 1967, I met my future husband, Teny Quill and we were married back in the states in 1968.

During my time in Sam Thong, the original seven nurses, myself, and Carol Mills received the King's personal Medal for Service to his country. Carol Mills, an ex-IVSer was "Pop" Buell's office assistant. Edgar "Pop" Buell, a former IVSer, was the Area Coordinator of Xieng Khouang Province where Sam Thong was located.

On July 4, 2013, in St Paul, MN, there was a Hmong nurses, medics and USAID reunion. About 200 people were there. It had been 40 years since I last saw many of the nurses. I was really proud when I heard that almost all of them had nursing careers after relocating to the USA. That day brought back many memories of Laos that I have cherished.

Gary Alex, IVS/Laos (1968–1972)
—2020 Return to the Scene

In 2020, I visited the ENI campus [Ecole Normale d'Instituteurs or Teacher Training School where he taught as a volunteer]—now renamed the Ecole Normale Supérieure. I talked to current students and some graduates from the ENI, but did not have a chance to talk with faculty or to meet any of my former students. I was quite impressed. The campus looks much the same as in the 1970s. The USAID dormitories, classrooms, and offices were in good condition and fully utilized and the campus in general seemed well maintained. The fish pond too looked very much the same—considerable potential, under-utilized and poorly-maintained— and likely for the same reasons—difficulties with water control, inability to control "midnight harvesting", and inadequate management attention. Alas, I did not see any campus vegetable gardens.

The students I met were quite positive and engaging. The standards for entrance have changed, and it is now a higher-level educational institution, though I wasn't able to figure out the exact entrance or curricula requirements. Students were from all over the South with many from rural areas. In the travel around Pakse, I chanced to meet several ENI campus graduates, who had small businesses, worked in the tourism industry, or were with government. They seemed quite proud of their school and quite competent in their jobs. One thing seemed the same as in the 1970s. The school is designed to train primary school teachers, but many students aspire to other jobs.

Off the campus, a day's drive across the Bolovens Plateau to Ban Houei Kong suggested that we had many things right in the IVS rural development program. Coffee, introduced by the French, is King on the Plateau. IVS saw coffee's potential, but did not work much with it as marketing was a problem during the war. Other diverse crops are also being produced and have ready markets. Irrigated rice, which IVS tried to introduce, is now grown. The saw mill had been a good idea, but now the forests are pretty well logged out so that is gone. Houei Kong itself has developed as a central market town and now has a daily market and a number of shops and businesses.

INFLUENCE ON NATIONAL OR DEVELOPMENT PROGRAMS AND POLICIES

Influence on national and donor policies and programs was less common and their substantial impact harder to assess. Such impacts are typically not expected. Still, the IVS presence at the local level with its understanding of conditions and needs had an impact on the approach or style of national operations, donor agencies, and leaders of those agencies. Certainly, when IVSers went on to work for developmental or other agencies, they took with them the grass-roots orientation, language, and cultural understanding they had acquired. Other chapters of this book give examples of changes exerted, for example, in USAID strategy, approach, and program design. Surely the impact on U.S. policy in Vietnam is part of this, as outlined in Chapter Seven. On a national, political level, Richard Berliner shares his story of how on-the-ground local voices can influence higher level decisions.

RICHARD BERLINER, IVS/Vietnam (1966–1968)
—*Romney Fact-finding Missions*

As IVS volunteers we lived with Vietnamese, spoke their language, and soon developed a reputation in some quarters as being very independent thinkers. Our experience and language skills gave us a unique perspective on the war, and for that reason we were occasionally asked by the IVS leadership to meet with visiting U.S. politicians making fact-finding visits to the war zone. On two different occasions I was asked to arrange meetings with Vietnamese youth, one with Senator Birch Bayh from Indiana and another with Governor George Romney from Michigan. Each visitor wanted to get a perspective from some young Vietnamese who were not a part of the government establishment.

The meeting with Romney was particularly noteworthy, because he was also a candidate for president in 1968. The message he heard from the youth was that Viet Nam needed to determine its own future, that the U.S. was only prolonging the struggle and exacerbating the suffering of the people, and that the U.S. should withdraw immediately. This message, coupled with the evidence he saw for himself that the U.S. was losing the war, contradicted the official line he received from the embassy and top military command. When Romney came back to the U.S. to report his findings he said, "I'd just had the greatest brainwashing that anybody could get." Unfortunately for him, the press focused on his use of the term "brainwashing," a message that effectively killed his chances of being president.

It was clear to most observers that he was referring to being told repeatedly that the U.S. was winning the war and only needed more time and more troops, which he did not believe. But the message in response to the press reports was that anybody who would allow themselves to be brainwashed did not qualify to be president.

Personal Influence On Volunteers

The impact that was most often cited by volunteers, and perhaps most profound, involved how volunteering influenced their careers, personal perspectives, interests, confidence, contacts, and world views. These are not generally what funding agencies are looking for from international volunteerism, as they pursue impacts on social and economic development and/or international goodwill.

Nearly all volunteers testify that experiences in IVS have been a major influence on the rest of their lives. As with many Peace Corps alums, the IVS experience led many volunteers into various forms of international engagement. Whether national or international careers emerged after IVS, every stage in life led to the next, so all are a part of the volunteer's life story.

In addition, the personal impact of volunteerism can be seen in the context of development strategies by academics and leaders of development organizations that have used IVS experience in developing new approaches.

Erwin H. Johnson (EJ), IVS/Laos (1966–1968)
—*Acceptance and Remembering Is a Great Gift*

After teaching agriculture for a few months at a Lao Teachers Training School just outside of Pakse, Laos, I transferred from the IVS/Laos Education team to IVS/Laos Rural Development. IVS volunteer David Teller and USAID employee Fred Hubig recruited me to work on the Bolovens Plateau in southern Laos. After a very brief time (about two weeks) of working together with them, David returned to the U.S. and Fred transferred to another assignment.

With Sae Senpaty, my IVS assistant, the entire venture in the Houei Kong area (44 villages) was suddenly in our province. Working with tribal villagers (Nha Huen and Laven), we built bridges, roads, schools, and an irrigation dam and canal system. We trained a cadre of local tribal young men as medics to provide basic medical care to the villagers. We developed an agricultural training program (crops, livestock, Lao language, extension, etc.) for boys 14-15 years old to come, live and train on our demonstration farm. We introduced corn and cattle production and American style pigs (boars) to the area. We even purchased a Massey-Ferguson 165 tractor plus implements to till the rich soils of the flat area. Raised beds for vegetable production were created and taught in the school and villages. It was a dynamic, exciting time in my life. Keeping "on top" of all the activities, logistics, and personnel even as the war was going on around us was a challenge. I reveled, excelled, and grew in this remote assignment as a volunteer.

We used resources and ideas from USAID, IVS, NGOs, and the CIA to conduct our projects and work. We had large amounts of creativity and ambition to accomplish the rural development work, but the war held much of our efforts back. The villagers were willing collaborators and understood hard work due to their slash and burn crop production practices and daily foraging or hunting to satisfy their food needs.

Three things stand out in my mind from my time spent with IVS in Houei Kong. First, I developed a positive sense of self. Secondly, I learned to like who I was and gained confidence in my talents and abilities. We were so isolated and removed from the language, culture, and environment from the world that I grew up in (even the outside world of Laos) while serving in Houei Kong. When I write these thoughts, it sounds like a contradiction, but it was a tremendous growing experience for me as an individual.

Thirdly, credit needs to go to the people in Houei Kong who worked and cooperated with us in our projects and activities. Upon returning to Laos on two separate trips, we traveled to the Houei Kong area in the years 1998 and 2002. On both ventures in the area, we were able to locate villagers and co-workers who remembered us from the late 1960's. Those individuals spent months and years in the "re-education" camps imposed on them by the Communists in part because they worked with the Americans. Amazingly, they remembered me and greeted me back into their lives as we shared meals, lao hai wine, laughter, and conversation together. Their acceptance and remembering is a great gift to me!

WILLIAM W. "BILL" SAGE, IVS/Laos (1969–1970)
—One Door Closes, A New One Opens

The experience of living and working in a rural, isolated tribal area shaped me in many ways but perhaps the most important value it taught me was that "cultures" are different because people's experiences are vastly diverse and have been formed by historical events, generations of traditions, and local environmental conditions. Most cultures have developed different ways of dealing or coping with basically the same problems in the context of survival and forging community through their individual customs, traditions, practices, and different resources available to them that allowed them to survive and in some cases thrive. Living among the Nya Heun and Laven, I observed that the differences often were dictated by the same goal of surviving and maintaining that survival with safeguarding values promoted through culture, customs, and traditions. I also learned, at least in the context for which I was operating, that there was less resistance by the people I was working with toward small incremental changes than toward big complex ones, which are slow to be accepted and less likely to create momentum to make the bigger more impactful changes that are often really needed.

My first encounter with refugees and displaced persons was in Houei Kong. I met Alak and Sapuan families living in Nya Heun villages, north of Houei Kong, while working with those villages. I learned that they had fled from their traditional homelands at the northeast base of the Plateau before I came to Houei Kong. They fled because of the war in their home areas. They fled with only the clothes on their backs, according to the stories they shared with me. I became aware of the hardship and uncertainty associated with becoming a "displaced person" or a "refugee" according to today's international definition of refugee. They had lost their home, their traditional livelihood as well as their land where generations before them had lived and maintained a way of life. This experience was the introductory point for my lifelong work with refugees. Over the next five decades, my life's work almost exclusively involved working with and assisting refugees in programs of refugee protection and promoting refugee resettlement programs in Western countries. I still look back on that first experience in Houei Kong and remember the stories I heard about the uncertainty faced by those refugee families, wondering at the time if they would ever be able to return home.

RAY BORTON, IVS/Viet Nam (1958–1960)
—*What We Learned on the Way Home*

Following our two years of work with IVS Agriculture in South Vietnam in 1960, four of us pooled our return home [U.S.] tickets and used the money to purchase a VW Microbus and proceeded to drive home. When we all reached home seven months later we had not only seen many great scenic and historic sights but also had visited with a list of development programs and people that added to our IVS experience in many ways. . . .

All of us added further qualifications to our bios. Gerry Theirstein became a research staff member at Colorado State, Bob Falasca found a career with the U.S. Seed Association, Paul Sutton became a Tennessee Agricultural Extension agent and I went on to work with The Agricultural Development Council in New York and The Philippines and with Stanford Research Institute in Ethiopia. I later finished my career with the California State Department of Food and Agriculture as a way of staying in one place long enough to raise a family.

LARRY WOODSON, IVS/Laos (1964–1971)
—*Jump Start to a Great Life*

My first two years [teaching] in the Luang Prabang basically gave me maturity, experiences, Lao language, and multi-cultural relationships with Lao, French, English and other social events like attending events at the Palace, such as Lao New Year with the King and his family.

A full lifetime of experiences compacted in eleven years in Laos. It also contributed to the remainder of my career with the State of Kansas and the elective assignments with Elk Township, Rural Water District and finally as the County Commissioner with Osage County (population 18,000). Twenty-nine years with the Kansas Department of Agricultural as a Program Director for Agricultural Products, Weights and Measures and Food Inspector for the Meat and Dairy Industry. Worked with several Governors, Secretary of Agricultural Departments, and was elected to be a Program Director with the United States Veterinarians Association and served as the National President of the States Meat And Food Safety Programs. Represented the State Directors to two National Secretaries Annual Meetings.

A great career! Thanks to IVS for the experience that provided the jump start to a great life!

WILLI MEYERS, IVS/Viet Nam (1963–1965; 1966–67), IVS/Washington (1965–66)
—*Small World*

In 2017, I was visiting the Vietnam National University of Agriculture to discuss a collaboration with the University of Missouri. As we departed, one of the Vietnamese professors asked me "have you ever been here before?" I said, "Yes, I was at this University in January 1994 to teach at a workshop on agricultural market economics." He stopped, looked at me and said, "I was one of the college students who attended that workshop."

Among the many post-IVS Vietnam experiences distributed over the years, this January 1994 trip was a highlight that bridged the old and the new, since it was 27 years after my IVS departure, 23 years after my IRRI-sponsored visit to Viet Nam and just before the opening of diplomatic relations between the U.S. and Vietnam. Les Small, a Rutgers University professor and IVS alum, and I, then an Iowa State University professor, were both teaching at this workshop which was the first agricultural market economics workshop in Vietnam after Vietnam opened its economy. . . .

How was it that IVS led me back to Vietnam and to advising two graduate students from Vietnam while a professor at University of Missouri? The first step was IVS board member John Mellor, a world class agricultural economist at Cornell University, who advised me during my second tour in IVS that a footloose mathematician could find a meaningful life as an agricultural economist. The second step was that I chose UP Los Banos over Ohio State for my MS studies, because I wanted to stay in the region and do NGO work next. However, agricultural economics captured my attention, so after marriage to a Los Banos lass we went off to University of Minnesota for my PhD and on to a research and teaching career at USDA, Iowa State, and University of Missouri.

Don Cohon, IVS/Vietnam (1965-1967)
—Bridging the Gap

The IVS experience of teaching English at Vũng Tau High School in South Vietnam from 1965-1967 significantly shaped the rest of my life—both in a professional career and in personal relationships. . . .

My experience as an IVS volunteer broadened my worldview and uniquely qualified me to understand the nuances and challenges of bridging the gap between our Western approaches to healing psychological problems and the healing traditions of SE Asian cultures. The situation made for an exciting and complex set of problems directing a project with multi-cultural staff whose backgrounds ranged from someone with an M.D. degree and another who had no high school and was from a pre-literate culture. "Talk therapy" was not familiar to most SE Asians. And there were within-country differences to consider, especially between northern and southern Vietnamese where tensions persisted. Another challenge was how to match clients with mental health workers—for example, an older man would have difficulty talking freely to a younger female. We could not change these factors and could only discuss them as openly as possible among ourselves. I developed a cross-cultural training curriculum that employed psychologists, psychiatrists, and social workers offering courses and individual supervision to refugee trainees. Fortunately, because of my recently completed post-doc, many professional contacts willingly volunteered time to teach and provide supervision to the newly hired refugee staff.

Bernard Wilder, IVS/Laos (1963-68)
—Literacy Changed My Life

I learned that USAID wanted to find out what the literacy rate of Laos was. . . I wasn't ready to go home right at the end of my fifth year, so I made a proposal to USAID to conduct a literacy survey of the country. IVS and USAID agreed to my contract extension. Before the English students left for home at the end of the school year, we trained the whole two top years to administer the tests. They were to do the surveys when they got home and bring the results back to the National Education Center when they returned to school in the fall. The conduct of the study was a turning point in my career, and I am forever grateful to IVS for going along with me on it. It was recognized at the time as the best country-wide literacy study ever done. We did 11,000+ interviews and gave USAID not one but 86 literacy rates. They were by sex, specific areas, and age groups. . . .

Every aspect of my career for the next five years grew out of this study. As a PhD candidate I began to do consultancies and gave several speeches on literacy and rural adult education in the developing world. My PhD thesis was based on it. My PhD got me consultancies. My consultancies got me known. And in the middle of an AID downsizing when many AID people were being RIFed [terminated or reduction-in-force], AID came to me and offered me a job to help to improve their programs in rural education.

Brian O'Conner, IVS/Laos (1963–1965)
—I Am No Longer Under Cover

After IVS, I worked for another year in Laos with USAID, then joined the CIA and went back to Laos with them for another 4 years, then on to Cambodia, Thailand, France, Mali and more. I worked for the CIA for 46 years as a staff officer and then as a contractor. I am no longer under cover so I have no problem with this being in print, but my suggestion would be not to include these details in the book. I suspect it will offend some IVSers and might give some people the wrong impression about IVS. The bottom line is that IVS really did change my life.

INTERNATIONAL GOODWILL

Improved international understanding is nearly always cited as an important reason for international voluntary service and in some cases may be a primary justification. From the U.S. Government perspective, international understanding seeks to improve attitudes towards the United States and democratic governance. In seeking to win friends for the U.S. or build credibility for a local government, impacts are extremely hard to measure. On the side of the volunteer, their experience often leads to life-long interest and attachment to the country in which they served. This comes through in many of the volunteer stories, as in the following two examples.

Tom Fox, IVS/Vietnam (1966–1968)
—Language Fluency Touches Lives

Learning Vietnamese was a rewarding experience. Few foreigners become "fluent," but I grew capable in speaking ordinary conversational Vietnamese. People were nearly always dumbfounded hearing Vietnamese coming out of the mouth of a blue-eyed, hairy American. The hair on my arms was a never-ending object of delight for the children.

IVSers, Mennonite and Quaker volunteers gained nation-wide reputations for speaking Vietnamese. It seemed it was no small matter. Face to face conversations, without interpreters, added a deeper, more personal dimension to communication. Moreover, a sense of the language helped us delve more deeply into the Vietnamese psyche. Knowing Vietnamese also helped us understand Vietnamese myth, proverbs and poetry, key ingredients of their romantic culture, one governed by Confucian minds, Buddhist hearts and animist souls.

How important was it to Vietnamese to hear an American converse in their language? IVSer Hope Harmeling tells the story of being called into a Nha Trang-based U.S. military hospital during the Tet offensive. She was asked to speak with Northern Vietnamese soldiers and tell them they would be operated on before being taken prisoner. "Even those who were taking their last breath smiled and told me I spoke beautiful Vietnamese," she said, "and thanked me for learning it. I will never, as long as I live, forget their absence of anger and their willingness to be so cordial to me."

RENE MOQUIN, IVS/Vietnam (1966–68)
—*Maybe I Did Have An Impact*

How much did my time in Vietnam change my life? I was able to become fully familiar with one Asian culture, which led me to explore the similarities and differences in others. My IVS experience left a powerful impression. I cannot tell what impact my meager IVS contribution may have had, but the benefit to me was incalculable. It opened the world to a 26 year-old man. . . .

I had journeyed to Vietnam as an idealistic young man, unsure of what type of impact I might have on our host culture. I became immediately aware of the appreciation felt by my Vietnamese friends. They appreciated that I attempted to learn their language, albeit never very successfully. . . .

International volunteers always ask the question, "Did I make a contribution?" I think I did but one is never sure. In 1972, after I had secured my first professional job in Elkhart, Indiana, there were a number of Vietnamese students studying at Goshen College. Periodically I would visit with them. One day I received a call from one of the students informing me that An, one of my former students in Vietnam, had secured a scholarship to study in the United States and was visiting them. Joanne and I invited him to our home. I still see him holding our twin daughters. In my conversation with An, I assumed that he would be going back to Vietnam to pursue a career in engineering. His response amazed me. "Rene I would like to go back to my country and do what I think you were trying to do." I don't know what ever happened to An, but maybe I did have an impact.

LINDA DURNBAUGH, IVS/Laos (1970–1972)
—*Learning to Listen, Taking Time to Chat*

In Laos, I not only became politically aware, I became more aware of myself as a citizen of the world community. I not only had the opportunity to experience and to be a part of a traditional culture, but also to become unwittingly a part of the international foreign community—volunteers from other foreign NGO's, a variety of people in official capacities for embassies, consulates, and organizations; and the "world travelers" (often referred to as W.T.'s), the passers-through from around the globe, who shared their stories with me. Upon my return to Cleveland, I acutely missed not only Laos and its gentle traditions that I had identified with, but also the marvelous cast of international characters who had given me insights into their lives....

Mark Twain once wrote that: "Travel is fatal to prejudice, bigotry, and narrow-mindedness, and many of our people need it sorely on these accounts. A broad, wholesome, charitable view of men and things cannot be acquired by vegetating in one little corner of the earth all one's lifetime." Fortunately, IVS provided me an opportunity to leave my little corner. I was one of the *Fortunate Few*. IVS may no longer exist as an official organization but its premise of helping others in faraway lands by sharing skills across cultures—people-to-people, heart-to-heart, without exploitation or proselytization—is alive and well. The torch still burns and the world still spins.

From Anecdotal Testimonies To Their Implications

Most volunteers conclude that the volunteer experience in IVS was more impactful in their own lives than in the lives of those whom they served or with whom they worked during their IVS days. Yet, many volunteers have seen former students (Ambassador Chamberlin in the foreword) or former co-workers (Steve Stone in this chapter) who have made significant contributions at least partly influenced by how and when IVS touched their lives. IVSers who went to work for USAID or other development agencies in the same or different countries surely applied their experience and had impacts on those efforts and even on the organizations themselves. IVSers who bore personal witness to U.S. policymakers and ordinary citizens on what they experienced about the nature of the war in Vietnam may have had an impact on the course of events. Most IVSers would likely feel, and may also say, that their impact was at the personal level, which is exactly what would be expected in the people-to-people approach stressed by IVS.

If we were able to take a survey of IVSers today, a large majority would likely say that the IVS experience changed the course of their lives and strengthened their interest and career paths in the direction of international engagement. But this international engagement also took many forms, from U.S. Government service to service in international agencies, to international business entrepreneurship, to academic careers, to private voluntary organizations of many forms and persuasions. Most political, economic, and religious persuasions can be found among IVS alumni.

This diversity was a strength of IVS and remains a strength of the alumni who have retained close connections, long after IVS ceased operations in 2002.

All these stories reveal the impacts of IVSers and those with whom they lived and worked, but what can we say about the impact of IVS, Inc as an organization during the 50 years of its existence? It is difficult to imagine anything more important than its influence on the creation of the Peace Corps, which was closely modeled on 10 years of IVS experience. In fact, some would suggest that the combination of Peace Corps success and the later elimination of the U.S. draft were major factors in the decline of opportunities and funding for IVS programs in the later years. But aside from leading to the Peace Corps, during its last 29 years IVS launched national volunteer programs in Bangladesh, Ecuador, Bolivia, Honduras, Botswana, and Zimbabwe offering volunteer opportunities to nationals in those countries as well as to those from the U.S. and other countries. The total number of voluntary agencies around the world also grew during the last decades of IVS. The implications for the future of volunteering for development are explored in the final chapter of this book.

IVS ORGANIZATIONAL IMPACTS

Moving from impact assessment of individual volunteer assignments to that of programs or the organization as a whole becomes quite subjective. Phases of IVS activities are described throughout this book, often chronologically. The following table summarizes, very subjectively, the impacts of IVS programs during its several phases of service.

Phase of IVS Program	Direct Service Impact	Human and Institutional Capacity Impact	Broad Policy and Program Impact	Volunteer Personal Impact	International Understanding Impact
Establishment (1953-1963)	Substantial	Minimal	Substantial	Moderate	Uncertain
Indochina (1957-1975)	Substantial	Moderate	Moderate	Substantial	Moderate
Expansion (1970-1985)	Moderate	Moderate	Minimal	Substantial	Uncertain
Transition (1985-2002)	Moderate	Moderate	Minimal	Minimal	Minimal

Source: authors

The major impact of IVS's establishment phase was on development policy and thinking in its proof-of-concept of international volunteerism. As mentioned, this undergirded the formation of the Peace Corps and the expansion of other private voluntary organization (PVO) programs. Volunteers performed well on programs, which led to program expansions. Unfortunately, many projects were curtailed for political reasons, and there was too little time to see substantial impacts.

The Indochina programs provided a wealth of experience to the many volunteers who served there. War greatly affected programs. Depending on the time and conditions, volunteers were able to make substantial contributions to rural development, refugee relief, and education, both in direct service provision and institutional and human capacity development. At other times, war erased any hope of positive impact. Also, depending on the time, volunteers were quite effective in improving international understanding ("winning hearts and minds") or in influencing U.S. policy. Impact and influence were expanded by the easy availability of other developmental resources from USAID.

As IVS expanded international volunteer programs in multiple countries, volunteers demonstrated an ability to work effectively (i.e., have impact) in widely different activities, in difficult country environments, and with different partnership arrangements. The impact of volunteers' direct work assignments was generally acceptable. Project evaluation studies were done for some USAID-funded projects, often where IVS had a supporting role. These reports evaluated the social or economic objectives of the project and tended to be positive regarding volunteer contributions. Evaluations noted delays in volunteer placements, limited support, and other constraints. Country capacity impacts were common but often compromised by the short duration, varied disruptions, and funding uncertainties in projects.

For the final transition phase of IVS, international volunteers were minimal. Local staff and volunteers implemented activities. Capacity development impacts were at least moderate, as this had become the primary objective of projects, increasingly targeting community level organizations serving disadvantaged groups, rather than larger public sector organizations more common in earlier programs. It is uncertain how lasting capacity impacts have been. There was some enthusiasm for local IVS spin-off organizations that could continue work started by IVS, but most of these did not survive long after the end of IVS support. Programs were of modest size and impacts were most notably at the individual level. Since there were few, if any, international volunteers, there was little potential for impact on international understanding.

The IVS experience in terms of impact on international volunteer programs suggests three lessons. (1) An overall program strategy for work in a specific sector provides a focus and mission for volunteer work. This also facilitates sound technical support and interchange of lessons learned and volunteer experience building on work of predecessors and colleagues. Conversely, volunteers scattered across multiple projects and sectors have much less opportunity for shared learning and innovation and can easily be left feeling isolated. (2) Critical mass itself is important in having enough volunteers on a program to spread administrative costs, command attention from stakeholders, permit experimentation with different approaches to assignments, and facilitate greater professionalism. (3) Longer term projects are also necessary for greater impact, allowing for applying lessons learned and building on consecutive volunteer assignments with the same community or organization.

None of this is surprising as these are issues common to other development programs. They do, however, introduce a tension in that larger, longer, focused volunteer programs may tend to usurp ownership and direction from the host institutions intended to benefit.

A final reflection on IVS impact might look at it in market terms. Effective programs should draw continued funding. IVS's initial partners (the USG and Peace Churches) and key stakeholders (developing countries and their institutions) presumably expected IVS impacts to further their own objectives. If they did so, funding should have continued. It did not. One explanation could be that IVS met needs of the 1950s that no longer existed. Still, as discussed in Chapters Nine and Eleven, USAID and churches continue with international volunteer programs, so there must be some felt need. Alternatively, IVS may have inspired other voluntary organizations that became more effective (i.e., had more impact) than IVS. Whatever the reason, it appears that as IVS evolved, it did not do so in a way that provided the value-added impacts desired by its stakeholders.

SECTION III
International Voluntary Services Partners

9

MISSION AND SERVICE
THE AMERICAN CHURCHES AND IVS

WILLIAM W. SAGE

The formation of International Voluntary Services, Inc. (IVS), as detailed in Chapter One, was from the beginning greatly aided by three American church service organizations: The Mennonite Central Committee (MCC) of the Mennonite Church; the Brethren Service Committee (BSC) of the Church of the Brethren; and the American Friends Service Committee (AFSC) of the Religious Society of Friends (Quakers). Known as the "Historic Peace Churches", each denomination had a long history of humanitarian and development services working person-to-person in other countries. They welcomed the opportunity to provide volunteers to complement the Truman Administration's Four Point Program that promoted "peace and freedom" abroad. They offered IVS experienced organizational know-how, funds, and volunteers for the IVS mission and remained steadfast throughout the fifty years of IVS.

This chapter seeks to provide an abbreviated history and background of these three churches. Understanding each church's history provides an appreciation not only of their successes in volunteer service activities over their long histories but also how their volunteer activities aligned with faith convictions and influenced the shaping of IVS principles, values, and programs.

ENGAGEMENT ABROAD BY AMERICAN CHURCHES BEFORE WORLD WAR I

In general, churches in America have engaged in mission and service since colonial times. After America's independence from England in the eighteenth century, they included missions abroad in addition to service and benevolent activities here in the United States.

In the nineteenth century, missionaries were sent to foreign lands primarily to evangelize and establish Christian schools, colleges, clinics, and hospitals. Exposure to human suffering in these lands weighed heavily on their evangelizing mission, while reaffirming the vital need to create education and health systems that would alleviate human misery. When the missionaries were exposed to humanitarian tragedies, their efforts usually turned to informing their home foreign mission boards and home constituencies. Missionaries brought to their home churches news and information about appalling human conditions abroad, such as famines, plagues, and natural disasters including floods, typhoons, and earthquakes. Their evangelizing began to develop into relief work and humanitarian assistance.

Prior to the late nineteenth century, news from locations abroad took a long time to reach a wide audience in the U.S. Had it not been for the missionaries in some parts of the world at that time, the awareness about such tragedies would have escaped the consciousness of much of the public in the western world, and measures for providing humanitarian relief to those effected by the tragedies would not have materialized.

An important example of American and European missionary efforts was the alarm they sounded to their home constituents concerning the 1876 famine in China. The famine extended over three years and took the lives of millions in north China. Thousands of people in that area of China had already died before the news reached Beijing, the capital. Even when missionaries learned of the famine, got the news back home, and had relief supplies reach the port of Tientsin, supplies remained on the docks because of logistics. Transporting the food, largely grains, over hundreds of miles of primitive roads and paths was slow to impossible, leading to many deaths from starvation.[1]

It was also an era when many orphanages were established in China to save orphaned, homeless, defenseless children from starvation and death.[2] The establishment of orphanages became an important mission objective that involved providing volunteers trained as health care workers to respond and save lives.

Before World War I, the missionaries relied primarily on their home mission board or the designated agency within the structure of their church for any support for humanitarian relief. After World War I, the realization set in that more could be done to help victims of war through cooperative efforts between the churches, making it possible to reach more victims and provide more help and relief to the people in need while adhering to their respective doctrines of faith and convictions. Among the shared convictions was the acceptance of the dignity of all persons regardless of background or religion and the understanding that the Spirit would guide discernment of all collective actions.

The following sections will provide a short history for each of the three peace churches, focusing on their witness to peace and their adherence to their religious principles of nonresistance,[3] humility, and simplicity, which were always the core principles and convictions for their response to the alleviation of human hardship and despair. All three had extensive experience with service projects in the U.S. due, in part, to the social and economic needs stemming from industrialization and urbanization taking place in the later part of the nineteenth century. Overseas experience was added when they responded to provide relief to persons and communities: devastated by World War I, World War II, the Spanish Civil War, and the Korean War; impacted by unjust social and political systems that brought about crushing poverty; or displaced because of natural or human-caused calamities.

Religious Society Of Friends
American Friends Service Committee (AFSC)

The 1650s through the 1670s were times of social upheaval, political unrest, civil strife, and religious intolerance in England and continental Europe. In 1647, when George Fox (1624-1691) spread his evangelical Christian message of "Christian perfection" (the process of achieving spiritual maturity or perfection), he drew opposition and contempt from the English clergy and laity. Yet, there were some among various disillusioned groups of soldiers, farmers, and common towns' people who were attracted to his message and preaching. Fox's message spread south from northern England to London and beyond. These early followers joined together to form the Religious Society of Friends, more commonly known as Friends or Quakers. The origin of the society's name came from the Bible's Gospel of John.[4] They were given the moniker, Quakers, because of the physical trembling that came over them during prayer.[5,6]

English Laws and Persecution

George Fox was imprisoned for the first time in 1650. He would be imprisoned numerous times over the coming decades. Charges for imprisonment were sometimes for causing disturbance and at other times for blasphemy. Other Quakers were also imprisoned. In 1662, the British Parliament enacted the Quaker Act, which made it unlawful for Quakers to refuse to take the "Oath of Allegiance to the Crown". The Conventicle Act[7] of 1664[8] upheld the 1662 law and made it a punishable crime to hold secret meetings. Despite these two laws, Friends continued to meet because they believed they were testifying to their convictions, and they were prepared to face the risks of punishment regardless of the severity of consequences. Some Quakers chose not to face punishment but to search for a new homeland where they could practice their religion freely and without persecution. Some Quakers went to the Netherlands, some to the English Massachusetts Bay Colony, and still others to New Amsterdam.[9]

In 1689, the English Parliament passed the Toleration Act which allowed for freedom of conscience and religious practice. Even with this law, Quakers were not widely understood or accepted by their English countrymen. They felt vulnerable and unprotected even with the new law.

Emigration

In response to legal suppression, emigration became important to members. In 1657, the first Quakers departed England and took up residence in Amsterdam. Like the Mennonites, they found the Netherlands a sanctuary of tolerance. However, with time the level of Dutch tolerance ebbed and a growing number of Dutch Quakers in Amsterdam contemplated yet another migration. Emigration from England and Amsterdam resulted in members finding new homes in the American colonies: Providence Plantations, later Rhode Island; Massachusetts Bay Colony; New Amsterdam (New York); and Pennsylvania. Providence Plantations was established in 1636 by Roger Williams (1603-1683) intending it to be a place of greater religious freedom. Some even emigrated to the Puritan Massachusetts Bay Colony, but they were not accepted as they originally had expected. They were considered heretics and sometimes jailed or banished from the colony.[10] Pennsylvania was settled by William Penn (1644-1718), a well-known early convert.

New Amsterdam (Re-named New York in 1664)

Arriving in New Amsterdam in 1657, one of the early New Amsterdam Quaker preachers, Robert Hodgson, preached to large crowds. He was arrested, flogged, and imprisoned by Governor Peter Stuyvesant (born c. 1592-1672) who also condemned other Quakers with harsh treatments of fines or imprisonment. Those who harbored Quakers faced the same measure of punishment. Edward Hart, the town clerk of Flushing, New York Colony, a settlement of thirty Quaker families, submitted a protest petition known as the "Flushing Remonstrance" in 1657, citing the Flushing town charter of 1645 (originally settled by Dutch Reform Church members) in which residents were promised "liberty of conscience".[11] Hart was jailed for nearly three weeks while others who had signed the petition were forced to recant. Quakers continued to meet, and in 1662, Stuyvesant arrested a farmer named John Bowne for holding Quaker meetings in his farmhouse. Bowne, after release, sailed to Amsterdam where he pleaded the case of religious tolerance before the Dutch West India Company, which had called the Quaker religion "abominable". Unexpectedly, in 1663, the Dutch West India Company overruled Stuyvesant and ordered him to "allow everyone to have his own belief". The next year, 1664, the Dutch surrendered New Amsterdam to the English.

Pennsylvania Colony

Among the early well-known converts in England was the previously mentioned aristocrat, William Penn (1644-1718). His mother was Dutch, so he first visited Amsterdam in 1671 and observed a growing religious intolerance there. When he visited again in 1677 to find no improvement, he decided to emigrate to the colonies. In 1682, he arrived by ship and worked to establish religious safety in the English Pennsylvania Colony. Quaker emigration from Europe continued, with many destined for the English Pennsylvania Colony.[12,13] Penn made guarantees that it would be a place of religious freedom. This attracted Quakers from other New England colonies.[14] Penn called his colony the second "holy experiment" and promoted extensive involvement in voluntary benevolent associations while electing to remain apart from government programs. He encouraged the building of schools, hospitals, and asylums for the mentally ill.

Migration, Social Values, and Concerns

Like many other religious groups in colonial America, the Quakers migrated to frontier areas and other colonies. Eventually they moved from Pennsylvania to New Jersey, Virginia, the Carolinas, and Georgia. Migration often brought into sharp focus compelling social issues existing in these colonial areas. This growing awareness brought about more active engagement with the society at large to address social concerns, including the need for institutions of higher learning which they eventually established.[15]

Slavery

Slavery was a deep concern for Quakers both in England and the colonies. By 1688, Quaker open opposition to slavery was published in Germantown, Pennsylvania. Not until 1758, however, did Quakers reach full unity (spiritual consensus) that slavery was wrong. Much of the convincing came about by John Woolman, a Quaker farmer, merchant, and tailor from New Jersey, who himself was convinced that slavery was inhuman and published, "John Woolman's Journal." There, he wrote, "Slaves of this continent are oppressed, and their cries have reached the ears of the Most High."[16] Quakers had always opposed mistreatment of slaves, and some Quaker slave owners also evangelized them and taught them Christian principles. Even William Penn owned slaves. Other prominent Quaker businessmen owned slaves who made fortunes in the slave trade in Barbados, or they owned ships that carried slaves from the British West Indies to the colonies. *John Woolman's Journal* convinced Quakers that slavery was wrong and eventually no Quaker would be a slave owner. Another historical point relevant to these churches is their work in England to eliminate slavery. In England, a Quaker coalition also worked with William Wilberforce to pass laws to eliminate slavery. Final abolition law passed in 1833.

Mental Illness

The treatment of the mentally ill was another social issue of deep concern to Quakers. In Philadelphia in 1752, they were the first in the English colonies to organize efforts to care for the mentally ill. In 1813, The Asylum for the Relief of Persons Deprived of the Use of Their Reason was opened under Quaker auspices as a private mental hospital in Philadelphia.[17]

Pacifism and Non-violence

The Quaker convictions of pacifism and non-violence were tested during times of war. Before the French and Indian War of 1754 to 1763, some Quakers struggled to gain and preserve peace with the Native American tribes. They strived to keep communications open with the tribes and encouraged the Pennsylvania legislative body to provide the tribes with material aid. During the American Revolution, their struggle was between patriotism and their rejection of war and non-violence. With the entry of the United States into World War I in April of 1917, the Quakers foresaw an approaching crisis for young Quaker men who would be subject to the draft. They met in Philadelphia to search for a way to exempt conscientious objectors (CO) from participating in the war effort in any form. In their first meeting, they discussed what alternatives for humanitarian service might be possible. Ultimately, they chose the battle zone in northern France as a place where those conscientiously opposed to war might provide alternative service in neutral, humanitarian ways.

Eventually the Quakers, Mennonites and Brethren worked together to convince the U.S. Government to allow exemption for conscientious objectors. This effort was largely unsuccessful, although some selective service boards cooperated to release conscientious objectors for alternative service. At that time, the term CO was not yet used; rather "serve non-violently" was used. Haverford College, in Philadelphia, founded by Friends in 1833, became a training center for one hundred Quaker conscientious objectors who would join the British Friends Society in the war zone in France.

Establishment of the American Friends Service Committee (AFSC)

The tragedy and anguish of the first world war resulted in the creation of the American Friends Service Committee (AFSC), previously the Friends National Service Committee, (FNSC). AFSC became the service arm of the Religious Society of Friends. AFSC was founded to enable Quakers and other young pacifists to serve during the war while being faithful to their conviction of nonviolence, but as the service arm of the church, AFSC also collected relief supplies for people displaced from their homes and villages in France and for other regional needs.

AFSC brochures and records from that time indicate some members supported these efforts by growing fruits and vegetables, canning them, and sending them to the AFSC warehouse in Philadelphia for shipment to France. Others sewed and knitted garments which, along with used clothing, were collected in Philadelphia and made ready for shipment abroad. Relief efforts of AFSC continued beyond the end of the war into the 1930s when efforts were directed towards helping escapees from Germany. During the same period, AFSC helped famine victims in the Soviet Union and orphans in Serbia and Poland. In the 1930s the U.S. Government authorized AFSC to provide relief to Germans by establishing kitchens and centers to feed starving children, particularly orphans. AFSC also provided relief for children during the Spanish Civil War.

AFSC operated several Civilian Public Service camps during the Second World War. After the war, AFSC helped many Japanese Americans resettle and rebuild their lives in American cities. Relief efforts in Europe, Japan, and China continued and expanded with the partition of India, which generated massive population movements between India and Pakistan in August 1947.

After the State of Israel was established in May 1948, conflict between Palestinian Arabs and Jews generated hundreds of thousands of Arab Palestinian refugees. In December 1948, AFSC was approached by the Director of the UN Relief for Palestine Refugees to organize a one-year relief program for Palestinian Arab refugees. The program involved 50 volunteers that distributed food, implemented public health interventions (distribution of medicines, malaria control), and organized education programs (establishing schools). Not all volunteers were Quakers, but most were from pacifist backgrounds. The program reached thousands of Palestinian Arab refugees sheltered in Gaza. In the absence of a political solution to the repatriation of the refugees and the declining AFSC resources, AFSC transferred the entire program to the newly created United Nations Relief and Works Administration (UNRWA) in 1950.

THE MENNONITE CHURCH
MENNONITE CENTRAL COMMITTEE (MCC)

The Mennonite Church and its service organization, MCC, made important contributions to the fabric and well-being of America both before and after American Independence. Mennonite history has been extensively documented by scholars and church historians. The intent here is to offer a background about their migration to North America and their service contributions to the creation of a world of understanding and peace. Their extensive mission and service abroad fully equipped and prepared them as founders and supporters of IVS.

The Anabaptist movement began in the early part of the sixteenth century with the Protestant Reformation in Europe. Anabaptists believed in delaying baptism until the candidate confessed his or her faith in Christ as opposed to infant baptism. The Protestant Reformation began in 1517 and ended with the 1555 Peace of Augsburg. In the 1520's, the Anabaptists disagreed with influential reform leaders like Ulrich Zwingli regarding the subjects of infant baptism, separation of church and state, and nonresistance/non-violence. Anabaptists suffered bitter persecution, yet their movement spread to parts of Germany, Austria, Switzerland, and the Netherlands. There were serious divisions amongst the leaders of the Anabaptist movement until a former Dutch Roman Catholic priest, Menno Simons, assumed leadership. The movement grew, taking the name of Menno; thereafter the followers were known as Mennonites. With growth in Europe, some Anabaptist groups split from the Mennonite mainstream and became known as the Hutterites and Amish. The Hutterites advocated communal living while the Amish practiced a more conservative Mennonite lifestyle based on simplicity, reverence, and devotion to God through piety.[18] During the 1600s, wars devastated parts of Europe, particularly Germany. In the wake of armies plundering crops, stealing livestock, and torching homesteads, famine ravaged entire communities. To this already agonizing situation, religious disputes also drove people to leave their homes because the rulers chose which church confession they would allow in their territory of control. Many Germans with strong pious convictions found the situation impossible to bear. They eventually sought a refuge where they could practice religious freedom. The early 100,000 migrants of German heritage that came to the English American colonies included Mennonites.

Mennonite Jan Lensen arrived in 1683 along with twelve German Quaker families who were weavers. They eventually organized a village north of what is now Philadelphia and called their town, Germantown. Following Lensen, at least twenty other families from Germany and the Netherlands settled in Germantown. By 1708, Swiss Brethren began arriving. They were called Anabaptists by their persecutors and, like the Mennonites, insisted that only believers should be baptized. Jailed, beaten, fined, or banished in Europe they resolved to leave for the Pennsylvania Colony. Dutch Mennonite followers helped them find passage to Pennsylvania, which had been founded by the English Quaker William Penn in 1681 under a land grant from King Charles II, who owed money to Penn's deceased father. Over time, the English colonial governors associated the Swiss with their Dutch brethren and called them Mennonites as well. This remained so as they eventually settled further inland from Germantown.[19] By the 1730s some families had settled in the Pennsylvania Cumberland Valley while others ventured further south down the valley into Virginia settling in the Shenandoah River region.

In the 1860s, a group of Mennonite immigrants settled in Iowa. The population grew rapidly, as Mennonite congregations elsewhere who wanted more progressive programs, such as missions in higher education plus more liberal disciplines, chose to move to Iowa.[20]

The first large wave of Mennonite emigrates to the U.S. and Canada from Imperial Russia took place in the 1870s, when their complete exemption to military service was threatened by the Tsarist government. Another wave of Mennonites left Russia for North America because of compulsory economic and cultural requirements, such as the obligation to use only the Russian language. About a third of the original Russian Mennonite population remained in Russia because a system of alternative military service was negotiated, whereby they could perform forestry or other government sanctioned services in lieu of military service. In 1920, the remaining population faced starvation because of famine resulting from the civil war. The North American Mennonite communities galvanized to respond to the famine, ultimately forming the Mennonite Central Committee (MCC) service organization in July of 1920. One of the great lessons learned by the Mennonites from their international service work during these war and post-war years was that cooperative efforts brought greater results.

The General Conference of the Mennonite Church, the largest branch of Mennonites, had established the Emergency Relief Commission (ERC) in 1899. During World War I, the ERC raised and donated funds to the American Friends Service Committee (AFSC) for relief and reconstruction work in France, where the reconstruction work was carried out by Mennonite volunteers. A second branch of the Mennonites established their own Mennonite Relief Commission for War Sufferers (MRCWS) in December of 1917, just months after the U.S. entered the war on April 6, 1917. By April of 1919, church funds were supporting some 54 Mennonite relief workers in Clermont-en-Argonne, France, an area devastated by the battle of Verdun. Volunteers were also sent to the Middle East through the American Committee for Armenian and Syrian Relief. The Mennonite Brethren branch also established an organization known as United Orphanage War Relief (UOWR).

Inspired by a common mission and established beliefs and principles, the three Mennonite relief groups, the ERC, the MRCWS and the UORW, met in January 1918 in Goshen, Indiana, to discuss ways of promoting more vigorous relief efforts. What emerged was an agreement to carry on a vigorous campaign for relief through the existing organizations while planning to expand their relief work in France. They also expanded their relief work in the Middle East by supporting the Armenian and Syrian Relief efforts with relief funds, and by January 1919, thirty-two Mennonite volunteers were working in the Middle East. By late 1920, MCC had emerged as the main Mennonite relief organization even as the other three Mennonite relief organizations carried on relief work in various foreign lands. During the war, they recognized the massive need to help the victims in Europe, particularly France. Following the war's end, the massive destruction and devastation caused by the Great War and the famine in the Soviet Union created the imperative to cooperate more closely than ever before. These experiences and the inter-Mennonite cooperation led to the discovery of a common identity running through the complex Mennonite community. It also led to recognition of an eagerness of many Mennonite youth to carry out their steadfast gospel convictions in practical ways through volunteerism and service.

MCC devoted much of its relief efforts to helping thousands of Mennonites emigrate from the communist Soviet Union in the 1920s. Emigration was the answer for many seeking religious freedom, food, and social security, bringing them to join those Mennonites who had emigrated from Russia to North America almost a half-century before.

During the First World War, there was no provision for deferment and alternative service for conscientious objectors despite efforts made by the peace churches to convince the U.S. Government to make such provisions for deferment. The Civilian Public Service (CPS) system of service camps was not established until the Second World War. Mennonite conscientious objectors found options for volunteering with AFSC reconstruction projects in France from late 1917 until the end of the war. After the Armistice of November 1918, more Mennonite volunteers served in France. In the summer of 1917, Mennonites were disappointed when they learned the option of farming and food production as a deferment and alternative to participation in war effort had been denied. They continued to press federal authorities to liberally interpret the Selective Service Act of May 18, 1917, by exempting conscientious objectors from all military related service. When this did not transpire, those who refused to serve in the military were forced by conviction to seek other ways to help those experiencing hardship and devastation. Some served in the AFSC reconstruction projects, often volunteering to work in hospitals or orphanages in France. Domestically, some served in the military but in non-combatant positions such as clerical workers or kitchen personnel. Nevertheless, in January of 1918, delegates representing the Mennonite branches held a conference to draft a resolution to be presented to President Wilson reaffirming their loyalty to the U.S. as their "beloved country" and seeking deferment from either combat or non-combatant service by requesting instead to be deferred for agriculture work.

At the start of the Second World War, MCC looked for different options, notably through working with other historic peace churches to design, win, and operate programs of government-approved civilian alternative service programs during the war. The National Service Board for Religious Objectors (NSBRO)[21] was the U.S. government agency responsible for overseeing the administration of the Civilian Public Service (CPS) system of camps. Some of the U.S. camps were operated by the Mennonites with the provision that camp residents would meet conscientious objector status. Camp residents were involved in forestry and conservation activities and other government approved public service projects such as hospitals and public health programs. These projects met both the requirements of the NSBRO and the convictions of conscientious objectors.

CHURCH OF THE BRETHREN BRETHREN SERVICE COMMITTEE (BSC)

As mentioned, the 1600s was an era of wars in Europe giving rise to extreme hardship, devastation, and frequently famine. The Reformation did not bring religious tolerance as hoped, but often resulted in persecution that targeted those who disagreed with the officially established state-church selected by the local nobility.

The Anabaptist movement continued to spread in Europe, particularly in Germany and the Netherlands. The movement was further influenced by seventeenth-century Pietism which was unacceptable to the officially recognized churches: Catholic, Lutheran, or Reformed in local districts in Germany.[22]

The history of the Brethren began in 1708 when a group of eight Christians organized themselves into a church under the leadership of Alexander Mack (1679–1735).[23] Five adult men and three women gathered in the German Town of

Schwarzenau at the Eder Brook for baptism, as an outward expression of their new faith.[24] One member of the group baptized Mack, who in turn baptized the other seven.

The Schwarzenau Brethren as they became known, believed that the reformed churches emerging from the Reformation missed the point of true Christianity as taught by Jesus in the Sermon on the Mount and revealed in the New Testament. They sought a church that taught New Testament discipleship and rejected some doctrines and practices of the state church, e.g., the practice of infant baptism and the use of force to punish dissenters. They decided to form their own church. The eight referred to themselves as "brethren" or New Baptists. They endured persecution and hardship for their beliefs, as had the earlier Anabaptists—the Mennonites who twenty-five years earlier had emigrated to Pennsylvania. The message of the State-Churches to all other groups was "Convert, leave or die."

The Brethren emigration to the Pennsylvania Colony (established in 1681), began in 1719. There, they practiced their religion freely and enjoyed the bounty of available, abundant land.[25] Most Brethren had left Europe by 1740. On arrival in Germantown, they reorganized and by Christmas 1723 had founded their first congregation. From the Pennsylvania colony they migrated to western areas of Lancaster and York counties in Pennsylvania (Pennsylvania meaning Penn's Forest), central Maryland, the Shenandoah Valley of Virginia, Tennessee, the Carolinas, western Pennsylvania, Ohio, Indiana, Illinois, Iowa, Kansas and eventually the American west coast.[26]

Initially they became known as German Baptist Brethren, although this name was not recognized until the Annual Meeting in 1836. In 1871, they adopted the name German Baptist Brethren Church until 1908 when the name "Church of the Brethren" was officially adopted at their Annual Meeting in Des Moines, Iowa. The name change was justified by citing the predominant use of the English language and the fact that the name "German Baptist" frustrated mission work.

Service to others was always an important Brethren principle since arriving in the English colonies. Early charitable activities included: support for a home for the elderly, rebuilding a farmhouse or barn that had burned down, caring for the family of a brethren who was injured or ill or suffered from a crop loss and food insecurity. Then, events abroad before World War I drew the attention and response by the Brethren to the hardship and suffering taking place in other parts of the world, including India in 1894 and China in 1908.[27]

One of the first significant outpouring of compassion and relief was their response to the 1915-1923 Armenian Genocide, in which an estimated 1.5 million Armenians perished because of the atrocities carried out by Ottoman Turks. By 1917, Brethren began responding to the enormous humanitarian needs of surviving Armenian refugees by creating a special Relief Committee to raise funds for Armenian assistance.[28] A temporary staff was added to the American Committee for Relief in the Near East (ACRNE)[29] to ensure that support for Armenian survivors and refugees would be carried out without interference of authorities and with dispatch.[30] In 1918, the Mennonite Relief Commission for War Sufferers (MRCWS), forerunner to MCC, established in 1920, was also raising funds for the American Committee for Armenian and Syrian Relief (ACASR). In early 1919, the first Mennonite volunteers were dispatched to the Middle East. Later, thirty men and two women volunteers served in the region as part of the humanitarian relief effort. The Brethren Near East Committee assigned volunteers to the Marsh district of Syria, where a program of relief primarily focused on providing clothing and shoes to orphanages, on the rehabilitation of vineyards, and on reconstruction of homes.

Brethren response to the starvation in Russia was channeled through the American Friends Service Committee and Mennonite agencies. However, with the outbreak of the Spanish Civil War in 1936, the Brethren Service was again galvanized to provide overseas relief. In addition to personnel and relief funds, the Brethren joined with the Mennonites and AFSC in sending, for the first time, "gifts-in-kind," later referred to as material aid. This became a feature of later relief and emergency responses to humanitarian emergencies around the world. The first "gifts-in-kind" are reported to have been cases of shoes shipped in 1937.

Emergency humanitarian needs were swelling across the world and, recognizing the impending dark clouds of war on the horizon in Europe, a committee of Brethren leadership formed the Brethren Service Committee in November 1939. This service arm of the Brethren Church was to provide relief assistance, reconstruction aid, and volunteers. By 1940 this mandate expanded to include urgent assistance for refugees and displaced persons.

When the U.S. entered World War I in April of 1917, the three peace churches worked together to persuade the U.S. Government to provide complete exemption from military service for conscientious objectors. The effort ended in disappointment. Between 1936 and 1937 representatives of the three peace churches again worked together to secure a provision for alternative service for conscientious objectors before the start of World War II.[31] This time the Brethren Service Committee (BSC) along with their partners the Mennonite Church and Religious Society of Friends and other supporting faith-based groups were able to convince the U.S. Government to enact a lawful provision for alternative service. In October of 1940, the U.S. National Service Board for Religious Objectors (NSBRO) sanctioned the creation of the Civilian Public Service System, a U.S. Government program providing conscientious objectors with an alternative to military service. From 1941 to 1947, nearly 12,000 draftees, unwilling to serve in any combat or non-combat role in the military, accepted assignments in one of 152 Civilian Public Service (CPS) camps.

The first camps administered by the Brethren were in Indiana, Michigan, and Arkansas. Early program morale was high, as the men worked on forestry, conservation, and other public service projects that NSBRO considered constructive service to their country and faithful to individuals' religious convictions. Service assignments included work in mental hospitals, public health service, and other projects in the national interest. About one-fifth of all CPS Brethren were working in mental hospitals.[32]

In 1942, the Brethren Service Committee started the Heifer Project, in addition to the clothing, food and other relief supplies sent overseas to those in need. In 1953, the Heifer Project became an independent nonprofit corporation as Heifer Project, Incorporated (HPI). At the time of its founding, it was believed to be more practical to send bred heifers overseas than calves and milk cows. Recipients of heifers were asked to donate the first female offspring to another qualified family which would in turn do the same. Long term, more families would benefit with that approach.

The United Nations Relief and Rehabilitation Administration (UNRRA) was created on November 9, 1943, by a charter signed by forty-four nations. The Heifer Project was well underway by that time. A first shipment was made to Puerto Rico in May of 1944. Yet, when BSC proposed shipping heifers to Europe, UNRRA declined approval believing such an undertaking was too hazardous. One year later, as the war in Europe ended, UNRRA approved the shipment of livestock to rebuild the devastated dairy industry. In May 1945, the Brethren Service Committee volunteers were dubbed the "seagoing cowboys" when BSC became the recruiting agency for livestock tenders needed by the UNRRA for shipments of animals to Europe.[33]

Between 1945 to 1947, the United Nations Relief and Rehabilitation Administration and the Brethren Service Committee of the Church of the Brethren sent nearly 7,000 men and boys ages 16 to 72 across the oceans to deliver livestock to war-torn countries. These seagoing cowboys made about 360 trips on 73 different ships.[34]

In 1944, the Church of the Brethren purchased Blue Ridge College campus in New Windsor, Maryland. The facility operated as a processing center for relief goods being shipped to survivors of the war, and eventually became a training center for volunteers serving in the U.S. and abroad. Trainees represented 20 different Protestant denominations and Catholics, but the majority were Brethren. By June 1949, volunteers were being placed in Europe. The processing of goods, particularly clothing, increased following the war. Protestant churches shipped donations of clothing and blankets to the New Windsor warehouse where they were sorted and sent to locations in need. Church World Service (CWS),[35] established in 1946, and Lutheran World Relief (LWR) funded room and board for volunteers processing clothing at New Windsor. The cooperation between New Windsor, CWS, and LWR was an early expression of ecumenical cooperation which firmly continues to the present.

The BSC signed an agreement with UNRRA on July 15, 1946, to provide fifty volunteers with farming and mechanical experience to go to China. Brethren experience in China began in 1908 when five missionaries arrived in Shanghai. Their experience in China prompted UNRRA to approach the Brethren, since UNRRA had provided two-thousand tractors to accelerate the reclamation of farmland. The Chinese had virtually no experience with mechanized farming. Western farming technicians were needed to instruct farmers on the use of the equipment. Shipment of the tractors and the Brethren volunteers was coordinated by UNRRA.

Forging Ecumenical Cooperation International Relief And Development

Dr. David M. Stowe, who became the executive secretary of the Department of Foreign Missions of the National Council of Churches, USA, (NCCUSA) and had served on the China Mission, spoke at the 1963 General Assembly of the NCCUSA in Philadelphia, and observed that "after World War II, a large world service enterprise of churches developed in separation from the program of missions" to address the "reconstruction, relief and rehabilitation needs throughout Europe." Through this program, great new resources became available first through special campaigns in the churches and then through grants and surplus commodities of the United States Government.[36] The tremendous human and material needs of Europe brought a much clearer, deeper, and comprehensive understanding to the meaning of volunteer service. "Service seeks to serve without intending to convert" and "service is the outreach of human compassion."[37]

World War II ended in Europe on May 8, 1945, and in the Asia Pacific on August 15,1945. Over one million Japanese from all over Asia were repatriated back to a shattered Japan. Over ten million people of German ancestry that had settled in

Eastern Europe required resettlement and relief assistance. Vast armies of soldiers returned to their homeland only to find their homes destroyed and families scattered. Needs were overwhelming and urgent.

American churches were also aware of other humanitarian crises in other parts of the world due to the partition of India in 1947, the rise of Communist China in 1949, and the Korean War 1950–1953. In 1952, there were five million North Korean refugees in South Korea, more than 350,000 Palestinian Arab refugees in the Middle East, and one million Chinese refugees in Hong Kong. In other parts of the world, independence movements against colonial rule had led to civil strife, generating large refugee movements and community displacement through the late 1960s. Natural disasters—famine, floods, and geological disasters—caused additional hardship and misery. These international developments required a humanitarian response by the American churches. In 1954, for example, MCC was providing material and food aid to Vietnamese refugees who had fled from north to south Vietnam.[38]

During the Second World War, there was growing acknowledgement that churches working together could more effectively reach victims and survivors and use church resources more efficiently. Those resources included both financial and diverse material and human resources, including volunteers with expertise in the medical, social service, agriculture, and educational fields needed in many unstable and turbulent locations around the world. The churches had a history of missionary and volunteer service in lands now ravaged by conflict, as in the Middle East, China, North Asia and Southeast and South Asia. As countries in Africa became independent in the 1960s,[39] the need for development assistance would be required as much as humanitarian relief assistance. The combination of financial resources, competency in specific skills, and geographic and cultural experience and expertise would be powerful tools the churches could provide to rebuild the social and economic fabric of nations torn apart by war, conflict, strife, famine, and population displacements.

Such efforts to bring closer ecumenical cooperation were evident as early as 1944, when the U.S. Church Committee on Overseas Relief and Reconstruction (CCORR) was carrying on the work of the Christian relief agencies begun four years earlier. Nine agencies[40] supported CCORR famine relief work in China, Burma (Myanmar), and India. Twenty-one Protestant church denominations and eight Christian agencies formed committees to foster increased giving for war victims in Europe and victims of famine in Asia.[41] This collaborative approach to giving eventually became known as "One Great Hour of Sharing" which continues today with participation by some Protestant denominations.[42]

On May 4, 1946, the U.S. Federal Council of Churches, the Foreign Missions Conference, and the American Committee of the World Council of Churches jointly established Church World Service (CWS) as a body representing ecumenical service. This grew out of the recommendation by a committee of church relief agency leaders in an effort to accomplish what they recognized as a biblical imperative. Seventeen American Protestant denominations were invited to appoint delegates to represent them on the governing body of CWS. In addition to the 17 governing body members, twelve denominations and church agencies adopted an affiliate relationship with CWS. CWS would thereafter become a conduit for the Churches' collaborative action. In that spirit of cooperation, they would also provide financial support to IVS and IVS programs in the years after 1953.

SOME THOUGHTS ON WHY TCA ENCOURAGED THE THREE PEACE CHURCHES TO FORM IVS

By the time the Technical Cooperation Administration (TCA later became USAID), encouraged MCC, BSC and AFSC to form IVS, the TCA had already recognized the unique resources the three church organizations could provide for successful implementation of the Truman Administration's Point Four agenda and timely healing of broken parts of the world. The three could play an important role in constructive and peaceful social and economic development in countries emerging from the destruction and deprivation of war and countries weakened by underdevelopment.

TCA recognized that the three organizations already had a long, distinguished history of cooperation in many joint efforts and relief activities beginning with World War I and continuing through World War II until 1953. Cooperation sometimes involved assigning volunteers to meet humanitarian needs of specific crises, such as in France during World War I, the relief needs from the Armenian genocide, the humanitarian needs during the Spanish Civil War, or urgent needs in Europe, the Middle East and Asia. In all these collaborative efforts, the three organizations assigned volunteers to humanitarian relief efforts, raised funds to support volunteers, and provided relief supplies in the form of food, clothing, shelter, medicines, livestock, and other material needs. The collaboration was extensive and historic.

With their long history of mission and relief work in foreign lands, the three churches had geographic experience and expertise for cultural understanding including language proficiency and knowledge for working with local communities of diverse cultures and religions. The principle and experience of working on a one-on-one basis was an important element to the success of their volunteer service.

The three organizations generated bountiful resources by and from their own churches and made these available in cooperative and mutually reinforcing ways for relief and rehabilitation and eventually for development activities in newly independent nations. They were able to generate material resources in generous supply such as clothing, shoes, bedding supplies, kitchen utensils, milk, grain, hospital supplies, and eventually livestock through the Heifer project.

The three organizations had provided volunteers and administrators to various projects in Europe, the Middle East and Asia. Often the volunteers were "generalists". Over time the need for volunteers with specific competencies evolved in areas such as agriculture, animal husbandry, farm management, social work with vulnerable groups like orphans, the mentally ill, the elderly, public health, mental health, education, and many more. All of these specialized skills were part of the abundance of resources made available over the years to both local neighborhood, community, and overseas projects. Even the organizations' experience with the resettlement of refugees from the Spanish Civil War to Cuba and Mexico was a model for the resettlement of refugees from Europe to North and South America and Australia.

The three organizations worked with the government to authorize alternative service for conscientious objectors before the Second World War. This cemented their cooperative approach, trust, and commitment for working together. Eventually, the approach succeeded in establishing the Civilian Public Service (CPS) system which provided the opportunity for conscientious objectors to serve in domestic projects recognized and approved by the NSBRO. Following federal regulations, the three organizations provided civilian oversight as administrators of some of the 152 CPS camps. The three organizations' experience with volunteer work camps on U.S. Indian reservations and in Mexico provided the concept and credibility for the idea of establishing the CPS camps.[43]

Once IVS was legally recognized, the U.S. churches provided financial support through the nearly 50-year history of the organization. The IVS board consisted mostly of members from Protestant church denominations and some Catholic agencies. Over the life of IVS, church financial support varied. During some periods, churches supported IVS directly and at other times supported IVS financially through an ecumenical organization like CWS which remained for the most part constant through the years.[44] IVS primarily functioned with U.S. Government contracts but was still reliant on church support and nonprofit and private donors. Birthed by church organizations, there was always an attempt to maintain church support, sometimes, easier than at other times but always a part of the identity of IVS.

The Faith Community And Volunteerism Today

Volunteerism has been a vital and steadfast value in American life going back to the first immigrants and the early colonial years. The Pennsylvania Colony, for example, saw volunteer benevolent associations emerge that promoted education, hospitals and asylums. Later, urbanization and industrialization led to a surge in the formation of civic service groups addressing social issues utilizing the energy and commitment of volunteers to sustain their compassionate efforts.[45]

The opportunities available to those who choose to volunteer and serve with a faith-based organization are practically unlimited. All faith-based organizations and faith communities value volunteers because the volunteers want to make a difference and because they want to be "doers" and not observers. Their convictions and ideals are generally the basis for a volunteer commitment. All commitments are important and highly valued by both the volunteers and the communities' hosting volunteers that are working on an activity or project. Volunteer involvement may be at a church food pantry, or tutoring in an after-class neighborhood school, or helping with resettlement of a refugee family, or cleaning up after a natural disaster locally or in another country, such as the 2004 Tsunami in Banda Aceh, Indonesia. Volunteers also commit to overseas opportunities like projects of building schools, constructing clinics and water systems, working with orphans in orphanages or working on farm, agriculture, or animal husbandry activities.

Every day of every year, there is a need for volunteers. There are never enough. The opportunity can be nearby and local or far away or abroad, short-term or long-term. The opportunity may be for generalists with no specific skills required, only time and commitment, or for specialized competencies, such as medical or social service professional, agriculture, information technology, conservation projects, construction, or renovation engineering, just to list a few. Sponsoring faith-based organizations might provide a stipend for living costs, or they may provide accommodations at a work. Each year, hundreds of thousands of volunteers of all ages, of all backgrounds and competencies, contribute their time, talent and treasure to be actively involved in a project that makes a difference in their neighborhood, in a community or in the world. The types and locations of volunteer opportunities have evolved over the years to meet a changing world and changing needs of communities but the opportunity to volunteer and serve continues to provide an infinite range of opportunities today.[46]

To explore volunteer opportunities, check the website of the organization of your interest. There is usually a tag which might say, for examples, "Get Involved" or "Jump-In and Volunteer" or "How You Can Make a Difference." Each faith-based organization will list the kinds of opportunities available and the requirements for placement.

10

IVS And The Origins Of The Peace Corps*

E. Timothy Smith

When Senator John F. Kennedy spoke at the University of Michigan during his 1960 presidential campaign, he proposed the creation of a Peace Corps. He challenged the 10,000 students assembled that October night to "contribute part of your life to this country." He asked those who were going to be doctors if they were willing to spend time in Ghana, or if those planning to be technicians or engineers were willing to work in the Foreign Service or share their skills working around the world.[1] In general, Kennedy has been credited for the creation of the Peace Corps, but what few people know is the long history of youth service that contributed to its creation. There were many people and groups, both in and out of the U.S. Government, that led to the Peace Corps. Perhaps the most important of them is the subject of this book, International Voluntary Services (IVS).

The idea of youth service in America dates to the nineteenth century. Some of that history has been explored in other chapters of this book. Numerous church-related and private voluntary agencies established projects for youth that contributed to the development of the Peace Corps. By the time the Peace Corps was established in 1961, there were approximately fifty American voluntary agencies working on assistance programs abroad and approximately 500 young people in programs ranging from social development, agricultural extension, community development, education, and animal husbandry to public health, emergency relief, and refugee resettlement.

Two groups were the most important in the creation of the Peace Corps—IVS and Brethren Voluntary Service (BVS). BVS may well have planted the seed of the idea in the mind of Senator Hubert Humphrey, who played a major role in pushing the idea and passing it on to Kennedy in 1960. It was IVS, however, that became the

---

*The author has also written on this topic in "Roots of the Peace Corps: Youth Volunteer Service in the 1950s" Peace & Change, Volume 41, Issue 2, April 2016.

model on which the Peace Corps was built. In the early 1950s, IVS received government funding for projects that aimed at community development (see Chapter One) and became increasingly important in U.S. policy during the 1960s. Over the long-term, community development policies of the U.S. government were viewed as a failure, although historians differ on the reasons.[2] However, the youthful volunteers, like those in IVS, worked on a people-to-people basis with small goals centered on their humanitarian interests and their technical skills. They sought to improve the lives of the people they worked with one village at a time. They became the face of America to those villagers.

The Peace Corps was also the result of the Cold War. As Elizabeth Cobbs Hoffman has noted, "The Peace Corps was a tool of the Cold War. . . ." However, she also noted that "it reflected a compound of motivations." It attempted "to represent and build upon the most charitable and humane traditions of the United States" and "was at odds with much other foreign policy in the 1960s."[3] By the mid-1950s the Cold War polarization had essentially stabilized in Europe with two military alliances: the North Atlantic Treaty Organization (NATO, a 30-nation alliance of democracies); and the Warsaw Pact (the Soviet Union and seven Eastern Bloc socialist countries). As a result, the U.S.-Soviet conflict became increasingly focused on influencing the developing world, including areas where IVS was particularly focused.

In November 1960, near the end of the presidential campaign, Kennedy gave a speech in San Francisco where he was critical of the Foreign Service. He noted that 70 percent of the new service officers spoke only English and were unable to communicate with the people of the nations where they were posted. He warned that the Soviets "were doing a better job endearing themselves to the developing world" and he again called for a peace corps of talented youth to counter the Russian efforts in the developing world.[4] Kennedy's San Francisco speech reflected ideas in a widely read political novel published in 1958, *The Ugly American*, written by William Lederer and Eugene Burdick. The novel, and its factual epilogue, argued that what the U.S. was offering in the developing world was not the right kind of help. Instead, they felt that the U.S. should send a small, well-trained force willing to give up comforts, speak the native language, and have an expertise in the nation they were helping.[5]

Fearful that U.S. foreign policy and its representatives abroad were not taking the correct approach to dealing with the threat of Soviet communism, some politicians felt that the United States had an obligation to help the poorer nations of the world, not through an arms buildup but through economic assistance. Two of those politicians were Sen. Hubert Humphrey (D-Minnesota.) and Rep. Henry Reuss

(D-Wisconsin). Beginning in 1957, the two men pushed for the creation of a voluntary organization that would place American youth in the developing world in local projects run on a people-to-people basis. Both were influenced by BVS and IVS, and the idea of a peace corps began to emerge with their efforts.

BVS, Humphrey, And The Seed

Humphrey was influenced toward the creation of a voluntary youth organization by a chance speech given by actor Don Murray at a campaign stop by 1956 Democratic Vice-Presidential candidate Sen. Estes Kefauver (D-Tenn.) in Hibbing, Minnesota, and the subsequent letters Humphrey and Murray exchanged. Hibbing was the birthplace of Greyhound Busses and Don Murray had just starred in the 1956 movie "Bus Stop" with Marilyn Monroe, so he was invited to join the delegation in Hibbing. Kefauver's plane was delayed, so Murray was asked to say a few words to keep the event moving. Humphrey and several other political and labor leaders were there and heard Murray's talk, but it wasn't about Hollywood as everyone expected. Instead, Murray spoke about his experiences working with the Brethren Volunteer Service (BVS). (See Chapter Nine on the Brethren Service Commission, BVS, and their importance in the founding of IVS). Murray spoke for a half hour about various volunteer projects. Humphrey was impressed and began to explore the idea of some type of youth service program.[6] After leaving BVS, Murray remained in Europe, first in Naples where he worked with refugees living like those around him—unlike the U.S. government officials portrayed in *The Ugly American*. Eventually, with social worker Beldon Paulson, W. Harold Row of the Brethren Service Commission, and the Congregational Christian Service Committee, Murray helped found the Homeless European Land Program (HELP). HELP purchased land in Sardinia to resettle European refugees.[7] The program received the support of Humphrey, and he wrote to Murray saying that he was "fighting a battle...that can be of great importance in other areas of the world" and offered Murray "all possible help". He also spoke on the Senate floor about how such programs like HELP could "contribute toward our winning this real struggle" for the minds of men.[8]

In the context of the Cold War, Humphrey viewed a youth service program as a different type of diplomacy—one that would win over the peoples of developing countries and peacefully help to achieve the goal of containing communism. The seed of a peace corps had been planted and Humphrey helped to make it grow.

International Voluntary Service, Inc

Congressman Henry Reuss also became interested in the idea of youth voluntary service as a part of U.S. foreign policy. He believed that the United States too often emphasized military alliances and provided military hardware to reactionary leaders who turned those weapons on their own people. He also believed that there was too much of an emphasis on grandiose projects and that U.S. officials abroad lived in enclaves away from the people of the nation that they were trying to assist. It was IVS that influenced Reuss to support the idea of some type of voluntary service by young people. He had seen IVS projects in operation travelling through Southeast Asia on a tour with a House subcommittee in November 1957.[9]

The story of IVS's inception in Chapter One notes that from the very beginning it involved people-to-people contact, and not the "grandiose" projects that Reuss objected to. An example was shown in the first IVS project done in conjunction with World Neighbors in Afadra, Egypt. Volunteer Kenneth Imhoff wrote about a donkey ride to villages that could not be reached by jeep. In the spirit of people-to-people connections, there was no better way of getting closer to the people than "to put yourself as near their level as possible." Imhoff also noted the importance of learning Arabic so that he could talk with the people in order "to understand their problems and customs."[10] Daniel Russell, an IVS field program officer, explaining what IVS did in a brochure addressed to potential volunteers, wrote that the volunteers lived and worked directly with the village and rural people introducing a "unique spirit of good will and understanding that came through being a good neighbor."[11]

IVS was funded first by the Technical Cooperation Administration (TCA) in the execution of the Truman Point Four program. The TCA was replaced by the Foreign Operations Administration (FOA), and later the International Cooperation Administration (ICA). By 1959 Oliver Popence, Deputy Director of Special Projects in the ICA, noted that the young volunteers cost far less money than what the ICA was spending for personnel. He also noted, according to IVS's executive director, John Noffsinger, that "these boys are frequently much more effective than ICA people because they are out in the country working with the people and not sitting in the capitol writing memos to each other." Popence also praised the agricultural work done by IVS in Egypt. He noted that at the time of the Suez Crisis the Egyptians were calling for more "like these boys" who were known "from one end of the Nile to the other". Popence indicated that not all ICA people supported the use of IVS. There was considerable opposition within the ICA to having technical assistance provided by outside groups. However, Popence wrote that he considered this totally wrong, and there was the potential for expansion of IVS's role if more money were made available.[12]

Popence was not the only supporter of IVS. Stanley Andrews, who had been the director of the TCA from 1952-1953, was a close observer of IVS. Although

Andrews had left the government by this time, he said that the ICA was trying to eliminate IVS support. Yet, Harold Weiss, who was the Egyptian country director under President Dwight Eisenhower, stated that IVS "was the most effective little group of people that we've ever dealt with." Andrews was able to convince Harold Stassen, Director of the FOA, to allocate a million dollars. Stassen told Andrews to "Go ahead and make it great."[13]

According to Andrews, the new head of the ICA, John B. Hollister, chopped off the million dollars. Andrews stepped in and pushed the IVS board to continue. Hollister was soon replaced by Jim Smith, who told Andrews that he was "interested in seeing these young people have a chance to work" and that he would approve anything they did. Under Smith and his successor, Dennis Fitzgerald, IVS programs were continued by the ICA.[14]

Both inside and outside of the government, Andrews remained supportive of IVS and wrote IVS Executive Committee member, W.Harold Row, that he believed the IVS program had "done much more to bring this concept of service to people further along that I or anybody else in the government have the right to be given credit for." He told Row that foreign aid had tended to take what he called the "monument approach" to assistance "rather than the educational and technical and long time working with people approach." He wrote Row that IVS was "able to do and are doing what the government sponsored work ought to do but aren't doing."[15]

In 1956, IVS began to send teams into Southeast Asia. The volunteers in Laos and Vietnam believed that they were playing a role in the U.S. foreign policy objectives in that region. For example, Richard Peters, writing in 1960, said that while they seldom thought of it in this way, their work was, in part, "to counter the advance of communism". He wrote that the answer to communism "can be found through the improvement of the standards of living of the people."[16] That was the goal of IVS. And ultimately the goal of the Peace Corps.

REUSS, HUMPHREY AND THE CREATION OF THE PEACE CORPS

The experiences and funding struggles of IVS provided an example for a different approach to foreign policy which ultimately led to the Peace Corps. Along the way, there were several detours and different visions that had to be reconciled. When Rep. Reuss was in Southeast Asia studying the U.S. foreign aid program, he was "struck by the oft-observed contrast between the militarism-encased-in-concrete approach and the Johnny-Appleseed approach." He noted the large amount of military assistance given to the Cambodian government, but the only time it was used was when the government was dealing with internal dissent. He also observed the economic assistance program with a superb U.S. built highway. But for the Cambodian peasants, its best use was its shoulder that could be used as a trail for their water buffalo.[17] In contrast, Reuss was struck by the good that a team of four young American school teachers associated with IVS were doing setting up elementary schools in the jungles. He felt that young Americans needed a sense of purpose, and the greatest challenges and adventures were in the developing nations of Asia and Africa. He felt that young Americans would "want to become involved in it." The U.S. would be well-served, he argued, if thousands of young Americans were "willing to help with an irrigation project, digging a village well, or setting up a rural school."[18] With the Cambodian experience and ideas influenced by what he saw IVS doing, Reuss decided to take the first step in the direction of the Peace Corps in what he called initially the 'Point Four Youth Corps'.

In addition to BVS and the HELP work that Murray was doing, Humphrey was also impressed with the work of IVS, which he called "the organization which has the experience most directly relevant" to a Peace Corps. He noted that IVS volunteers spent "most of their spare time with the local populaces" and had been "goodwill ambassadors" for the United States. When Humphrey proposed the Peace Corps in 1960, he argued that IVS volunteers were idealistic young people oriented toward the people-to-people approach and had had tremendous success. Specifically, he pointed out the work of an IVS agricultural specialist team in Laos that so impressed the Laos government that it requested eleven more teams. Humphrey also referred to the Suez Crisis, noting that after the crisis one of the first requests from the Egyptian government was to get IVS back and to send ten more teams just like them. The senator stated that what the U.S. needed was an imaginative and constructive plan that emphasized the "humanitarian ideal" of the nation.[19]

Between 1957 and 1960 both Humphrey and Reuss, joined by Senator Richard Neuberger (D-Oregon) until his death in March 1960, attempted to persuade Congress to support the establishment of a youth volunteer service program sponsored by the U.S. government. Humphrey introduced the first Peace Corps-type legislation in 1957, but it was met with little enthusiasm by fellow senators. In his autobiography, Humphrey wrote that traditional diplomats "quaked" at sending young people all around the world. Even liberal senators "thought it a silly and unworkable idea."[20]

Nonetheless, Humphrey continued his efforts and urged President Dwight Eisenhower to institute some type of national program of voluntary service. Eisenhower did send Kevin McCann, the president of Defiance College, to meet with Don Murray to discuss BVS. McCann was supportive and heartily recommended to

Eisenhower that he "support a federally funded program that would enable American youth to volunteer for service." Eisenhower's advisers, however, convinced him that it would not work, fearing that it would leave "egg on the face of the administration," and so Eisenhower rejected the idea. However, Humphrey continued discussing it in Democratic Party circles. Peter Grothe, an advisor to Humphrey, compiled a review for the senator on the experiences of organizations like the Brethren Service Commission, the American Friends Service Committee, and the Mennonite Central Committee on their various service projects abroad. Humphrey introduced his bill for a 500 person corps the first year that would grow over a five-year period to 5,000. Humphrey's bill was the first to use the name "Peace Corps" and he advocated it in his 1960 run for the Democratic nomination for President.[21]

Meanwhile, Reuss continued his efforts to establish some type of volunteer agency. In November 1959, in a memorandum to the Director of the Legislative Reference Service, Reuss proposed that the ICA "determine the feasibility of establishing a 'Point Four Youth Corps.'" Reuss argued that it would have a two-fold purpose. First, it would further U.S. foreign policy by creating goodwill for the United States by dispelling the image of the "Ugly American". Second, it would offer young people the chance to serve their country and broaden their understanding of the world. Reuss suggested that the ICA study could determine what types of projects would be undertaken and discussed the role that private groups, like church organizations, might have in working with a government sponsored youth corps and with the ICA.[22]

In late December, David Anderson of Reuss' office wrote to John Noffsinger of IVS requesting information about IVS experience, asking what assistance they needed, wondering how they could expand their current programs, and what types of people they could use.[23]

Reuss introduced his first peace corps-type legislation in January 1960. His called only for a study of the advisability and practicability of establishing what he still called the 'Point Four Youth Corps'. The bill was attached as a rider to the Mutual Security Act (MSA) of 1960 and authorized $10,000 for the study. While IVS, BVS, and other such groups carried out their voluntary programs primarily for humanitarian reasons, Humphrey and Reuss very much had the Cold War in mind. When Reuss introduced his MSA amendment, Reuss noted that the main theater of the Cold War in the 1960s would be in the developing nations of Asia, Africa, the Middle East, and Latin America. Reuss argued that the way the United States played its role in this theater "will help to determine whether our civilization will survive."[24]

Writing for Reuss, Arthur H. Darken, a foreign policy analyst in the Library of Congress, elaborated on the Reuss proposal. He noted how "economic development and technical assistance programs have become major instruments of our foreign policy directed at helping" newly independent nations develop themselves free from foreign domination. But there were problems with those programs. One was getting enough Americans to make the program a success. Another was the "Ugly American" problem. On the other hand, he noted private groups have many more student applications than they have positions for them to work. 'A Point Four Youth Corps' would help solve those problems and multiply the number of Americans who have knowledge of the real problems in the less developed world.[25]

Reuss' idea of a study eventually gained the endorsement of House and Senate Committees, and the MSA with his amendment passed both houses. The Study was contracted by the ICA to Professor Maurice Albertson of the Colorado State University Research Foundation and was to be completed by March 1961. Reuss felt that the idea of a youth corps was popular with the public, but Vice President Richard Nixon criticized the ideas as a "haven for draft dodgers".[26]

Humphrey also placed youth service in the context of the Cold War. When he introduced the Peace Corps legislation in June 1960, he said it was "not meant primarily as an anti-Communist measure." He stated that the West should not think about only negative policies to stop communism but also "creative efforts which reflect our own elevating visions of the kind of world in which we would like to see mankind live." Despite that assertion that it was not an anti-Communist measure, he placed it clearly in the Cold War context arguing that his was a positive program to fight the Soviets in the developing world. Humphrey noted that the people of the developing nations want to live like the people of the United States and 'helping them along to economic self-sufficiency" is a very effective statement against the Soviet Union.[27]

During the primary and presidential campaigns of 1960, Senator Kennedy became more familiar with the idea of some type of youth volunteer corps. Once Humphrey withdrew from the contest in June, he sent his files for his proposed Peace Corps to Kennedy. Kennedy then brought it up in his October 13 speech at the University of Michigan and again in San Francisco on November 3, where he used the term Peace Corps. Once elected, however, it was not a priority despite the huge wave of enthusiasm that followed Kennedy's proposal in October. As the idea circulated from campus to campus, Kennedy received over 30,000 letters expressing interest in the idea. As president-elect, Kennedy asked Professor Max Millikan, the director of the Center for International Studies at the Massachusetts Institute of Technology, to study the issue and submit a paper on youth service. Along with the Albertson ICA study and the Millikan study, Samuel Hayes of the University of Michigan circulated a report. Students, too, kept pressuring to establish a Peace Corps.[28]

THE CREATION OF THE PEACE CORPS

Millikan reported back to the President-elect on December 30, 1960, with a cautious approach to the establishment of a youth volunteer agency. He noted that the problem was "to devise a new government instrument which can help match the apparent needs of the underdeveloped countries for trained manpower with the swelling supply of dedicated American young people eager to participate in constructive activities in the underdeveloped countries." His proposed solution was the International Youth Service Agency (IYSA) with a director reporting to the coordinator of U.S. development programs and with a board "representative of the major private groups with experience and interest in the employment of young people overseas." However, the MIT professor stated that the "program should be launched on a limited pilot basis" with only a few hundred participants. Although he recognized that there were in operation several privately sponsored youth volunteer programs which served useful purposes, he argued that they did not sufficiently contribute to solving manpower problems of host countries to justify including them in a program financed by the U.S. government. Instead, the IYSA should be part of a broader U.S. government effort to assist the underdeveloped countries to build institutions essential to self-confident nationhood. However, he emphasized, it should be "a small semi-autonomous government organization" operated through grants and contracts to a variety of private organized programs. He wanted a small, experimental program that reported to the director of the U.S. foreign aid program.[29]

In addition to the Millikan study and the ICA Colorado State study, Samuel Hayes of the University of Michigan circulated his report. Hayes included a discussion of many earlier programs including IVS, which he noted "was organized by people committed to the idea that American youth could make an important contribution to U.S. foreign policy by establishing person-to-person contacts with people of other countries."[30]

Students remained active in their effort to see the Peace Corps established. The Americans Committed to World Responsibility sought to organize a conference in Washington at the end of March 1961. They felt that "the aim of the Peace Corps was to help people in the way that they want to be helped.... It should have no political, economic" dogma and "would increase "mutual understanding and appreciation."[31]

Reuss continued to work with Maurice Albertson and his staff to call together various organizations for all day meetings in a House Office Building on December 15, 19, and 20, 1960, to discuss the Point Four Youth Corps. On December 20, the meeting included eighty-eight people representing six government agencies, thirty-eight nongovernmental organizations, eight colleges and universities, and representatives from seven Congressional offices. Those attending included Harold Row of the BSC and IVS. IVS was also represented by John Noffsinger, Dale D. Clark, and John Reisner. Various other groups running volunteer programs were also in attendance, including Crossroads Africa, the Mennonite Central Committee, and the American Friends Service Committee. Drawing from their wealth of experience, the participants made various recommendations on how to recruit, select, train, and supervise youthful volunteers in overseas projects.[32]

While inclined to accept the Millikan report recommendation of a small pilot project, Kennedy appointed his brother-in-law R. Sargent Shriver to head a task force to study the idea. Shriver and Harris Wofford got the task force started, and they began to solicit advice from a wide variety of sources. Soon they were "inundated with a variety of plans, often in contradiction with one another." Some favored the smaller, cautious approach, but Wofford and Shriver wanted a larger, bold plan.[33]

Shortly after the task force began its work, IVS executive director Noffsinger wrote to Shriver introducing him to IVS and inviting collaboration. The two men then began a series of meetings, and over the next few months IVS's contact with the task force continued. According to Paul Rodell, it "cannot be overemphasized... how closely [the] Peace Corps actually copied IVS." As the Peace Corps evolved it had many things in common with IVS. "Peace Corps volunteers were young college graduates...who made a two-year commitment to live among their co-workers in urban or rural areas." They learned the local language and culture and worked on a people-to-people basis. They were "required to refrain from political or religious proselytizing". They received a minimal salary and were "advised that they might be sent to areas of the world where living may be very difficult and physical amenities few."[34]

While the task force was working, Shriver and Wofford abandoned the Millikan report. Wofford wrote that it was "contrary to every bone in Shriver's body and every cell in his brain." Shiver believed that if the Peace Corps were to have a chance, it could not be "a cautious little experiment within the foreign aid program", because that kind of slowness is what had earned a bad reputation for U.S. overseas aid.[35]

The bolder plan Shriver sought "came in an unsolicited memorandum from two young foreign service officers, Warren Wiggins and William Josephson." They were well aware that there were many volunteer programs operating overseas on a small level. To be a "genuine departure in foreign policy," any new program would have to be "on an entirely different scale from . . . its predecessors."[36] Wiggins, who was 34 years old, was the deputy director of the Far Eastern operations for the ICA. Josephson, who was 26 years old, was a counsel for the ICA's Far East section. Wiggins was "appalled" by the U.S. foreign assistance programs where U.S. diplomats were living well, oblivious to the poverty around them. In late 1960, Wiggins told Josephson that he felt the Peace Corps might be the opportunity to reform U.S. foreign aid programs and proposed drafting a paper on the Peace Corps. They did so and submitted it to Shriver on February 5, 1961. The next day Shriver told the Task Force, which now included Wiggins, that they should all read the report "because it comes the closest to representing what I think should happen."[37]

The report was titled "A Towering Task: The National Peace Corps," drawing from Kennedy's January 30, 1961, State of the Union address that had referred to problems in achieving the goal of constructing a sound economy for the non-communist world as "towering". The paper gave a brief history of the efforts by Humphrey and Reuss to establish a Peace Corps, the Colorado State University study, and the Millikan report, noting that "many with overseas experience tend to be overly cautious in their approach to it." The cautious approach, they noted, was proposed by many because of the possibility of a fiasco, and those who proposed it were the most experienced. For example, voluntary organizations suggested that if government money were available, they could double the number of youths in their programs. That would mean 500 more volunteers in their existing programs. Wiggins and Josephson argued that for a variety of reasons a small and cautious National Peace Corps "may be worse than no Peace Corps at all." The purpose of their paper, they wrote, was "to advocate consideration of a 'quantum jump' in the thinking and programming concerning" the Peace Corps. They called for initiating the program with several thousand Americans participating in the first 12-18 months. They felt that one of the things that should be done would be to appoint a new ICA Deputy Director to serve as the Peace Corps Administrator.[38]

As the task force moved from discussion of the Wiggins and Josephson paper to the creation of the Peace Corps, there were changes in direction, discussions about leadership, and on-going advice from youth volunteer groups, especially IVS. Shriver differed with "A Towering Task" concerning its recommendation that the Peace Corps be administered by the ICA, which he felt would "identify the Peace

Corps with the public, political and bureaucratic disabilities which grew up in recent years." Starting the Peace Corps as another ICA operation ran the risk of losing its new appeal. Instead, Shriver believed, the Corps "should be administered by a small new agency operating as one component in our whole overseas operation" drawing on universities, voluntary agencies, and foundations.[39] Ultimately, when created in March 1961, the Peace Corps was an independent agency under the Department of State.

Both IVS and BVS had some input into the Kennedy administrations development of the Peace Corps. Noffsinger sent a letter to Kennedy on February 13, 1961, noting that the legislative proposals in Congress were drafted after a careful study of IVS projects abroad. He also included a fact sheet on IVS for the president. Kermit Eby sent a letter to Shriver that included an article co-written with Don Tonjes called, "The Brethren Are Already There." In his letter, referring to BVS, Eby said that the Peace Corps "might learn from the experiences of an organization which has been extensively engaged in peace-corps type activity for some years."[40] Stanley Andrews noted the importance of IVS on Peace Corps development in his 1970 interview. He said that Shriver toured all the IVS missions and talked with the volunteers. Andrews said in that interview that Shriver "set the Peace Corps up on the basis of this IVS demonstration."[41]

IVS and BSC might have had an even greater influence if Harold Row had taken the job as the director. Shriver's task force report raised the issue of who was going to run the corps. In the report, "Shriver had recommended several academics who had had experience placing students in programs in developing countries." Kennedy rejected them all because he felt that "an ivory tower academic would not project the adventurous image" he wanted for the Peace Corps.[42] Meanwhile, according to Kreider in his book on the BSC, Row and his staff had been meeting with Kennedy. According to Kreider, during those White House discussions, Kennedy had asked Row to serve as the director of the Peace Corps. According to his brother, whom he talked to by phone after being offered the position, Row declined the offer because he felt "there would be too much political pressure associated with the position, and he would not be free to guide the organization as he thought it should operate."[43] Despite his concerns about nepotism, Shriver took on the position himself as the first Director of the Peace Corps. While turning down the offer of the directorship, Row became a consultant for the creation of the organization.

It is evident that IVS and religious based volunteer organizations like BVS had a major impact on individuals who initially proposed the corps as well as on the creation of the organization itself. IVS submitted a paper with suggestions to Albertson's study. Other organizations submitted suggestions to Shriver's task force. It was IVS, however, that repeatedly was most often described as "the prototype" of the Peace Corps, even by Shriver.[44]

The Peace Corps was established by a presidential executive order on March 1, 1961. Congress formalized its creation by legislation that was signed September 22, 1961. In the Congressional hearings on the legislation, the role of the voluntary organizations was often discussed. On the House floor Reuss noted that the Peace Corps was fortunate "to draw on the experience of various American voluntary organizations." The most prominent, he noted, was IVS which "has done a superlative job in its limited but thoroughgoing overseas ventures." Representative John Brademas (D-IN), in discussing BVS noted that the BSC has been "effectively operating a voluntary program … similar to the Peace Corps plan" and "I think it would be immensely valuable to consider its counsel in establishing the Peace Corps."[45]

IVS had an important impact on the emerging Peace Corps through its on-going personnel contacts with the developing program. Congressman Reuss, in February 1961, noted the role of John S. Noffsinger, IVS Executive Director. Reuss, in an Extension of Remarks in the Congressional Record, noted that "In carrying out the Peace Corps program," we are fortunate to be able to draw on voluntary organizations. "Prominent among these is International Voluntary Services, Inc." He makes specific reference to the role of Noffsinger as the executive director and that IVS had done a "superlative job" in its overseas ventures. But that was not the end of Noffsinger's influence. He was 76 years old in 1962 and had been working for the Peace Corps for six months as a recruiter of older Americans to join the Peace Corps. As Shriver told the President, the Corps had more grandparents in the Peace Corps than there were teenagers. There were thirty-nine men and women over fifty years old working abroad and there had been 177 inquiries from older people in the previous month. As Shriver noted about Noffsinger, "His efforts have gotten results." Later, at the fifth anniversary dinner of the Peace Corps, Noffsinger was hailed by Shriver as a "Peace Corps Pioneer".[46] But IVS is where he had his greatest impact. Arthur Z. Gardiner, Executive Director of IVS at the time of Noffsinger's death in 1966, told the Brethren magazine *Messenger* that Noffsinger left a big mark on IVS "and through IVS a bigger mark in the establishment of the Peace Corps, which is so obviously patterned on IVS."[47]

Harold Row, still representing IVS and the BSC and not in the Peace Corps, nonetheless still influenced the development of the Peace Corps. Speaking in support of the legislation to establish the Peace Corps on June 23, 1961, before the Senate Committee on Foreign Relations in its hearings on S. 2000 (the Peace Corps bill) Row succinctly explained the importance of the private voluntary agencies in the establishment of the Peace Corps:

> *I have been actively participating in other groups related to the proposed Peace Corps, such as International Voluntary Services. . . .*

Row stated that it had been mentioned frequently that there is little new in the Peace Corps. In one sense that is true. He continued:

> *Voluntary and private agencies, including church and educational efforts overseas long have been engaged in leadership training and community development in almost every country of the world. And our Government, especially through its foreign aid and predecessor programs, for decades now has been carrying forward extensive and significant programs in the categories roughly analogous to the proposed Peace Corps types of activities. So in this case, the Peace Corps is nothing new.*

Row did go on to say, however, that it is new, "almost breath-takingly so," because it is the first time the Government has undertaken a "national community effort in this direction" and has caught the imagination of our people.[48]

11

USAID
Recent Volunteer Service Involvement

Jack Hawkins

The key role of predecessor agencies of the U.S. Agency for International Development (USAID) in the establishment of IVS is described in Chapter One. The forty years of USAID funding support to IVS is chronicled in subsequent chapters. Why USAID reduced funding for IVS voluntary service projects may be somewhat obscure, but its support for international volunteerism continues, perhaps influenced by the IVS experience. In recent years, USAID has promoted volunteer service abroad by skilled professionals: sometimes on behalf of another U.S. government agency, as an initiative of the White House, or through its own volunteer service activities.

Two high-profile programs are highlighted in this chapter: (1) the Farmer-to-Farmer program, which has been managed by USAID with funding provided to the U.S. Department of Agriculture since 1985, and (2) Volunteers for Prosperity, a White House national service initiative coordinated by USAID from 2003 to 2009. In addition, this chapter briefly reviews USAID's own Volunteers for Economic Growth Alliance (VEGA) Leader with Associates Award (LWA),[1] which ran from 2004 through 2018, and Volunteers for International Security and Prosperity Annual Program Statement (VISP APS), which has been operational since 2017.

Farmer-to-Farmer Program
An Impactful Peer-to-Peer Volunteer Service Program

The Farmer-to-Farmer (F2F) Volunteer Program[2] has been USAID's longest running volunteer activity. Initiated in 1985, over 19,000 volunteer assignments[3] have been carried out in 112 countries.[4] The average assignment is slightly less than three weeks, although length is variable and might be up to a year. Volunteers are, with few exceptions, American, generally experienced mid-to-late career specialists. Through 2014, they assisted an estimated 11,000 host organizations and directly benefitted 1.2 million people.[5] The program name is slightly misleading because volunteers come from many occupations (farmer, business, finance, education, government) and assist many types of host organizations (individual farmers, cooperatives, agribusinesses, financial organizations, technical agencies, NGOs).

The F2F Program is implemented through grants and contracts with NGOs and other institutions that recruit and place volunteers worldwide. The grants or contracts are typically awarded competitively for five-year periods. Implementing organizations establish country offices with staff to identify volunteer opportunities, develop scopes of work, prepare host organizations to use volunteers, facilitate volunteer work, and follow up with hosts after the assignment. Assignments differ widely across countries, host organizations, and disciplines. The implementing agencies collaborate in a flexible "community of practice" that has strengthened volunteer management practices, which are summarized in an F2F implementation manual.[6]

F2F Program evaluations are carried out approximately every five years and have typically been quite positive. The most recent one in 2017 found that 90 percent of 978 stakeholders surveyed were satisfied with the project due to it being "needs based."[7] A former USAID F2F program manager believes the strength of the program lies in: the committed and well-qualified pool of volunteers it draws from; the diverse and innovative implementing organizations; and the host organizations that request and make use of volunteers through the demand-driven program.[8]

The Program's origin helps to explain its longevity. The idea for Farmer-to-Farmer volunteers was conceived by Congressman Doug Bereuter while visiting USAID projects in Latin America. He approached USAID with the idea but received a less than encouraging response. He then arranged to fund the program in the U.S. Farm Bill budget for the USDA PL-480 Food for Peace program. A pilot project in 1976 and later programs proved successful, so dedicated funding continues under the U.S. Farm Bill. USAID country missions do provide additional funding for volunteers and complementary input costs (grants, equipment, consultants, training), but Farm Bill funding—all of which is for volunteer costs—covers the core program.

With its emphasis on agriculture and rural development, community approaches, and local civil society capacity-building, the F2F program is, at least indirectly, continuing the IVS legacy.

Volunteers For Prosperity (VFP)
A Promising White House National Service Initiative

Volunteers for Prosperity (VFP) was established by President George W. Bush on September 25, 2003, through Executive Order 13317 as "a call to service to support major U.S. initiatives that promote health and prosperity around the world."[9] The program envisioned highly skilled Americans serving abroad as volunteers to help achieve U.S. objectives for "providing clean water to the poor, promoting demographic governance, developing economic freedom, promoting free and open markets, and stemming the spread of HIV/AIDS."[10]

VFP's establishment was prompted by the terrorist attacks on the United States on September 11, 2001, and the Peace Corps' inability to match the heightened interest among Americans to serve abroad as volunteers that immediately followed. Notably, Peace Corps applications were up nearly twenty percent by the end of 2002.[11] In short, as the Peace Corps could only accommodate roughly 7,500 volunteers annually post-9/11, the Bush Administration conceived of VFP as a flexible alternative that would allow skilled Americans to volunteer for "Peace Corps-like" assignments of generally two-to-three weeks in duration through a network of volunteer-sending organizations sponsoring international development projects.

Launch, Scope, Management, and Structure

VFP was officially launched on September 29, 2003, at an event held in Washington, DC and co-hosted by the Administrator of the U.S. Agency for International Development (USAID), Andrew S. Natsios, and White House Domestic Policy Advisor and Director of the USA Freedom Corps, John Bridgeland. In attendance at the event were representatives of the forty U.S. non-governmental organizations (NGOs) that had signed on as inaugural partner organizations of VFP.

By design, skilled Americans interested in participating in VFP would seek to volunteer for short-term assignments typically lasting two-to-three weeks through VFP partner organizations (volunteer-sending organizations) engaged in projects broadly consistent with the "U.S. global prosperity agenda" or directly relevant to the following initiatives: the President's Emergency Plan for AIDS Relief (PEPFAR); the Trade for Africa Development and Enterprise Initiative; the Water for the Poor Initiative; the Digital Freedom Initiative (DFI); and the Middle East Partnership Initiative (MEPI). The President's Malaria Initiative was added to the VFP portfolio in 2005.

Per executive order 13317, VFP was to be managed by USAID's Office of

Volunteers for Prosperity (formally established in October 2003; VFP Office), which, in turn, was to report to, and be accountable to, the USA Freedom Corps at the White House.[12]

Owing to its application to interagency Presidential initiatives reflecting the U.S. global prosperity agenda, the VFP organizational structure itself was "interagency", and thus there were VFP offices established at the Departments of State, Commerce, and Health and Human Services reporting to the host USAID office. Administrator Natsios appointed Jack Hawkins of USAID's Global Development Alliance Secretariat as VFP Director in November 2003. To ensure VFP's interagency profile, Hawkins was also detailed to the White House and the USA Freedom Corps.[13]

Early Implementation

The initial focus of the VFP Office was to aggressively build the network of partner organizations through which skilled American professionals could volunteer their time, energy, and expertise. By the end of November 2003, the staff had succeeded in expanding the network of partners to just over one hundred. Notably, this network had grown well beyond the initial forty U.S. NGOs to also include a number of volunteer-sending faith-based groups and corporations keenly interested in their employees' desire to "give back" through volunteer service. The active participation of faith-based groups proved critical to VFP's ultimate success and impact. Not surprisingly, IVS, which was founded in 1953 by the Mennonite, Brethren and Quaker churches, may have served as a model for the work and engagement of faith-based VFP partners.

Apart from simply increasing the partner network, the VFP Office sought to meet the challenge of directing interested skilled Americans to potential volunteer assignments via a new searchable directory—accessible through the Volunteers for Prosperity website—listing a host partner and its relevant development focus (e.g., economic growth, education, clean water, health).

Concurrently, the VFP Office, with support from the White House and the USA Freedom Corps, a White House office established to promote voluntary service, commenced building relationships across the Federal government by holding meetings with key staff of State, Commerce, and Health and Human Services (HHS). The primary goal of these meetings was to find ways of incorporating VFP and the utilization of skilled American professional volunteers in support of the various other Presidential initiatives "owned" by USAID and/or State, Commerce, and HHS and comprising the "U.S. global prosperity agenda".

Further, daily meetings were held with USA Freedom Corps staff to further strengthen White House support for VFP. The detail of Hawkins to the White House and the USA Freedom Corps helped to ensure VFP had a prominent role to play in national service. By mid-2004, the VFP was in a position to actively promote volunteer service abroad by skilled American professionals. Its network of partner organizations could help professionals find volunteer opportunities that matched their personal skillsets, interests, and schedules.

Role in the Southeast Asian Tsunami

On December 26, 2004, a massive earthquake under the Indian Ocean released a series of massive tsunami waves that struck coastal areas of Indonesia, Sri Lanka, India, and Thailand resulting in the deaths of nearly 230,000 people. Among the deadliest natural disasters in recorded history, the event prompted a rapid and comprehensive U.S. response to deploy U.S. government resources to the affected areas and provide for survivors.

In the early days of the response, the Bush Administration convened an interagency task force led by the Department of State. Working in connection with the USA Freedom Corps, the VFP Office became an active member of the task force. The Southeast Asian Tsunami highlighted VFP's potential utilization in global disaster response and relief, going well beyond the original focus on skills-based volunteering and advancing international development in the context of the "global health and prosperity agenda".[14]

While the VFP Office was broadly tasked with responding directly—and in a timely fashion—to offers of assistance from all Americans moved by what they read or heard from news reports about the widespread devastation and suffering of so many people in the region, it quickly focused on finding ways to directly engage those whose professional training and background were appropriate to global disaster response and relief.[15] A case in point, was the VFP Office referral of a retired West Coast fire chief to advise the task force.[16]

Despite having to focus on the processing of inquiries and offers of assistance from those with only the most appropriate backgrounds, the VFP Office also recognized the importance of responding to those whose backgrounds were not suited to the challenge, but who were, nevertheless, motivated to reach out with compassion. Among the many offers of assistance came one from a mother and wife who offered the assistance of her family to help "clear road debris" in Banda Aceh, among the hardest hit areas with the highest death toll.

The "lesson" of the Southeast Asian Tsunami later prompted the VFP Office to explore the development of a platform that could facilitate the immediate engagement of leading international companies in a streamlined response and relief effort anywhere around the world at any time.

Numerous partner organizations in the existing VFP network had strong capabilities in global disaster response and relief and had effectively deployed resources, including trained volunteers, to Southeast Asia.

Role in National Security

Given its application to the six presidential initiatives, the "U.S. global prosperity agenda", and disaster response with the Southeast Asian Tsunami, the VFP was recognized as an effective instrument of "soft power". Simply put, it had demonstrated the compassion of the American people to make a difference in the lives of others around the world.

To wit, VFP was cited by the 2006 National Security Strategy for its role "unleashing the Power of the Private Sector."[17] Per the National Security Strategy:

> *The [Bush] Administration has sought to multiply the impact of our development assistance through initiatives such as…Volunteers for Prosperity, which enlists some of our Nation's most capable professionals to serve strategically in developing nations.*[18]

Recognition and Direct Support of Volunteers

As VFP was a "call to service," it was necessary for the VFP Office to explore ways of facilitating and supporting the work of skilled Americans volunteering abroad. Thus, in addition to enabling prospective volunteers to identify organizations and assignments that met their interests, skills, and schedules, the VFP Office sought to highlight the actual work and impact of the individual as well as directly address the challenges of assignment costs.

Through the President's Volunteer Service Award, the VFP Office was able to recognize volunteers for their commitment and contributions to improving the lives of others through their assignments and service. Over the course of VFP's existence, dozens of skilled American volunteers became recipients of various levels of the award.[19] In several instances, the VFP Office Director traveled to events hosted by partner organizations to formally present awards. Local media covered these events and produced stories about volunteers and their service.

Working closely with partner organizations and volunteers, the VFP Office was able to discern an array of possible challenges to making VFP a much more robust initiative.

One issue of great concern to partner organizations and prospective volunteers alike was the cost of volunteer assignments. Indeed, the vast majority of VFP partner organizations lacked the resources needed to directly fund basic volunteer assignment expenses, such as airfare and local lodging. Similarly, it was found that most prospective volunteers lacked the personal wherewithal to self-fund volunteer assignments.

Recognizing the pervasiveness of the assignment cost challenge, VFP Office leadership, in March 2008, launched a matching grant program called VFPServ to enable volunteers to raise funds from "family and friends" in amounts that could be matched by the VFP Office, up to $1,000. To participate, a prospective volunteer would have to identify or develop a volunteer assignment with a participating VFP partner organization, establish an assignment budget, and direct "family and friends" to donate using a customized donation platform, developed and managed by the online philanthropy GlobalGiving.

For purposes of establishing a pilot program, VFPServ was capitalized by USAID with $100,000. During the pilot phase, VFPServ facilitated the assignments of 113 volunteers, who, in turn, had raised roughly $150,000 from "family and friends."[20] The pilot program proved to be a successful public-private partnership. Notably, among the earliest assignments made possible by VFPServ, was one jointly developed by several volunteers of a leading faith-based organization.

Impact at Five Years

Per the 2008 Annual Report to the White House—released September 25, 2008, the fifth anniversary of the signing of EO 13317—the VFP network had grown to nearly 300 partners, through which nearly 120,000 compassionate American professionals had given their time and talent to improving the lives of others around the world.[21]

During 2008 alone, a total of 268 VFP partners—up 10 percent from the 2007's 244 partners—deployed more than 43,000 volunteers, an increase of more than 25 percent over 2007's total of 34,000.[22]

An Effective Call to Service Generates Calls for Permanence

Given VFP's impressive growth and development after five years, interest grew to make the initiative permanent through legislation. In remarks delivered September 8, 2008, on the South Lawn to commemorate national volunteer service, President George W. Bush summarized VFP's impact as follows:

> We've helped Americans answer the call by creating a program called Volunteers for Prosperity. This initiative matched skilled American professionals with service opportunities—a lot of them in the developing world. This year we mobilized more than

> 43,000 doctors, teachers, engineers, and other skilled volunteers. That's a pretty good start for an important program, it seems like to me. These men and women save babies from malaria on the continent of Africa. They bring modern information technology to Afghanistan. They live out one of America's strongest beliefs—that to whom much is given, much is required.[23]

On September 11, 2008, First Lady Laura Bush also highlighted the effectiveness of VFP in a keynote speech to the Service Nation Summit held in New York City.[24] With these endorsements, the Bush Administration had called on Congress to make VFP permanent.[25]

On September 12, 2008, Senators Edward M. Kennedy (D-MA) and Orrin Hatch (R-UT) introduced legislation to expand national service through the "Serve America Act of 2008" (S. 3487).[26] While seeking to expand volunteer opportunities for Americans at every stage of life and apply volunteer service to specific national challenges, they sought to authorize the Volunteers for Prosperity initiative as well as expand VFPServ, the matching grant program piloted by the VFP Office.[27]

The Kennedy Serve America Act was signed by President Obama on April 21, 2009.[28]

Authorization and "Sunset"

The Kennedy Serve America Act acknowledged VFP's impact as an important national service initiative and sought to build upon its key features, including a significant expansion of the VFPServ matching grant program.[29]

However, while VFP was authorized for FY2010 through FY2014, it never received an appropriation, nor did it receive any financial support from host USAID during the Obama Administration. Eventually, the legislated Volunteers for Prosperity program was never implemented.

Noting the numbers of partner organizations and the rising numbers of American professionals serving as volunteers through those organizations over the course of at least five years during the Bush Administration, VFP clearly had an impact. And that was not just the sentiment of the White House, but also the sense of the U.S. Congress.

VFP's authorization expired or "sunset" at the end of FY2014.

USAID Sponsored Activities

The Volunteers for Economic Growth Alliance (VEGA) was established in 2004 as a consortium of volunteer-sending organizations engaged in international economic growth and development. It was created as a procurement mechanism with an ultimate ceiling of $380 million that "allowed USAID missions and bureaus to procure services and activities directly from VEGA's [volunteer-sending organization] members through a streamlined competitive process managed by a secretariat based in Washington."[30] While it was used to implement 45 activities in 41 countries, VEGA's actual utilization of skilled professionals as volunteers was minimal. By the time operations had ceased at the end of 2018, it was found that VEGA had deployed only about 1,500 volunteers in connection with development projects.[31]

The Volunteers for International Security and Prosperity Annual Program Statement (VISP APS) was created in August, 2017, to "help USAID mobilize the creative capacity of volunteers in support of USAID's development objectives."[32] It allowed any volunteer-sending organization to propose the utilization of skilled professionals for a development activity to be funded and managed by a USAID operating unit (e.g., office, bureau, mission) and funded and managed by that operating unit. The VISP APS was envisioned as a vehicle for engaging skilled professionals as volunteers helping USAID to achieve development outcomes.

Currently, the VISP APS has no central funding within USAID. To date, USAID has made only one grant (cooperative agreement) under the VISP APS to a volunteer-sending organization.[33]

In sum, VEGA, as a fully funded program, never had the impact of Farmer-to-Farmer, in terms of volunteer numbers or international development. In contrast to VFP, VEGA was greatly cost-ineffective. For its part, the VISP APS, which was conceived as a cost-effective alternative to VEGA,[34] certainly lacks, to date, any real financial support or public profile, as it has not attracted the interest of the White House and is unknown beyond USAID.[35]

USAID Volunteer Funding And Program Design Assessing the Future

Leaving aside the Farmer-to-Farmer program because it is funded through the U.S. Department of Agriculture, the experiences of Volunteers for Prosperity (VFP), the Volunteers for Economic Growth Alliance (VEGA), and Volunteers for International Security and Prosperity Annual Program Statement (VISP APS) point to uncertainty over future USAID funding for international volunteers. Consider the following:

1. The experience of VEGA was that USAID had provided significant funding to an ambitious volunteer sending activity that, in all actuality, engaged only a relatively small number of volunteers.

2. Although USAID funding in support of volunteer service in connection with VFP was rather limited, it did catalyze additional financial support from the public in a far greater amount.

3. Lacking any centralized funding from USAID, the decision to commit any financial resources to a volunteer service activity under the VISP APS will be at the sole discretion of the operating unit involved.

It is worth noting that while the VEGA experience can be viewed as far too expensive a proposition (i.e., 45 activities in 41 countries utilizing only 1,500 volunteers over a 14 year-period), the Kennedy Serve America Act would have required that no more than 10 percent of the appropriated funds could be used to cover USAID's administrative costs.[36] Thus, with an authorization of appropriately $10 million, $9 million would have supported the VFPServ matching grant program during FY 2010.

In sum, it seems highly unlikely that USAID would ever return to VEGA-type levels of funding for a volunteer program. However, the alternative to VEGA, the VISP APS, given its lack of centralized funding, represents the other extreme. It seems highly unlikely that USAID's operating units, primarily country Missions, will fund volunteer-based programs on their own.

Without significant funding, any future USAID volunteer service activity would be better served by focusing on facilitation rather than direct management. To wit, VFP lacked any real funding but played an impactful role facilitating—and promoting—skilled volunteering around the world. VEGA, on the other hand, represented a direct management model, but despite significant funding, utilized relatively few volunteers.

Apart from issues relating to USAID funding, future volunteer service program design may be influenced by the recent (and still raging at the time of this writing) COVID-19 pandemic. Simply put, most future volunteer service may have to be conducted "virtually," as it is not only more cost-effective but "safer" in terms of public health.

The American volunteer spirit lives on. USAID and the United States Government (USG) more broadly have attempted to facilitate volunteer engagement in international relief and development programs. This has at times proven highly effective, but the financial sustainability of such volunteer programs has proven problematic.

Separately, and regardless of funding, it is entirely possible that IVS has influenced the USAID and USG volunteer programs described above. Certainly, a number of faith-based organizations became active participants in VFP, and a faith-based organization served as an implementing partner of VEGA. In short, the contributions of these organizations to the programs highlighted were consistent with the work of IVS and its volunteers.

SECTION IV
Implications And Questions For Future
International Voluntary Services

12

LESSONS LEARNED
IMPLICATIONS FOR THE FUTURE OF
VOLUNTEERING FOR DEVELOPMENT

CLIFF ALLUM AND BENJAMIN J. LOUGH

As a pioneer in the expansion of international voluntary services, IVS's influence on the broader international volunteerism sector of volunteers, hosting organizations, communities, and countries is worthy of consideration. Although there is much academic research on the value and impact of international volunteer service in general, this book provides specific supplemental lived experiences and stories by volunteers.

EMERGENT THEMES AND LESSONS LEARNED

Throughout its life, IVS operated amid affecting trends of the day that contributed to the evolution of international voluntary service. In 1972, Arthur Gillette analyzed the trends of his day—dynamics that still impact the forms and functions of international service.[1] His assessment described five significant changes in international volunteering: (1) the expansion of government-sponsored funding for international volunteering, (2) innovation and diversification in the variety of voluntary programs and volunteers' activities, (3) a wider geographical distribution of international volunteering, (4) a greater focus on social development and capacity building activities alongside initial economic development and modernization, and (5) greater collaboration and cooperation among discrete International Volunteer Cooperation Organizations (IVCOs) leading to higher professional standards, better volunteer safety, and more equitable benefits for volunteers.

These trends exerted tensions on IVCOs globally including IVS. IVS began with the initial engagement of young and low-skilled volunteers for peace and development projects and concluded with challenges brought on by globalization and the 'fourth industrial revolution' of digital and technical progress.

The Challenge of Young and Low-skilled Generalist Volunteers

The preceding chapters in this book chart the development of IVS as an initial expression of youth service going back to the early 1950s. Young and idealistic American volunteers supplied emergency assistance and economic relief to many newly independent countries during the "era of development" that emerged from decolonization. Several factors paved the way for volunteer participation by these young people. First, assistance was needed in rural locations where national officials and foreign experts were typically unwilling to live and work. In contrast, young IVS volunteers were often drawn from rural farm backgrounds. Second, these young people came from religious backgrounds, reflecting the involvement of church groups in the formative years of IVS, which can be seen to have generated idealistic and humanitarian instincts. Finally, volunteers were generally viewed by governments as generalists who were cost effective and potential cultural ambassadors.

However, tension existed between volunteers' objectives to assist communities and their objectives in learning and experiencing a new culture and country. This inherent contradiction was evident from the earliest days of state-supported international volunteer activities in the U.S. and other countries.[2] But the 'development decade' of the 1960s, alongside its focus on development outcomes, eventually outweighed the issue of personal enhancement. This resulted in a general trend to recruit older and more professional volunteers described in earlier chapters of this book—a movement that began to reverse course only toward the end of the 1990s.

For many IVCOs focused on technical cooperation, the average age of volunteers increased gradually until the 1990s, when the diversification of programs resulted in new models of youth volunteering schemes.[3] The professionalization of volunteers was a clear trend in the industry. However, many volunteers were unprepared to take on roles essentially equated with consultants or advisors to increasingly large organizations and institutions. This trend was also evident in the early days of IVS. As described in Chapter Four, the first two decades of IVS primarily recruited recent college graduates but later shifted to recruiting volunteers with more professional and international experience, which ultimately altered its model towards more highly qualified volunteer specialists. Case examples from this book relating the IVS experience in Vietnam, Sudan, and Morocco each describe the benefits and challenges of moving away from recruiting volunteers embodied with "the brashness of youthful idealism" towards recruiting older and more skilled and experienced volunteers with professional experience. The pushback towards this trend, as described in Chapter Five, continues to drive debates about the human-centered role of volunteers, both local and international, and their distinctive value contributions to development.[4]

Because youth-based international volunteering is often viewed as "supply-oriented" rather than "demand-oriented", involving young international volunteers in development is not universally supported and has been a topic of much debate and criticism over the years. While the two-year model, which became widespread amongst IVCOs in the 1960s, is still a typical duration for government-sponsored programs, there is a far wider variety of options available for young volunteers today. The key reasons for this sectoral trend were twofold. First, young volunteers were less often willing to serve for periods of up to two years and sought more flexible arrangements. Second, governments and donors began to more explicitly fund programs aiming to develop marketable skills and global citizenship in their young citizens, which they believed could be accomplished in shorter time periods.[5] In addition, while privately funded organizations have been facilitating short-term international volunteering since the early twentieth century, this was relatively uncommon for government funded IVCOs until recent decades.

This change reflects new values for international volunteering that move beyond its role as a distinctive model for development cooperation. In recent history, internationalization and globalization have been driving demand for a labor force that is better prepared to work in international contexts and with populations from various nations and cultures. International volunteering is viewed as an effective way to prepare young people to work in a global marketplace. In addition, governments increasingly value international volunteering for its contributions to citizen diplomacy and nurturing cosmopolitan global citizenship.

Against this backdrop, governments from many nations—particularly in the Global North—are altering funding patterns and priorities for international service to prepare young people for new global realities. For instance, governments in the UK, Germany, Canada, the U.S., and Australia, have in recent times provided grants to commercial, civil society, and faith-based organizations to facilitate short- and long-term international volunteer placements. While this has the potential to benefit young people, it has also sparked a global debate about whether government funding may be creating a supply of international volunteers without a commensurate demand for these volunteers in host communities. We will return to these themes later in this chapter.

DIVERSIFICATION OF IVS ACTIVITIES
RESPONSE TO CHANGES IN CULTURAL AND HISTORICAL CONTEXTS

Beyond the funding diversification evident in the 1980s, the 1990s were years of programmatic experimentation and diversification for IVS and other IVCOs operating across the globe. Complementing longer-term placements, models of more specialized short-term volunteer placements were also institutionalized within many organizations. The concerns described in several chapters about the short-term nature of projects associated with funding timelines (e.g., see the case examples from Morocco, Yemen, and Botswana) have not necessarily been resolved in contemporary discussions of the virtues and vices of international volunteering. While some international volunteer programs have historically placed volunteers for two years or longer as an exclusive practice, most programs now accommodate the short-term expediency and priorities of their volunteers and funders. While this is not necessarily detrimental when short-term volunteers have specialized skills, it reflects continuing tensions between the needs and interests of funders and the communities that volunteer service programs are intended to benefit.[6]

In addition to changes in the duration of volunteer programs, chapters in this book highlight diverse volunteer activities and the recruitment of a more international volunteer base. This diversification of IVS program activities reflected global trends in other industrialized countries as well. However, the initial focus of IVS on food security, agriculture, and rural development marked a somewhat distinctive focus. Most international service programs operating in the 1960s focused initially on education and health services. It was not until the 1970s that agriculture and rural development activities became more mainstream for most IVCOs.[7]

The issue of sector also plays to an urban-rural split, which is evident in the histories of health and agricultural volunteering by Australian Volunteers International (AVI)[8] volunteers as compared with the location of educational activities, often located in an urban setting. While funder priorities played a part in the balance of those programs, the issue of security influenced more urban program placements. This would echo elsewhere in other IVCOs, as urban areas became the most likely opportunity for volunteering in areas of overt conflict. The reputation of volunteers as risk-takers and desiring to experience the 'real' people and country lessens with the urbanized security of volunteer campuses. IVCOs may variously focus on community living (urban and rural) and locations in large institutions or rural communities. The tradition of the placement of volunteers in rural contexts, which can be seen in the IVS tradition is perhaps best illustrated in more recent times in the model used by the Peace Corps, which is further addressed later in this chapter.

The previous section described the expansion of IVS activities to support greater organizational development and other technical and industrial crafts that increasingly required professional volunteers. Contemporary discussions continue to question how the demand for volunteers by communities intersects with the supply of volunteers, especially when addressing specific skills. To their credit, IVCOs have increasingly responded to community needs and recruited the types of volunteers that could meet community requirements and aspirations. The early stages of IVS saw an emphasis on rural poverty—matching the source of volunteers—but the movement of IVS programs into urban settings might be seen to address investment in education or business development. In this light, it is important to recognize how the IVS move in the 1990s towards social justice, reducing inequalities, and the empowerment of minority and indigenous ethnic groups was in some ways a return to that earlier period. It is also interesting to consider how this has become a core focus for many IVCOs globally.

Localization of IVS Programs

As illustrated in Chapter One, the IVS mission had a consistent emphasis on local "people-to-people" engagement from its origins. However, the programmatic implementation of this agenda was challenging and changed over time. Stories by volunteers in this book reflect changes in development philosophy that affected the growth and development of IVCOs in their approach to international volunteering and development projects. These stories raised critical questions about the value of volunteers as international actors intervening in local spaces.

The 1980s witnessed a growing skepticism about the virtue of international technical cooperation with its focus on infrastructure, industrialization, and rural development. This skepticism, combined with a heightened belief in the essential role of citizen participation, led to the promotion of self-help, domestic involvement, and a more targeted emphasis on capacity building and national volunteering on top of the previous ideological recognition of its importance. As described in Chapter Five, some IVS programs even closed, after converting programs into independent national chapters. Likewise, as indicated in the case study of Honduras, while volunteers provided specialized and technical support to established NGOs, the plan was for it to focus on the sustainability of local nonprofits.

Localization is used in different ways throughout the book. Chapter Two indicates the challenges of adapting imported technologies to local conditions in Iraq. Most volunteers and programs reflected some level of commitment to align volunteer services with local needs and conditions. Localization was also illustrated through the use of local volunteers to establish or strengthen local voluntary agencies. Overall, the concept demonstrated a historical trend for local services to eliminate a need for expatriate volunteers from abroad. It relates to who takes the lead on the development process, who is involved, and what their roles are. Locally driven programs that engage local people, including volunteers, often engage international volunteers to support the aspirations and ambitions of local communities.

It is interesting to consider how goals to support domestic development intersect with volunteers' English language instruction activities. These activities may historically be considered a dimension of the promotion of cultural values.[9] Although English language learning programs were common activities for IVS volunteers, the case example from Chapter Four unpacks some of the ongoing challenges with international volunteers teaching English and local empowerment. As noted in this chapter, "Some volunteers questioned the developmental value of teaching English, and others felt volunteers were simply filling positions that Algerians could have filled." This case example reflects ongoing critiques levied against international volunteering, which challenged volunteers' influence on national language and identity, local empowerment, and capacity development.

Questions regarding volunteers' support of local empowerment were not unique to IVS historically. These principles were emphasized in the first Universal Charter of Volunteer Service, which recognized the importance of supporting the growth of local and national volunteer programs.[10] Likewise, in 1971, Dorothea Woods, a scholar on international volunteering, wrote a forward-looking report about the contemporary and future patterns of volunteers in development. This report estimated that cooperation between international and national volunteers was the most propitious way to accomplish sustainable community development.[11] Some critics contend that this should be the goal of most international volunteering programs, which should eventually close as local capacity increases in parallel with national empowerment and identity.

Alongside the localization of development cooperation, several case examples in this book described diversification in the recruitment of IVS volunteers from outside the U.S., as well as the promotion of domestic volunteering for development. As summarized in Chapters Two and Three, during the first two decades of IVS, most volunteers were American. IVS then moved to a more international and diverse corpus of volunteers, a move that seems to have been a productive direction for development effectiveness, although perhaps not for the organization's ultimate survival. For example, the Village Volunteer Program and related National Volunteer Program in Bangladesh emphasized how the skills and expertise developed in one village could be transferred to other villages. This example clearly demonstrates the value of South-to-South volunteer cooperation in strategic support of a domestic development agenda.

Despite a generalized recognition of the virtues of South-to-South (and South-to-North) volunteer cooperation, these types of exchanges remain under-practiced and under-funded. Most governments and private organizations across the globe continue to administer a North-to-South model. While the variety of countries that send and receive international volunteers has dramatically expanded over the past 60 years, the typical international volunteer in the twenty-first century comes from countries in Europe, North America, and Asia (esp. Japan and Korea) and serves in countries in Sub-Saharan Africa, South and Southeast Asia and the Pacific, and Latin America. Considering current factors influencing the development sector, it is possible that some IVCOs may follow the example of IVS in Bangladesh and other countries that prioritized national development and volunteering—perhaps leading to the eventual demise of these IVCOs as international volunteers train themselves out of a job.

Challenges Confronting IVS And The U.S. Government

This section investigates challenges evident in the preceding chapters as IVS struggled to navigate its relationships with the U.S. government including: its drive to diversify resourcing from public funding; the continual search to redefine the IVS value proposition, including maintaining its distinctiveness from Peace Corps volunteers and USAID personnel; and differentiating IVS's diplomacy and development objectives.

Resourcing the Drive to Diversify IVS Resourcing from Public Funding

Patterns of resourcing identified in this book reflect the challenges that many international volunteer organizations have faced during this time. Volunteer organizations that were initially sponsored by private donors found substantial support from governments beginning in the 1960s. This can be seen across the northern globe and by 1965 included USA, Canada, UK, Belgium, Japan, Australia, West Germany, Denmark, and Norway.[12] Some of these organizations were new, having been established around 1960, but others were longstanding, and public funding produced issues of balancing highly desired resources with issues of independence.

As described in Chapter One of this book: "Even in this first formal meeting, the issue of IVS independence was discussed in the context of a potential conflict with government priorities. In retrospect, this discussion was quite prescient."

Similar to many other international volunteer organizations globally, the infusion of government funding into IVS initiatives tended to bring the role and scope of volunteering programs into the arena of government policy, which left the challenge of how social movements could best respond. Most government-sponsored IVCOs attempted to avoid tying their operations to their government's foreign policy objectives and sustained a level of independence. While this tension also emerged at the level of individual volunteers, many examples in this book indicate how volunteers supported goals that aligned with the U.S. government's political priorities. While in some cases, this might have been a conscious decision, such an alignment could occur without a volunteer's awareness or intention. Allegiance to common values did not necessarily mean allegiance to practice in policies or programs.

By the late 1980s, neoliberal reforms had led to a retrenchment in some countries of official development assistance. These reforms resulted in a reduction in the state's contributions to development efforts combined with the promotion of more market-based mechanisms to advance liberal democratic values. As with other IVCOs, IVS was pressured to seek funds from outside the state sector. The case example of Bangladesh described in Chapter Five (where funding to IVS from USAID gradually decreased from 100% in the first decade (1972-1982) to 0% by around 1990) was not necessarily widespread, but it was indicative of a tightening of focus of donor funding. In reality, many IVCOs remained highly dependent on public financing, and this has not fundamentally changed when viewed from a global perspective.

However, to maintain funding, many IVCOs internationally had needed to find ways to reach an accommodation with state donors, which demanded tighter reporting and a direct focus on development outcomes rather than program volunteer numbers. While diversification was not uncommon, this was often driven by reliance on some level of state funding. There are instances where a reorientation away from volunteering for people-to-people development towards, for example, development projects or consultancy was evident. Or, in some cases, simply a struggle to survive on a small scale.

The attempt by IVS to continue working independently, while having some parallels with other agencies working internationally, was not the approach taken by most IVCOs who survived from the 1960s. For instance, JOCV (Japan) and DED (Germany) have been fully absorbed into the state development agencies of their countries, while APSO (Ireland) closed, as did Progressio and Skillshare International (UK) when state funding ceased. As described in Chapter Six, the 1971

Harper's Ferry decisions to reduce IVS reliance on U.S. government funding clearly had both advantages and disadvantages; as it increasingly moved away from receiving state funding, it is unclear whether IVS was able to maintain a clear value proposition for both the U.S. government and other key donors.

Maintaining IVS Distinctiveness
Differences in IVS, Peace Corps and USAID Personnel

Chapter Ten describes traceable links between IVS and the development of the U.S. Peace Corps in the context of people-to-people support and program models. Both programs also had direct funding links to the U.S. government, with many similarities in the personalities involved in their creation and administration. The growing interest in gaining support from the state for volunteering programs was a shared agenda across countries and indeed operated internationally.[13] However, different governments responded in different ways, some by establishing a state-led provision and others by funding organizations outside the state sector. In the U.S., the location of the Peace Corps as an arm's length organization from established government structures was similar in some ways to the use of the Lockwood Committee in the UK, which coordinated the state-funded volunteer programs of different organizations, giving the state-funded program coherence.

On the other hand, the institutional arrangements for the Peace Corps seemed to leave increasingly little space for the other U.S. volunteering agencies. This was undoubtedly true for IVS, which moved from a partner to a competitor for USAID funding. For instance, when in supposed partnership with the Peace Corps, IVS was pushed out of Liberia. The Peace Corps was left as the lead agency of volunteer choice with USAID.[14] In most countries that partnered with a lead IVCO (leaving aside the emergence of private sector providers), the state tended to partner with a single agency, leaving other volunteer agencies to struggle. Therefore, there was insufficient space for both the Peace Corps and IVS in the framework of governmental-IVCO relationships. Although the Peace Corps had taken much of its founding ideas and approach from IVS and took these ideas to an overwhelming scale in the 1960s, this challenged IVS to continue providing a distinctive offer.

This challenge was reinforced by on-the-ground experience with USAID staff and volunteers, making IVS volunteers not just indistinguishable from the Peace Corps but also from many USAID staff. This was further exacerbated by the unclear representations of volunteers in the communities where they served. As described in Chapter Four: "Everyone is told that volunteers are USAID personnel." Indeed, the sense of self-identity held by IVS volunteers may have either conflicted with or reinforced this. There were concerns about the term 'volunteer' being perceived as amateur, and several case examples illustrate a sense of movement away from the language of 'volunteer' identification among some international volunteering organizations.

Indeed, dropping the designation and language seemed to be associated with loss of the distinctive volunteer proposition: working harder, sacrifice, pro-social motivations, willingness to go into areas that consultants may not be willing to go to, relationship-focused rather than a strict technical focus, etc. In addition, Chapter Seven illustrated how the themes of risk, rapport, responsibility, resourcefulness, and romance all played out in the stories and experiences of IVS volunteers. These themes frame the ways that volunteers encounter, learn, and bring back lasting impacts from their experiences abroad. In many ways, these themes also represent qualities that express the unique value of volunteers compared with other professionals and consultants working in the space of international development cooperation. The initial willingness of IVS volunteers to go into areas where USAID staff or Peace Corps volunteers were unwilling to enter may have been one reason why they continued to operate despite increasing similarities between programs. However, this distinctiveness lost value over time.

The inability of IVS to clearly articulate its value proposition, compared to USAID consultants and U.S. Peace Corps volunteers, was evident by the 1980s, as reflected in the ways that other IVCOs adopted a diversity of terms to emphasize the professional quality of their contribution. In response, IVS tried to reinvent itself with too late an effort. As argued in Chapter Five: "With its reinvention, IVS lost its uniqueness and ability to offer a specialized volunteer service different from other contractors or NGOs."

Alongside these challenges, case examples in these chapters also illustrate the opportunities provided by IVS to advance both development and diplomacy objectives. Although the diplomatic components of the model could perhaps have accentuated distinctive elements of international volunteering, this objective was not without detractors and critics. The following section discusses some of these opportunities and challenges.

IVS's Diplomacy and Development Objectives

From the initial interventions in the Middle East to those in Southeast Asia, the connection of the work of IVS with U.S. foreign policy is contextually related. This is by no means unusual for international volunteering programs. The intervention of governments in the funding of international volunteer activities presents a way of parceling the globe based on spheres of interest. It was no coincidence to find IVS operating in the Middle East after the formation of Israel, nor its involvement in Southeast Asia in the area of communist insurgency. The Cold War was fought across the globe, and Chapter Ten (IVS and Peace Corps) alluded that one reason for state support for people-to-people volunteers was a concern about countering the relative success of the Soviet Union.

Volunteers were not the only means of intervention. However, people-to-people diplomacy provided distinctive value for international understanding, and in some cases, was described as the primary purpose of international volunteering. As described in Chapter Three: "The main purpose behind the presence of IVS here is to bridge the 'last six inches' in the extension of American diplomacy." Such interest-based parceling was founded on strategic interests and was no more coincidental than the assignment of UK volunteers to English-speaking Africa or French volunteers to francophone countries; or in more recent times, how Chinese volunteers are sent to the 'front line' of the 'Belt and Road' initiative.

These 'last six inches' could see volunteers on the front line and potentially exposed to security risks, but it also potentially enabled them to develop an affinity with the people they were living with and brought allegiances into question. There was some suggestion of this in the case study accounts of IVS in Southeast Asia. It poses an interesting contradiction that IVCOs and state funders still face today: that while the fact of international volunteering demonstrates the commitment of a country and meets public diplomacy objectives, the experience of that assignment may not make that a lived experience for the volunteer exposed to the consequences of their home country's foreign policy in their day to day living alongside their host community. But this was a complex issue. While this was seen as incompatible in some cases, in others it was experienced as a positive relationship.

These tensions play out at the individual and organizational levels. Therefore, IVCOs had to manage that space and strategically decide if it was possible or desirable to link volunteers with governments' strategic priorities. In the extreme context of Southeast Asia described in the 1960s and 1970s, it is hard to imagine how such tensions could be managed, especially in the surround sound of anti-war campaigning in the latter part of that period. However, the decision of "delinking foreign assistance from broader foreign policy objectives" was not necessarily followed in other countries. For instance, IVCOs in the UK continued to campaign against apartheid in South Africa, all the while maintaining programs in front-line states funded by the UK government.[15] This volunteer work continued despite the UK government's tacit support for the South African regime.[16]

Given these concerns, several case examples from this book illustrate that a close identification between IVS and other U.S. government programs was perceived to be incompatible with the values and ideals of IVS. As a result, IVS programs distanced themselves from USAID when they perceived that this relationship was too close for comfort. The case example in Chapter Three, describing how IVS began working in closer cooperation with the Lao government, is a good example of how IVS responded to these challenges. Other cases suggest that their response was perhaps not sufficiently quick or drastic. For instance, the case of Cambodia illustrated a clear association between U.S. politics and IVS volunteers, which ultimately led to the ousting of U.S. volunteers by the Cambodian monarchy.

In other cases (such as Sudan, Ecuador, and Zimbabwe), participation by volunteers in community activities suggests potential alignment between volunteers and local politics. Such an alignment did not necessarily represent the position of IVS as an organization. Case studies suggest that IVS volunteers could be catalysts to instigate changes to the social and political order of countries—particularly those volunteers working in countries with weak or threatened democracies. However, the appropriate role for IVS volunteers in political action seemed ambiguous across countries and programs. Even at the time, scholars and government leaders questioned whether international volunteers' involvement in local and national political struggles was appropriate—seeing this as a local responsibility and a potential danger to intergovernmental political relations.[17]

As the case example from Vietnam illustrated, this contention was not easily resolved even within IVS teams, which became increasingly polarized regarding the direction of the war and its effect on volunteer activities. When such questions were uneasily resolved, they were sometimes ignored—to the ultimate detriment of IVS programs. For example, the case example of Laos illustrated how IVS leaders "put on blinders and ignored the military and political ramifications of volunteer work..." ultimately leading to challenges that could not be overcome.

These challenges were not limited to international volunteers. By association, national volunteers and local staff were also exposed to risks. The Bangladesh end-game experience described in an earlier chapter is one example of the dangers. The role of IVS in sensitive programs does not mean that the risks to local staff ended with the program.[18]

SAFETY AND SECURITY CONCERNS OF IVS VOLUNTEERS

The distinctive contributions of IVS volunteers raised questions of safety and security for volunteers: such as going into difficult or rural areas that the Peace Corps or

USAID might avoid, engaging in local struggles and political tensions, and perceptions of IVS volunteers as directly connected to the U.S. governmental interventions. In Laos, for instance, a key challenge for administration seemed to be a constant reexamination of what IVS was doing in Laos and whether volunteers were exposed to an unacceptable amount of danger.

Issues of safety and security, along with the consequences of engaging in challenging spaces, were evident in many of the stories contained in this collection. With a strong spirit of idealism and adventure, IVS volunteers tended to feel passionate about their assignments, even in challenging circumstances when realities on the ground often prevented them from completing their tasks. Where destabilization, political turmoil, or war disrupted volunteer placements, this appeared to leave volunteers with some emotional trauma or regrets as case examples in some chapters exemplify.

Many of the distinctive attributes of volunteers continue to be connected to their willingness to serve in more informal (in relation to governments), rural or otherwise unpopular destinations, and less structured circumstances. However, the ongoing challenges of mitigating safety and security concerns associated with these unique positions remain today. These issues will be further explored below when discussing the future of international volunteering.

The Long-term Legacy Of IVS

In models of international volunteering, there is typically a defined time and task. But the sense of being part of a whole-encompassing commitment limited by programmatic rather than personal decisions tends to frame the inevitable question: 'What happens when I leave?' This is closely followed by a more reflective question: 'What difference did I make?'

This sense of personal questioning is evident in the stories of IVS volunteers contained in these chapters. It links to the challenge of sustainability, and a fear that things will simply go back to the way they were before the volunteer's service. One example of this challenge is explicitly described in the Yemen experience, where "volunteers encountered the common dilemma of sustainability" and questioned the value of their service. Indeed, the dilemma of whether IVS was involved in sustainable capacity development or local displacement is apparent throughout these chapters. Concerns about who would replace them when they left co-existed with related concerns about filling a position that should be held by a local person: "Volunteers were simply filling positions that Algerians could have filled."

The aspiration about what is left behind when the individual volunteer leaves (or indeed when IVS leaves as a whole) from a given locality is not necessarily the completion of a task. More satisfactory in meeting aspirations is how by working together IVS volunteers and local people created something that continued to operate and became sustainable without IVS volunteers. This is evident in the way such successes are described, not just the fact that they happened. The tone of this account is as revealing in some ways as its content:

"IVS volunteers working with Bangladeshis created The Friends in Village Development, Bangladesh (FIVDB). . . . This program was so successful that eventually, FIVDB was run by Bangladeshis with no outside assistance. FIVDB was also able to raise its own financial support. IVS volunteers had worked themselves out of their jobs."

This is not simply a legacy of individual volunteers or of a volunteer group: it is the legacy of a social movement, which like all such movements, is inevitable for its time. The circumstances in which IVS developed and grew are unlikely to be repeated. The general legacy of IVS can perhaps be best understood in terms of the experience of walking in others' shoes and an awareness of 'how others see us', generating a level of understanding about our own identities, which informs what international volunteers do for the rest of their lives in their own communities. Learning to recognize that we may never know what difference we made during our service as an international volunteer is one side; what we subsequently did with that experience is perhaps a better way to consider our legacy. The passion evident in the accounts of IVS volunteers, and their desires to ensure that these stories are told, are testaments to the volunteers and the communities they lived with and worked alongside.

THE FUTURE OF INTERNATIONAL VOLUNTEERING

The various country case examples described in these chapters reflect a unique expression of international service specific to a particular historical and cultural context. In this sense, the evolution of IVS was specific to each time and place where the volunteers served. On the other hand, these changes also reflect many of the historical trends common to other global IVCOs, as international volunteering changed over the course of their formation in the 1950s or '60s to their eventual demise. IVCOs that survived these changing tides had to continuously adapt. In some ways, the nature of international volunteering remains the same; in other ways, it is hardly recognizable.

Looking only at the most recent changes, scholars have highlighted several ways that international volunteering has changed over the past decade. First, many governments are no longer willing to provide core funding to IVCOs and have instituted competitive contracting systems that pit IVCOs against each other and against organizations outside of the sector for funding. This is often linked to complex reporting systems and an emphasis on delivering outcomes, such as development targets.[19] Second, international volunteering is increasingly commoditized with private and corporate sector engagement. The 'international volunteer experience' can now be purchased where local communities primarily benefit from ensuring the experience meets the volunteer's requirements.[20] Third, heavy promotion of short-term international volunteering from Northern countries—primarily with young people and older adults—has replaced the longstanding trends towards older and longer-term volunteer placements that were evident in many case examples throughout this book. And finally, donors seem interested in funding international service programs that develop the marketable skills of volunteers combined with continued objectives for public diplomacy and international understanding.[21] We will likely continue to see these directions accentuated in the coming years.

The digital environment has also opened new opportunities and challenges. Innovations in communication and information technology are central to many new forms of international volunteering. The availability of Internet technology has revolutionized IVCOs' training and communication capacities. These tools are used to recruit and support traditional forms of international volunteering and to develop new forms of volunteering. Online campaigns have made it easier to advocate for volunteers to participate in global causes without leaving their home country.

COVID-19 has accelerated shifts towards online volunteering. However, the pandemic's influence on accelerating virtual volunteering and decelerating face-to-face international volunteering may not be as radical as some might initially think. Research during the pandemic indicates that face-to-face international volunteering is still seen as desirable by volunteers and while online volunteering is expected to grow, it is not believed to be a replacement for face-to-face volunteering. Indeed, some models only achieve their objectives by returning volunteers being able to share their experiences and support fundraising and awareness in their home communities and institutions.[22] However, the same studies suggest that a greater reliance on local and national volunteers may be the wave of the future—consistent with longstanding trends in the sector—as a way of sustaining development interventions. Local volunteers embedded within the social relations of their communities may be more cost effective and do not necessarily need not be commoditized. The IVS experience suggests that the sustainability of local volunteering may still be threatened if they are entirely dependent on international donor funding. This greater reliance on local volunteerism as a strategy for managing risk is evident in the approach of some IVCOs, local partners, and donors.[23]

As international volunteers were repatriated, leaving local volunteers in place, questions have arisen about IVCOs responsibilities for the well-being of all volunteers—regardless of whether they are domestic or international. The stories throughout this book illustrate how some of these threats to safety were more acceptable and common—and in some ways, marked the distinctive value of IVS volunteers over other international actors in the development space, such as Peace Corps volunteers and USAID consultants. Contemporary IVCOs now offer a suite of services and protections designed to safeguard volunteers, along with systems for collecting and communicating information to minimize potential threats. These safety and security practices begin with the screening and selection of volunteers and continue through training and development, housing practices, and protections for volunteers' physical and psychological well-being. This contrasts with some traditional views of volunteer security as being based upon relationships in-country, acknowledging that secure compounds for volunteer accommodation also have a long history in some IVCO programs.

The disparity in guaranteed protection between domestic and international volunteer development programs is not necessarily new. As some of the case studies in this collection illustrate, domestic volunteers often receive few protections, even when serving in counterpart with international volunteers. This has long been a source of concern for practitioners.

In addition to accelerating virtual volunteering and providing support and safety protections for local volunteerism, the global pandemic also highlighted the benefits of decreased international travel on the environment. This was not an issue of importance during the IVS years but has emerged as a major priority in the twenty-first century. Recognizing the growing concern about the effects of carbon emissions and consumption on the planet, the future of international volunteering must certainly reconcile its practices with climate change and climate justice. Any international volunteering programs concerned with development will need to balance their goals to achieve the 2015-2030 UN SDGs (particularly climate action and responsible consumption) with the negative influence of international travel on carbon emission targets.

The role of churches in the international volunteering landscape has also changed over time. Faith has a strong history with international development volunteering and continues as a strong feature in associations within countries such as Switzerland (e.g., Unité) and Germany (e.g., AKLHÜ e.V.). In these cases, the state has continued to work in partnership with faith-based associations and volunteer organizations. However, in many situations where the state has taken a lead role in facilitating international development volunteering, the state has supplanted faith-based development volunteering. As described in Chapter Nine, faith remains a strong motivator for a section of international volunteers and individual IVCOs even if explicit religious institutions no longer maintain the same level of involvement as in the past.

Another area that has become increasingly important for international volunteering is the engagement of the private and corporate/commercial sector. New high-wealth philanthropy from private foundations and corporate partnerships has diversified and expanded the support base for international volunteering beyond resources obtained from the public sector. While developing partnerships with private companies began as a trend in the 1980s and was described in multiple chapters as a historical phenomenon, it has become even more popular today. At the local level, this is often referred to as developing sustainable marketplaces at the "bottom of the pyramid" in the name of social development. Consistent with the historical analysis in prior chapters, many critics today are concerned about the practical implementation of 'neoliberal' principles of self-reliance, self-help, and empowerment that drive localization activities that champion market principles. Nonetheless, the rise of corporate social responsibility in the twenty-first century has opened new opportunities for IVCOs and international volunteers.

Conclusion

Looking back over the decades of IVS, it seems appropriate to consider whether the future is optimistic or pessimistic. During the time when IVS was most active, there was a coalescence, sometimes an accommodation, of views between IVS, its volunteers, the host government, and the U.S. government. This coalescence is critical to enable all to stay engaged in the undertaking. The varied motivations of these different parties present a challenge in aligning different interests for volunteering to operate effectively internationally. Although it may be possible to configure other clusters to incorporate contributions from private sector investors and philanthropic capital, the process remains complex.

For over twenty years, IVCOs have been challenged to align their activities and measures with the UN Millennium Development Goals (MDGs) and the Sustainable Development Goals (SDGs). Over time, IVCOs have become, and in some cases still aspire to become, recognized as part of the development ecosystem. IVCOs continue to struggle to raise the profile of international volunteers' distinctive contributions to the SDGs. While some IVCOs have attempted to find alternative ways to demonstrate their contribution to development outcomes, this singular focus on development targets such as the SDGs may devalue the distinctive value proposition of international volunteering as a model for human-centered development. Modern IVCOs are working to develop and promote a more distinctive value proposition. But what should this value proposition be?

Perhaps the most forthright approach in recent years was articulated by the 'Valuing Volunteering' research conducted by the UK-based Voluntary Service Overseas (VSO) and the Institute for Development Studies (IDS). Based on three years of research, this study concluded that the relational nature of volunteering was its distinctive value rather than volunteers' skills or technical contributions.[24] Conclusions from this study get at the heart of the problem directly: is the distinctive value of international volunteering primarily about skills development and capacity building or relationships and mutual learning? For IVCOs, it's all of the above. Therefore, the focus is not entirely clear going forward; the emphasis varies depending on who asks the question. For IVCOs and international volunteering to survive, priorities may need to change. Governments may one day view international volunteering as a more valuable tool for citizen diplomacy, nation branding, and soft power, and IVCOs may need to find more effective ways to advance that agenda.

However, this picture does not necessarily capture the positivity and sense of commitment evidenced by the IVS volunteers in these chapters. Volunteers from IVS faced challenges of a different order and magnitude than other players in the development architecture. IVS volunteers showed how to embrace the essence of international volunteering. Ultimately, IVS held values and relationships at its core, often at the expense of organizational survival. In this way, the IVS pioneers who forged the path of international volunteering will continue to be recognized for their dedication and commitment. Whatever the future holds for international volunteering, modern IVCOs must articulate a clear value proposition and let that clarity guide their future directions.

Appendix A: IVS Country and Regional Programs
Years and Numbers of Volunteer Assignments

Country/Regional Program	Year Start	Year End	No. of Volunteer Assignments*
Algeria	1963	1977	122
Bangladesh	1973	2002	58
Bolivia	1975	2001	30
Botswana	1975	1988	33
Cambodia	1960	1963	25
Cape Verde	1987	1988	1
Caribbean (Antigua, Dominica, Grenada, St. Kitts & Nevis, St. Lucia, St. Vincent)	1983	1989	8
Colombia	1975	1976	3
Congo (Zaire)-I	1970	1974	13
Congo (Zaire)-II	1986	1989	6
Ecuador	1974	1974	48
Egypt	1953	1957	4
Ethiopia	1984	1984	1
Ghana	1960	1961	2
Honduras	1975	1987	27
Indonesia	1974	1975	2
Iraq	1954	1957	20
Jordan	1955	1962	2
UNRWA (Jordan, Syria, Lebanon, Gaza)	1963	1965	8
Laos	1954	1975	384
Liberia	1960	1963	24
Libya	1971	1973	2
Madagascar	1975	1977	1
Malaysia (Sabah)	1965	1987	3
Mali	1988	1988	2
Mauritania	1975	1979	11
Morocco	1968	1972	12
Nepal	1956	1958	4
Papua New Guinea	1975	1984	39
Southeast Asia (Vietnam, Cambodia, Thailand)	1991	2002	3
Sudan	1966	1983	43
Vietnam	1956	1972	416

Yemen	1971	1979	13
Zimbabwe	1983	1992	21
Country of assignment unknown			28
Total			1419

* Based on best available information from the IVS Alumni Association database. Includes international volunteers and some country staff but does not generally include national volunteers. Assignments are based on information on countries served for 1368 individual volunteers. Assignments were typically two years, but many extended for multiple years, and some had shortened assignments. At least 48 served in two countries and three in three countries. The identity of the one volunteer in Ethiopia is not known but the number of volunteers with unknown countries is reduced to account for this.

Appendix B: IVS Corporate Objectives and Strategy

Certificate of Incorporation of International Voluntary Services, Inc. (1953)

We, the undersigned, all citizens of the United States and a majority citizens and residents of the District of Columbia, desiring to associate ourselves as a corporation for benevolent, charitable, and educational purposes pursuant to the provision of Title 29 of Chapter 6 of the District of Columbia Code (1951), and not for pecuniary profit, do hereby certify as follows:

First   The name or title by which this corporation shall be known in law shall be the International Voluntary Services, Inc.

Second   The term for which it is organized shall be perpetual.

Third   The particular business and objects of said corporation shall be:

a) To utilize the services of volunteers on an organized basis to combat hunger, poverty, disease, and illiteracy in the underdeveloped areas of the world and thereby further the peace, happiness, and prosperity of the peoples thereof.

b) To strengthen the bonds between the United States of America and other freedom loving countries and peoples.

c) To recruit personnel to serve in projects undertaken by the corporation.

d) To operate, direct, and maintain, either alone or in conjunction with other agencies health, training and demonstration centers; model farms and other demonstrations of rural activity; schools for artisans and trainees; hospitals, dispensaries and other health establishments; and any other means and agencies which from time to time may seem expedient to its directors.

e) To establish projects for assistance to displaced persons, homeless orphans, and other victims of unsettled conditions.

f) To maintain facilities for central administration and for receiving and training recruited personnel prior to departure to foreign assignment.

g) To make provision for maintenance, supervision and administrative support of its representatives in the field.

h) To advise and/or contract with the United States Government and its various departments and bureaus, and/or with state or other local governments or groups, and/or with societies, foundations, and trusts with reference to the furtherance of the objectives of the corporation.

i) To establish, conduct and maintain such educational, social, economic, and charitable enterprises as may assist in the advancement of the foregoing objects.

j) To contract with other persons, corporations, associations or governmental bodies for the use by such persons, corporations, associations or governmental bodies of the property and facilities of this corporation upon such terms and subject to such terns and subject such restrictions as may be provided for in the by-laws or by resolution of the directors.

k) To take, receive and hold any property, real, personal, or mixed, and to use, invest, dispose and convey the same.

l) To undertake and perform such other projects as may be for the general advancement of the purpose set forth above.

FOURTH The number of its trustees, directors, or managers for the first year of its existence shall be not less than three nor more than fifteen.

IN TESTIMONY WHEREOF, we have this 16th day of Feb. 1953 hereunder set our hands and seal.

Duane H. Ramsey /s/
333 N. Carolina Ave. S.E.
Washington, 3, D.C.

The following document, entitled "Purposes and Policies" and dated 1953, provided a statement of the organization's first principles. This original declaration of purpose was restated in the "IVS Reporter" newsletter of March 1970, as a reminder of origins and raison d'etre for IVS.

IVS Purposes and Policies

The Policy

The Act for International Development stipulates that "participation of private agencies and persons shall be sought to the greatest extent practicable" in carrying out the Point 4 program. The aim of International Voluntary Services, Inc. is to help effectuate the idea underlying this policy. As Secretary of State Dulles has said, there must be an "enlarged role for individuals as against governments." He has spoken of the need for intensifying private benevolence on an international scale and stated that "perhaps the best that (the new administration) can do will be to encourage and make place for the individual and group efforts which are the most precious jewels of freedom."

Background

Voluntary action has in the past been a principal factor in our relations with people of less developed areas. Missions and foundations and other non-government organizations have carried on service projects designed to improve health and well-being and raise the level of literacy. Health centers, schools, and agricultural demonstration stations have been established in remote parts of the world. These undertakings have gained respect and support from the native peoples and reflected credit on the United States of America.

The Point 4 program has given new focus to these activities. Emphasis on grass roots approach and "people-to-people" cooperation makes it clear that private agencies may be particularly effective in supplementing and augmenting the efforts of Government operated programs.

The Point 4 program was quick to utilize the experience and facilities of private voluntary agencies. Several agencies were brought into cooperative relationships with TCA and are now carrying out village improvement and other projects pursuant to contract.

The needs, however, are limitless. Both public and private programs are needed abroad, and the two should be coordinated.

It was with a view to working out a more suitable mechanism for coordination between governmental and private agency effort that a group of private agency representatives, with experience in foreign aid programs, sought solution through the newly established International Voluntary Services, Inc.

The Opportunity

The Point 4 program of sharing our skills and techniques with the peoples of underdeveloped areas has been given such genuine approval by the American people that many non-governmental organizations, professional groups, church-connected service agencies, and individuals would contribute voluntarily to promote its success. American generosity and goodwill should be released in a people-to-people cooperative endeavor at mutual improvement.

TCA supported programs can extend their effectiveness by joining hands with non-government organizations. The energies of highly specialized experts in a foreign country can be magnified by the presence of IVS demonstration workers at village levels who can teach improved production, conservation and health practices.

Such participation vitalizes American interest in our international role, and it stimulates greater public understanding and support.

Organizing for the Job

The administrative difficulties encountered in taking advantage of volunteered assistance which is diverse, disbursed, and sporadic, are considerable. It was believed the problem would be simplified through the presence of a mechanism which unites voluntary energies of willing groups and individuals and provides for orderly planning, uniform procedures and common training facilities.

International Voluntary Services, Inc. is a mechanism established with a view to utilize experience and resources of voluntary agencies for foreign projects. These projects may be closely related to TCA programs.

IVS is registered as a non-profit organization under the laws of the District of Columbia. Permanent headquarters office is in Washington, D. C. An operations center is located at New Windsor, Mary land, some 65 miles distance. Here there are ideal facilities for training and administrative support activities which include offices, dormitories, warehouses and equipment used in extensive overseas rehabilitation work carried on by Church World Service following World War II. A training and orientation program for persons assigned to foreign rural improvement teams may be conducted at New Windsor, wherein special lectures and consultants living in Washington, D. C. might be utilized. It is planned that voluntary contributions of tools and supplies in support of field teams will be processed through the facilities at New Windsor.

Control and direction of IVS is in the hands of a Board representative of broad public interest.

Objectives

The objectives of International Voluntary Services, Inc. may be summarized as follows:

a) To provide a channel for "people-to-people" cooperation and facilitate the efforts of groups who desire to meet some need abroad.

b) To provide a legal and administrative mechanism through which voluntary efforts and contributions can be coordinated with the aims and operation of governmental and multi-lateral technical assistance programs abroad.

c) To provide administrative services in meeting common objectives among private agencies, regularizing procedures and conducting negotiations with Point 4 and foreign government representatives.

d) To provide facilities for assembling, organizing and training teams of village and rural improvement workers for assignment to approved projects abroad.

e) To select suitable projects and disseminate information about them to interested groups and the public.

f) To serve as a responsible agency for preparing reports and insuring compliance with regulations of U.S. and foreign government agencies.

Some Guiding Principles

a) Voluntary Service on a voluntary basis is emphasized. Participants will make sacrifice in salary but adequate maintenance and allowances will be provided.

b) "Grass Roots"—Personnel selection will be directed mainly to service at village levels. Volunteer workers will frequently be young men with background of farm or vocational experience. Some married couples will serve, and where possible nationals of the countrywho have been educated in America. There will be some specialists in fields of health, education, agriculture, home economics and home construction.

c) Language—Knowledge of native language will be emphasized. For some cases intensive language instruction will begin in a training course before departure and continue in the field.

d) Operational IVS is not a "broker" or "holding company" for member agencies nor is it an instrument of the government. It is an independent, public operational entity.

e) Non-Denominational—Participants may include professional, trade, service and church groups and individuals. Cooperating private groups will assist in selection of workers and advise IVS in the conduct of the program.

f) Inter-Cultural—Progress has been made in enlisting some native workers who have been educated in the U. S. They can perform invaluable liaison and guidance for team members in the field and also give language instruction.

Training Future Leaders

The International Development Advisory Board has recommended that the government provide opportunities for competent, trained young technicians who do not yet have a background of government experience and find it difficult to get a foothold in the field of international development even though they have trained themselves for it. The program of IVS will benefit

those who give as well as those who receive. It will direct the energies of young men into fields of foreign service, give them invaluable experience and opportunity for service.

Utilization of a selected number of native students trained in the United States serves another potential contribution of IVS. These trained people constitute a valuable potential asset, but they are frequently not utilized when they return to their countries of origin. The great waste in talent is generally recognized and is a cause of concern among officials and educators dealing with this problem. The effect of American education has been in many cases to "specialize" foreign students out of a job when they get home. The U. S. trained students' problem of applying American methods in his native environment is complex and frustrating. Native technicians anxious to bring modern knowledge to play in a native environment, have expressed their desire for an apprenticeship in the field with a team of similarly trained and highly motivated Americans.

Appendix C: IVS Leadership
Executive Directors and Board of Directors Chairmen

IVS Executive Directors (1953-2002)

John S. Noffsinger, 1953–1961
Russell Stevenson, 1961–1964
John Provinse, 1964–1965
Arthur Z. Gardiner, 1965–1970
Richard J. Peters, 1971–1974
Anthony Lake, 1974–1976
John Rigby, 1976–1980
Nan Borton, 1981–1989
David R. Smock, 1989–1991
Linda Worthington/Don Luce, 1991–1993
Don Luce, 1993–1996
Parker F. Hallberg, 1996–1997
Anne D. Shirk, 1998–2002

Chairmen of IVS Board of Directors (1953-2002)

The Board of Director's leadership position was variously termed President, Chairman, Honorary Director, and Director. Archival documentation lists the following as Board leaders:

1953	Roy A. Burkhart, World Neighbors	
1954	Carl C. Taylor, Ford Foundation	
1954	Captain William H. Tuck—former director of international refugee program during World War II	
1954–1962	John H. Reisner, Executive Secretary of the Agricultural Missions, Inc. in New York and former Dean of agricultural college in China	
1962–1964	Mervin G. Smith, Department of Agricultural Economics and Rural Sociology, Ohio State University	
1964–1966	Monsignor Edwin W. O'Rourke, Executive Director of National Catholic Rural Life Conference	
1969–1971	Carl C. Taylor, Agricultural Economist	
1971–1977	Nicholas Katzenbach, former U.S. Attorney General	
1978	June Pulcini (interim), IVS Cambodia 1963, Vietnam 1964-65, Laos 1965-70	

1979–1984 Donald Fraser, Mayor of Minneapolis; former U.S. House of Representatives, Minnesota

1985–1992 Charles Whalen Jr., former U.S. House of Representatives, Ohio

1992–1997 Hugh Manke, IVS Vietnam 1967–71; Updike. Kelly and Spellacy Law Firm

1998–2002 Jeanette Goodstein, non-profit sector both in the U.S. and abroad

Chairmen of IVS Board Executive Committee

The Executive Committee was key to IVS operations for much of its lifetime. Available archival documentation indicates the following as Executive Committee chairpersons:

1953–1955 H. Harold Row, Church of the Brethren Service Committee

1956–1959 William T. Snyder, Executive Director, Mennonite Central Committee

1960–1961 H. Harold Row, Church of the Brethren Service Committee

1972–1979 William T. Snyder, Executive Director, Mennonite Central Committee

1980–1984 Ben Stephansky. Deputy United States Representative to the Organization of American States

1985–1986 Walter Carrington, United States Ambassador Extraordinary and Plenipotentiary to Senegal and Nigeria

1987–1992 Charles Whalen Jr., former U.S. House of Representatives, Ohio

1993–1994 Hugh Manke, IVS/Vietnam 1967–71; Updike. Kelly and Spellacy Law Firm

1995–2002 Stephan Nichols, IVS Vietnam 1967–1968.

Notes

Most of IVS documents cited in notes below are available in the IVS Collection of the Mennonite Church USA Archives, 3145 Benham Ave., Elkhart, IN 46517. Contact: Jason Kauffman or Roberta Yoder, archives@mennoniteusa.org or tel. 574-523-3080.

Chapter 1: IVS Origins And Early Years—1953–1957

1. Based on IVS Alumni Association database as summarized in Appendix A.

2. www.trumanlibrary.gov/library/public-papers/19/inaugural-address, accessed August 20, 2020.

3. Ibid.

4. Stephen Macekura, "The Point Four Program and U.S. International Development Policy," Political Science Quarterly, Vol. 128, No. 1 (Spring 2013) pp. 134-135.

5. Dean Acheson, Present at the Creation: My Years in the State Department, New York, 1969, p. 265 and Robert Schlesinger, White House Ghosts: Presidents and Their Speechwriters, NY: Simon & Schuster, 2008, pp. 60-63. "Benjamin H. Hardy Papers," Truman Library and Museum, www.trumanlibrary.org/hstpaper/hardybh.htm, accessed August 23, 2020.

6. Sam Rushay, "Truman's Point IV Program Provided Needed Aid," The Examiner (Independence, MO) February 16, 2019, www.examiner.net/opinion/20190216/trumans-point-iv-program-provided-needed-aid, accessed September 2, 2020.

7. On the origins of the AFSC, see www.afsc.org/story/origin-afsc while the story of the Nobel Peace Prize honor it received in 1947 can be found at www.nobelprize.org/nobel_prizes/peace/laureates/1947/friends-committee-history.html, September 2, 2020

8. Melvin Gingerich, Service for Peace: A History of Mennonite Civilian Public Service, Mennonite Central Committee, Akron, PA, 1949, pp. 16 and 420.

9. "Beliefs" www.brethren.org/about/beliefs (official website of the Church of the Brethren, Elgin, IL) accessed 9/30/2020.

10. "Oral History Interview with Stanley Andrews," conducted by Richard D. McKinzie on October 31, 1970. www.trumanlibrary.gov/library/oral-histories/andrewss, accessed 10/25/2020.

11. Interview of Dale D. Clark by Robert Zigler for the Association for Diplomatic Studies and Training, Foreign Affairs Oral History Collection, Foreign Assistance Series, October 14, 1998, pp. 12-13. Loc.gov/item/mfdipbib001694/ accessed 14 October 2020. Hereinafter cited as "Clark interview Oct. 1998."

12. Ibid., pp. 13 and 30. Unfortunately, Clark did not say exactly when he and the peace churches representatives met in the TCA office or when this informal meeting was held, and there is no written record of either in the IVS archives located at the Mennonite Church USA Archives, Elkhart, Indiana.

13. Ibid., pp. 13-14. 'Hyphenated project' refers to a joint project. In this case between IVS and World Neighbors.

14. Minutes of the IVS Board of Directors, July 8, 1953, pp. 1-5 plus two exhibits. Exhibit I was the agreement on the Iraq program between the ICA and IVS of June 30, 1953, p. 6, and an unsigned and undated copy of the IVS Certificate of Incorporation. These two exhibits were sent to the Board members in September with a cover letter of the fourth by the office manager, Ruth Early whose services were provided on loan by the Brethren Service Committee. See, International Service Records, Box 1, folder 2. International Voluntary Services Records, 1952-2010, XI-014, Mennonite Church USA Archives. Elkhart, Indiana.

15. Minutes of the Operations Advisory Committee for July 28 and August 3, 1953 in International Service Records, XI/o14, Series 1, Box 1, folder 2.

16. Minutes of the Operations Advisory Committee for August 28, 1953 in International Service Records, XI/o14, Box 1, folder 2.

17. Minutes of Board of Directors for September 11, 1953, in International Service Records, XI/o14, Box 1, folder 2.

18. Minutes of the Operations Advisory Committee for October 20, 1953, and November 18, 1953, in International Service Records, XI/o14, Box 1, folder 2.

19. Paul A. Rodell interview of Dale D. Clark, Bountiful, UT, July 13, 2002. Tape recording in possession of the interviewer.

20. Paul A. Rodell, "John S. Noffsinger and the Global Impact of the Thomasite Experience," in Corazon Villareal, ed., Back to the Future: Perspectives on the Thomasite Legacy to Philippine Education, Quezon City, American Studies Association of the Philippines, 2003, pp. 63-79.

21. Minutes of Board of Directors, January 8, 1954 in International Service Records, XI/o14, Box 1, folder 2.

22. Minutes of the Executive Committee, January 26, March 5, April 21 and June 21, 1954 in International Service Records, XI/o14, Box 1, folder 2.

23. Minutes of the Board of Directors meeting, July 9, 1954 in International Service Records, XI/o14, Box 1, folder 2. For Dale Clark's family banking business and his involvement, see his August 23-24, 2008 obituary in the Deseret News in Salt Lake City, UT that was reprinted by Legacy in its funeral notice, https://www.legacy.com/obituaries/deseretnews/obituary.aspx?n=dale-duncan-clark&pid=116185623.

24. Minutes of the Executive Committee meeting, January 3, 1955 in International Service Records, XI/o14, Box 1, folder 2.

25. Minutes of the Executive Committee meeting, March 30, 1955 in International Service Records, XI/o14, Box 1, folder 2.

26. Minutes of the Board of Directors meeting of April 27, 1955 in International Service Records, XI/o14, Box 1, folder 2.

27. Minutes of the Executive Committee meeting of August 1, 1955 in International Service Records, XI/o14, Box 1, folder 2.

28. Minutes of the Executive Committee meeting of December 14, 1955 in International Service Records, XI/o14, Box 1, folder 2.

29. Minutes of the Board of Directors portion of the meetings of April 9, 1956, p. 3 in International Service Records, XI/o14, Box 1, folder 2.

30. The minutes for the Executive Committee, Luncheon speaker, Board, and Board meetings plus budgetary details, and a leadership roster and all in International Service Records, XI/o14, Box 1, folder 2.

31. Minutes of the Executive Committee meeting of May 24, 1956 in International Service Records, XI/o14, Box 1, folder 2.

32. Minutes of the Executive Committee meeting of September 7, 1956 in International Service Records, XI/o14, Box 1, folder 2.

33. Ibid.

34. Minutes of the Executive Committee meeting of December 18, 1956 in International Service Records, XI/o14, Box 1, folder 2.

35. The minutes for the Executive Committee, Luncheon speaker, Executive Committee and Board Meeting March of March 27, 1957-September 1, 1960 in International Service Records, XI/o14, Box 1, folder 3.

36. Ibid.

37. Minutes of the Executive Committee meeting on May 24, 1957 in International Service Records, XI/o14, Box 1, folder 3.

38. Minutes of the Executive Committee meeting on October 3, 1957 in International Service Records, XI/o14, Box 1, folder 3.

39. Minutes of the Executive Committee meeting on , 1957 in International Service Records, XI/o14, Box 1, folder 3.

40. Ibid.

CHAPTER 2: INITIAL PROGRAMS—Set-up, Structure And Experience

1. IVS Executive Board meeting, August 3, 1953. Pax was a Mennonite program offering an alternative to military service.

2. Kreider, J. Kenneth. 2001. A Cup of Cold Water: The Story of Brethren Service. Brethren Press. p. 366.

3. Two married couples, Howard and Alice Mills and Ted and Joan Kimmel, arrived in Baghdad shortly after the first three volunteers. The Mills were assigned to Mahawil but found the harsh living conditions difficult for a young family and within the first month were transferred elsewhere. Ted and Joan Kimmel were assigned to Shaqlawa. Joan had medical problems and stayed in Baghdad to be near medical care not available in Shaqlawa and after a couple of months returned to the US. Ted remained for several months. This flexibility appeared a good way to handle the issues with the married couples.

4. Ed's parents, Dr. William and Charlotte Wiser were Presbyterian Missionaries in northern India in the 1920-40's and authored the classic sociological book, "Behind Mud Walls", that was considered 'must reading' for anyone doing research at the village level.

5. IVS Executive Committee Meeting, January 30, 1958

6. IVS Executive Committee Meeting, April 21, 1958.

7. IVS Board of Directors Meeting Minutes 2/26/1963.

8. Cliff Doke Report of Field Visit, March 25, 1965–May 14, 1965.

CHAPTER 3: VOLUNTEERS AND THE COLD WAR - Conflict In Southeast Asia

1. Goldstein, Martin E. (1973). American Policy Toward Laos. Rutherford; Madison, Teaneck: Fairleigh Dickinson University Press. p. 107-108.

2. Goldstein, Martin E. (1973). American Policy Toward Laos. Rutherford; Madison, Teaneck: Fairleigh Dickinson University Press. p. 128.

3. The Foreign Operations Administration (FOA) became the International Cooperation Administration (ICA) on June 30, 1955 and was renamed the U.S. Agency for International Development (USAID) on September 4, 1961. The Technical Cooperation Administration (TCA), established on September 8, 1950, to oversee Point Four, was subordinated to the Director of Mutual Security on June 1, 1953. On August 31, 1953, its functions were transferred to the Foreign Operations Administration (FOA). Subsequently, on June 30, 1955, the aid program was transferred to the State Department's International Cooperation Administration (ICA). The United States Operations Missions (USOM) were established as ICA's administrators of aid. In 1961, USOM became the U.S. Agency for International Development (USAID) (see National Archives). Throughout this chapter the term USAID is mostly, but not always, used in lieu of TCA, FOA and USOM.

4. USAID. 1962. American Aid to Laos, FY 1955-FY 1962. Vientiane: 115-166.; Benson, Frederic C. (2015). "Indochina War Refugee Movements in Laos, 1954-1975: A Chronological Overview Citing New Primary Sources." In Journal of Lao Studies, Special Issue 1. March 2015, Center for Lao Studies, http://www.laostudies.org/sites/default/files/public/6%20Benson.pdf, last accessed June 25, 2021. p. 28-29.

5. United States House Committee on Government Operations 1959b. United States Aid

Operations in Laos. Hearings Before a Subcommittee of the Committee on Government Operations, House of Representatives. 86th Congress, 1st Session. Washington, DC: US Government Printing Office, March 11, 12, 13, 17, 18, 19, 20, 23, 24, April 13, 14, 15, 16 17, 21, 22 27, May 4, and June 1, 1959. 3.

6. Minutes. Executive Committee Meeting. Washington, D.C.: International Voluntary Services, Inc., January 3, 1955.

7. Minutes. Executive Committee Meeting. Washington, D.C.: International Voluntary Services, Inc., March 30, 1955; Minutes April 27, 1955)

8. Minutes. Executive Committee Meeting. Washington, D.C.: International Voluntary Services, Inc., April 27, 1955.

9. Rolston, W. Wendell. 1956. Xieng Khouang Development Project: Progress Report, February 3 to August 3, 1956. International Voluntary Services, Inc., Vientiane. p. 1-2.

10. Rolston, W. Wendell. 1956. Xieng Khouang Development Project: Progress Report, February 3 to August 3, 1956. International Voluntary Services, Inc., Vientiane. p. 1.

11. Bowman, Dean (ed.). 1959. Annual Report 1959: Xieng Khouang Development Project. International Voluntary Services. p. 1.

12. IVS. 1959. Xieng Khouang Development Project, Laos: Fourth Progress Report, January 20, 1959. Washington: International Voluntary Services, Inc. p. 1.

13. IVS. 1959. Xieng Khouang Development Project, Laos: Fourth Progress Report, January 20, 1959. Washington: International Voluntary Services, Inc. p. 6.

14. Minutes. Executive Committee Meeting. Washington, D.C.: International Voluntary Services, Inc., September 9, 1959.

15. ICA country offices were known as 'USOM' for U.S. Operations Mission.

16. Reisner, John H. (1960). International Voluntary Services, Inc.: Report of Annual Inspection, January 1 – February 23, 1960. Washington: International Voluntary Services, Inc. p. 7.

17. Reisner, John H. (1960). International Voluntary Services, Inc.: Report of Annual Inspection, January 1 – February 23, 1960. Washington: International Voluntary Services, Inc. p. 7.

18. IVS. 1959. Xieng Khouang Development Project, Laos: Fourth Progress Report, January 20, 1959. Washington: International Voluntary Services, Inc. p. 9-10.

19. Beery, Galen. 1966. International Voluntary Services, Inc. Progress Report July 1965–June 1966: Laos Rural Development Team. Washington: International Voluntary Services, Inc. p. 7.

20. Minutes. Executive Committee Meeting. Washington, D.C.: International Voluntary Services, Inc., September 1, 1960.

21. Minutes of Executive Committee Meeting. Washington, D.C.: International Voluntary Services, Inc., September 1, 1960.

22. Minutes. Executive Committee Meeting. Washington, D.C.: International Voluntary Services, Inc., February 8, 1961.

23. As a point of interest, thus far (as of July 1961) IVS had operated eleven projects overseas in nine different countries—in Egypt, Jordan, Iraq, Nepal, Vietnam, Laos, Cambodia, Ghana and Liberia. Eight of these projects were under contract with USAID, and one each under contract with World Neighbors, Arabian American Oil Company and the Rockefeller Brothers Fund (Minutes July 10, 1961).

24. Minutes. Executive Committee Meeting. Washington, D.C.: International Voluntary Services, Inc., September 1, 1960.; See also: Minutes. Executive Committee Meeting. Washington, D.C.: International Voluntary Services, Inc., March 29, 1960 and Minutes. Executive Committee Meeting. Washington, D.C.: International Voluntary Services, Inc., June 2, 1960.

25. Maxwell, Dayton. Email to the author dated September 3, 2016.; Russell, Daniel (1959). 1959 Summary Report. Washington, International Voluntary Services.: 1; Beery, Galen (1966).

International Voluntary Services, Inc. Progress Report July 1965–June 1966: Laos Rural Development Team. Washington: International Voluntary Services, Inc.

26. Beery, Galen. 1966. International Voluntary Services, Inc. Progress Report July 1965–June 1966: Laos Rural Development Team. Washington: International Voluntary Services, Inc.

27. IVS 1967a. Annual Report IVS Laos 1966-1967. Vientiane: International Voluntary Services. p. 40.

28. See: Stuart-Fox, Martin. 2008. Historical Dictionary of Laos. The Scarecrow Press, Lanham, MD. p. 167.

29. Mann, Charles A. (1964). Country Assistance Program FY 1966 – Laos, Section II, USAID, Vientiane, December. p. 168-169.

30. USAID. 1962. American Aid to Laos, FY 1955-FY 1962. Vientiane: 115-166.; Benson, Frederic C. (2015). "Indochina War Refugee Movements in Laos, 1954-1975: A Chronological Overview Citing New Primary Sources." In Journal of Lao Studies, Special Issue 1. March 2015, Center for Lao Studies, http://www.laostudies.org/sites/default/files/public/6%20Benson.pdf, last accessed June 25, 2021. p. 28-29. p. 116.

31. USAID. 1962. American Aid to Laos, FY 1955-FY 1962. Vientiane: 115-166.; Benson, Frederic C. (2015). "Indochina War Refugee Movements in Laos, 1954-1975: A Chronological Overview Citing New Primary Sources." In Journal of Lao Studies, Special Issue 1. March 2015, Center for Lao Studies, http://www.laostudies.org/sites/default/files/public/6%20Benson.pdf, last accessed June 25, 2021. p. 28-29. p. 137.

32. Minutes. Executive Committee Meeting. Washington, D.C.: International Voluntary Services, Inc., May 31, 1961.

33. Beery, Galen. 1966. International Voluntary Services, Inc. Progress Report July 1965–June 1966: Laos Rural Development Team. Washington: International Voluntary Services, Inc. p. 7-8.

34. Minutes of Executive Committee Meeting. Washington, D.C.: International Voluntary Services, Inc., September 8, 1961.

35. Beery, Galen. 1964. Annual Report of International Voluntary Services, Inc., Rural Development Division Team (VARDA) Laos: July 1963 - June 1964. Washington: International Voluntary Services, Inc. p. 42-43.

36. Minutes of Executive Committee Meeting. Washington, D.C.: International Voluntary Services, Inc., September 8, 1961.

37. USAID. 1962. American Aid to Laos, FY 1955-FY 1962. Vientiane: 115-166.

38. Mann, Charles. 1969. Development of the Rural Economy: Support for the Commission of Rural Affairs. Project Appraisal Report. USAID, Vientiane, March 20: 64-81, https://repository.asu.edu/items/38318, last accessed on September 1, 2020.: 1-A or 83.

39. Mendenhall, Joseph. 1965. Country Assistance Program Laos FY 1967—Part II, Section One, USAID, Vientiane, December. p. 169.

40. Mendenhall, Joseph. 1965. Country Assistance Program Laos FY 1967—Part II, Section One, USAID, Vientiane, December. p. 169.

41. IVS 1970. Annual Report 1969-1970. Vientiane: International Voluntary Services, Inc.

42. IVS 1967a. Annual Report IVS Laos 1966-1967. Vientiane: International Voluntary Services. p. 40.

43. IVS 1967a. Annual Report IVS Laos 1966-1967. Vientiane: International Voluntary Services. p. 40.

44. Beery, Galen. 1966. International Voluntary Services, Inc. Progress Report July 1965–June 1966: Laos Rural Development Team. Washington: International Voluntary Services, Inc. p. 7.

45. Malia, James. "We Want to Build; They Want to Destroy: The Dilemma of Volunteering in

Laos." Pages 89-100. Lawrence Kessler (editor). Southeast Asia Review of Asia Studies. Vol. XX, 1998. Southeast for Asian Studies, Southeast Conference. p. 95.

46. Mu Ban Samaki (Lao version of the strategic hamlet). See https://history.state.gov/historicaldocuments/frus1964-68v28/d42.

47. Mendenhall, Joseph. 1965. Country Assistance Program Laos FY 1967 – Part II, Section One, USAID, Vientiane, December. p. 168.

48. Mann, Charles A. 1964. Country Assistance Program FY 1966 – Laos, Section II, USAID, Vientiane, December. p. 142.

49 See: IVS 1964c. Annual Report 1963-1964, IVS Rural Development Team. Vientiane: International Voluntary Services.

50. Mann, Charles A. 1964. Country Assistance Program FY 1966 – Laos, Section II, USAID, Vientiane, December. p. 121, 123.

51. USAID. 1968. United States Aid to Laos, May: 694-732. P. 727-728.

52. Mann, Charles A. 1964. Country Assistance Program FY 1966 – Laos, Section II, USAID, Vientiane, December. p. 062-26.

53. Mann, Charles A. 1964. Country Assistance Program FY 1966 – Laos, Section II, USAID, Vientiane, December. p. 062-25.

54. Mann, Charles A. 1964. Country Assistance Program FY 1966 – Laos, Section II, USAID, Vientiane, December. p. 121, 140.

55. Beery, Galen. 1966. International Voluntary Services, Inc. Progress Report July 1965–June 1966: Laos Rural Development Team. Washington: International Voluntary Services, Inc., p. 8.

56. IVS1964b. IVS Laos Newsletter for June 1964. IVS/RDD Team, USAID RD Division, Vientiane, Laos.

57. Beery, Galen. 1964. Annual Report of International Voluntary Services, Inc., Rural Development Division Team (VARDA) Laos: July 1963 - June 1964. Washington: International Voluntary Services, Inc. p. 4, 6, 27.; IVS 1964a)

58. Beery, Galen. 1964. Annual Report of International Voluntary Services, Inc., Rural Development Division Team (VARDA) Laos: July 1963 - June 1964. Washington: International Voluntary Services, Inc. p. 4.; IVS1964a. IVS Laos Newsletter for May 1964. IVS/RDD Team, USAID RD Division, Vientiane, Laos.

59. Brockmueller, Gordon. 1964. Semi-Annual Report of IVS Field Projects, May, 1964, IVS.

60. Beery, Galen. 1966. International Voluntary Services, Inc. Progress Report July 1965–June 1966: Laos Rural Development Team. Washington: International Voluntary Services, Inc., p. 8.

61. Beery, Galen. 1964. Annual Report of International Voluntary Services, Inc., Rural Development Division Team (VARDA) Laos: July 1963–June 1964. Washington: International Voluntary Services, Inc.

62. IVS 1969a. IVS Reporter May 1969. Washington, D.C.: International Voluntary Services.

63. Collected IVS Stories 2020: 199.

64. Ramsey, Gordon B., Charles A. Sanders, Leland W. Voth, Thomas Wilson, William H. McCluskey, Percy J. Avram, Charles F. Wilding-White, Paul J. Maynard, Dayton L. Maxwell, Hunter A. Fitzgerald, Edwin T. McKeithen III, FHWA PASA Team, Robert T. Dakan, Gary E. Alex, Lawrence J. Berger, John Kennedy, Ernest C. Kuhn, John A. Huxtable, Gerald L. Nell, Sanford J. Stone, Robert E. Zimmerman, Don F. Wadley, Theodore L. Lewis, Walter F. Stettner, Staff of the Office of Laos Affairs. 1976. (Overview) Termination Report—USAID Laos, USAID, Washington, DC, January 9: 1943-2309, http://digital.library.wisc.edu/1711.dl/SEAiT.Documents, last accessed September 1, 2020.

65. IVS 1969b. IVS Reporter December 1969. Washington, D.C.: International Voluntary Services.

66. Gardiner, Arthur Z. "Seasons Greetings: To the Volunteers and Friends of International Voluntary Services, Inc." Christmas 1967.

67. Beery, Galen. 1965. International Voluntary Services, Inc., Annual Report: July 1964–June 1965. Rural Development Team (VARDA). Washington: International Voluntary Services, Inc. p. 8.

68. Haffner, Loren E. 1967. [Memo to] all Forward Area Team Members. USAID, Vientiane, Laos, October 20. p. 2.

69. IVS 1970. Annual Report 1969-1970. Vientiane: International Voluntary Services, Inc. p. 5.; See Malia, James. "We Want to Build; They Want to Destroy: The Dilemma of Volunteering in Laos." Pages 89-100. Lawrence Kessler (editor). Southeast Asia Review of Asia Studies. Vol. XX, 1998. Southeast for Asian Studies, Southeast Conference.

70. IVS 1970. Annual Report 1969-1970. Vientiane: International Voluntary Services, Inc. p. 5.

71. IVS 1968. IVS Reporter February 1968. Washington, D.C.: International Voluntary Services.

72. IVS 1970. Annual Report 1969-1970. Vientiane: International Voluntary Services, Inc. p. 7.

73. IVS 1970. Annual Report 1969-1970. Vientiane: International Voluntary Services, Inc. p. 7.

74. IVS 1971. IVS Reporter December 1971. Washington, D.C.: International Voluntary Services.

75. IVS 1970. Annual Report 1969-1970. Vientiane: International Voluntary Services, Inc. p. 7.

76. IVS 1970. Annual Report 1969-1970. Vientiane: International Voluntary Services, Inc. p. 5.

77. IVS 1970. Annual Report 1969-1970. Vientiane: International Voluntary Services, Inc. p.

78. IVS 1967b. IVS Reporter August 1967. Washington, D.C.: International Voluntary Services.

79. IVS 1969b. IVS Reporter December 1969. Washington, D.C.: International Voluntary Services.

80. Steiner, Ken. "My Tour in Indo-China." In Bulletin of the Peace Studies Institute, Vol. 31 (2001). North Manchester, Indiana: Manchester University.

81. IVS 1970. Annual Report 1969-1970. Vientiane: International Voluntary Services, Inc.

82. Collected Laos/Vietnam IVS Volunteer Stories (2015).

83. IVS 1972a. International Voluntary Services Laos: Annual Report 1971-1972. Vientiane: International Voluntary Services, Inc. p. 5.

84. IVS 1972a. International Voluntary Services Laos: Annual Report 1971-1972. Vientiane: International Voluntary Services, Inc. p. 2, 30, 34.; IVS 1972d: 8)

85. IVS 1972a. International Voluntary Services Laos: Annual Report 1971-1972. Vientiane: International Voluntary Services, Inc. p. 5.

86. IVS 1972d. IVS Reporter November 1972. Washington, D.C.: International Voluntary Services. p. 8.

87. IVS 1972a. International Voluntary Services Laos: Annual Report 1971-1972. Vientiane: International Voluntary Services, Inc. p. 33-39.

88. IVS 1972a. International Voluntary Services Laos: Annual Report 1971-1972. Vientiane: International Voluntary Services, Inc. p. 2.

89. IVS 1972a. International Voluntary Services Laos: Annual Report 1971-1972. Vientiane: International Voluntary Services, Inc. p. 2.

90. IVS 1972b. IVS Reporter August 1972. Washington, D.C.: International Voluntary Services.

91. IVS 1973. IVS Reporter Spring 1973. Washington, D.C.: International Voluntary Services.

92. IVS 1972a. International Voluntary Services Laos: Annual Report 1971-1972. Vientiane: International Voluntary Services, Inc. p. 2.

93. IVS 1972c. New Directions 1972. Washington, D.C.: International Voluntary Services.

94. IVS 1972a. International Voluntary Services Laos: Annual Report 1971-1972. Vientiane: International Voluntary Services, Inc. p. 20.

95. IVS 1971a. IVS Reporter April 1971. Washington, D.C.: International Voluntary Services. p. 6.
96. Dommen, Arthur J. 1985. Laos: Keystone of Indochina. Boulder: Westview Press. p. 99.
97. Simons, Lewis M. 1975. "U.S. AID's Legacy in Laos." The Washington Post, June 16, 1975. P. A18.
98. IVS 1975. IVS Reporter Summer/Fall 1975. Washington, D.C.: International Voluntary Services. p. 1.
99. Collected IVS Stories 2020: 169.
100. Collected IVS Stories 2020: 129.
101. Steiner, Ken. "My Tour in Indo-China." In Bulletin of the Peace Studies Institute, Vol. 31 (2001). North Manchester, Indiana: Manchester University.
102. Malia, James. "We Want to Build; They Want to Destroy: The Dilemma of Volunteering in Laos." Pages 89-100. Lawrence Kessler (editor). Southeast Asia Review of Asia Studies. Vol. XX, 1998. Southeast for Asian Studies, Southeast Conference. p. 100.103. Goldstein, Martin E. (1973). American Policy Toward Laos. Rutherford; Madison, Teaneck: Fairleigh Dickinson University Press. p. 327.
104. Shirk, Anne D. 2003. International Voluntary Services, 1953-2003.Harpers Ferry, West Virginia. p.1.
105. For a detailed description of the program see: Thomas, Winburn L. 1972. "The Vietnam Story of International Voluntary Services, Inc., IVS. Washington.
106. See Volunteer Bill Camp's account of working with street kids in Chapter 7.
107. Brockmueller, Gordon. 1964. Semi-Annual Report of IVS Field Projects, May, 1964, IVS.
108. Linn, Jim. 1971, "An Analysis of the Termination of IVS in Vietnam, in "IVS Reporter: A Quarterly' Account of IVS and Its People," December 1971. International Voluntary Services, Inc.
109. Miller, Robert W. 1972. "The Role and Contribution of the Foreign Voluntary Agencies in South Viet Nam—1966-1971". Submitted to The Faculty of the Graduate School of Public Affairs in partial fulfillment of the requirements for the degree of Master of Public and International Affairs. University of Pittsburgh.
110. Manke, Hugh. Undated. "IVS and USAID in Vietnam: Who Left Whom?", included in Collected IVS Stories 2020 in IVS archives.
111. Brockmueller, Gordon. 1964. Semi-Annual Report of IVS Field Projects, May, 1964, IVS.
112. Elkind, Jessica. 2016. Aid Under Fire: Nation Building and the Vietnam War. University Press of Kentucky, Lexington, Kentucky. p. 208-209; IVS. 1971b. IVS Reporter December 1971. Washington, D.C.: International Voluntary Services.
113. IVS. 1971a. IVS Reporter April 1971. Washington, D.C.: International Voluntary Services. p. 8.
114. IVS. 1971a. IVS Reporter April 1971. Washington, D.C.: International Voluntary Services. p. 1.
115. IVS. 1971a. IVS Reporter April 1971. Washington, D.C.: International Voluntary Services. p. 5.

CHAPTER 4: GOING GLOBAL WITH A MATURING VOLUNTEER PROGRAM

1. IVS Reporter, March 1970.
2. Minutes of Meeting of IVS Board of Directors and Staff at Harpers Ferry, February 19-21, 1971.
3. David Blanchard letter of August 15, 1962 to family and friends from Zorzor, Liberia.
4. Brockmueller, Gordon. 1964. Semi-Annual Report of IVS Field Projects, May, 1964, IVS.
5. A. Z. Gardiner, executive Director, report on Algeria—February 24-25, 1966.

6. Rawlings, Stuart (Editor). 1992. "The IVS Experience—from Algeria to Vietnam". International Voluntary Services, Inc. Washington.
7. Minutes of Meeting of IVS Board of Directors and Staff at Harpers Ferry, Plenary Session #3 February 20, 1971.
8. IVS Board Meeting Minutes, 2/29/1971.
9. W. Furtick, W., W. Krueger, J. Grayzel, and P. Crawford: 1984. Rangeland Management Improvement Project—Project Mid-Term Evaluation, January 1984. USAID.
10. IVS Reporter Newsletter: A Quarterly Account of IVS and Its People, August 1972.
11. Scott Endsley letters of November 1987 in IVS Archives.
12. Annual Report: International Voluntary Services, Inc. 1990.
13. USAID. National Sorghum and Millet Crop improvement Project Paper, Annex 8. 12/15/1975.
14. University of Arizona. 1979. Fourth Semi-Annual Report: National Sorghum and Millet Project. Sept. 16, 1979 through March 15, 1979.
15. IVS. Undated. "IVS in the Sudan: A Brief Overview", IVS archives paper. Despite some references to an initial IVS engagement in Sudan in 1966-67, no information on such was found in the IVS archives.
16. USAID. 1980. Wadi Haifa Community Development Project Evaluation Summary. USAID.
17. USAID Project Evaluation Summary (PES) Yambio Research Station Rehabilitation (OPG), April 29, 1982.
18. Agency for International Development. 1975. Development Assistance Program—FY 1975 Section Three: Senegal, Mali, Mauritania. USAID. Washington.
19. The Reporter (IVS newsletter), Fall 1974.
20. The Reporter (IVS newsletter), Fall 1974.
21. John Rigsby personal communication.
22. "The Reporter- a newsletter for IVS volunteers", Vol. 3, 1980.
23. John Rigsby email of August 20, 2021 to Michael Chilton on the subject of the "IVS Legacy Project."

CHAPTER 5: REINVENTING IVS—NEW APPROACHES AND THE END GAME

1. "The Reporter – a newsletter for former IVS volunteers." Vol. 1, No. 1, May 1978.
2. "The Reporter – a newsletter for former IVS volunteers." Vol. 2, Summer/Fall 1979.
3. VS Thirty-Fifth Anniversary Brochure.
4. IVS Newsletter, Vol. 2, No. 2; July-August, 1985.
5. Nagle, William A. 1981, Evaluation of International Voluntary Services, Inc. USAID.
6. "IVS Developments" newsletter, First Quarter 1988.
7. "Developments from International Voluntary Service", Vol. 6, No. 4, Fourth Quarter 1989.
8. Smoot, David and James Cawley. 1990. "IVS Experience with Rural Development—some comparative reflections".
9. IVS, 1993. IVS Report to AID Cooperative agreement OTR-0158-A-00-8156-00, July 1, 1992 –June 30, 1993. IVS, Washington.
10. "IVS Alumni Link: newsletter, Summer, 1997.
11. Gary Alex memo on "Action Plan for IVS Renewal" to IVS Executive Committee, dated June 18, 1999.
12. Also called "Association of Voluntary Agencies in Bangladesh" (AVAB) by Char Cuento-Jeggle (Rawlings, 1992) and "Agricultural Development Agencies for Bangladesh" (ADAP) in "The Reporter - A newsletter for former IVS volunteers" Vol. 1, No. 2, December 1978.
13. A.K.M. Ferdous Choudhury, "An Assessment of an International Voluntary Services Project:

a Potential Model for Agricultural and Rural Community development", submitted to the Faculty of the Graduate College of Oklahoma State University in partial fulfillment of the requirements for the Degree of Doctor of Education, May, 1980.

14. See "The Fortunate Few" annex describing the program.

15. David French letter dated 1998 to Anne Shirk, IVS/Washington.

16. Olson, Craig, Kenneth Koehn, Ruth Ammerman-Yabes, Peter Doan, David Goh, and Donald Jackson. 1985. Private Voluntary Organizations and Institutional Development: Lessons from International Voluntary Services, Inc. and the Institute for International development. Inc. Development Alternatives, Inc. and Cornell University. USAID.

17. Annual Report: International Voluntary Services, Inc. 1984.

18. IVS. Undated. "International Voluntary Services 35th Anniversary".

19. Appleby, Gordon, John Richey, and Martha Cruz de Yafies. 1991. International Voluntary Services, Inc. Mid-Term Program Evaluation under Cooperative Agreement ORT-158-A-008156-00. USAID.

20. Ogara, William O. and Sailesh Chakravarty. 2000. An Assessment Report of IVS-National Volunteer Program (NVP) in Bangladesh. International Voluntary Services Inc.

21. Chemonics International. 2001. "Bangladesh Enterprise Development Assessment Report Task Order No. 817 Under the GBTI IQC No. PCE-I-00-98-00015-00; Volume Two: Annexes M - BB Submitted to: USAID Dhaka, Bangladesh.

22. Buzzard, Shirley. 1993. Final Evaluation Under Cooperative Agreement ORT-158-A-008156-00, for A.I.D./FHA/PVC. Draft Report, draft 25 June 1993, Appendix A.

23. IVS Executive Committee Meeting – September 8, 2001.

24. IVS Board of Directors Meeting Minutes – September 25, 1999.

25. Abdul Matin email of 1/22/02 to Anne Shirk forwarded to Gary Alex on 1/22/02.

26. Anne Shirk email of 1/22/2002 to Gary Alex: "Notes on conversation with Jan Emmert, USAID, Bangladesh – 22 January 02."

27. Email from Matin, IVS/Bangladesh to Anne Shirk, dated 6/2/2004.

28. "To Whom It May Concern" Letter from Anne Shirk, dated 10/9/2004.

29. Gary Alex "Trip Report on Visit to IVS/Bangladesh" memo of 4/17/2002 to Anne Shirk, IVS Executive Director.

30. Panel Discussion of the 40th Anniversary Celebration of IVS at Harpers Ferry in 1993.

31. IVS News December 1974/January 1975.

32. IVS Annual Report – 1985.

33. IVS Annual Report – 1990.

34. DAI. 1985. "Private Voluntary Organizations and Institutional Development: Lessons from International Voluntary Services, Inc. and The Institute for International Development, Inc., USAID.

35. IVS Annual Report – 1991-92.

36. Project Completion Report: Horticultural Development Project, Project 633-0215. USAID. https://pdf.usaid.gov/pdf_docs/PDAAQ320.pdf.

37. Project Completion Report: Horticultural Development Project, Project 633-0215. USAID. https://pdf.usaid.gov/pdf_docs/PDAAQ320.pdf.

38. The Reporter, IVS, Summer/Fall 1977.

39. Annual report – 1985 International Voluntary services, Ins.

40. Arthur Kelly, IVS/Honduras, Final Report.

41. Buzzard, Shirley. 1993. Final Evaluation Under Cooperative Agreement ORT-158-A-008156-00, for A.I.D./FHA/PVC. Draft Report, draft 25 June 1993, Appendix A.

42. IVS 1990 Annual Report.

43. IVS 1990 Annual Report.

44. IVS Annual Report—1991-92

45. Nan Borton email of Aug 17, 2021 to Michael Chilton on the subject of "The Legacy of IVS / Executive Contributions."

46. IVS. 1986. Annual Report.

47. IVS. 1990. Annual Report.

48. DAI. 1985. "Private Voluntary Organizations and Institutional Development: Lessons from International Voluntary Services, Inc. and The Institute for International Development, Inc," US-AID.

49. "IVS Developments" newsletter, First Quarter 1988.

50. Buzzard, Shirley. 1993. Final Evaluation Under Cooperative Agreement ORT-158-A-008156-00, for A.I.D./FHA/PVC. Draft Report, draft 25 June 1993, Appendix A.

51. IVS News, Vol. 2., No. 3, April, 1972.

52. "IVS: a time of transition" in the "The Reporter – a newsletter for former IVSers." Vol. 3, 1980.

53. IVS, 1993. IVS Report to AID Cooperative agreement OTR-0158-A-00-8156-00, July 1, 1992 –June 30, 1993. IVS, Washington.

54. Buzzard—Final Evaluation, draft 25 June 1993, Appendix A—Buzzard, Shirley. (June 25, 1993). Final Evaluation Under Cooperative Agreement ORT-158-A-008156-00, for A.I.D./FHA/PVC. Draft Report.

55. Developments for International Voluntary Service, Vol. 8, No. 6, Fourth Quarter 1991.

56. Buzzard, Shirley. 1993. Final Evaluation Under Cooperative Agreement ORT-158-A-008156-00, for A.I.D./FHA/PVC. Draft Report, draft 25 June 1993, Appendix A.

57. Nagle, William L. 1981. Evaluation of International Voluntary services, Inc. 12/11/81. US-AID.

Chapter 6: Administration Challenges—Running A Nonprofit NGO

1. Norris, John. 2021. The Enduring Struggle: The History of the U.S. Agency for International Development and America's Uneasy Transformation of the World. Lanham, MD: Rowman & Littlefield. 102.

2. IVS. 1971. IVS Reporter: A Quarterly Account of IVS and Its People. (August 1971). Washington, DC.

3. IVS. 1970. IVS Reporter: A Quarterly Account of IVS and Its People (December 1970). Washington, DC.

4. U.S. Congress. Congressional Record. The Harpers Ferry Charter for International Voluntary Services, Inc. in the 1970's, Henry S. Reuss, March 18, 1971.

5. IVS. 1971. IVS Reporter: A Quarterly Account of IVS and Its People (April 1971). Washington, DC.

6. U.S. Congress. Congressional Record.

7. IVS (1976-1977). Annual Report. Washington, DC.

8. IVS (1980-1981). Annual Report. Washington, DC.

9. Nagle, William J. (December 11, 1981). Evaluation of International Voluntary Services, Inc. Contract No. PDC-0100-S-00-1148-00 of September 30, 1981, as amended. Contract with U.S. Agency for International Development, 3-4.

10. Ibid. 11.

11. Ibid. 12.

12. IVS (1991-1992). Annual Report, Washington, DC.
13. Ibid.
14. Unknown (December 31, 1982). Report to AID, International Voluntary Services, Inc., Matching Grant PDC-0236-G-SS-2076-01. January 1, 1983-December 31, 1983. 2.
15. IVS (1985 July-August). Newsletter. Vol. 2 No 2. Washington, DC.
16. IVS (1991-1992). Annual Report. Washington, DC.
17. (Luce, Don and Linda Worthington) (Undated). IVS Priorities According to Don and Linda.
18. IVS. June 1993. International Voluntary Services, Inc.: Report to AID Cooperative Agreement, OTR - 0158 -A - 00 - 8156 – 00, July 1, 1992 – June 30, 1993.
19. This impression of IVS leadership was at odds with other observers. The 1990 World Development Report found that: "During the past three decades the developing world has made enormous economic progress. This can be seen most clearly in the rising trend for incomes and consumption: between 1965 and 1985 consumption per capita in the developing world went up by almost 70 percent. Broader measures of well-being confirm this picture; life expectancy, child mortality and educational attainment have all improved markedly. Viewed from either perspective income and consumption on the one hand, broad social indicators on the other the developing countries are advancing much faster than today's developed countries did at a comparable stage." ┼World Bank. 1990. World Development Report: Poverty. World Bank. Washington.20. IVS. 2000. International Voluntary Services Organizational and Management Structure. 21. Beery, Galen S. 1969. A Brief History of International Voluntary Services, Inc.22. IVS. 2000. International Voluntary Services Organizational and Management Structure.23. IVS. 1977.. IVS Reporter (Summer-Fall 1977), Washington, DC.

24. IVS. 1978. IVS Reporter: A newsletter for former IVS volunteers (May 1978). Vol. 1 No. 1 Washington, DC.
25. Buzzard, Shirley. 1993. Final Evaluation Under Cooperative Agreement ORT-158-A-008156-00, for A.I.D./FHA/PVC. Appendix A. Draft Report. 10-11.
26. IVS. 1993. International Voluntary Services, Inc., Report to AID Cooperative OTR - 0157 - A - 00 - 8156 – 00, July 1, 1992- June 30, 1993. Washington, DC.
27. IVS. Undated. "Officers and Members of the Board - International Voluntary Services, Inc.
28. IVS. 1988. The History of International Voluntary Services - 1953-1988 (Draft).
29. Norris, John. 2021. The Enduring Struggle: The History of the U.S. Agency for International Development and America's Uneasy Transformation of the World. Lanham, MD: Rowman & Littlefield. 103.
30. USAID. 1922. Office of Private and Voluntary Cooperation (PVC) New Directions. See https://pdf.usaid.gov/pdf_docs/Pdabu153.pdf. Last accessed April 19, 2022.
31. Nagle, William J. 1981. Evaluation of International Voluntary Services, Inc. Contract No. PDC-0100-S-00-1148-00 of September 30, 1981, as amended. Contract with U.S. Agency for International Development, 3-4. 1.
32. Shook, Cleo F. 1979. Evaluation: International Voluntary Services, Inc., Contract No. AID/SOD/PDC-C-0241-6/7/79. 2.
33. Ibid. 18.
34. Nagle, William J. 1981. Evaluation of International Voluntary Services, Inc. Contract No. PDC-0100-S-00-1148-00 of September 30, 1981, as amended. Contract with U.S. Agency for International Development, 3-4. p. 8-9.
35. IVS. 1983. Newsletter (1983 September-October). Washington, DC.
36. IVS. 1984. Newsletter (1984 March-April). Washington, DC.
37. Ibid.
38. Olson, Craig, et al. 1985. Private Voluntary Organizations and Institutional Development:

Lessons from International Voluntary Services, Inc. and The Institute for International Development, Inc. Development Alternatives, Inc. (DAI). Washington, DC. xiv.

39. Ibid. xiv.
40. Ibid. 69.
41. IVS. 1986. Newsletter (1986 August). Washington, DC.
42. Ibid.
43. IVS. (Undated). International Voluntary Services – 35th Anniversary. Washington, DC.
44. Borton, Nan. 1987. AID Proposal, 1988-1993. Memo to IVS Board of Directors. Washington, DC.
45. Ibid.; Buzzard (June 25, 1993). 1; Borton (March 15, 1988). Amended Matching Grant. Washington, DC.
46. Appleby, Gordon, John Richey, Martha Cruz de Yanes. 1991. International Voluntary Services, Inc., Mid-Term Program Evaluation, Under Cooperative Agreement ORT-158-A-008156-00. For USAID/PVA/PVC. iii.
47. Ibid. vii.
48. IVS (January 22, 1959). Executive Committee Minutes. Washington, DC.
49. IVS (First Quarter 1990). Developments. Vol. 7, No. 1. Washington, DC.
50. Fox, Thomas H. (April 2, 1982). Action Memorandum for the Assistant Administrator, FVA.
51. U.S. Congress. Congressional Record.
52. IVS (August 1972). IVS Reporter: A Quarterly Account of IVS and Its People. Washington, DC.
53. IVS (March 1972). IVS Reporter: A Quarterly Account of IVS and Its People. Washington, DC.
54. IVS (Spring 1973). IVS Reporter: A Quarterly Account of IVS and Its People. Washington, DC.
55. (Unknown). IVS in the 1970s.
56. IVS (April 1971). IVS Reporter: A Quarterly Account of IVS and Its People. Washington, DC.
57. IVS (Spring 1973). IVS Reporter: A Quarterly Account of IVS and Its People. Washington, DC.
58. IVS (Winter 1974). IVS Reporter: A Quarterly Account of IVS and Its People. Washington, DC.
59. IVS. 1980. The Reporter: A newsletter for former IVS volunteers (Vol. 3, 1980), International Voluntary Services, Inc. Washington, DC.; Buzzard (31 October 1991) The Coop Agreement Between AID and PACT (PDABP827).
60. Ibid. (IVS Vol. 3, 1980).
61. Ibid.
62. Fox, Thomas H. (April 2, 1982). Action Memorandum for the Assistant Administrator, FVA.
63. IVS. 1984. Newsletter (1984 March-April).. Washington, DC.
64. Nagle, William J. 1981. Evaluation of International Voluntary Services, Inc. Contract No. PDC-0100-S-00-1148-00 of September 30, 1981, as amended. Contract with U.S. Agency for International Development, 3-4.
65. IVS. 1982. Newsletter (1982 Fall). Washington, DC.
66. IVS. 1982. Newsletter (1981 Summer). Washington, DC; Fox, Thomas H. (April 2, 1982).
67. IVS (Vol. 3, 1980).
68. IVS. 1985. Newsletter (1985 July-August). Vol. 2 No 2. Washington, DC.
69. IVS. 1988. Report to AID: International Volunteer Services, Inc., Matching Grant, AID/

PDC - 0206 – GSS - 5069. Report Period: July 1, 1987–June 30, 1988 and Final Report: July 1, 1985 – June 30, 1988. IVS: Washington, DC.

70. Borton, Nan (August 31, 1987).

71. IVS (First Quarter 1989). Developments. Vol. 6, No. 1. Washington, DC.

72. IVS. 1989. International Voluntary Services, Inc., Report to AID Cooperative OTR - 0157 - A - 00 - 8156 – 00, July 1, 1988- June 30, 1989. Washington, DC. (PDAAZ391). 34.

73. Ibid.

74. IVS (1993-94). Annual Report. Washington, DC.

75. IVS (June 1992). International Voluntary Services, Inc., Report to AID Cooperative OTR - 0157 - A - 00 - 8156 – 00, July 1, 1991- June 30, 1992. Washington, DC. ii.

76. IVS (June 1993). International Voluntary Services, Inc., Report to AID Cooperative OTR - 0157 - A - 00 - 8156 – 00, July 1, 1992- June 30, 1993. Washington, DC.

77. Buzzard, Shirley. 1993. Final Evaluation Under Cooperative Agreement ORT-158-A-008156-00, for A.I.D./FHA/PVC. Appendix A. Draft Report. 10-11.

78. Ibid. 26.

79. Ibid. 2.

80. Ibid. 3.

81. Ibid. 26.

82. Ibid. 1.

83. Manke, Hugh J. (July 6, 1993). IVS Draft Evaluation. Memo to Shirley Buzzard. New Haven: Conn.

84. IVS 1993. Developments (August 1993).. Vol. 10, No. 2. Washington, DC.

85. IVS. 1993. Developments (May 1993).. Vol. 11, No. 1. Washington, DC.

86. IVS 1995. Developments (November 1995).. Vol. 13, No. 2. Washington, DC.

87. IVS. 1995. Annual Report. Washington, DC.

88. IVS. 1997. Annual Report. Washington, DC.

89. Hugh Manke, personal communication.

90. IVS (April 11, 1997). International Voluntary Services Executive Committee of the Board. Washington, DC.

91. (Unknown). (Undated). International Voluntary Services. Annexes A to F. Draft IVS brochure.

92. Hallberg, Parker F. (September 9, 2000). International Voluntary Services, Minutes of Executive Committee Meeting. Washington, DC.

93. Hallberg, Parker F. (February 10, 2001). International Voluntary Services, Executive Committee Meeting. Washington, DC.

94. Nichols, Stephen C. (April 6, 2001). Memo to Gary Alex. IVS: Washington, DC.

95. Hallberg, Parker F. (April 27-28, 2001). IVS Board of Directors Meeting. Washington, DC.

96. Ibid.

97. Hallberg, Parker F. (September 8, 2001). International Voluntary Services, Executive Committee Meeting. Washington, DC.

98. Hallberg, Parker F. (November 17, 2001). International Voluntary Services Board of Directors Meeting. Washington, DC.

99. Ibid.

100. Shirk, Anne (February 20, 2002). IVS Again? E-mail to Gary Alex; Hallberg, Parker F. (November 17, 2001).

101. Goodstein, Jeanette and Stephen Nichols. (November 30, 2001). Memo to IVS Alumni and Friends, Washington, DC.

102. IVS (September 8, 1958). Minutes. Executive Committee Meeting, International Voluntary Services, Inc. Washington DC.

CHAPTER 7: VOLUNTEERS OUT OF THEIR COMFORT ZONE

1. Unless otherwise cited, volunteer stories are excerpts from volunteer contributions of their experience in 2015 or 2020 that are available in the IVS archives located in the Mennonite Church USA Archives (Elkhart, Indiana).

2. All examples come from international volunteers, mostly American, and none are from the national and regional volunteers from the later years of IVS. The local and regional volunteers undoubtedly had many of the same types of experiences, although one might theorize that these may not have been as intense. This might be an interesting area for research on local volunteers.

3. Rawlings, Stuart (Editor). 1992. "The IVS Experience—from Algeria to Vietnam". International

4. Additional information is available in: Nuttle, David. 2022. Shadow Walker. Kindle Edition eBook.

CHAPTER 8: IMPACTS OF INTERNATIONAL VOLUNTARY SERVICE

1. Unless otherwise cited, volunteer stories are excerpts from volunteer contributions of their experience in 2015 or 2020 that are available in the IVS archives locates in the Mennonite Church USA Archives (Elkhart, Indiana).

2. Office of Development Effectiveness. 2014. "Evaluation of the Australian Volunteers for International Development (AVID) program". Department of Foreign Affairs and Trade, Canberra, 2014. online at www.ode.dfat.gov.au.

3. Lough, Benjamin J. 2015. The Evolution of International Volunteering, Written for presentation at the International Volunteer Service Exchange Conference, 12-13 October 2015, Beijing, China. United Nations Volunteers (UNV) programme, Bonn, Germany.

4. All examples come from international volunteers, mostly American, and none are from the national and regional volunteers from the later years of IVS. The local and regional volunteers undoubtedly had many of the same types of experiences, although one might theorize that these may not have been as intense. This might be an interesting area for research on local volunteers.

CHAPTER 9: MISSION AND SERVICE—THE AMERICAN CHURCHES AND IVS

1. Harold E. Fey, Story of Church World Service. p. 15.

2. John Earl Baker, Fighting China's Famine, an unpublished manuscript dated 1943 in the Missionary Research Library, New York.

3. Nonresistance or non-resistance is the principle or practice of passive submission to a constituted authority even when unjust or oppressive. The Mennonite Article: Peace, Justice, and Nonresistance.

4. John 15:14: "You are My friends if you do what I command."

5. Jean Kinney Williams, The Quakers. p. 7.

6. George Fox, founder of the Society in England, recorded that in 1650 "Justice Bennet of Derby first called us Quakers because we bid them tremble at the word of God." It is likely that the name was originally derisive by those who ridiculed the Quakers.

7. An unlawful secret religious meeting.

8. Rufus Jones. The Quakers in the American Colonies. p. 417.

9. In the spring of 1664, the English Duke of York supplied a fleet and an army of 300 men to sail to New Amsterdam harbor as an act of intimidation. On August 29, 1664, the Dutch army agreed

to depart leaving the English in charge. The name, New York, was given by the Duke of York, later to become James II, 1685-1688.

10. The first Quakers are thought to be Mary Fisher and Ann Austin who arrived in 1655 from Barbados. The two were thrown into confinement upon arrival for "dangerous, heretical and blasphemous opinions." Five weeks later they were sent back to Barbados. www.quakersintheworld.org/quakers-in-action/187

11. Flushing is in the New York City, Borough of Queens or Queens County.

12. Penn first arrived at New Castle, Delaware on 27 Oct. 1682 after a nine-week voyage, in which thirty of the one hundred passengers died of smallpox.

13. Rufus Jones. The Quakers in the American Colonies, pp. 410-420.

14. "A Declaration of the Sad and Great Persecution and Martyrdom of the People of God called Quakers in New England for Worshipping God." Title page of a book on Quaker persecution in New England.

15. Guilford College, North Carolina, 1837; Earlham College, Indiana, 1847; Swarthmore College, Pennsylvania, 1864; Bryn Mawr College, Pennsylvania, 1885.

16. John Woolman, The Journal of John Woolman. p. 137.

17. <https://www.nps.gov/places/friends-asylum.htm> (accessed 7/6/2022).

18. Gerlof D. Homan. American Mennonites and the Great War 1914-1918. p. 29.

19. Founded by German, Quaker, and Mennonite families in 1683 as an independent borough, it was absorbed into Philadelphia in 1854.

20. Ibid. p. 32.

21. The NSBRO was established in October 1940 and initially called the National Council for Religious Conscientious Objectors. One month later, it was renamed the NSBRO.

22. Anabaptists believe baptism is valid only when candidates freely confess their faith in Christ and request to be baptized; thus, infants are not able to make a conscience decision to be baptized. Pietism and Radical Pietism is "one who studies God's word and leads a holy life in accord with it. Donald F. Durnbaugh. Brethren Beginnings: The Origin of the Church of The Brethren in Early Eighteenth Century Europe. p. 1.

23. Donald F. Durnbaugh. Fruit of the Vine; A History of the Brethren, 1708-1995. p. 28.

24. Now Bad Berleburg in North Rhine-Westphalia, Germany.

25. Ibid. p 74.

26. Brethren Historical Library and Archives.

27. Donald F. Durnbaugh. pp. 357-362.

28. Ibid. p. 430.

29. The Near East Foundation, founded in 1915 as the American Committee on Armenian Atrocities, later the American Committee for Relief in the Near East, and after that the Near East Relief, is a Syracuse, New York-based American international social and economic development organization, originally dedicated to helping Armenian and Assyrian victims of the Ottoman Empire.

30. "Armenian Genocide Sparked 100 Years of Brethren Response to Disaster and Conflict", Church of the Brethren Newsline, May 8, 2015.

31. Electronic communication from Ron Sensenig, former MCC volunteer.

32. Kenneth J. Kreider. A Cup of Cold Water: The Story of Brethren Service. p. 18.

33. Ibid. p. 132.

34. "The Seagoing Cowboys Delivering Hope to a War-Torn World", newsletter posted November 14, 2014. https://seagoingcowboys.com/seagoing-cowboys/cowboy-stories/.

35. Church World Service was established in 1946 as an ecumenical grouping of Protestant Churches.

36. Harold E. Fey, Cooperation in Compassion: The Story of Church World Service. p. 173.

37. Ibid. p. 174.

38. MCC. "Remembering MCC Vietnam: Carrying a Weight Beyond Its Numbers: Fifty-Five Years of People-Centered Development in Vietnam".

39. 1945: Indonesia; 1948: Sri Lanka, Burma; 1950 Laos; 1953: Cambodia; 1957: Malaysia; 1960: Nigeria, Cameroon, Upper Volta, Cote d'Ivoire, Chad, Madagascar, Benin, Niger, Mali, Senegal, Togo, Central African Republic, Gabon, Mauritania; 1962: Kenya, Jamaica, Trinidad and Tobago, Uganda, Algeria, Burundi, Rwanda.

40. Harold E. Fey. p 26. The American Bible Society, American Committee for Christian Refugees, American Friends Service Committee, Central Bureau for Interchurch Aid, Church Committee for China Relief, International Missionary Council-Orphans Missions Fund, World Student Christian Federation-Emergency Relief and Reconstruction, YMCA-War Prisoners Aid and YWCA-World Emergency and War Victims Fund.

41. Ibid. p 24.

42. Ibid. p 24.

43. Kenneth J. Kreider. Cup of Cold Water. p. 116.

44. Church World Service is specifically mentioned here as one of the ecumenical agencies that provided funding for IVS programs.

45. "Rev. Raquel Lettsome, Associate Minister, Methodist Episcopal Church, Warwick, N.Y. in sermon of January 30, 2022 titled "Conjunction. What's Your Function."

46. The U.S. Department of Labor, Bureau of Labor Statistics in 2017 reported roughly 62.6 million people volunteered for one or more organizations in the U.S. The Bureau estimated that about 33.1% were faith-based organizations.

CHAPTER 10: IVS AND THE ORIGINS OF THE PEACE CORPS

1. https://www.peacecorps.gov/about/history/founding-moment/, accessed May 29, 2021.

2. See Michael E. Latham, Modernization as Ideology: American Social Science and Nation Building in the Kennedy Era (Chapel Hill: University of North Carolina Press, 2000), Jeremi Suri, Liberty's Surest Guardian: Rebuilding Nations After War from the Founders to Obama (New York: Frere Press, 2011), Michael E. Latham, The Right Kind of Revolution: Modernization, Development, and U.S. Foreign Policy from the Cold War to the Present (Ithaca, NY: Cornell University Press, 2011), and Amanda Kay McVety, Enlightened Aid: U.S. Development as Foreign Policy in Ethiopia (New York: Oxford University Press, 2021).

3. Elizabeth Cobbs Hoffman, "Diplomatic History and the Meaning of Life: Toward a Global American History," Diplomatic History, Vol. 21, No. 4 (Fall 1997): 518.

4. Scott Stossel, Sarge: The Life and Times of Sargent Shriver (Washington: Smithsonian Books, 2004), 171.

5. See William J. Lederer and Eugene Burdick, The Ugly American (Greenwich, Conn: Fawcett Publications, Inc., 1958), 239-240.

6. J. Kenneth Kreider, A Cup of Cold Water: The Story of Brethren Service (Elgin, Ill.: press, 2001), 460-461, Letter from Murray to the author, January 19, 1998, Hibbing Daily Tribune, November 5, 1956, and Stevenson-Kefauver Campaign, Information Bulletin, Saturday, October 1956, Hubert H. Humphrey Papers, Senatorial Files 1949-1964, 150.D.5.1 (B), Minnesota State Archives, St. Paul, MN.

7. Don Murray, "The People Nobody Wanted," Gospel Messenger, November 4, 1961, 8-10, Kreider, A Cup of Cold Water, 302-304, and Murray to the author, April 14, 2009.

8. Humphrey to Murray, February 10, 1958, copy in possession of the author, Humphrey to Murray, December 29, 1958, copy in possession of the author, and The Congressional Record, 85th

Cong., 2nd sess., August 5, 1958, p. 16194.

9. Henry S. Reuss, When Government was Good: Memories of a Life in Politics (Madison, Wisc.: University of Wisconsin Press, 1999) 58-59.

10. Kenneth Imhoff, "Way Down in Egypt Land—No. 3, October 16, 1953", Box 1, file 3, IVS Collection, and Imhoff, "Way Down in Egypt Land, 6th report on World Neighbors' Project at Assiut, Egypt," April 10, 1954, Box 1, file 1, IVS Collection.

11. Daniel Russell, "So You Want to be a Volunteer," found in an extension of remarks by the Hon. Olin E. Teague, Congressional Record, 87 Cong., 1 sess., Mar. 6, 1961, A1533-A1534.

12. Oliver Popence, June 10, 1959, WHO, OSANSA, OCB Series, Subject Subseries, Box 3, IVS file, Eisenhower Library, Abilene, KS.

13. Oral History Interview with Stanley Andrews, Alamo, Texas, October 31, 1970, Harry S. Truman Library and Museum, Independence, MO., https://www.trumanlibrary.gov/library/oral-histories/andrewss, accessed June 1, 2011.

14. Andrews Oral History interview.

15. Stanley Andrews to W. Harold Row, December 10, 1956, Box 1 folder 1, IVS Collection.

16. Richard J. Peters, IVS in Vietnam, April 10, 1960, Box 1, file 6, IVS Collection.

17. Henry S. Reuss, "A Point Four Youth Corps," Commonweal, May 6, 1960, p. 146.

18. Reuss, "A Point Four Youth Corps," 146 and Reuss, When Government was Good, 59.

19. Humphrey, Congressional Record, 86 Cong., 2 sess., June 15, 1960, 12636.

20. Hubert H. Humphrey (ed. By Norman Sherman), The Education of a Public Man, My Life and Politics (Garden City, NY: Doubleday and Co., Inc, 1976, 250

21. Kreider, A Cup of Cold Water, 461, Murray to the author, January 19, 1998, E. Wilson, Uphill for Peace: Quaker Impact on Congress (Richmond, IN: Friends United Press, 1975), 177, and Gerard T. Rice, The Bold Experiment: JFK's Peace Corps (Notre Dame, IN: University of Notre Dame Press, 1985), 11.

22. Reuss to director, Legislative Reference Service, November 5, 1959, Henry S. Reuss Peace Corps Records, series 3, Box 2, Legislative History file, Marquette University, Department of Special Collections and Archives, Milwaukee, Wisconsin.

23. Office of Reuss (submitted by David Anderson) to Mr. Knopsinger [sic.], Executive Director International Voluntary Services, December 22, 1959, Series 3, Box 2, Legislative Papers, Reuss papers.

24. Rice, The Bold Experiment, 10-11 and Reuss, The Congressional Record, 86 Cong., 2 sess., January 14, 1960, 574.

25. Arthur Darken, "Proposal for a Point Four Youth Corps," March 18, 1960, Series 3, Box 2, Legislative History, Reuss Papers.

26. See Reuss, When Government was Good, 59 and Theodore M. Vestal, "A Peace Corps History," speech delivered April 28, 2001, Tulsa, OK.

27. Humphrey, The Congressional Record, 86 Cong., 2 sess., June 15, 1960, 12635.

28. Latham, Modernization as Ideology, 133. Many individuals have taken credit for introducing Kennedy to the idea of a peace corps. Milton Shapp claims to have put the idea into Kennedy's head and "'selling'" the President in advancing the idea. General James M. Gavin discussed the idea before a group in Miami Beach in October 1960 and Ted Sorensen also noted additional sources, including the Mormon Church's requirement of voluntary service by its youth as well as other youth volunteer programs. See Harris Wofford, Of Kennedys and Kings: Making Sense of the Sixties (New York: Farrar, Straus, Girous, 1980), 245, Milton Shapp to Robert Kennedy, October 25, 1960 and Milton J. Shapp to Sargent Shriver, March 1, 1961, RG 490, Correspondence of the Office of the Director, Box 6, file S 1961, National Archives and Records Administration, College Park, MD (hereafter referred to as NARA), and James M. Gavin to Samuel F. Hayes, December

14, 1960, Box 1, Correspondence File, Samuel Hayes Papers, Kennedy Library, Boston, MA. In response to the Kennedy speech, students at the University of Michigan formed concern for our world responsibility." The idea spread to other campuses and over the next few weeks the Kennedy campaign received over 30,000 letters expressing interest in the idea. See W. Arthur Milne, Jr. to Senator John Kennedy, October 30, 1960, Box 1, Correspondence file, Hayes Papers, JFK Library and Peter Shapiro (ed.), "The Peace Corps is Born: 1960-1962, A History of National Service in America," from the Center for Political Leadership and Participation, 1994 at http://www.academy.umd.edu/publications/NationalService/peace_corps.htm , accessed May 9, 2007, and Vestal "A Peace Corps History." See also W. Arthur Milne, Jr. to Senator John Kennedy, October 30, 1960, Box 1, Correspondence file, Hayes Papers, Kennedy Library, Vestal, "A Peace Corps History," and Stossel, Sarge, 194.

29. Max F. Millikan, "Memorandum on an International Youth Service," December 30, 1960, RG 490, Office of Evaluation Program Planning Evaluation Files 1961-1967, Box 4, file: Colorado State University, NARA.

30. Samuel P. Hayes, "Promise and Problems of a Peace Corps," in Pauline Madow (ed.), The Peace Corps (New York: H.W. Wilson Co., 1964), 36.

31. Steve Bosworth, Chairman, Americans Committed to World Responsibility to "Friends," February 14, 1961, Samuel Hayes Papers, Correspondence File, Box 1, Kennedy Library.

32. "Attenders at Point Four Youth Corps Discussion Meeting," December 20, 1960, Reuss Papers, Series 5, Box 2, Marquette University Special Collections, Milwaukee, Wisconsin, and Wilson, Uphill for Peace, 178.

33. Elizabeth Cobbs Hoffman, All You Need is Love: The Peace Corps and the Spirit of the 1960s (Cambridge: Harvard University Press, 1998), 42

34. Paul Rodell, "John S. Noffsinger and the Global Impact of the Thomasite Experience," in Corazon D. Villareal (ed.), Back to the Future: Perspectives on the Thomasite Legacy to Philippine Education (American Studies Association of the Philippines, Manila, 2003), 68

35. Harris Wofford, Of Kennedys and Kings: Making Sense of the Sixties (New York: Farrar, Straus, Giroux, 1980), 252-53.

36. Hoffman, All You Need is Love, 42-43.

37. Stossel, Sarge, 199-202.

38. Warren W. Wiggins, "A Towering Task: The National Peace Corps," Draft—February 1, 1962, http://archive.peace corps.gov, Peace Corps 50th Anniversary Digital Library, assessed June 8, 2009.

39. "Report to the President on the Peace Corps," from Sargent Shriver, February 22, 1961, JFK Papers, President's Office Files, Departments and Agencies, Box 85, Kennedy Library.

40. Noffsinger to Kennedy, February 13, 1961, RG 490, Correspondence of the Office of the Director 1961 K-N Box 4, file N, NARA and Kermit Eby to Shriver, May 29, 1961, RG 490, Correspondence of the Office fo the Director, Box 2, File E, NARA.

41. Oral History Interview with Stanley Andrews, Alamo, Texas, October 31, 1970 (by Richard D. McKinzie) Harry S Truman Library and Museum, Independence, Missouri, http://www.trumanlibrary.org/oralhist/dndrews.htm, accessed June 1, 2011.

42. Stossel, Sarge, 209.

43. Kreider, A Cup of Cold Water, 462.

44. Shriver to James O'Sullivan (U.S. Ambassador in Malaya), April 12, 1961, RG 490, Letters Sent by Shriver, Moyers and members of the Executive Secretariat 1961-1965, Box 1, file April 1961, NARA.

45. Extension of Remarks by Henry S. Reuss, Congressional Record, 87th Cong., 1 sess., February 28, 1961, A1482 and Extension of Remarks of John Brademas, Congressional Record, 87th Cong., 1 sess., March 7, 1961, A1884.

46. "Extension of Remarks by Hon Henry S. Reuss," February 28, 1961, Congressional Record, 87th Congress, 1 sess., March 3, 1961, A1482, "Memorandum for the President, from Sargent Shriver, June 18, 1962, JFK Papers, President's Office File, Departments and Agencies, Box 86, Peace Corps file, Kennedy Library, and "In the Foreshadow of the Peace Corps," Messenger, June 23, 1966, p. 15 [Noffsinger Obituary].

47. "In the Foreshadow of the Peace Corps, 15.

48. W. Harold Row, June 23, 1961, The Peace Corps, Hearings before the Committee on Foreign Relations, United States Senate, 87th Cong., 1st sess., on S. 2000, U.S. Government Printing Office, Washington, D.C., 1961.

Chapter 11: USAID—Recent Volunteer Service Involvement

1. A Leader with Associate award is a grant for a specified worldwide activity (i.e., the leader award) that includes language allowing other operating units (country missions or offices) to make separate awards (i.e., associate awards) to the leader award recipient for similar types of activities without further competitive procurement procedures.

2. The formal name is "John Ogonowski and Doug Bereuter Farmer-to-Farmer Program" in honor of one of the pilots killed September 11, 2001, and of former Congressman Bereuter, who initially sponsored the program.

3. Many individual volunteers have carried out multiple assignments.

4. Farmer-to-Farmer website, https://farmer-to-farmer.org/about/history (7/7/2021).

5. Summary Meta-Review of Reports on the Farmer-to Farmer Volunteer programs (2014).

6. Muldoon, Michelle, Eric Johnson, and Ron Wendt. 2017. "Evaluation: Managing International Volunteer Programs —A Farmer-to-Farmer Program Manual of Good Practices." (2016). https://pdf.usaid.gov/pdf_docs/PA00M95H.pdf.

7. Mid-term Theory of Change and Impact Learning Evaluation of the Farmer-to-Farmer Program (https://pdf.usaid.gov/pdf_docs/pa00n1s6.pdf).

8. Gary Alex, personal communications.

9. https://www.federalregister.gov/documents/2003/09/30/03-24919/volunteers-for-prosperity

10. Ibid.

11. 9/11 Drives Americans to Answer Peace Corps Call to Service (https://www.peacecorps.gov/news/library/911-drives-americans-to-answer-peace-corps-call-to-service/)

12. https://www.federalregister.gov/documents/2003/09/30/03-24919/volunteers-for-prosperity

13. Hawkins notes

14. Hawkins notes

15. Hawkins notes

16. Hawkins notes

17. National Security Strategy of the United States of America; March 2006; p.32 (https://www.comw.org/qdr/fulltext/nss2006.pdf)

18. National Security Strategy of the United States of America; March 2006; p.32 (https://www.comw.org/qdr/fulltext/nss2006.pdf)

19. Hawkins notes

20. Hawkins notes

21. Volunteers for Prosperity Annual Report to the White House, 2008; p.2 (https://pdf.usaid.gov/pdf_docs/Pdacm414.pdf)

22. Volunteers for Prosperity Annual Report to the White House, 2008; p.4 (https://pdf.usaid.gov/pdf_docs/Pdacm414.pdf)

23. Remarks by President George W. Bush, September 8, 2008, South Lawn; p.1183 (https://www.govinfo.gov/content/pkg/WCPD-2008-09-15/pdf/WCPD-2008-09-15-Pg1181.pdf)

24. Remarks by First Lady Laura Bush, September 11, 2008, Service Nation Summit, New York, NY (https://georgewbush-whitehouse.archives.gov/news/releases/2008/09/20080912-13.html).

25. The Bush Record - Fact Sheet: USA Freedom Corps: Strengthening Service to Meet Community Needs (archives.gov) (https://georgewbush-whitehouse.archives.gov/infocus/bushrecord/factsheets/needs.html#:~:text=Volunteers%20for%20Prosperity%2C%20also%20created,opportunities%20in%20the%20developing%20world.)

26. Serve America Act of 2008; (https://www.congress.gov/bill/110th-congress/senate-bill/3487/text)

27. Serve America Act of 2008; Title II-Volunteers for Prosperity Program (https://www.congress.gov/bill/110th-congress/senate-bill/3487/text)

28. Edward M. Kennedy, Serve America Act Signed. https://obamawhitehouse.archives.gov/photos-and-video/photos/edward-m-kennedy-serve-america-act-signed

29. Serve America Act of 2008; Title II-Volunteers for Prosperity Program (https://www.congress.gov/bill/110th-congress/senate-bill/3487/text)

30. *Performance Evaluation of the Volunteers for Economic Growth Alliance* (VEGA) Leader with Associates Award; May 2019; USAID; p.vi (https://pdf.usaid.gov/pdf_docs/PA00TRKW.pdf)

31. *Performance Evaluation of the Volunteers for Economic Growth Alliance* (VEGA) Leader with Associates Award; May 2019; USAID; p.16. (https://pdf.usaid.gov/pdf_docs/PA00TRKW.pdf)

32. GRANTS.GOV (https://www.grants.gov/web/grants/view-opportunity.html?opId=296974)

33. Hawkins notes. However, several awards have been made under addenda to the VISP APS.

34. Hawkins notes

35. Hawkins notes

36. https://www.congress.gov/111/plaws/publ13/PLAW-111publ13.pdf

Chapter 12: Lessons Learned
—Implications For The Future Of Volunteering For Development

1. A. Gillette, "Aims and organization of voluntary service by youth," Community Development Journal, vol. 7, no. 2, pp. 99–129, 1972.

2. Bird, D, "Never the same again: A History of VSO" p.38, 1998 (Lutterworth Press)

3. The reference to an increasing average tends to obscure that there were some volunteers who were young and some who were closer to retirement or retired. This was true in both the US and abroad. For example, when the Norwegian Volunteer Service was disbanded and replaced by FK Norway (now NOREC) at the end of the 1990s, one focus was the way in which the generation of 1960s volunteers were still volunteering in the 1990s.

4. Devereux, P. 2010. International volunteers: cheap help or transformational solidarity toward sustainable development: Vol. PhD thesis. Murdoch University.

5. The issue of addressing social exclusion also appears in other countries, e.g. the UK governments Platform 2 program, which attempted to address the engagement of young people who did not have the educational levels normally associated with international volunteers.

6. Lough, B. J. 2015. Balancing donor priorities and the civil society function: A challenge for modern IVCOs. International Forum for Volunteering in Development.

7. Lough, Benjamin J. 2015. The evolution of international volunteering. United Nations Volunteers.

8. Australian Volunteers International

9. In more recent times, the teaching of English language may be seen as part of necessary

commercial and technical development as that language has developed as an international form of communication.

10. CCIVS / UNESCO. 1968. The universal charter of volunteer service. Coordinating Committee for International Voluntary Service.

11. Woods, D. E. 1971. Volunteers in community development. Coordinating Committee for International Voluntary Service, UNESCO.

12. Between 1964 and 1968, several global Inter-Agency Meetings on Youth were held by governments around the world to discuss schemes for international voluntary service by young people. As a result, some have argued legislation authorizing governmental resources to support international voluntary services lifted many of the previously poorly-financed IVCOs from marginal to mainstream organizations. UNV, United Nations Volunteers: History and concept. Geneva: United Nations Volunteers, 1985.

13. See for instance the representations made to the Council of Europe in 1962 in Allum, C "Forum: the early years" (forthcoming)

14. The sharp elbows of Peace Corps also impacted on the volunteer programs of other countries see Bird op cit Ch 3

15. Founded as SCI in 1920, IVS was established in 1963 as the British Branch of SCI. See Moyes, A. "Volunteers in Development," ODI, 1966. There is no known organizational link between the UK-based organization and IVS USA.

16. Judge, E. (ed), "To Whom It May Concern," Skillshare International, UK, 2004

17. C. Ball, J. M. Hammer, and V. Yeghiayan, "Voluntarism: The real and emerging power," ACTION, Washington D.C., 1976.

18. Due to their sensitive nature which might put individuals at risk, such examples are not included in this book

19. The focus on development targets in the sector has become widespread since 2000 initially with the MDGs and then the SDGs. This has arguably driven a focus on outcomes rather than process in the minds of donors, which tends to make it difficult for IVCOs to demonstrate the value of volunteering.

20. One aspect of this is the construction of projects which directly meet volunteer felt needs, e.g., the creation of orphanages in which volunteers are placed to work with 'orphans.'

21. N. Georgeou, Neoliberalism, development, and aid volunteering . New York: Routledge, 2012.; C. Allum, "Youth international volunteering and development: An opportunity for development, international understanding or social inclusion?," International FORUM on Development Service, Ottawa, Canada, 2012.; M. Baillie Smith and N. Laurie, "International volunteering and development: Global citizenship and neoliberal professionalization today," Trans. Inst. Br. Geogr., vol. 36, pp. 545–559, 2011.

22. Perold, H, Mati, JM, Allum, C., and Lough, B. J. 2021. COVID-19 and the future of volunteering for development. International Forum for Volunteering in Development.

23. ibid

24. Burns, D. & Howard, J. 2015. "What is the unique contribution of volunteering for international development?" IDS Bulletin, Vol 46 No 5 Wiley, Blackwell, UK

Readings on Volunteerism, IVS, and IVS Volunteers

Appleby, Gordon, John Richey, and Martha Cruz de Yafies. "International Voluntary Services, Inc. Mid-Term Program Evaluation under Cooperative Agreement ORT-158-A-008156-00". USAID. 1991.

Benson, Frederic C. "IVS Volunteers in Rural Laos, 1956-1969," in The Journal of Lao Studies, Volume 7, Issue 1, December 2020. Pgs. 1-36, http://laostudies.org/content/volume-7-issue-1-december-2020, last accessed 7/25/2022. 2020.

Branfman, Fred. *Voices from The Plain of Jars, Life Under an Air War*. Harper & Row, Harper Colophon Books. 1972.

Burns, D. & Howard, J. "What is the unique contribution of volunteering for international Development?" IDS Bulletin, Vol 46 No 5 Wiley, Blackwell, UK. 2015.

Buzzard, Shirley. "Final Evaluation Under Cooperative Agreement ORT-158-A-008156-00, for A.I.D./FHA/PVC". 1993.

Cayer, Marc. *Prisoner in Viet Nam*. Washington, D.C., Asia Resource Center. 1990.

Chatterjee, Amal. "Story of a lifetime of Anil in English", Chapters 1 to 4 on IVS/Vietnam and IVS/Algeria). <https://storyofalifetimeofanil.wordpress.com/page/2/>. 2017.

DAI. "Private Voluntary Organizations and Institutional Development: Lessons from International Voluntary Services, Inc. and The Institute for International Development, Inc., USAID." USAID. 1985.

Elkind, Jessica. *Aid Under Fire: Nation Building and the Vietnam War*. University Press of Kentucky, Lexington, Kentucky. 2016.

Finnell, Loren. *Still a Country Boy: After Embracing the World From Peace Corps Volunteer to Founder & CEO of the Resource Foundation, A Life of Service*, Mayfair Publishing. 2011.

Gilbert, Marc Jason (editor). *Why the North Won the Vietnam War*. New York: Palgrave. 2002.

Gillette, A, "Aims and organization of voluntary service by youth," Community Development Journal, vol. 7, no. 2. 1972.

Gruhzit-Hoyt, Olga. *A Time Remembered—American Women in the Vietnam War*. Presidio Press. 1999.

Huffman, Franklin E. *Monks and Motorcycles: From Laos to London by the Seat of my Pants*. 1956-1958. iUniverse, Inc. 2004.

Hunting. Jill. *Finding Pete: Rediscovering the Brother I Lost in Vietnam*. Wesleyan. 2009.

Kreider, J. Kenneth. *A Cup of Cold Water: The Story of Brethren Service*. Brethren Press. 2001.

Lewin, Howard. *Sunsets, Bulldozers, And Elephants: Twelve Years in Laos, The Stories I Never Told*. Howard S. Lewin. 2005.

Lough, Benjamin J. "Balancing donor priorities and the civil society function: A challenge for modern IVCOs. International Forum for Volunteering in Development". 2015.

Lough, Benjamin J. "The Evolution of International Volunteering", Written for presentation at the International Volunteer Service Exchange Conference, 12-13 October 2015, Beijing, China. United Nations Volunteers (UNV) programme, Bonn, Germany. 2015.

Luce, Don and John Sommer. *Vietnam. The Unheard Voices*. Cornell University Press. 1969.

Malia, James. "We Want to Build; They Want to Destroy: The Dilemma of Volunteering in Laos." Pages 89-100. Lawrence Kessler (editor). Southeast Asia Review of Asia Studies. Vol. XX, 1998. Southeast for Asian Studies, Southeast Conference. 1998.

Manke, Hugh. "IVS and USAID in Vietnam: Who Left Whom?", included in Collected IVS Stories 2020 in IVS archives. c. 2016.

Nagle, William J. "Evaluation of International Voluntary Services, Inc. Contract No. PDC0100-S-00-1148-00 of September 30, 1981", as amended. U.S. Agency for International Development. 1981.

Neese, Harvey and John O'Donnell (editors). *Prelude to Tragedy: Vietnam, 1960-1965*. Naval Institute Press. 2000.

Norris, John. *The Enduring Struggle: The History of the U.S. Agency for International Development and America's Uneasy Transformation of the World*. Lanham, MD: Rowman & Littlefield. 2021.

Olson, Craig, Kenneth Koehn, Ruth Ammerman-Yabes, Peter Doan, David Goh, and Donald Jackson. "Private Voluntary Organizations and Institutional Development: Lessons from International Voluntary Services, Inc. and the Institute for International development. Inc". Development Alternatives, Inc. and Cornell University. USAID. 1985.

Paul Rodell, "John S. Noffsinger and the Global Impact of the Thomasite Experience," in Corazon D. Villareal (ed.), *Back to the Future: Perspectives on the Thomasite Legacy to Philippine Education* (American Studies Association of the Philippines, Manila). 2003.

Phillips, Rufus. *Why Vietnam Matters*. Annapolis, Naval Institute Press. 2008.

Poole, Richard. *The Inca Smiled*. Oxford, Oneworld Publications. 1993.

Rawlings, Stuart (Editor). "The IVS Experience -- from Algeria to Vietnam". 1992.

Schanche, Don A. *Mister Pop, the Adventures of a Peaceful Man in a Small War*. New York, David McKay Company, Inc. 1970.

Sherraden, Margaret Sherrard, John Stringham, Simona Costanzo Sow. and Amanda Moore McBride. 2006. "The Forms and Structure of International Voluntary Service". in: Voluntas: International Journal of Voluntary and Nonprofit Organizations, June 2006, Vol. 17, No. 2 (June 2006), pp. 163-180. Published by: Springer Stable. https://www.jstor.org/stable/27928015.

Shook, Cleo F. "Evaluation: International Voluntary Services, Inc., Contract No. AID/SOD/PDC-C-0241-6/7/79". 1979.

Woods, D. E. "Volunteers in community development". Coordinating Committee for International Voluntary Service, UNESCO. 1971.

Index

A

Abewickrame, Bandu, 159
Abewickrame, Su, 159
Afadra, 48, 49, 282
Agricultural Credit, 121, 122
Agricultural Rehabilitation, 132
Agricultural Research, 62, 91, 132, 133, 134
Ahfad University College for Women (AUCW), 132
Alex, Gary, 244
Algeria, 42, 117, 118, 119, 144, 192, 212, 216
American Committee for Relief in the Near East (ACRNE), 271
American Friends Service Committee (AFSC), 26, 259, 261, 265, 267, 268, 269, 271, 275
Andrews, Stanley, 25, 26, 36, 39, 40, 45, 51, 106, 282, 290
Ansell, Christine, 127, 205
ARAMCO (the Arab American Oil Company), 23, 35, 44, 49, 50
Archer, James, 154, 224, 239
artificial insemination, 53, 55, 56, 58
Asia Foundation, 92, 106, 141
Associacion Indigena Evangelista del Napa (AIEN), 159, 203
Association of Development Agencies in Bangladesh (ADAB), 152, 154, 156
Assuit, Egypt, 29, 30
Attard, Mary, 170
Atwood, Tracy, 104
Augspurger, Dick, 242

B

Badan Urusan Tenage Kerja Sukaela Indonesia (BUTSI), 129, 130, 131
Baile, Jim, 50, 54
Ban Me Thuot, 41, 91, 215, 226
Bangladesh, 112, 142, 144, 145, 150, 151, 152, 153, 154, 155, 156, 157, 158, 172, 174, 175, 176, 177, 178, 184, 188, 189, 191, 193, 195, 196, 197, 199, 239, 240, 241, 254, 312, 313, 314, 318, 320
Bangladesh Rural Advancement Committee (BRAC), 152, 155
Barwick, John, 43
Barwick, Peter, 53, 56, 64
Beestman, George, 116
Benson. Frederic C., 71, 181
Berliner, Richard, 94, 245
Blanchard, David, 114, 115

Board of Directors, 31, 34, 36, 122, 157, 183, 187, 190, 199, 200
Bolivia, 145, 148, 150, 160, 161, 162, 163, 174, 176, 177, 184, 186, 189, 191, 196, 197, 198, 202, 254
Bolovens Plateau, 40, 42, 43, 217, 218, 245, 246
Bordsen, Mark, 130
Borton, Nan, 174, 189, 190, 195
Borton, Ray, 248
Botswana, 142, 150, 163, 164, 165, 175, 176, 184, 188, 189, 191, 193, 195, 254, 310
Bowman, Jim, 106
Bread for the World, 155
Brethren Service Committee (BSC), 259, 269, 271, 272, 273, 275, 288, 290, 291
Brethren Voluntary Service (BVS, 279, 281, 284, 285, 290, 291
Brockmueller, Gordon, 40
Burke, Eldon, 38, 41, 52
Burkhart, Roy A., 29, 30
Burma, 33, 35, 37, 42, 44, 140, 274
Bushong, Benjamin, 27, 29
Business Development, 132, 135, 138, 151
Buzzard, Shirley, 156, 196, 197

C

Call, Michael, 67
Cambodia, 35, 37, 38, 44, 71, 73, 74, 91, 103, 104, 105, 106, 111, 171, 172, 197, 202, 251, 318
Camp, Bill, 230
Canar project, 159
Capacity development, 242, 243, 255
Cape Verde, 141
CARE, 114, 129, 130, 131, 243
CARE-MEDICO, 130
Caribbean, 23, 168, 169, 174, 176, 177, 189, 191
Caribbean Advisory and Professional Services (CAPS), 169, 191
Castillo, Carol, 167
Catholic Church, 23, 37, 39, 90, 141, 159, 168, 187, 234, 266, 269, 276
Caycedo, Hans, 160
CEDEN, National Evangelical Committee for Development and Emergency, 167
Chao Chin, Wang, 166
Charitas-Australia, 158
Chase Manhattan Foundation, 158, 160
Cheng Ching Kui, 166
Chevallier, Willem and Corrie, 137
Chilton, Mike, 232
Chota Valley, 158

Church Committee on Overseas Relief and Reconstruction (CCORR), 274
Church of the Brethren, 25, 26, 31, 259, 270, 272
Church World Service, 141, 199, 273, 275
Civilian Public Service (CPS), 268, 269, 272, 276
Clarke, Dale D., 26
Cluster Program, 78
coca crop substitution, 163
Cohon, Don, 250
Cold War, 24, 65, 72, 83, 176, 182, 196, 280, 281, 285, 286, 317
Colombia, 141, 160, 168
Colyer, Dave, 214
Comilla Model, 152
Commission for Rural Affairs (CRA), 77
Community Development, 38, 45, 51, 53, 62, 63, 65, 69, 72, 79, 95, 134, 156, 164, 170, 230
Community Development Center (CDC), 53, 54, 55, 57, 58, 59, 60, 63
Congo (see also Zaire), 121, 122, 123, 125, 143, 144, 192
Conneely, Dudley, 162
conscientious objector, 26, 34, 94, 106, 214, 264, 268, 269, 271, 272, 276
Cooperatives, 106, 135, 152, 161, 163, 170
Cripe, Gordon, 166
Cuento-Jeggle, Char, 152

D

Damaske, David, 122
de Creveling, DeWa, 68
de Paul, Carter, 37
de Pedro, Freddie, 154
Disaster Preparedness, 151
diversification, 163, 170, 307, 308, 310, 312, 314
Doke, Cliff, 114
Dominica's National Development Foundation (NDF), 169
Dongdok, 75, 78, 88
Durnbaugh, Linda, 252
Dutch Interchurch Organization for Development Cooperation, 155

E

Ea Kmat, 91
Early, Ruth, 30
Eason, George, 103
Ecole Normale d' Instituteurs (ENIs), 78
Ecole Superieure de'Pedagogie, 75
Ecuador, 142, 148, 150, 158, 160, 161, 174, 175, 176, 177, 184, 186, 189, 191, 197, 198, 199, 203, 254, 318
Education, 32, 72, 74, 75, 77, 78, 86, 89, 92, 93, 103, 113, 118, 119, 130, 132, 141, 167, 192, 246, 250
Education Team, 75, 77, 78
Edwards, Chandler, 82
Egypt, 28, 29, 30, 31, 33, 35, 37, 40, 41, 42, 47, 48, 49, 144, 282
EMPOWER, 172, 173
Endsley, Mary and Scott, 125
Eng, Jean, 139
English teaching, 32, 75, 77, 92, 115, 118, 119, 127, 129, 130, 243
Enterprise Development, 163, 168
Erbil province, 52
Erwin H. Johnson (EJ), 246
Esman, Milton J., 36
Esser, John, 216
Ethiopia, 141, 148, 190, 248
evaluation, 85, 128, 134, 149, 155, 156, 164, 165, 175, 178, 184, 188, 189, 191, 195, 196, 197, 237, 238, 255
Evangelical and Reformed Center for Vocational Education (CEVER), 167
Evans, E.B., 30

F

Farmer-to- Farmer, 293, 301
Ford Foundation, 29, 35, 36, 37, 40, 42, 45, 48, 151
Foreign Operations Administration, 30, 36, 72, 73, 282, 283
Forward Area Teams (FAT), 81
Fox, Diane, 216
Fox, Robert, 170
Fox, Tom, 233, 251
Francis, David, 115
Francis, George, 114
Francisco, Feliciano, 153, 154
Fraser, Donald M., 184
French, David, 154
Friends In Village Development, Bangladesh (FIVDB), 153, 154, 193, 320
Funding, 48, 49, 51, 65, 67, 72, 89, 103, 113, 117, 120, 121, 126, 129, 132, 136, 138, 141, 151, 156, 158, 161, 163, 166, 168, 170, 171, 176, 188, 192, 195, 196, 301, 313

G

Gardiner, Arthur Z., 81, 291
Gaza, 41, 67, 265
Ghana, 141, 279

Gingerich, Jim, 86
Gono Shasthya Kendra (GK), 152
Goodfellow, Don, 54
Goodstein, Jeanette, 200
Gordon Ramsey, 87
Goulden, James, 38
Government funding, 148, 174

H

Haffner, Loren, 82
Hallberg, Parker F., 187
Ham, Rudman, 53
Harmon, Edward D Jr., 62
Harper, Reg, 132, 133
Harris, Franklin S., 30
Hawkins, Jack, 296
Heffron, Peter, 153
Heifer Project, 26, 27, 37, 45, 48, 49, 50, 58, 59, 60, 272
Henderson, Loring, 123
Hickey, Margaret, 29
Hidalgo, Ariel, 159
Hill, Patty, 158
Hiteshew, Roy L., 29
HIV/AIDS Prevention, 171
Holloway, Albert, 53, 56, 216
Horticulture, 163, 164, 165, 193
Humphrey, Hubert, 279, 280
Hussey, Stephen, 170
Hutcheson, Betty, 54, 61, 63

I

ICCO (Interchurch Organization for Development Cooperation), 151
Imhoff, Kenneth, 48, 282
impacts, 24, 120, 131, 135, 140, 238, 239, 242, 243, 245, 246, 251, 253, 254, 255, 256, 316
Indonesia, 42, 43, 44, 45, 129, 130, 131, 144, 216, 277, 297
Inter-American Foundation, 162
International Agency Development Board, 27
International Cooperation Association (ICA), 23, 38, 39, 40, 41, 44, 45, 50, 62, 73, 74, 75, 76, 113, 114, 183, 187, 188, 192, 200, 282, 283, 285, 286, 287, 289, 290
International Voluntary Services in Bangladesh (IVS/B), 157
International Volunteer Cooperation Organizations (IVCOs), 307, 308, 309, 310, 311, 313, 314, 316, 317, 320, 321, 322, 323, 324
Internationalization, 142

Iraq, 29, 30, 31, 33, 35, 36, 38, 40, 41, 42, 43, 44, 47, 50, 51, 52, 53, 56, 59, 60, 62, 63, 64, 69, 70, 144, 192, 214, 216, 311
Iraq Community Development Agency, 40
Ireson, Randall, 81, 84
IRIS Project - University of Maryland, 151, 156
Ito, Yoshikazu, 126
IVS strategy, 149, 175
IVS/ Vietnam, 214, 232, 233
IVS/Algeria, 117, 119, 216
IVS/Washington, 102, 128, 138, 153, 156, 157, 176, 178, 189, 191, 195, 199, 249

J

Jantzen, Carl, 52, 53, 206
Jenne, Everett, 52, 53
Jennings, James, 153, 154
Jericho, 28, 29, 30, 32, 35, 37, 38, 39, 41, 44, 45, 49, 50
Job Opportunities and Business Support (JOBS) Project, 156
JOCV (Japan), 314
Johnson, Ronald, 113
Jordan, 28, 29, 32, 33, 41, 42, 47, 49, 50, 54, 65, 67, 68
Josephson, William, 289

K

Kaufman, Jacques, 65
Kelly, Arthur, 167
Kennedy Serve America Act, 300, 302
Kerse, Alan, 135
Kong Le, 76, 78
Korea, 33, 34, 140, 274, 313
Kumar, Lala A., 164
Kweneng Rural Development Association (KRDA), 164

L

Lamb, David, 167
Laos, 35, 36, 37, 38, 40, 41, 42, 43, 44, 45, 71, 72, 73, 74, 75, 76, 77, 78, 79, 80, 81, 82, 83, 84, 85, 86, 87, 88, 89, 97, 103, 104, 105, 106, 107, 111, 144, 148, 172, 178, 182, 183, 188, 192, 214, 216, 217, 219, 220, 224, 225, 239, 241, 242, 243, 244, 246, 247, 249, 250, 251, 252, 253, 283, 284, 318, 319
Lease, Gareth, 65
Lebanon, 37, 67
Lee, Henry, 166
Legacy, 110, 146, 180, 258, 278, 304, 306, 319

Levi Strauss Foundation, 151
Lewin, Howard, 85
Liberia, 42, 111, 113, 114, 115, 116, 143, 144, 192, 315
Libya, 141
Livestock, 91, 214
local empowerment, 312
Localization, 311
Long, Jeffrey, 83
Luce, Don, 97, 105, 187
Luche, Tom, 109
Lutheran World Federation, 137
Luxembourg office, 143

M

Madagascar, 141
Mahawil, 51, 63
Malaria Suppression Team, 93
Malaysia (Sabah), 141
Malia, Jim, 88
Manke, Hugh, 71, 197, 232
Mann, Charles, 80
Marcus, Russell, 241
Mark,s John, 164
Marshall Plan, 24, 151
Marshall, General George C., 24
Martin, Tina, 118
matching grant, 156, 176, 196, 197, 299, 300, 302
Matin, Abdul, 157
Matsheng Village Woodlot Project, 165
Mauritania, 136, 138, 144, 184, 219, 220
Max Goldensohn, 136, 219
Max Millikan, 286, 287, 288, 289
Mayo, Nolina, 171
MCC - Mennonite Central Committee, 259, 266, 267, 268, 269, 271, 274, 275
McKeithen, Win, 88, 217
Mennonite Central Committee, 26, 27, 44, 49, 50, 243, 259, 266, 267, 285, 288
Mennonite Relief Commission for War Sufferers (MRCWS), 271
Meyers, Willi, 129, 249
micro-enterprise development, 170
Middle East, 23, 27, 31, 32, 33, 34, 35, 36, 38, 39, 40, 41, 42, 45, 47, 64, 65, 69, 71, 182, 184, 268, 271, 274, 275, 276, 285, 295, 316, 317
MISEREOR, 168
Mitchell, Don, 54, 57, 59, 64
Mobile Science Teams, 93
Montagnard, 92, 100, 226, 227, 228
Moquin, Rene, 98, 252
Morocco, 42, 120, 121, 143, 144, 308, 310

Mu Ban Samaki, 78
Mummert, Dennis, 82
Murray, Don, 281, 284
Musa Bey Alami, 30, 32, 49

N

National Catholic Rural Life Conference, 36
National Education Center (NEC), 75
National Voluntary Services (NVS), 94, 95
National Volunteer Program (NVP), 155
Near East Church Council Committee for Refugee Work (NECC-CRW), 67
Neese, Harvey, 215
Nepalgunj, 65, 66, 67
Nguyen, Tin Sy, 125
Nichols, Stephen, 200
Noble, Francicso, 155
Noffsinger, John S., 31, 32, 33, 34, 35, 36, 37, 40, 41, 43, 44, 50, 73, 282, 285, 288, 290, 291
Norris, Richard A., 32
Nutrition, 86, 138, 160
Nuttle, David, 92, 226
NVA, 90, 91, 100, 101

O

O'Conner, Brian, 251
Office of Inter-American Affairs (OIAA), 25
Oi, Jiro, 80, 224
Olie, Koen, 172
Olsen, Lawrence, 88, 220
Operating Program Grants (OPGs), 182
Operations Advisory Committee, 29, 31, 32
Organization of Rural Associations for Progress (ORAP), 170, 171

P

Pacifism, 264
PACT, 149, 151, 183, 194, 197, 198
Pakistan, 33, 35, 36, 44, 140, 148, 151, 265
Papua New Guinea, 138, 140, 148, 184, 189
Pathet Lao, 76, 81, 82, 87, 242
Pax Program, 48
Peace churches, 24, 25, 26, 27, 178, 261, 268, 269, 271
Peace Corps, 77, 94, 111, 113, 114, 118, 121, 126, 129, 138, 142, 144, 145, 160, 164, 182, 188, 193, 200, 224, 238, 246, 254, 255, 279, 280, 283, 284, 285, 286, 287, 288, 289, 290, 291, 292, 295, 310, 313, 315, 316, 317, 318, 322
Peter and Anne Clark, 159
Peters, Dick, 108, 194

Peters, John L., 36
Philippines, 31, 32, 33, 71, 101, 115, 143, 152, 154, 155, 157, 159, 164, 168, 248
Pilot National Volunteer Program in Ecuador, 160
Popence, Oliver, 282
President John F. Kennedy, 23, 279
private funding, 69, 106, 118, 144, 176, 194, 195, 196
Private funding, 101, 156
Private Voluntary Organization (PVO), 46, 188, 255
Public Health, 121, 138

Q

Quill, Dianna (Dee) and Dick, 244

R

Range management, 120
Rapti Valley Village Development Center, 66
Rawlings, Stuart, 99
Readers Digest Foundation, 151
refugee, 38, 47, 64, 65, 67, 68, 77, 80, 81, 90, 95, 102, 108, 151, 242, 243, 248, 250, 255, 274, 277, 279
Reinvention, 174
Reisner, John H., 28, 29, 30, 34, 35, 45, 74, 75, 288
Relations with USAID, 124, 143
Religious Society of Friends (Quakers), 25, 259
Reuss, Henry, 280, 281
Right Reverend Luigi G. Ligutti, 36, 37, 38, 40, 45
Rigsby, John, 145
Rockefeller Foundations, 23
Rodell, Paul, 23, 288
Rodriguez de Moscoso, Antonia, 162
Rolston, W. Wendell, 73
Row, Harold, 27, 28, 31, 33, 37, 281, 283, 288, 290, 291
Rowe, Otis, 48
Royal Lao Government (RLG), 74, 76
Ruge, Marian Cast, 139
Rupel, Martha, 52, 53
Rural Development, 51, 65, 66, 72, 74, 75, 78, 86, 103, 104, 136, 149, 152, 158, 164, 169, 191, 192, 246
Rural Youth Program, 93
Russell, Daniel, 191, 282

S

Sage, William W., 97, 247
Scarborough, Jay, 83
Seepersaud, Michael, 169

Senor de Mayo Project, 161
SERRV International (Sales Exchange for Refugee Rehabilitation and Vocation), 26
Shafer, Lem, 99
Shaqlawa, 51, 52, 53, 55, 57, 60, 63, 64, 69, 70
Shirk, Anne, 23, 149, 157, 187, 199
Shriver, R. Sargent, 288
Smock, David, 187, 191
Snyder, William T., 29, 33
Soil Conservation Service, 117
Sommer, John, 229
Southeast Asia, 23, 33, 36, 37, 40, 42, 43, 44, 46, 47, 71, 72, 104, 106, 109, 111, 119, 143, 152, 171, 174, 191, 282, 283, 297, 298, 313, 316, 317
St. Lucia's National Research and Development Foundation (NRDF), 169
St. Vincent Organization of Rural Development (ORD), 169
Stillman, Art, 82
Stone, Steve, 243, 253
Street Boy Project, 230
SubCentral de Cooperativas Agropecuarias Villa Paraiso, Ltda. (SUCAP), 162
Sudan, 132, 133, 134, 135, 143, 144, 148, 184, 188, 189, 193, 195, 205, 308, 318
Sulaymaniyah Sub-center, 62
Sumner, Don, 214
Swift, Steve, 96, 241
Syria, 67, 68, 271

T

Tacadeo, Andres, 128
Taylor, Carl C., 29
Technical Cooperation Administration (TCA), 23, 25, 26, 27, 29, 30, 31, 36, 45, 275, 282
Tet Offensive, 100
Thailand, 27, 33, 37, 42, 44, 73, 88, 104, 105, 140, 171, 172, 173, 197, 240, 251, 297
Thananya, 173
Thomas, Winburn T., 86, 107
Thomasites, 32
Tuck, Captain William H., 28
Turner, J. Sheldon, 51

U

Ullum, Ken, 80
UN Relief and Works Agency (UNRWA), 67, 68, 69, 265
UNICEF, 53, 60, 151, 171
United Nations Reconstruction Agency, 34
United Nations Volunteers Program, 144

United States Operations Mission (USOM), 33, 71
UNRRA, 272, 273

V

VARDA Project, 75, 76, 77, 79
Viet Cong, 92, 96, 97, 100, 101, 107, 215, 226, 235
Vietnam, 33, 34, 35, 37, 38, 40, 41, 42, 43, 44, 71, 73, 74, 76, 79, 81, 83, 86, 87, 89, 90, 91, 92, 93, 94, 95, 96, 98, 99, 100, 101, 102, 103, 104, 105, 106, 107, 108, 109, 111, 130, 143, 144, 148, 171, 172, 178, 182, 183, 188, 192, 197, 198, 214, 215, 216, 226, 229, 230, 232, 233, 234, 235, 241, 243, 245, 248, 249, 250, 251, 252, 253, 274, 283, 308, 318
Vietnamese Advisory Board, 96
Village Development Training Program (VDTP), 153
Village Level Workers, 53, 54
Village Life Improvement Program, 52
Village Volunteer Program (VVP), 155, 156
village water system, 56
Volunteer assignments, 144, 239
Volunteer support, 142
Volunteers for Economic Growth Alliance (VEGA), 293, 301, 302, 303
Volunteers for International Security and Prosperity (VISP), 293, 301, 302
Volunteers For Prosperity (VFP), 295, 296, 297, 298, 299, 300, 301, 302, 303

W

Wadi Halfa, 133, 134, 135
Wardle, Chris, 124
Wau Ecology Institute, 140
Well-Baby Clinics, 60
Welsh, Frank, 131, 216
Wiggins, Warren, 289
Wilder, Bernard, 78, 250
Willard Patton, 65, 66
Wiser, Ed, 54, 63
Wolf, Louis, 225
Women and Development Unit (WAND), 169
Woodcock Mitchell, Cherie J., 54
World Neighbors, 23, 28, 29, 30, 31, 35, 36, 42, 48, 282
Worthington, Linda, 187

X

Xieng Khouang, 38, 42, 74, 77, 244

Y

Yemen, 126, 127, 128, 129, 143, 144, 184, 188, 192, 193, 195, 310, 319
Yost, Charles, 40
Young, Dorothy, 119
Youth Corps, 284, 285, 286, 288

Z

Zaire (see also Congo), 42, 121, 123, 124, 125, 190, 192
Zimbabwe, 170, 171, 174, 176, 177, 191, 197, 204, 254, 318

About the Authors

Gary Alex grew up on a farm in northern Illinois and studied Agricultural Sciences at University of Illinois and Cornell University. He served as an IVS volunteer in Laos for four years teaching agriculture and community development. After IVS, he worked forty years in international agricultural and rural development with USAID and the World Bank. During that time, he managed the Farmer-to-Farmer Volunteer Program for twelve years.

Cliff Allum is writer, researcher, and consultant in International Development, specializing in volunteering. In 2017, he joined the Third Sector Research Centre at the University of Birmingham, UK as an Associate Fellow. He has written on issues impacting on volunteering for development, most recently on climate change and on the impact of COVID-19. Until 2016, Cliff was CEO of Skillshare International, a UK-based International Volunteering and Development Organization, and prior to that Director of Skillshare Africa, which had originally been part of the UK IVS. He was also President of the International Forum on Volunteering for Development between 2002-2008 and formed the Forum Research Group in 2009. Cliff has an MA and PhD from the University of Warwick and worked in adult education and community and economic development in the UK before working internationally. He is active in his local community, in Birmingham UK and a national trustee of the WEA, the largest voluntary sector provider of adult education in the UK.

Frederic C. Benson earned his BA in History and Asian Studies at St. Olaf College in Northfield, Minnesota (which included a semester at Chulalongkorn University in Thailand and the University of Oslo's International Summer School in Norway), MBA at Thunderbird School of Global Management (Glendale, Arizona), and MLIS at the University of North Carolina/Greensboro. He worked in Laos from 1968 to 1974, two years with International Voluntary Services, Inc. (IVS) and four years with the United States Agency for International Development (USAID). After leaving Laos he pursued a career in international business, which involved postings in Southeast Asia and extensive travel worldwide.

Michael Chilton grew up on a small farm in SE Iowa and completed a graduate degree in botanical sciences Iowa State University. He served five years as a volunteer and team leader with IVS in Vietnam, after which he served six years as a remote area security development specialist in Thailand with the Border Patrol Police and then four years in Vietnam in public and private development sectors. After returning to the U.S. in 1975, he worked eight years with an agricultural company in Salem, Oregon on technical upgrading and then founded Agricultural Alternatives, Ltd.in 1985 to produce specialty seed and plant materials for a range of internationally marketed plant products. Mike has visited over eighty countries and lived or worked in nineteen.

Jack Hawkins has held senior positions in the US government relating to national volunteer service. From 2003 to 2009, he was founding director of Volunteers for Prosperity (VFP), a Presidential initiative to promote international volunteer service by skilled American professionals that helped mobilize 120,000 volunteers through a network of 300 US nonprofits and companies. VFP became law under the Kennedy Serve America Act. Jack has held senior positions in the private sector in nonprofit management, information and communications technology, management consulting, and financial services and served on boards of national and global nonprofit organizations. Jack has a BA in political science from the University of Pittsburgh and a master's degree in international affairs from the University of Pittsburgh's Graduate School of Public and International Affairs (GSPIA).

Benjamin J. Lough is a Professor of Social Work and Business Administration, and Director of Social Innovation at the Gies College of Business, University of Illinois Urbana-Champaign. He also holds positions as Senior Research Associate with the Center for Social Development, University of Johannesburg, and Faculty Director of International Service at the Center for Social Development, Washington University in St. Louis. Dr. Lough's research and teaching interests include volunteerism, international community development, and non-profit management. He was lead researcher and author of the UN State of the Worlds Volunteerism Report 2018 and is currently researching the contributions of international volunteers to gender equality from the perspectives of partner organizations. Ben is a member of The International Forum for Volunteering in Development 'Research, Practice, and Policy Group', and has produced several publications for this Forum and the United Nations Volunteers (UNV) program. He earned his PhD in Social Work from the Brown School at Washington University in St. Louis in 2010.

Hugh I. Manke is a senior principal with Updike, Kelly & Spellacy, P.C. and has represented the State of Connecticut, cities and towns, Tweed New Haven Airport Authority and private clients since 1975. He is both a transactional and litigation attorney. He has held executive positions with several professional organizations and served as Secretary of Junior Achievement of Southwestern New England and past-Board Chair of the Greater New Haven Chamber of Commerce. He received his J.D. from the State University of New York School of Law in Buffalo, where he was on the Buffalo Law Review, and received an A.B. from Princeton University. His science background in college led him to a unique science education program as a volunteer in South Vietnam with International Voluntary Services. After two years in that capacity, Hugh served as Chief of Party in 1969 for two years. He was a Board member of IVS/Washington and Board Chair for several years during his tenure from 1988 until IVS's termination in 2002.

Willi Meyers grew up as a Mennonite preacher's kid in Souderton, Pa, and studied Mathematics at Goshen College. He was in the IVS-Vietnam Hamlet School program and Mobile Science program, Recruitment Officer in DC, and Team Leader in Vietnam before leaving IVS to protest the war. He later earned an MS in the University of the Philippines-Los Banos, and a PhD at University of Minnesota. He served as an Agricultural Economist at the USDA, Iowa State, FAO and the University of Missouri for 44 years.

Cherie J. Woodcock Mitchell grew up on a dairy farm in New York and graduated from Cornell University with a BS in Home Economics, before joining the IVS/Iraq team in 1955 as home economics extensionist. In 1957, she married Don, who worked for USAID in Thailand, Laos, Turkey, and the Philippines. While in Laos, she worked on the IVS/Education team and in other posts taught in schools. She worked with resettling refugees in Virginia and, in 1989, moved to Oregon to develop a cut flower business. She served two terms on the Southwest Oregon Community College Board of Directors. She died March 28, 2020.

Don Mitchell grew up on an irrigated farm in Idaho and graduated from the University of Idaho with a degree in Agriculture. He was Idaho's first International Farm Youth Exchange delegate, going to the Netherlands in 1950. He served two years in the U.S. Army and then joined the IVS team in Shaqlawa, Iraq. He completed an MS in Human Development and joined USAID as an Agricultural Officer, serving in Thailand, Laos, Turkey, and the Philippines. He farmed in Virginia and Oregon, where he and Cherie established Flora Pacifica to produce and market commercial cut flowers. He was active in local economic affairs, serving on boards of directors.

Paul A. Rodell is Emeritus Professor of History at Georgia Southern University specializing in Southeast Asia and the Philippines. He served with the Peace Corps in the Philippines (1968-71) in agriculture extension and has written two articles about IVS. He is currently Treasurer of the Association of Global South Studies (2019-present). He was chair of the Philippine Studies Group, Association for Asian Studies (2009-2011) and executive director for the Association of Third World Studies (1996-2002). He has written thirty-nine articles and book chapters and edited an anthology on Southeast Asia (2000). His Culture and Customs of the Philippines won the 2002 Cecil B. Currey Book Award of the Association of Third World Studies.

William W. Sage has worked with and for both governmental and non-governmental organizations and agencies including the United States Agency for International Development, the International Rescue Committee, Catholic Charities, the Northern California Ecumenical Council, the Churches Auxiliary for Social Action, New Delhi, India, Church World Service, the International Catholic Migration Commission, Action of Churches Together, and International Orthodox Christian Charities. He served as Adjunct Professor at Arizona State University for nearly a decade and previously served as Senior Consultant to the United Nations High Commissioner for Refugees Office in New Delhi, India. He has a BA in Political Science from Arizona State University and is currently an Independent Consultant.

E. Timothy Smith, Professor Emeritus of History at Barry University, retired in 2021 after 36 years of teaching. He received his B.A. in history and political science from Manchester University in Indiana and his MA and Ph.D. in history from Kent State University. He specialized in diplomatic history publishing on Cold War Issues including NATO, opposition to the containment policy, and the roots of the Peace Corps.

Ann Wright-Parsons [Archives Research] completed a BA from Grinnell College before serving as an IVS English teacher at Dong Khanh Girls high school, Hue, Vietnam. She then worked in the IVS/Washington office and later taught English in schools and to adults while living in the Philippines, Indonesia, Thailand, and Bangladesh. She worked as a volunteer at the Museum Pusat, Jakarta and the Bangkok National Museum and as editor of the Ganesha Volunteer magazine in Thailand. She completed an MA in Anthropology/Southeast Asian Studies at Northern Illinois University and worked in the Anthropology Department of the American Museum of Natural History in New York and as Director of the Anthropology Museum at Northern Illinois University until she retired in 2010.

THE FORTUNATE FEW
IVS VOLUNTEERS
FROM ASIA TO THE ANDES

THIERRY SAGNIER

6" x 9," 371 pages
ISBN: 0-9771435-7-0
$24.95
b&w photo plates

Distributed by Ingram
Available from bookstores, Amazon and other internet retailers

The Fortunate Few is first and foremost a book about the men and women who volunteered their time and skills to improve the lives of millions through the International Voluntarary Services (IVS).

Nearly one hundred of these volunteers recount their service years and the impact their work had on their futures and the people they served, often at great cost to themselves. About a dozen volunteers died, victims of the armed conflict that raged across Southeast Asia with the war in Vietnam.

The effectiveness of IVS volunteers would eventually lead to the creation of a number of other international volunteer agencies including the Peace Corps.

Everyone interested in the history of American develoment efforts—from the Thomasites' work in the Philippines to projects initiated by IVS in the Andes—will value having *The Fortunate Few* in their libraries. Volunteers today will find in these stories a rich source of inspiration.

www.ingramcontent.com/pod-product-compliance
Lightning Source LLC
Chambersburg PA
CBHW071235160426
43196CB00009B/1073